Healthy Getaways
& Complementary Health Centres
throughout Ireland

First published in 2001 by Marino Books
16 Hume Street Dublin 2
Tel: (01) 6615299; Fax: (01) 6618583
e.mail: books@marino.ie
an imprint of Mercier Press
PO Box 5, 5 French Church Street, Cork
Tel: (021) 4275040; Fax: (021) 4274969
e.mail: books@mercier.ie
Website: www.mercier.ie

Trade enquiries to CMD Distribution
55a Spruce Avenue
Stillorgan Industrial Park
Blackrock County Dublin
Tel: (01) 294 2556; Fax: (01) 294 2564

© Jenifer Miller and Ann Bracken 2002
Foreword © Jan de Vries 2002

ISBN 1 86023 145 4

10 9 8 7 6 5 4 3 2 1
A CIP record for this title is available from the British Library

Cover photographs courtesy of Inchydoney
Lodge and Spa, Cork
Cover design by Mercier Press
Printed in Ireland by ColourBooks
Baldoyle Industrial Estate, Dublin 13

This book is sold subject to the condition that it shall not, by way of trade or otherwise, be lent, resold, hired out or otherwise circulated without the publisher's prior consent in any form of binding or cover other than that in which it is published and without a similar condition including this condition being imposed on the subsequent purchaser.

No part of this publication may be reproduced or transmitted in any form or by any means, electronic or mechanical, including photocopying, recording or any information or retrieval system, without the prior permission of the publisher in writing.

Healthy Getaways
& Complementary Health Centres throughout Ireland

Jenifer Miller and Ann Bracken
Foreword by Jan de Vries

Contents

	Foreword by Jan de Vries	7
	Acknowledgements	8
	About This Book	9
County Antrim	Non-residential	13
County Clare	Residential	19
	Non-residential	24
County Cork	Residential	26
	Non-residential	35
County Derry	Residential	49
County Donegal	Residential	50
	Non-residential	52
County Down	Residential	53
	Non-residential	54
County Dublin	Residential	55
	Non-residential	59
County Fermanagh	Residential	118
County Galway	Residential	120
	Non-residential	130
County Kerry	Residential	137
	Non-residential	140
County Kildare	Non-residential	144
County Kilkenny	Non-residential	147
County Laois	Non-residential	150

County Limerick	Non-residential	151
County Louth	Non-residential	152
County Mayo	Residential	153
	Non-residential	157
County Meath	Residential	161
	Non-residential	164
County Offaly	Non-residential	168
County Roscommon	Residential	169
	Non-residential	170
County Sligo	Residential	171
	Non-residential	173
County Tipperary	Residential	175
	Non-residential	178
County Waterford	Residential	179
	Non-residential	182
County Wexford	Residential	184
	Non-residential	188
County Wicklow	Residential	190
	Non-residential	196
	Glossary	199
	Directory of Resources	231
	Directory of Practitioners	235
	Index of Centres	257
	Index of Centres by County	260
	Index by Therapy Type	263

Foreword

Over the years, the popularity of complementary health has grown enormously, which has shown that, overall, there is a tremendous need for further guidance in this area. *Healthy Getaways & Complementary Health Centres throughout Ireland* gives a very concise indication as to what healthy living is all about. I have known Ann Bracken well for a number of years, and she and Jenifer Miller use their extensive knowledge and experience to provide a comprehensive guide to holistic healing therapies. An individual has three aspects: the physical, mental and emotional. The holistic approach to complementary therapy looks at these three aspects when treating problems.

Complementary medicine is more popular than ever in today's society, and although there are still some misunderstandings and misgivings about it, this form of medicine has proved to be very successful. There are now the beginnings of integration between alternative and orthodox medicine.

It has been said that orthodox medicine is 'male', often a bit harsh, sophisticated and sometimes aggressive. Alternative medicine, on the other hand, is considered to be 'female', as it is more gentle, friendly and intuitive. To help tackle human suffering, a happily 'married' system of the two would be most beneficial.

Healthy Getaways & Complementary Health Centres throughout Ireland is another guide to the union of orthodox and alternative medicine to the benefit of others, and I am very happy that I was asked to contribute to the book, which I am sure will find a place in many households throughout the country.

Jan de Vries

Acknowledgements

I would like to thank Robert Doran for encouraging me to pursue this project; my family for their love, encouragement and very practical assistance; Uncle Andreja Atanackovic for his many emergency rescues; my great-aunt Janet, who told me that writing was a better occupation than bartending; Siobhán Cooney and Theresa Carton for repeatedly telling me I can do it; Moira Brown for her invaluable computer expertise; Eoin O'Byrne for the meals, warmth and support; Isabelle Soudry, Akiko Yoshida, Ayura Kazama and Annie B. for the chanting, pints and spiritual succour; and Daisaku Ikeda for continuing – as ever – to show me the way to a healthy, happy life.

Jenifer Miller

I would like to thank my precious flowers Sinead and Leighann for being such wonderful children; Stefan, the true love of my heart, for his encouragement and support; my family for being there for me in my light and darkness; my friends, who are my walking angels on Earth; Emma, Laserfiona, Sara, Siobhan, Jenifer, Cori, Richard, Marina, Suleima, Kathleen, Amisha, Rosemary, Charlotte, Sinead, Liz, Sean, Lisa, Jean, Vanessa, Goff, Eunice, Jenny, Rosemary, Chrissie and Ronan; and Daisaku Ikeda and Nichiren Daishonin's Buddhism for guiding me towards my highest potential.

Ann Bracken

About This Book

Creating harmony and balance within and without is a gift we owe ourselves, through caring for our physical, psychological and spiritual aspects. This book is aimed at helping you achieve optimal health and vitality the natural way.

Health is more than a note in a medical file saying that all systems are in working order. When an individual decides to take the necessary action towards achieving good health, profound results can occur. Through genuinely, gently and gradually working to achieve health in mind, body and spirit, a person can begin to discover who they really are, relate to others better and embrace and enjoy life. By adopting a positive attitude towards your own life, you naturally overcome various subtle and perhaps deep-rooted negative tendencies which may lead to ill-health in body and mind. When you begin to feel a sense of well-being within, this wholesome effect ripples outwards into the environment, affecting the world – if only in a small way – for the better.

Well-being occurs on many levels. The knowledge required to attain it is innate and the vibrant potential for it resides within all of us. We already know what to do. Most people understand that they should eat balanced meals with plenty of fresh fruit and vegetables, drink lots of water, avoid smoking and excessive alcohol intake, establish a regular exercise routine and connect with their higher self through meditation or prayer. It is establishing a routine and keeping to it that is sometimes difficult to achieve. This book is about taking the time to get away from the daily grind in order to rest and recover from everyday stresses, and it is about empowering yourself to adopt a healthier lifestyle.

We must be our own healers – both for ourselves and for society at large. The individual who gazes at the stars is gazing at a part of him- or herself. The decision to heal ourselves lies before us.

Health Centres Featured in This Book

Just as each person is different, so are each of the centres listed in this book. The closest some people may want to get to the world of holistic health is to receive an Indian head massage after a monthly hair appointment. Others may crave a week-long immersion in a detoxifying programme of daily yoga, vegan food, therapeutic body-work and morning walks in the country air – all in the absence of television, radio and mobile phones. In order to provide an experience to suit a broad range of lifestyles, we have included in these pages centres that are right for all bodies and all budgets. In selecting centres for inclusion, we talked to the various owners and managers about their philosophies in relation to health. We looked for places with dedicated and well-trained staff, comfortable surroundings and a commitment to helping people. We avoided centres that offered quick fixes or dubious cures.

The centres and getaways listed in this book represent a broad range of approaches, all of which aim to help you rediscover your body's natural rhythms and gain greater control of your health. Each of the places listed in the book was chosen for one main reason: to help you embark on the journey to well-being.

How to Use This Book

This book includes more than a hundred and sixty healthy getaways and complementary health centres – in both Northern Ireland and the Republic – organised alphabetically by county. Each listing provides a narrative description of the centre, its programmes and – where possible – the philosophy of the owners. After the general description comes practical information, such as days and hours of operation, accommodation, rates, credit cards accepted, meal plans, therapies offered, recreational activities, facilities, staff and directions to the centre. Prices are in euro, except for centres in Northern Ireland, for which prices are in pounds sterling. When phoning any of the centres from outside Ireland, dial '00 353' and drop the '0'. For Northern Ireland, dial '00 44' and drop the '0'.

At the end of this book you will find a glossary and resource guide. The glossary defines most of the services and treatments listed in this book, as well as those that may not yet be offered in Ireland. Referring to it may help you understand what various centres are offering and what may be offered in the future. The resource guide lists complementary-health associations, educational facilities and environmental organisations. Also in the back of the book are three indexes of centres – alphabetical, by county and by therapy type – that will help you find a centre in an area or with an approach that appeals to you.

How to Choose the Place That Is Right for You

Choosing the centre that is best for you means determining first what you would like to get from the experience. Do you want to go away for a few days or weeks, or do you want to find out who in your neighbourhood might help you address a particular health concern that conventional doctors do not seem able to resolve? Are you prepared to travel for a few hours to get to a centre or do you want to stay close to home? Do you require privacy and seclusion? Are you comfortable with group situations? Are you able to handle a diet of fresh fruit and vegetables? Do you want vigorous exercise or to perform yoga or walk each day?

Try to choose a centre that offers programmes that encourage you to continue your journey towards health once you return home. Do not expect overnight results, and be wary of anyone who promises them. If the centre is non-residential, find out who the practitioners are and what sort of education and experience they have. If it is a residential centre, find out whether the programme is flexible or fixed, what the meal plan consists of and exactly what is included in the cost of a stay. Request a brochure and if possible try to speak to the owner or manager. Can you establish a rapport with the individual? Do you feel that your questions are answered adequately? Are you confident in the ability of the staff to address your unique needs?

Whatever you finally decide upon, keep your mind open to the experience of healing, as the results can be far broader than you may have imagined.

The changes you eventually make will have far-reaching effects on both you and your loved ones.

Publisher's Note

Prices are correct at time of going to press but are subject to change. The authors have made every effort to ensure that information given in this book is correct but cannot accept responsibility for any errors contained in it. The publishers will be happy to correct any such errors in future printings of the book.

Aaron Acupuncture & Physiotherapy Clinic

17 Hightown Road
Glengormley

Tel: 04890 836 216

Through a unique combination of physiotherapy and acupuncture, therapists at the Aaron Clinic aim to determine the cause of an ailment, as opposed to merely treating its symptoms. Acupuncture was added to the thirty-year-old clinic's list of services nearly ten years ago in order to address certain chronic illnesses that were not responding to physiotherapy. Stress-management techniques may also be employed, depending on the patient's condition.

Staff at the clinic strive to take a holistic approach in relation to clients and help them examine lifestyle factors that may be contributing to their ailment. 'As a health psychologist, I am acutely aware that the diseases we have today are chronic ones,' says Dr Lynn Dunwoody. 'With chronic illness, you get quite a lot of stress. If somebody comes here with a bad back, we don't just treat the back, we want to know what caused it. Sometimes an individual can't tell us, so we ask about the job they do, whether they sit at a computer all day, what sort of activities they engage in while relaxing, and the like. From that, we can usually help a person in pinpointing what triggered the back problem and help in rehabilitating them by giving them exercises and so on.'

Days and Hours of Operation: Appointments are normally scheduled between 10 am and 5 pm, Monday to Saturday, and during the evenings by prior arrangement.
Rates: Acupuncture costs £28 Stg per session; physiotherapy costs £20 Stg for a thirty-minute session.
Credit Cards: None accepted.
Services: Chinese acupuncture, Western acupuncture, physiotherapy, stress management and relaxation techniques.
Facilities: Two private treatment rooms.
Staff: Two full-time physiotherapists and acupuncturists, and one part-time psychologist and acupuncturist.
Special Notes: The centre is accessible for people with disabilities.
Getting There: The centre is twelve minutes by car from Belfast.

Chinese and Complementary Medicine Clinic

80 Upper Lisburn Road
Belfast BT10 0AD

Tel: 04890 600 600
Fax: 04890 403 582

Established in 1994, the Chinese and Complementary Medicine Clinic aims to bring a truly holistic form of medicine to the people of Northern Ireland. The emphasis is on treating the body as a whole and on strengthening the patient's immune system, thereby correcting any imbalances of the internal organs. Herbal treatments are given in the form of tea, powders, tablets or lotions and are used to correct symptoms of illness. Staff at the clinic use acupuncture to stimulate vital energy points, end stagnation of energy and relieve pain. For clients who are afraid of needles, the clinic provides acupressure and electrotherapy, both of which work on the same principles as acupuncture but do not use needles.

Days and Hours of Operation: Monday, Wednesday and Friday, 9.30am to 6 pm. Tuesday and Thursday, 1 pm to 9 pm. Saturday, 9 am to 2 pm.
Rates: An initial consultation costs £14 Stg. Acupuncture, electrotherapy and back-and-shoulder treatment costs £29 Stg for the first visit, including consultation, and £22 Stg thereafter.
Credit Cards: Cash or cheque only.
Services: Herbal treatment, acupuncture, acupressure, electro-therapy, and back-and-shoulder and heat treatment.

Facilities: Include on-site car parking and wheelchair access.
Staff: Two doctors qualified in traditional Chinese medicine with over ten years' experience working in Chinese hospitals. Also two receptionists.
Getting There: Located midway between the King's Hall and Finaghy crossroads, with easy access from the M1 and M2.

The Complementary Health Clinic

First Floor
86A Stranmillis Road
Belfast BT9 5AD

Tel: 04890 809 888
E-mail: healthclinic@freeuk.com
Website: www.healthclinic.freeuk.com

Katherine McDonnell believes that she has achieved her main aim in life by establishing the Complementary Health Clinic. Previously, she had worked on world cruise liners and land-based salons as a beauty therapist and aromatherapist. Now, working with other therapists as part of a close-knit team, she combines beauty treatments with a range of holistic therapies. This gives people who may not have tried natural healing before an opportunity to experience it, in addition to benefiting from beauty treatments.

Days and Hours of Operation: Wednesday, Friday and Saturday, 10 am to 6 pm. Tuesday and Thursday, 10 am to 9 pm.
Rates: Prices for beauty treatments range from £20 to £30 Stg. Holistic treatments cost between £20 and £35 Stg.
Credit Cards: Visa.
Services: Aromatherapy, reflexology, beauty clinic, kinesiology, reiki, remedial massage, life enhancement, chiropody/podiatry, hypnotherapy, colour therapy, nutrition, counselling and neuro-linguistic programming (NLP). The centre is also a stockist of aloe vera, often known as 'the miracle plant' because of its nutritional and antioxidant qualities and for promoting cell growth and healing.
Facilities: Three treatment rooms, reception area and beauty-therapy area
Staff: Katharine McDonnell is qualified in beauty therapy and aromatherapy. Joan Larmour is qualified in psychotherapy, hypnotherapy and NLP and is a member of the Association of Psychotherapists and National Hypnotherapy Council. Paul Smith is qualified in kinesiology, reflexology and nutrition. Katharine is qualified in remedial massage, aromatherapy and chiropody/podiatry. Additional staff are fully trained and qualified.
Nearby Attractions: The centre is ten minutes' walk from Queen's University Belfast and the famous Botanic Gardens and is also close to the Ulster Museum.
Getting There: The clinic is situated in the heart of Stranmillis village.

Fortwilliam Reflexology

537 Angrim Road
Belfast

Tel: 04890 716 352

For the past nine years, clients have climbed the stairs to a private treatment room above the Fortwilliam Post Office to seek the services of Donal McDaniel. Specialising in reflexology, Bach flower remedies and the metamorphic technique, Donal opened the clinic as a result of his own positive experiences with complementary therapies in treating his illness. 'Spiritual healing was the one that worked best,' he says.

Donal trains twenty reflexologists a year at the local technical college. He is also one of only a handful of people qualified in Bach flower remedies, which he uses to complement the reflexology.

Donal aims to achieve results easily and at little expense to his clients. Although he is particularly skilled in treating lower-back pain, he addresses a gamut of ailments, including stress and emotional problems. 'The inspirational thing for me is just to get results with people who have not had success with ordinary medicine,' he says.

Days and Hours of Operation: Open Monday to Friday, 9 am to 7 pm, and Saturday, from 9 am to 1 pm.
Rates: A one-hour session costs £30 Stg. Half-hour treatments cost £15 Stg each.
Credit Cards: None accepted.
Services: Reflexology, Bach flower remedies and metamorphosis.
Facilities: One private treatment room.
Staff: Donal McDaniel owns and operates the centre on his own.

Special Notes: Clients must be capable of climbing three flights of stairs in order to reach the centre.
Getting There: The clinic is a mile and a half from Carlisle Circus on the Antrim road.

Hao Clinic for Traditional Chinese Medicine

16 Binham Street
Bangor BT20 5DW

Tel: 0289 146 3888
Fax: 0289 147 9858

After helping to set up the first Chinese medical centre in Northern Ireland, Ri Fang Hao went on to open two practices of her own. With over twenty-five years' experience in traditional Chinese medicine, Ri Fang Hao is one of the leading consultants in this area. She graduated from Beijing University of Traditional Chinese Medicine and is also a qualified doctor of Chinese medicine. She worked in Beijing, Mongolia, Poland and London before moving to Northern Ireland.

Traditional Chinese medicine offers effective treatment for many health problems. For diagnosis, Ri Fang Ho employs traditional Chinese pulse reading, examination of the tongue and, where necessary, medical tests as used in Western medicine. A program of treatment that fits the needs of each individual patient is prescribed, using herbs or acupuncture, or both. Advice on special diet and exercises may also be provided. In addition, the clinic uses ear acupuncture and moxibustion and cupping, which are also traditional aspects of Chinese medicine.

Days and Hours of Operation: Tuesday, 1.30 pm to 8.30 pm. Wednesday, 9.30 am to 1.30 pm. Thursday, 9.30 am to 5.30 pm. Friday, 9.30 am to 5 pm. Saturday, 9.30 am to 1.30 pm.
Rates: The first consultation costs £25 Stg, and repeat consultations cost £12 Stg. A first consultation and an acupunture session costs £42 Stg, with additional sessions costing £29 Stg each.
Credit Cards: Cash or cheque only
Services: Acupuncture, Chinese herbal medicine, moxibustion and cupping
Facilities: Four treatment rooms, reception area and waiting area. Also Chinese-style garden, and ample car-parking space.
Staff: One therapist qualified in traditional Chinese medicine, and two receptionists.
Getting There: Take right turn off the main street in Bangor onto Hamilton Road, then turn left.

Quintessence Complementary Clinic

327 Antrim Road
Belfast BT15 2HF

Tel: 04890 351 590

Holistic care and beauty are both catered for in this modern, purpose-built centre, which includes a complementary-healthcare clinic, hairdressers and beauty salon. The centre is owned and managed by three sisters, Geraldine, Mari-Celene and Christina McGuigan, who provide healing and beauty care from head to toe and for both the inside and the outside of the body. Each area of the clinic has a separate entrance to ensure privacy. The health clinic has three treatment rooms, which are used by various practitioners, allowing for a vast range of therapies to be provided. Prospective clients are advised to book therapy sessions in advance to ensure that notice can be given to the appropriate therapist.

Days and Hours of Operation: Monday and Tuesday, 9.30 am to 9 pm. Wednesday to Saturday, 9.30 am to 5.30 pm. Later appointments are available by arrangement.
Rates: Treatments cost an average of £25 Stg.
Credit Cards: Visa and MasterCard.
Services: Kinesiology, acupuncture, reflexology, aromatherapy, deep tissue massage, Indian head massage, reiki, bio-testing and Bach flower remedies.
Facilities: Three treatment rooms and reception area, one beauty salon and one hairdressers.
Staff: Kinesiologists, one acupuncturist, four reflexologists, three aromatherapists, one deep-tissue massage therapist, one bio-testing therapist, two reiki practitioner and one Bowen-method practitioner.
Nearby Attractions: Belfast Zoo and Belfast Castle are both located nearby.
Getting There: From north Belfast, take the Antrim road towards Glengormley; the clinic is opposite the Waterworks Park.

Therapy Matters

The Trees
31 Fortwilliam Park
Belfast BT15 4AP

Tel: 04890 777 830

According to Jean Sage, Therapy Matters has brought healing at a very deep level, both physically and emotionally, to clients who attend her clinic. Working in hospice care for nine years, Jean realised the benefits of healing with aromatherapy and reflexology, and on returning to Belfast in 1990 she established Therapy Matters to bring further healing to individuals. A healing room should be a comfortable and relaxing space, contends Jean. To add to the feeling of relaxation for clients in the Therapy Matters healing room, she has decorated it in a soft cherry colour in addition to having teak panelling to provide a subdued warmth.

Days and Hours of Operation: Open Monday to Thursday, 2 pm to 6 pm, and Friday, 8.30 am to 6 pm.
Rates: Treatments cost between €20.30 and €31.73.
Credit Cards: Cash or cheque only.
Services: Therapeutic massage, aromatherapy, reflexology and occupational therapy.
Facilities: Treatment room and waiting area.
Staff: Jean Sage is sole owner-operator of the centre.
Local Attractions: The centre is situated close to the sea and Cave Hill.
Getting There: Take the Fortwilliam exit off the M2, then head north until you reach Fitzwilliam Park.

Claureen Health Farm

One Mile Inn
Ennis

Tel: 065 682 8969
Mobile: 065 684 2970
Fax: 065 684 2970
E-mail: claureen.ennis@eircom.net
Websites: www.claureen.com
www.healthfarmsofireland.com

For nineteen years, guests have travelled to Claureen Health Farm to relax, revive and detoxify weary bodies. Proprietor Mary Howard's mother originally opened the centre as a way to extend her keen interest in health and fitness. Its reputation soon spread by word of mouth. It was only natural for Mary to take over operations, as she had always wanted to follow in her mother's footsteps.

No more than eight to ten guests at a time stay for an average of five days in the 180-year-old converted farmhouse. Modern refurbishments have added comfort to the single, twin and triple rooms, which meet all Bord Fáilte standards for Irish health farms.

The primary programme on offer emphasises detoxification, although individuals are given the freedom to set their own pace. 'Guests see their energy levels go up and they also lose weight,' says Mary. 'The diet is so strict that we make up for it in other ways. There is a lot of pampering that goes with it.' A typical day begins at 9 am with a breakfast of fresh fruits and juices. All meals are free of dairy products, meat and alcohol. From 10 am until 1 pm, guests are in the gym. Those who fear exercise need not worry – gym sessions can include a relaxing sauna and jacuzzi. A lunch of home-made soup, salad and fruit is followed by free time, which can include a walk through the unspoilt countryside or a scenic tour to the Cliffs of Moher, Ailwee Caves, the Burren or Bunratty Castle. In the afternoon, guests receive instruction in yoga, followed by a Swedish full-body massage. For those wanting a bit more pampering, ki massage, aromatherapy, Indian head massage and reflexology can be booked. Evenings usually consist of people sitting around the fireplace for a chat. 'People would have met each other here six years ago or so and arrange to come on the same week every year,' says Mary.

Days and Hours of Operation: Open for residential programmes all year round.
Accommodation: A combination of eight single, double and twin bedrooms accommodating no more than ten people in total. Four of the rooms are en suite.
Rates: Vary according to season and services. From March to October, a one-week stay averages €400 or a single person and €361.95 per person sharing. Price includes room, board, classes, use of equipment, afternoon bus excursions, sunbed, sauna and jacuzzi.
Credit Cards: None accepted.
Meal Plans: All meals are included in the price of the programme. No dairy products, meat or alcohol are served at the centre.
Services: Detoxification programme, stretch-and-tone courses, massage, reflexology, yoga, hypnotherapy, acupuncture, facials and beauty treatments.
Recreational Activities: Cycling, yoga and gentle exercise. Swimming, golf, fishing and horse-riding are available nearby.
Facilities: Fully equipped gym, bicycles, yoga room, sauna, jacuzzi, sunbed, several treatment rooms, video library, pitch and putt, walled garden.
Staff: Mary Howard is a qualified beauty and body therapist, with additional training in Indian head massage, Bach flower remedies, reiki and nutrition. The centre also employs a yoga instructor, an aerobics instructor, a full-time beauty therapist and several part-time therapists. All are fully licensed and/or qualified.
Special Notes: Claureen only accepts residential clients. A minimum stay of five days is recommended, but midweek and weekend breaks are available. Smoking is not allowed. No children. Book two to three weeks in advance.
Nearby Attractions: The Burren, Ailwee Caves, Cliffs of Moher, Lahinch beach, Bunratty Castle and Fun Park.
Getting There: Situated one mile from the centre of Ennis on the N85. Shannon Airport is fourteen miles away. Collection can be arranged from the airport, or train or bus stations.

Kilkee Thalassotherapy Centre & Guest House

Grattan Street
Kilkee

Tel:	065 905 6742
Fax:	065 905 6762
E-mail:	mulcahype@eircom.net
Website:	www.kilkeethalasso.com

Opened in June 1999, the Kilkee Thalassotherapy Centre is part of the forty-year-old tradition of seaweed baths in the region. The family-owned centre, located within walking distance of the Kilkee coast, offers a range of relaxing and rejuvenating spa treatments. Although it does not yet have a medical doctor on staff, there are plans to employ one. As the seaweed is at its best between the spring equinox and the summer solstice, the natural baths run from about mid-March until the end of October. In the off-season, guests can avail of therapeutic treatments, even though the baths may not be on offer.

Perhaps inspired by her mother's annual travels to the Lisdoonvarna Spa Wells for a cure, owner Eileen Mulcahy brings her great love of all things related to the sea to the services available at the centre. An experienced diver who knows the Clare coast well, Eileen had to hang up her diving gear forever after a serious car accident seven years ago. 'I know a lot from a layman's point of view about the different plants and things in the ocean,' she says. 'Just physically lying in a bath of heated seawater is therapy in itself.'

Days and Hours of Operation: From July to September, the centre is open Monday to Saturday, 10 am to 7 pm. From October to June, it is open Tuesday to Saturday, 10 am to 7 pm.
Accommodation: Five en suite rooms – one triple, a twin, a single and two doubles – in a Bord Fáilte-approved, three-star guest house.
Rates: Prices of treatments range from €15.24 to €101.58. A weekend package including two nights bed and breakfast, six treatments, use of sauna and complimentary robes and slippers is €381. During the week, the same package costs €285.75.
Credit Cards: MasterCard, Visa and Laser.
Meal Plans: Meals are on a B&B basis only. Dietary requirements are accommodated, with advance notice.
Services: Natural seaweed baths, balneotherapy, three types of seaweed body wraps, massage, six different types of facials, beauty treatments.
Recreational Activities: Horse-riding, dolphin-watching, golf, scuba-diving, hill-walking.
Facilities: Private bathing room with two tubs, sauna, steam room, relaxation area. Private parking, spectacular cliff walks, beach a hundred yards away.
Staff: Two full-time and three part-time licensed and qualified therapists.
Special Notes: The entire premises is non-smoking. Advance booking is advisable throughout July and August.
Nearby Attractions: EU Blue Flag beaches, Scattery Island in Kilrush, monastic settlements, the Loop Head drive and three eighteen-hole golf courses.
Getting There: The centre is accessible by main roads directly from Dublin and Galway. Bus Éireann offers a range of stops throughout the county.

Poll na Lobhar Holistic Treatments

Kilnaboy

Tel: 065 708 9120
E-mail: pgrimes@eircom.net
Website: www.hello.to/pulse

Fresh country air and the sound of birdsong will awaken guests staying in Poll na Lobhar in Clare. For those of you who wish to stay in authentic surroundings, you will enjoy staying in this converted farmhouse, which is over a hundred years old and set in an acre of scenic grounds, including beautiful gardens and quiet areas for reflection. With breathtaking views of Mullaghmore Mountain at the rear of the house and the Burren National Park, famous for its wildlife and flowers, located to the right, this is an ideal setting for nature lovers. The centre is run by Helen Bolger and Paul Grimes. Helen has spent most of her life working as a teacher in New Zealand and the Pacific Islands. She became interested in complementary health after she had a profound experience in the Pacific Islands, where she was healed by indigenous people using natural methods. Before working in the complementary-therapy field, Paul was a senior manager in the London Ambulance Service.

Days and Hours of Operation: 9.30 am to 8.30 pm every day. Workshops run between 10 am and 5 pm.
Accommodation: Two guest bedrooms, each suitable for a maximum of two people sharing.
Rates: Weekend workshops cost between €120 and €220 each. Treatments cost €35 and last approximately one hour.
Meal Plans: Organic vegetarian meals made with produce from the centre's organic garden.
Services: Aromatherapy, reiki, kinesiology, massage, body pulsing, and focusing.
Workshops: Reiki, body-mind balancing, energy balancing, focusing, mind-works and body pulsing.
Recreational Activities: Hiking or walking in the Burren and on Mullaghmore Mountain.
Staff: Paul Grimes and Helen Bolger are both reiki masters and qualified practitioners in the therapies offered at Poll na Lobhar.
Getting There: From Corrofin in County Clare, take the R476 in the direction of Kilfenora and Lisdoonvarna. After two miles you will reach Kilnaboy and see a sign on your right pointing towards Kilnaboy Church and School. Turn right there. After three miles, at a crossroads marked Green Road on the left, carry straight on. One mile later you will pass a large period house on the left. Half a mile further on, you will come to the driveway of Poll na Lobhar on the left.

Tinarana House

Killaloe

Tel:	061 376 966
Fax:	061 376 773
E-mail:	info@tinarana.ie
Website:	www.tinaranahouse.com

On the shores of Lough Derg, surrounded by three hundred acres of parkland, sits the hundred-and-twenty-year-old Tinarana House. Gentle gardens surround the Victorian mansion, which is approached from a winding, tree-lined road. A typical day on a healthy break at this tranquil haven, which opened ten years ago, begins with juice at 7.45 am, followed by a walk at 8 am. After breakfast comes an ozone bath, a detoxifying body wrap, a back massage and an aerobics, yoga or relaxation class. The day finishes with a dinner of fresh organic foods. Guests have full use of the steam room, sauna and gym. Herbal teas and juices are available throughout the day.

Also associated with Tinarana House is the East Clinic in Killaloe. Established more than twenty years ago, this sixty-room day clinic is staffed by Doctors Paschal and Frieda Carmody. The Carmodys specialise in treating chronic degenerative diseases through non-chemical therapeutic means, and particular emphasis is placed on preventive medicine.

Days and Hours of Operation: Open year-round for day-long and residential programmes.
Accommodation: Fourteen en suite guest bedrooms, primarily doubles and twins.
Rates: Prices vary. A one-day package with ozone bath, body wrap, facial, lunch and yoga session is ¤146.02.
Credit Cards: MasterCard, Visa and American Express.
Meal Plans: Breakfast, lunch and dinner; special diets catered for; organic vegetables.
Services: Medical consultation, full laboratory service, dietary therapies, homeopathy, herbal remedies, vitamin infusion, chelation therapy, fango, hydrotherapy, balneotherapy, ozone baths, colour therapy, light therapy, chiropractic, colonic irrigation, therapeutic massage, aromatherapy, body wraps, reflexology, yoga, reiki, metamorphosis, aerobics and full range of beauty services.
Recreational Activities: Horse-riding, cycling, hill-walking, water sports and golf.
Facilities: Guest bedrooms, sauna, steam room, solarium, gym, sunbed, private treatment rooms, adjoining conservatory, separate medical clinic, and pleasure gardens.
Staff: Three full-time fully licensed and qualified therapists. Part-time therapists are hired as needed.
Special Notes: To avoid disappointment, it is advisable to book treatments prior to arrival.
Nearby Attractions: The eighteen-hole East Clare Golf Course, Lough Derg marina and boating facilities and the East Clare Way.
Getting There: Half an hour drive from Shannon Airport, two and a half hours from Dublin, fifteen miles from Limerick.

The Burren Holistic Centre

Rock Forest
Tubber

Tel: 091 633 212
Mobile: 086 833 4188
E-mail: bridintwist@yahoo.com
Website: www.burrenholisticcentre.com

Bridín Twist worked as the national president of the Irish Countrywomen's Association, living life on the road every day and in Brussels every week before deciding to 'step off the treadmill' and open the Burren Centre. Transforming her family home, which is over a hundred years old, also transformed her life, and she uses this experience when working with others who come to the centre, to inspire them and offer healing in a beautiful, tranquil setting. The original cottage has been extended using limestone and decorated in bright, inviting colours. The centre is surrounded by the Burren, with its extraordinary flora and fauna offering a unique setting for healing workshops and retreats. Extensive gardens with water features and seating areas include a zen garden in a wooded area for meditation, a sweat lodge with a sacred fire space, a peace labyrinth and a yoga garden. These are all incorporated into the workshops, which offer a supportive, tranquil environment for personal growth, meditation and stress-management. The venue is also available to hire for groups for their own tailored programmes or for individuals who need some time out for quiet reflection.

Days and Hours of Operation: Workshop weekends start with dinner at 7 pm on Friday and finish at 4.30 pm on Sunday. Massage and reiki treatments by appointment, to suit clients.
Accommodation: Accommodation for sixteen: seven rooms, three en suite, with individual colour schemes in each room. Also two treatment rooms.
Meal plans: Wholesome vegetarian food made with local organic ingredients.
Rates: Weekend workshop, €190.46. Midweek workshop, €63.49 for one day, €82.53 overnight. Treatments, €38.09 each.
Credit Cards: Cash or cheque only.
Staff: At weekends, Bridín and one cook, one housekeeper and one facilitator for the course.
Facilities: Large workspace/yoga room in the original cottage with limestone walls and decorated in soft oranges, yellows and greens. Seven bedrooms. Dining room, sun room and deck area. Sweat-lodge with sacred fire space and peace layrinth on the grounds. Extensive gardens, with water features and seating areas. Yoga lawn for use in summer. Zen garden in wooded area.
Services: Reiki, integrated-energy therapy and combined massage with reiki. Workshops on 'Sacred Space', meditation, tantra work, animal imagery, 'Finding Your Purpose', 'The Challenges of Fear', 'Dancing the Spiral' and neurolinguistic programming. Also stress-management courses.
Nearby attractions: Ailwee Caves, the Cliffs of Moher, the Dolmen – Poolnabron, the Aran Islands, the Burren and Lisdoonvarna.
Getting there: Take the train to Galway or Ennis and then take the bus to Gort. Bridín will collect from Gort on request.

From Dublin: through Athlone to Loughrea into Gort and then into the Burren. From Galway: through Gort and into the Burren.

Lisdoonvarna Spa Wells Health Centre

Lisdoonvarna

Tel: 065 707 4023

Since 1845, Lisdoonvarna has been Ireland's premier natural spa, and it is now an operational spa. In recent years, the health centre has been expanded to include sulphur baths, sulphur water, wax baths, aromatherapy and reflexology. There is also a coffee shop, which serves light refreshments. Ever since the sulphur spring was accidentally discovered in the early 1700s, the sulphur water has been used to help cure rheumatism, arthritis and general aches and pains. It is also considered to be a remedy for chronic congestion of the liver. The original bath house was completed in 1946. Three underground holding tanks in front of the pump room hold 3,000 gallons of sulphur water, which is pumped to the roof of the bath house and held there for use in the sulphur baths.

Days and Hours of Operation: Open June to October only. Monday to Friday, 10 am to 6 pm in June, July and August. Monday to Saturday, 10 am to 6 pm in September and the first week of October.
Rates: A sulphur bath is €22.84, and holistic treatments vary between €15.23 for a light massage to €44.42 for aromatherapy massage.
Credit Cards: Cash or cheque only.
Meal Plans: Coffee shop open in September only. Light refreshments such as sandwiches, soft drinks, tea and coffee are served.

Services: Sulphur bath, aromatherapy, reflexology, wax bath treatment to hands or feet, light massage.
Facilities: Four ladies' bath cubicles, four men's bath cubicles, two treatment rooms, two saunas.
Staff: Three general staff, two massage therapists.
Nearby Attractions: Lisdoonvarna, a small, friendly town in north Clare, is a mecca for traditional Irish music and culture. It is situated on the edge of the Burren and is only four miles from the sea, close to the incredible Cliffs of Moher. There are many interesting walking tours nearby. Ask staff for details of the Bog Road Walk, Judge's Walk, Quarry Walk and Castle Walk.
Getting There: From Shannon Airport, take the Ennis road. Follow the Corofin road to Kilfenora and then on to Lisdoonvarna.

BLARNEY PARK LEISURE CENTRE

Blarney

Tel: 021 438 5248
Fax: 021 438 1506
E-mail: leisurecentre@blarneypark.com
Website: www.blarneypark.com/leisure

Blarney Park Leisure Centre is part of the Blarney Park Hotel. It offers a wide range of facilities and includes a twenty-metre swimming pool with a giant water slide, leisure lagoon and toddler pool. The gymnasium has the latest aerobic and resistance equipment, with professional instructors available to arrange a training programme tailored to clients' personal requirements. There is a wide range of exercise classes available in the air-conditioned aerobics studio. The studio is bright and airy, with views of the surrounding rural landscape. Those who prefer outdoor sport can avail of the tennis courts and become involved in the regular courses, tournaments and club sessions. The leisure centre is particularly suited to families, as it provides child-care facilities which stimulate and entertain the children, while parents can enjoy the sports and leisure facilities in the therapy centre. Pastel colours add to the relaxing atmosphere. Expert therapists will advise on the best treatment to take your cares away.

Days and Hours of Operation: 9 am to 9 pm, seven days a week. Book to avoid disappointment.
Accommodation: Ninety bedrooms, with a choice of standard en suite and superior en suite.

Rates: €88.83 B&B for a single en suite room. Treatments cost €25 for each half-hour session and €38 per hour-long session.
Credit Cards: Visa, Laser and MasterCard.
Meal Plans: The restaurant provides meals of the highest quality and variety. Special needs are also catered for, with healthy options and vegetarian meals available.
Services: Ki massage, therapeutic massage, reflexology, aromatherapy massage and Indian head massage.
Facilities: Two treatment rooms, twenty-metre swimming pool, and gymnasium.
Staff: All staff are qualified in one or more treatment areas.
Nearby Attractions: Local attractions include the Blarney Stone, Blarney Woollen Mills, Fota Golf Course, Fota Wildlife Park, Inniscarra Lake, Farran Forest Park and all the amenities of Cork City itself.
Getting There: From Cork (Dublin direction), go to the Glanmire roundabout, and go straight ahead at the roundabout. When you see Silversprings Hotel, take the next left and go over the bridge. Go straight through eight sets of traffic lights. At the T-junction, turn right towards Blarney.

Diamus

PO Box 244
Cork

Tel: 021 487 7120
Mobile: 087 412 5417
E-mail: foleydonna@hotmail.com
Website: www.diamus.com

Donna Foley wants to enable people to see the diamond within them. After studying and living in the United States, Australia and Guatemala, Donna returned to Ireland with qualifications in herbal medicine, massage, nutrition, body-centred psychotherapy and craniosacral therapy. For just over a year, she has organised residential weekends focusing on various aspects of health and well-being.

'I guess my philosophy is that we are all creatures of unlimited ability,' she says. 'I think our whole sense of self-empowerment is not so strong in Irish culture. I try to facilitate more of that to emerge. Like Nelson Mandela says, it doesn't serve you to stay small so that other people will feel more comfortable around you.'

A typical day on a course involves hands-on experiential work with a group for a total of about six hours. Because the group dynamic is important to the success of the workshop, people are encouraged to eat together and integrate. The programme presents an ideal opportunity for anyone considering a career in a particular therapy, as they can receive a brief introduction to it over the course of the intensive weekend. Although the residential courses are usually run in a rural setting, such as Myros Wood in west Cork, some may take place in Dublin.

Two of the workshops on offer in 2001, for example, were 'Food as Medicine' and 'Complementary Therapies for Children', both of which Donna facilitated. Participants in the 'Food as Medicine' course learned about various food groups and how to combine them. People with special dietary needs and allergies learned the skills needed to prepare interesting and satisfying meals. Parents participating in the 'Complementary Therapies for Children' discussed ways to improve their children's emotional and physical health using therapies such as aromatherapy, nutrition and homeopathy. Special focus was placed on children with attention-deficit disorder, allergies and behavioural problems.

Donna has been particularly influenced by the Esalen style of body-work, which was developed at the Esalen Institute in Big Sur, California. More information about the institute and its programmes can be gathered from its Website at www.esalen.org.

Days and Hours of Operation: Weekly workshops running from Friday to Sunday are held from September to April.
Accommodation: Between twenty and thirty adults are housed in a combination of single and shared rooms.
Rates: Programmes cost between €150 and €200.
Credit Cards: None accepted.
Meal Plans: Meals are included. Where possible, the food is vegetarian and organic.
Services: A range of personal-development courses centred on body-awareness seminars, massage and somatics.
Facilities: As the residential venue varies throughout the year, contact Donna Foley for information regarding specific facilities.
Staff: Guest speakers facilitate the workshops. The majority of these people are teachers visiting from Continental Europe or America who specialise in Esalen workshops, yoga, somatics and therapeutic body-work.
Special Notes: Smoking is not allowed.
Getting There: Contact Donna Foley for details.

Grove House

Longevity Centre and Spa
Shanballymore
Mallow

Tel:	022 25518
Fax:	022 25043
E-mail:	longevity@eircom.net

Grove House is a splendidly converted old farmhouse which provides accommodation of the highest standard in ye olde style in a remote, quiet country area of Cork. Proprietor Jacqueline Mary O'Farrell's bubbly, friendly personality quickly puts you at ease on your arrival. The health facilities are situated away from the family home and are clean, comfortable and tastefully decorated. They include a small swimming pool with views of the surrounding green, lush landscape, providing you with a sense of calm and serenity. The Canadian hot tub overlooking surrounding fields and oak trees is the perfect way to relax after your dip.

A wide variety of therapies is on offer. Grove House caters for individuals and groups, and residential and day visitors. Mary's main area of interest is nutrition, and nutrition advice and weight-management dietary plans are available on request. Walkers can delight in taking peaceful walks in the surrounding countryside. During a twenty-minute walk, I observed wild deer, ponies, pheasants, swans and the occasional dog! Areas of interest in the surrounding area are Doneraile Forest Park, megalithic tombs and the Famine Folly.

Hours and Days of Operation: Daily, weekend and weekly overnights. The centre can be reserved for private groups.

Accommodation: A maximum of ten guests in en suite bedrooms with pine floors and doors, high ceilings and pine furniture. Bord Fáilte-approved.

Rates: €39 per person sharing. Weekends from €180, including two treatments, B&B for two nights, and one dinner. Average price for individual therapies is €39. Gift vouchers are available.

Credit Cards: MasterCard and Visa.

Meal Plans: Breakfast, lunch and dinner available. Vegetarian and non-vegetarian cuisine. Please advise of any special dietary needs when booking.

Facilities: Indoor swimming pool, hydrotherapy spa, steam room. Conference room available.

Treatments: Body-scrub exfoliation, seaweed body wrap, reflexology, toning body wrap, frigid cold-wrap treatment, reiki, aromaceane, aromatherapy massage, rebalancing aromatherapy facial, Indian head massage and back, neck and shoulder massage.

Staff: Two professional massage therapists, two part-time beauticians, one reflexologist, one reiki master and one nutritionist.

Special Notes: Weekend courses available, at arranged times, on stress management, relaxation therapy, neurolinguistic programming, exercise and fitness, women's health, kinesiology, yoga and natural healing through detoxification, herbs and optimum nutrition.

Getting There: Grove House is twenty minutes from Mallow or Mitchelstown in Cork. A private or hired car would be the best form of transport, given the centre's countryside location.

Hagel Healing Farm

Coomleigh
Bantry

Tel: 027 66179

If anyone has managed to create a piece of heaven on earth, it is Janny and Fred Wieler. Their home, which offers stunning vistas of Bantry Bay and the green valleys undulating towards it, evolved into the eight-year-old Hagel Healing Farm. The couple started with one room and a few people winding their way through the back roads of County Cork up to the couple's small organic farm. 'We like being with people and sharing the lifestyle we lead ourselves,' says Janny. 'We always found that our place was well visited. Don't ask me how they got here – they just did. We thought that since that was happening anyway, we might as well make it a business.'

The couple moved to Ireland from Holland nearly twenty years ago in search of a healthier lifestyle. After several years of organic gardening, keeping cows and making cheese, they both trained in various complementary therapies. Janny eventually became a yoga teacher, then trained in aromatherapy, massage and reiki. Fred pursued his interest in art therapy and reiki and became a teacher in both disciplines. He also specialises in vegetarian cookery, running cookery courses and preparing all the meals at Hagel.

Set in the mountainous Bantry Bay area, the healing farm is surrounded by secluded and mature wild gardens on five acres of private land. The remoteness and quiet are important elements of a stay with the Wielers. 'People usually think they have driven too far and passed it,' says Janny. 'Part of being here is really to get back in contact with nature. This is for the type of person who likes to be out and away from things.'

A stay at the farm begins with either a sauna upon arrival or a footbath with essential oils or seaweed. Guests can curl up in front of the open fire in the living room with a cup of tea made from herbs picked in the garden. In the morning, guests can enjoy muesli, fresh fruit, yoghurt, juice and bread for breakfast, served either in bed or in the spacious conservatory, which offers views of the valley and ocean beyond. Depending on the programme, the day may then include an aromatherapy massage, a seaweed wrap and facial, a daily sauna or a seaweed or aromatherapy footbath, a reflexology or reiki treatment, walks, yoga or guided relaxation.

'Our approach is very individual,' says Janny. 'We can gear our programmes completely to the needs of the person. People come back year after year. I think they like the personal approach. We have time for people, time for a chat. They know they are a person and not Number 25 in the group.'

In addition to offering restorative retreats, Janny Wieler also runs a school for therapeutic massage and aromatherapy at the centre. Students are trained to receive ITEC certification during residential weekends and week-long intensive programmes over the course of nine months. When not at the farm, Janny may be found in the store she owns and operates, the Natural Health Care Centre & Shop at Anam Cara in Bantry.

Days and Hours of Operation: Weekend and week-long packages offered year-round. Closed at Christmas and New Year.
Accommodation: Three single and three double en suite rooms
Rates: Vary according to services. Weekend general health packages average €215.90 from Friday to Sunday.
Credit Cards: MasterCard and Visa.
Meal Plans: A diet of fresh, healthy wholefoods is included in the programme price.
Services: Therapeutic massage, aromatherapy, reiki, seaweed wraps, seaweed facials, reflexology, shiatsu, vegetable-and-fruit fasts, meditation, art therapy. Courses in reiki I, reiki II and vegetarian cooking.
Recreational Activities: Yoga, hill-walking.
Facilities: Sauna, jacuzzi bath, seaweed room, meditation room, garden.
Staff: The centre currently employs three fully licensed and qualified therapists, as well as occasional part-time therapists according to demand.
Special Notes: Smoking is not allowed.
Nearby Attractions: Bantry Bay, Beara Peninsula, heritage sites, fishing, boating, horse-riding.
Getting There: From Cork Airport, catch the bus to Bantry. A pick-up service is available from Bantry, with prior arrangement.

INCHYDONEY LODGE AND SPA

Clonakilty

Tel:	023 33143
Fax:	023 35229

E-mail: reservations@inchydoneyisland.com
Website: www.inchydoneyisland.com

Inchydoney is set on a headland with spectacular views of magnificent Blue Flag beaches. This contemporary four-star hotel is a winner of the AA Millennium Hotel of the Year and includes a thalassotherapy centre with highly sophisticated equipment and treatments. Although relatively new to Ireland, thalassotherapy, which uses heated seawater in the swimming pool and treatments to restore health and energy, is very popular in Europe. According to Dr Christian Jost of Inchydoney Lodge, the effect of heating the fresh seawater to a certain temperature opens the pores of the body and allows an exchange of minerals between the blood and the sea water, giving the person a sense of vitality. This treatment is particularly beneficial for those experiencing circulatory problems, arthritis, stress, fatigue or migraines. I certainly felt invigorated on my departure from the centre.

The staff are confident, friendly and efficient in their approach – and thankfully unobtrusive – as you relax away the stresses and strains of modern living in the soothing environment of the lodge and spa. The award-winning Gulfstream Restaurant, which overlooks the sea, provides the most delicious food I have tasted in some time. The highlight for me was swimming in the heated seawater pool, with its micro-bubble seats, neck showers and underwater jets.

Days and Hours of Operation: As the thalassotherapy centre is part of the Inchydoney Island Hotel, it is open daily between 8 am and 8 pm.

Accommodation: Sixty-seven ocean-view de luxe rooms and twenty apartments.

Rates: Double en suite luxury room €129 per person sharing per night. Weekend rate for two sharing – two nights B&B, one evening meal and six treatments – is €1,020 each. Treatments are approximately €39 each.

Credit Cards: Visa, American Express and Access.

Meal Plans: When the client is attending the thalassotherapy centre, Dr Christian Jost and the executive chef work together to prepare a health and dietary plan which allows the person both to enjoy and to gain an understanding of the food you eat. The food includes plenty of fresh vegetables and fruit – organic wherever possible – cereals and grains. Calorific and fat content is clearly marked on the menu.

Services: Balneotherapy, hydrojet treatment, pressotherapy, cryotherapy, algotherapy, brumisation, electrolysis, massage, reflexology and beauty treatments.

Facilities: Heated seawater pool with countercurrent swimming area, waterfall, geyser spa, air spa, micro-bubble seats, underwater massage seats, neck showers, underwater jets and aqua-gymnastic area. Eleven treatment rooms. Sauna and hammam steam room. Relaxation area, overlooking the ocean. Medical consultant and varied dietary system. Fitness centre incorporating cardio and muscular training. Beauty centre specialising in hair, face, bust and body.

Nearby Attractions: Twenty minutes away from the Old Head of Kinsale Golf Course. For the equestrian enthusiast, there is an excellent riding centre just two miles from the property, where you can enjoy an early-morning ride along the beach. Excellent walks.

Getting there: Thirty miles from Cork at the roundabout in Clonakilty, follow signs to Inchydoney.

Ki-Care Clinic

Fitzpatricks Fitness Centre
Silver Springs
Tivoli
Cork

Clinic Tel:	021 450 5128
Hotel Tel:	021 450 7533
Hotel Fax:	021 450 7641
E-mail:	silversprings@morangroup.ie
Website:	www.moranhotels.ie

Ki-Care Clinic is part of the four-star Silver Springs Moran Hotel, set in sylvan terraced grounds. The exterior architectural design is 1970s in style, with a contemporary, elegant hotel interior. Views overlook the upper reaches of the River Lee. Within the complex is an award-winning leisure facility, including a twenty-five-metre pool, fully equipped modern gymnasium, indoor tennis courts and nine-hole golf course. These facilities are all available to guests and members only. The clinic itself is open to guests and the general public. It offers a variety of therapies to help you de-stress, revitalise or generally pamper yourself.

Days and Hours of Operation: Monday to Friday, 10 am to 8.30 pm. Saturday, 10 am to 2 pm.
Accommodation: Available in four-star Silver Springs Hotel. A hundred and twenty-three executive bedrooms, eight luxurious suites. Fully air-conditioned, with ample car parking. Double or twin room €184.10 to €279.33. Includes full Irish breakfast and all taxes.
Rates: Therapies cost between €25 and €38.
Credit Cards: Visa only.
Meal Plans: Hotel restaurant with Irish and international cuisine and extensive wine list.
Services: Ki, therapeutic and Indian head massage, injuries and sports massage, reiki, reflexology, Hopi ear candles, Chinese medicine: acupuncture, herbs and cupping (covered by BUPA insurance).
Facilities: Three treatment rooms, reception and waiting area. Guests have access to the gym and swimming-pool area.
Staff: Karen Bourke: sports-injury massage, deep-tissue therapeutic massage and reflexology. Justin Dennehy: acupuncture, reflexology, ear candles, ki massage. Audra Furnell: Indian head massage, therapeutic massage, sports massage, ear candles. Rob Littlewood: traditional Chinese medicine, including acupuncture, ear candles, herbs and cupping. Tanya O'Keefe: deep-tissue massage, Indian head massage, sports-injury massage and ear candles.
Nearby Attractions: Fota House, Fota Wildlife Park, Cork City, Cobh town, Seapoint – the departure point of the *Titanic*.
Getting There: Ten minutes from Cork train station. Take a taxi in the direction of the Jack Lynch Tunnel. Cork International Airport is seven miles away.

Nature Art Centre for Drumming, Art and Healing

Ballybane
Ballydehob

Tel/Fax: 028 37323
E-mail: naturart@gofree.indigo.ie
Internet: www.holistic.ie/nature-art

The Nature Art Centre is a family-run workshop centre and environmental project. It is situated in a secluded, peaceful area of west Cork, surrounded by mountains and incredible views. Programme facilitators Thomas Wiegandt and Annette Patzold provide an atmosphere which is welcoming and condusive to the self-empowering workshops on offer. Thomas has been playing and performing music since 1973 and has been trained by West African and Balinese teachers. He is also an instrument maker and builds, repairs and sells drums and percussion instruments. Annette is a dancer and painter. They regularly invite special guest teachers to give workshops. There are no daily regimens guests must adhere to. Visitors are free to attend workshops or simply take walks through some of the breathtaking landscape which surrounds the centre. Several workshops throughout the year focus on healing; for instance, healing-drum workshops draw on shamanic traditions and Sufi chanting to restore inner harmony by clearing vibration blocks in the body, which manifest as emotional disturbance. Tibetan singing bowls feature in healing ceremonies that use vibration and sound massage as a source of healing. Voice and percussion workshops are also held, to connect individuals with their own voices in a safe space. Intuitive-painting workshops and vegetarian cookery classes are also on offer, making this a centre where people can access and express their inner creativity fully.

Days and Hours of Operation: Weekend workshops and personal retreats are offered in autumn, winter and spring. A more extensive range of workshops is available in the summer.
Accommodation: Although the accommodation is basic, it is reasonably priced and the owners are also open to having guests camp on the land. The holiday hostel sleeps up to six people and includes three bedrooms, a small kitchen and a bathroom.
Rates: July and August, €317.43. All other times of year, €190.46. B&B, €19.05. Self-catering accommodation, €12.70. Hostel, €10.16. Cost of courses: €32 per day. The maximum size of groups is six, to ensure individual attention.
Credit Cards: Cash or cheque only.
Meal Plans: Three wholesome meals per day, using fresh, organic ingredients. Vegetarian and special diets are catered for.
Staff: Thomas Wiegandt and Annette Patzold, with part-time invited teachers involved in various workshops throughout the year.
Services: Healing and personal-growth workshops, including African drumming, shamanism, belly dancing, Tibetan singing bowls, voice and percussion and intuitive-painting workshops. There is also the opportunity to learn how to cook wholesome vegetarian meals.

Recreational Activities: Three-hour guided tour of ancient Celtic sites. Visit the magic stone circle and ring fort, with its rare Bronze Age rock art.

Getting There: The Nature Art Centre is situated four miles north-east of Ballydehob and eight miles south of Bantry. It is worth checking their website for the map, given its remote location.

Anam Cara Natural Health Care Centre

First Floor
Warner Centre
Barrack Street
Bantry

Tel: 027 52020 or 027 66179

To extend their offering of therapeutic services in a non-residential setting, Hagel Healing Farm owners Fred and Janny Weiler also own and operate the Anam Cara Natural Health Care Centre in the scenic town of Bantry. The couple use their combined backgrounds in reiki, yoga and massage to provide a committed natural approach to health that complements conventional medicine.

Clients receive a high level of committed personal attention during therapies. For example, during aromatherapy sessions, individualised blends of oils are tailored to the person's needs. Upon request, the aromatherapist will produce a bottle of the mixture for use at home.

Days and Hours of Operation: From 10 am to 6 pm Monday to Saturday.
Rates: Treatments typically cost €38.09 per hour.
Credit Cards: MasterCard and Visa.
Services: Reflexology, aromatherapy, reiki, biodynamic therapy, counselling, yoga, shiatsu, holistic massage, sports-injury therapy, manipulative therapy, cranio-sacral therapy, classes in yoga, aromatherapy, massage and t'ai chi.
Facilities: Four private treatment rooms, yoga room, retail shop.

Staff: Eight fully qualified and licensed full- and part-time therapists.
Special Notes: Available through the shop is a wide range of skincare products, essential oils, soaps, crystals, relaxation music, videos, books, tapes, incense and more.
Getting There: The centre is within a five-minute walk of the Bantry bus stop.

Bon Secours Health Lodge

Western Road
Cork

Tel: 021 434 7351

The Bon Secours Health Lodge, located in the refurbished gardener's lodge of Cork City Hospital, has new therapy rooms and a small garden. Its founder, Sister Norrie Finan, spent three and a half years in training before setting up the centre, which was officially opened to all members of the community by Minister for Health Micheál Martin in July 2000.

Sister Finan initially became interested in holistic therapies while on missions in Peru. A qualified nurse, she became fascinated by how people used herbs to heal themselves in the absence of antibiotics or Western medicines. Meadbh MacSweeney, also a qualified nurse, worked with Sister Finan for a year before the centre opened. Both are trained and have qualified to practice reflexology and aromatherapy. Sister Finan also holds a diploma in humanities and holistic development, while Meadbh is qualified in both ki and remedial massage. In November 2001, another Sister, qualified in nutrition and stress management, will join the group.

Clients at Bon Secours are given the time to tell their story in full, and no one is ever rushed. 'Our philosophy is one of creating a sacred space where people can escape the effects of the bombardments and stresses of everyday living,' says Sister Finan. 'It's about allowing the body, mind and spirit time out, encouraging each individual to reach deep into their own psyche and activate the body's natural healing powers.'

The centre is linked to the Bon Secours Hospital through the oncology ward. Therapists at the centre work with cancer patients on a weekly basis.

Days and Hours of Operation: Monday, 9 am to 9 pm. Tuesday to Friday, 9 am to 6 pm. One Saturday per month, 9 am to 6 pm.
Rates: The cost of treatments typically ranges from €31.74 to €44.44 per one-hour session.
Credit Cards: None accepted at the moment.
Services: Aromatherapy, reflexology, therapeutic massage, infant and pregnancy massage, manual lymph drainage, coping skills, nutrition counselling, stress management, guided imagery and meditation.
Facilities: Meditation room and two private treatment rooms.
Staff: Three fully qualified and licensed therapists.
Special Notes: The centre is accessible for people with disabilities. Smoking is not allowed.
Getting There: The clinic is a twenty minutes' walk from the city centre.

Clinic of Oriental and Traditional Chinese Medicine

9 Oakfield Green
Glanmire

Tel/Fax: 021 866607
E-mail: cotcm@indigo.ie

The Clinic of Oriental and Traditional Chinese Medicine is run by Deirdre Mackesy, a highly qualified practitioner of traditional Chinese medicine and homeopathy. Deirdre qualified as a nurse in 1984 and worked as a staff nurse in emergency care, hospice care, medicine and surgery. She first discovered the benefits of complementary therapies when working with a medical aid agency in Africa. The agency used some complementary therapies to heal victims of famine and war. Following this, she embarked on a journey of study in the area of complementary health. She has studied in Dublin, London, China and Sri Lanka. Deirdre combines her training in the areas of reflexology, acupuncture, aromatherapy, massage, reiki, ear-candling, tui na and Chinese herbal medicine and homeopathy with her training in conventional medical care as a nurse and her understanding of anatomy and physiology gained while working in the pharmaceutical industry. Her primary medical focus is natural health care; having spent twenty-one years in the health-care sector, she brings a wealth of experience and insight to her healing.

The first appointment in the clinic lasts approximately ninety minutes, or up to three hours for homeopathy and acupuncture. During this time, Deirdre takes a detailed medical and lifestyle history. This includes questions regarding general health, family history and lifestyle choices. Subsequent sessions last between one and two hours.

Days and Hours of Operation: Monday to Friday, 9 am to 5 pm.
Rates: €57.11 for first consultation and €44.45 for subsequent sessions.
Credit Cards: Cash or cheque only.
Services: Acupuncture, homeopathy and vacuflex reflexology.
Staff: Deirdre Mackesy.
Getting There: Located in Glanmire, a suburban area four miles outside Cork City on the old main Dublin–Cork road. There is a good bus service to Glanmire from Cork City.

CRYSTAL CONNECTION

50 Cornmarket Street
Cork

Tel: 021 427 8243.

Johnathan Dawson and his wife opened the Inner Healing Centre in Cork six years ago, when they began offering reflexology and aromatherapy treatments as well as workshops in various aspects of holistic health. While shopping in Dublin, his wife bought a few crystals from a collector, who commented that it was about time someone began selling them in Cork. While the Dawsons had no intention of selling crystals, the idea slowly took root, and eventually they laid the odd, eye-catching stone down on the table, with a price tag attached, during workshops. Initial sales grew, and the Crystal Connection was born.

The shop, which is located on the ground floor, stocks a variety of stones, books and esoterica. Three private treatments on the first floor accommodate approximately twelve therapists specialising in various aspects of healing. 'Right from the start, the idea was to provide a space where people could come and find things that were authentic and to provide a service that was not found anywhere else,' Johnathan says.

Despite a fire in the summer of 2001 that forced the Dawsons to relocate, the shop and healing rooms continue to operate. 'We have always kept the two together,' Johnathan notes. 'On the one hand it is a shop, and on the other it is a place to have work done. The two feed each other.'

Days and Hours of Operation: The shop is open Monday to Friday from 11 am to 6 pm and on Saturday from 10 am to 6 pm. The healing centre is open by appointment, with the last treatment ending at 10 pm.
Rates: The average price for an hour-long session is €38.09.
Credit Cards: None accepted.
Services: Reiki and seichim, qi gung, aromatherapy, reflexology, Indian head massage, lymphatic drainage, yoga classes, reiki workshops, astrology, tarot readings, counselling, psychotherapy, Buddhist meditation.
Facilities: There are four floors in the building: the shop is on the ground floor and there are therapy rooms on each floor. The therapy rooms, which are used for workshops and therapies, can be accessed through the shop or via the side entrance.
Staff: Twelve therapists operate out of the healing centre.
Special Notes: Smoking is not allowed.
Getting There: The centre is located on the Coal Quay, which is a five-minute walk from Patrick Street.

Douglas Day Spa

Morris House
Douglas

Tel: 021 896622

Douglas Day Spa is essentially a beauty salon, offering skincare treatments for the face and body. The spa also provides some complementary therapies. It is ideal for those who want head-to-toe pampering.

Days and Hours of Operation: Monday to Saturday, 9.30 am to 6 pm, or later by appointment.
Rates: From €19.04 for back massage to €88.83 for ninety minutes' algae detox treatment, in which a marine algae mask is used to refine, hydrate and enhance the appearance of the skin.
Credit Cards: Visa, Laser, MasterCard and Access.
Services: Reiki, reflexology, Indian head massage, sports-injury massage, aromatherapy body massage, back massage, ultimate detox, algae treatment and beauty treatments.
Staff: Two qualified complementary therapists, two beauticians, and manager Martyna Cooney.
Facilities: Two treatment rooms.

Flowing Unity

28 Princes Street
Cork

Tel: 021-4222790
E-mail: flowingunity@yahoo.co.uk
Web: www.geocities.com/flowingunity

The subtle smell of incense greets clients as they walk in the door of the family-owned Flowing Unity holistic healing centre and shop, run by sisters Fionnuala Conroy, Ber O'Mahony and Karen Foley. Fionnuala, who teaches reiki at the College of Commerce and St John's College, offers reiki seichim and Indian head massage treatments and workshops. In addition to teaching tarot workshops, Ber specialises in rebirthing and cellular healing. Both these disciplines aim to provide a comfortable space in which people are able to empower themselves and interact more positively with the world at large.

Fionnuala is careful to cultivate a welcoming atmosphere in the shop, which sells a variety of rough and smooth cut crystals, miniature gems, feng shui accessories, hand-made goods imported from Nepal through fair-trade agreements, tarot cards, angel cards and goddess cards. 'People can pop in and have a chat,' she says. 'Anybody who is on in reception is qualified to offer at least one of the therapies, so they can talk to the person and guide them to what might be best for them.'

Days and Hours of Operation: Reception and shop hours are Monday to Saturday, 11 am to 6 pm. Therapies are available Monday to Saturday, 9 am to 10 pm. The shop is open on Sundays for therapies and workshops by special appointment.
Rates: The average price of a treatment is €32. Workshops cost €6.35.
Credit Cards: None accepted.
Services: Reiki, seichim, acupuncture, rebirthing, cellular healing, reflexology, chakra readings, aromatherapy, Indian head massage, sports injury massage, therapeutic massage. Workshops on shamanism, drumming, dream-work, reiki, angel meditation and tarot.
Facilities: Upstairs, on first and second floor: the shop room, a large room where workshops and groups are accommodated (this room can hold roughly twenty people), and a private treatment room.
Staff: Six full- and part-time therapists and workshop facilitators.
Special Notes: Smoking is not allowed.
Getting There: The centre is located in Cork City, just off Patrick Street.

Freedom Holistic Centre

1 Rockgrove
Midleton

Tel: 021 463 3421
E-mail: info@kinesiologycollege.com
Website: www.kinesiologycollege.com

After making her way first as a music teacher, then as a computer-software trainer, Ger Hunter changed hats yet again. In 1992, Ger began practising kinesiology, and in 1995 she opened the Freedom Holistic Centre, which she ran from home. Her qualifications include training as a 'Touch for Health' instructor with the International Kinesiology College in Zurich, as a wellness kinesiology instructor with Topping International Institute in Washington State and as a prana instructor with Gateways College of Natural Therapeutics in California. 'I trained as a kinesiologist in order to help people help themselves,' she says. 'It's about giving people the life skills to bring themselves into balance.'

Therapists at the centre take a decidedly holistic approach, examining ailments from structural, emotional and biochemical viewpoints. Also figured into the equation are environmental stresses. 'It's about caring for people and promoting self-healing,' says Ger. 'We're not healers. We help people to gain greater body-awareness.'

The clinic was soon bustling with satisfied clients; this clearly demonstrated to Ger the need for more qualified therapists in her field. In 1995, she founded the Kinesiology College of Ireland. In a large conservatory with wood floors and tall windows looking out onto a garden with a pond and waterfall, students study to receive the only kinesiology diploma in Ireland that is recognised by other international organisations. Also available through the college are weekend and mini three-hour workshops on kinesiology and related subjects, such as 'Touch for Health' and 'Perceptive Vision'. 'The emphasis of learning is really on fun – the ability to have fun with kinesiology,' says Ger. 'We teach very hands-on and we work with the way people learn. If a person is visual we will give a more visual presentation. All different learning styles are catered for.'

Days and Hours of Operation: Open Monday and Wednesday from 9 am to 9 pm, and Tuesday, Thursday and Friday from 9 am to 5 pm.
Rates: The average price of a treatment is €50.
Credit Cards: None accepted.
Services: Kinesiology, and workshops and courses in kinesiology, Tibetan energy healing, 'Touch for Health' and stress management.
Facilities: One private treatment room.
Staff: Two fully qualified and licensed kinesiologists and one administrator.
Special Notes: The centre is accessible for people with disabilities. Advance booking of three to four weeks is recommended. Smoking is not allowed.
Getting There: From Cork City, take the Midleton bus. The centre is located on many of the main Cork bus routes.

Jivan Clinic of Complementary Medicine

28 Princes Street
Cork

Tel: 021 422 2790
Mobile: 087 991 3564

Taking its name from the Sanskrit word for 'spiritual healing', the Jivan healing centre is situated one floor above the Flowing Unity bookshop and healing centre in Cork City. Paul Vaughan and Ann Clare McCarthy established Jivan to provide an inspiring setting in which to facilitate people's journeys to complete well-being. Having previously worked in health centres in Thailand and Australia, Paul specialises in spiritual healing, reiki and therapeutic massage. After studying resonance healing and dynamic journalling in the Netherlands, Ann Clare returned to Ireland to teach these disciplines through personal one-on-one sessions and workshops. Both Paul and Ann bring a profound sensitivity to their work, treating each client as a unique individual.

Days and Hours of Operation: Open Monday to Saturday, 9 am to 9 pm by appointment. Courses are on offer over the weekend.
Rates: The average price of a session is €25.40.
Credit Cards: None accepted.
Services: Ki massage, therapeutic massage, reiki, resonance healing, energy balancing, meditation, and workshops on resonance healing, journalling and goal-setting.
Facilities: The centre, which is located on the second floor of the building, has one private treatment room.
Staff: Paul Vaughan and Ann Clare McCarthy.
Special Notes: Smoking is not allowed.

L.A. Beauty Salon

29 Ash Street
Clonakilty

Tel: 023 34565

L.A. Beauty Salon proprietor Louise O'Connell caters to people on the run. 'The amount of forty-minutes back massage we do is unreal,' she says. 'And that would just be with people passing through.' The present two-storey, purpose-built salon opened five years ago, but Louise has owned the L.A. Beauty Salon for just over ten years. Beauty treatments are on offer on the ground floor, while therapeutic spa treatments take place upstairs.

'Nowadays people are so stressed out,' says Louise. 'This is a place where people can come to do the important jobs, such as getting their hair done, waxing and so on, but also just take time out for themselves without having to spend a day in a spa.' Louise does recommend, however, that clients wanting a serene and quiet atmosphere should be sure to schedule appointments in the evening, as the salon is often very busy during the day. Tourists drawn to Clonakilty by its abundant flowers and numerous tidy-town awards will have no difficulties getting slotted in, even for a half-hour reflexology quick fix.

Days and Hours of Operation: Open Monday to Saturday from 9.30 am to 6 pm. The salon is open until 9 pm on Thursday and Friday evenings by appointment.

Rates: A typical hour-long spa treatment costs an average of €44.44. Facials vary between €19.05 and €76.18.
Credit Cards: MasterCard, Visa, Laser, American Express.
Services: Full range of beauty treatments, aromatherapy massage, reflexology, facials, seaweed algae wraps, peppermint seaweed body twist, lymphatic drainage, toning, non-surgical facelifts.
Facilities: Seven private treatment rooms, two sunbeds, shower facilities.
Staff: Three full-time and two part-time therapists and aestheticians.
Special Notes: Smoking is not allowed. Children under eighteen must be accompanied by a parent. There are special offers on treatments once a month.
Getting There: The salon is located roughly thirty miles from Cork City off the main road to Clonakilty.

The Natural Healing Centre & Natural Healing Institute of Ireland

Thompson House
McCurtain Street
Cork

Tel: 021 450 1600

Established by Peter O'Donoghue and Mark Longfield in 1984, the Natural Healing Centre is a purpose-built centre for complementary therapies and has been decorated with the comfort of the client in mind. Sunshine yellow and warm primrose colours mixed with pine floors throughout give clarity of space, in addition to uplifting the mood. Classical music and delicate aromas of clary sage and lavender help alleviate any negativity and lift the spirits. With twenty years' teaching experience in the field of complementary health care, the centre's practitioners are some of the most highly trained therapists in the country, providing therapeutic and sports massage, zen deep-tissue therapy, acupuncture, reflexology and biocranial therapy. Diploma courses run at the centre are taught to a high practical standard. These include therapeutic massage, sports and remedial massage and reflexology. On conclusion of the course, the student takes a theory and practical examination, endorsed by the British Complementary Medicine Association. The Natural Healing Institute of Ireland, which is affiliated to the centre, was formed in 1996 to promote the professional interests of qualified practitioners and inform them of career prospects, group-insurance details and affiliated organisations. Most courses are run at weekends, and therapies are available throughout the week.

Days and Hours of Operation: Monday, 9 am to 6.30 pm. Tuesday, Thursday and Friday, 9 am to 9.30 pm. Wednesday, 9 am to 4.30 pm.
Rates: The average cost of a therapy is €50.76. Course fees include all books, charts, lecture notes, exam fees and refreshments. The course leading to the therapeutic-massage diploma costs €1,027.92, payable over five months. The reflexology diploma course and the sports- and remedial-massage diploma course cost €1,091.37 each.
Credit Cards: Cash or cheque only.
Services: Reflexology, therapeutic and sports massage, zen deep-tissue therapy, acupuncture, biocranial therapy, t'ai chi, yoga and karate.
Facilities: Four treatment rooms, reception area, kitchen, training room and yoga room, and lecture room.
Special Notes: Diploma courses in therapeutic massage, reflexology, and sports and remedial massage.
Nearby Attractions: Close to Cork Opera House, Everyman Theatre, shops and restaurants.
Getting There: The centre is ten minutes' walk from the main train station: go over Patrick's Bridge onto Bridge Street, then turn right onto McCurtain Street.

Natural Health Care Centre & Shop

Warner Centre
Barrack Street
Bantry

Tel: 027 52020

Nestled between the Cork and Kerry mountains in scenic west Cork, this centre is committed to a natural approach to health which complements rather than conflicts with conventional medicine. The natural-health therapists tend not to diagnose, but rather work towards correcting imbalance, which causes disease. These therapies support the body's own healing mechanism as part of a preventative health-care programme, as a way of dealing with chronic or short-term illness, or when convalescing after sickness. Therapies on offer are also available for relaxation and overall well-being. Books, relaxation music, meditation tapes, videos, aromatherapy oils, crystals, cards and candles can all be purchased in the Natural Health Care Shop, which is part of the centre.

Days and Hours of Operation: Monday to Saturday, 10 am to 9 pm.
Rates: Treatments vary between €25.38 and €50.76.
Services: Therapeutic massage, aromatherapy massage, reflexology, reiki, biodynamic therapy and shiatsu. Counselling sessions and yoga classes are also available.
Facilities: Three treatment rooms, one reception area, one shop, one yoga room. Rooms to rent by therapists.
Staff: Four massage therapists, three reiki practitioners, one shiatsu practitioner, two biodynamic therapists, two counsellors and psychotherapists, two yoga teachers.
Nearby attractions: Situated on Bantry Bay, with views of the Cork and Kerry mountains.
Getting There: One hour's drive from Cork on the N71.

Natural Therapy Centre

15–16 Westend
Mallow

Tel: 022 51595

Clients have been coming to the calm, quiet rooms of the Natural Therapy Centre, located in an old building on Mallow's main street in the Blackwater Valley, for therapeutic treatments for the last five years. Breda O'Sullivan opened the centre after completing courses in massage, reiki and traditional Chinese medicine. 'I started doing it professionally gradually and eventually made a clean break,' she says. 'I have never regretted it. I have gone from strength to strength.'

Clients range in age from a three-month-old baby to an octogenarian. As Longville House is only up the road, Breda receives a fair number of tourist clients, who come to her by referral. Ultimately, she aims to provide each client with a heightened sense of well-being. 'I would like this to be a light at the end of the tunnel for people wandering around trying to find some way to cure themselves after giving up on the medical profession,' she says. 'I think nearly everyone leaving here feels much calmer. They find a real sense of serenity while they are here. They love that.'

Days and Hours of Operation: Open Monday and Tuesday from 10 am to 8.30 pm, Thursday and Friday from 9 am to 7.30 pm and Saturday from 8 am to 1 pm.
Rates: A typical hour-long session costs €38.09.
Credit Cards: None accepted.
Services: Traditional Chinese medicine, therapeutic massage, reflexology, Indian head massage, reiki, vortex healing and homeopathy.
Facilities: Two private treatment rooms for acupuncture and homeopathy, plus one private treatment room for massage downstairs.
Staff: In addition to Breda, a fully licensed and qualified acupuncturist and a homeopath offer services from the centre.
Nearby Attractions: Fishing, golf and horse-riding.
Getting There: Coming off the N20 from Cork, head down towards the town centre; the Natural Therapy Centre is the second building on the right-hand side of the main street.

Natural Therapy Clinic

29 Hazelwood Avenue
Glanmire

Tel: 021 482 2258
E-mail: daverevins@oceanfree.net

As a young boy, David Revins worked on his father's hurt back; this eventually led him to develop a keen interest in natural therapies. 'People said I was good with my hands, so I decided to work at it,' he says. 'I got involved with sports massage and progressed from there.' Eventually, David trained at the Natural Healing Centre in Cork. Shortly afterwards, he converted part of his home to accommodate the Natural Therapy Clinic, which he opened seven years ago. 'When people come here, they find out how peaceful it is,' he says. 'They have to experience it for themselves. I like to give people time. I like to sit and listen to people and make them feel that they aren't rushed and can go away with peace of mind and a sense of well-being.'

Days and Hours of Operation: Open Monday to Thursday and every second Friday from 8.30 am to 8.30 pm.
Rates: The average price of a treatment is €31.74.
Credit Cards: None accepted.
Services: Reiki, reflexology, and therapeutic, sports and Indian head massage.
Facilities: One private treatment room.
Staff: David Revins owns and operates the centre on his own.
Special Notes: Accessible for people with disabilities.
Getting There: Located seven miles south of Cork City, towards Glanmire.

Quayside Holistic Health Centre

9 Sullivan's Quay
Cork

Tel: 021 431 0154
Mobile: 087 251 1562

In a small, private healing centre facing the quiet River Lee, clients can avail of any number of therapies, including reiki, nutrition counselling and therapeutic massage. The warm summer colours and wooden floors create a natural and relaxed setting that helps to put people at ease.

While working in a very stressful business environment, founder Ann Walsh turned to holistic therapies. Soon feeling the profoundly beneficial effects of these therapies, she decided to make a career-switch to the field of holistic health. After completing a course in holistic studies at the Cork College of Commerce, she opened the Quayside Centre two years ago. 'I found out how much it had helped me, so I began to appreciate a profound need for this type of work in society,' she says. 'I had a very good circle of people that I knew in the field and really we all merged together – and it's growing all the time.'

Services are designed to approach health in a holistic manner, targeting the mind, body and spirit. 'The counselling and body-work all integrates very well,' says Ann.

Also associated with the centre is Occupational Health Management, a company offering twenty-minute on-site chair massage in the workplace. OHM also provides on-site stress-management workshops, nutrition consultations, acupuncture, aromatherapy, t'ai chi, yoga, reflexology, shiatsu, chiropractic and acupuncture. For more information on OHM, phone 021 455 3677 or visit the website at www.ohm.50g.com.

Days and Hours of Operation: Open Monday to Saturday, 9 am to 9 pm, with the last appointment taken at 7.30 pm.
Rates: The average price of a treatment is €38.09.
Credit Cards: None accepted.
Services: Swedish massage, aromatherapy, reflexology, homeopathy, nutrition counselling, reiki, counselling, psychotherapy and professional stress management.
Facilities: Two private treatment rooms on the ground floor.
Staff: Around eight fully licensed and qualified therapists work from the centre at any given time.
Special Notes: The centre operates on a strictly appointment-only basis. Forty-hour notice of cancellation is required. Children under eighteen are not allowed. Smoking is not allowed.
Getting There: The centre is located beside FÁS, a three-minute walk from Patrick Street in Cork city centre.

SUREIA HOLISTIC CENTRE

3 The Mart
Coolbawn
Broderick Street
Midleton

Tel: 021 463 4566

Tuan Johore Jalill established Sureia Holistic Centre to combine Eastern and Western approaches to natural health care, providing the best possible service for his clients. Having grown up in the ayurvedic tradition of natural health care in Sri Lanka, he now applies this to his treatments. Tuan often travels to Sri Lanka, where he obtains his natural oils for aromatherapy massage. They offer a wide range of therapies in a very popular and picturesque part of Cork.

Days and Hours of Operation: Monday to Saturday, 10 am to 8 pm.
Rates: €38.10 for a one-hour session, €31.75 for forty-five minutes.
Services: Holistic massage, Indian head massage, acupressure, aromatherapy, reiki, reflexology and counselling.
Staff: One practitioner in these treatments, one counsellor.
Facilities: One treatment room, a waiting room and a changing room.
Nearby Attractions: Ballymaloe House restaurant, herbal garden centre and cookery school, Fota Wildlife Park and Botanical Gardens, Ballycotton fishing village and coastal walks and Cobh Cathedral. Sailing, tennis, golf and fishing are all available in close proximity to Midleton.

The Derrynoid Centre

The Rural College
Derrynoid
Draperstown BT45 7DW

Tel: 048 796 29100
Fax: 048 796 27777
E-mail: enquiries@derrynoid.co.uk
Website: www.creativebreaks.org

The Rural College was established six years ago as an educational resource for individuals and groups interested in continuing-adult-education workshops. A number of accredited courses are also offered through the college in association with institutions such as Queen's University Belfast and the National University of Ireland.

Courses take place in a gorgeous natural setting amidst two hundred and fifty acres of secluded woodlands on the site of the eighteenth-century Irish manor house Derrynoid Lodge. No previous experience in the topic is required for attendance. The average size of a class is about twenty people.

A number of subjects pertaining to holistic health are available throughout the year. 'The most popular is aromatherapy,' says programme director Alistair McGowan. One of the more interesting courses in 2001 was professional counsellor Judith Loder's workshop based on best-selling author Louise Hay's book 'You Can Heal Your Life'. Loder designed the workshop to help people break the habit of negative thinking and realise their true potential. Students practised awareness exercises, as well as guided meditation and visualisation. Loder's course on stress management taught students to increase their self-awareness through understanding the messages the body is sending, using the mind in a more creative way, making positive affirmations and releasing guilt.

Days and Hours of Operation: Open for residential and day courses throughout the year, with the exception of Christmas Day and St Stephen's Day.
Accommodation: B&B-style accommodation, with thirty en suite guest rooms. All rooms include direct-dial telephone, colour television, hairdryer and a tea- and coffee-making service.
Rates: Weekend residential courses, which run from Friday to Sunday, cost €125.70. This price includes meals, tuition and use of all facilities, including sauna and gym.
Credit Cards: MasterCard and Visa.
Meal Plans: All meals are included in the price of programmes. The centre offers a range of table d'hôte and à la carte meals. Vegetarians and people with special dietary needs can be accommodated with advance notice.
Services: Continuing-adult-education courses in a wide range of subjects, including stress management, aromatherapy, reflexology, wine appreciation, painting, image consulting, self-hypnosis, fishing and finanacial investing.
Recreational Activities: Hill-walking, golf, fishing, cycling, bird-watching, horse-riding and watersports.
Facilities: Hundred-and-fifty-year-old ancestral home; multimedia presentation theatre that seats up to a hundred and ten people; eight fully equipped syndicate rooms; PC stations, printers, photocopier and fax machine; library; resource room; restaurant and bar; fitness centre; and sauna and jacuzzi.

Staff: There is a full-time staff of nineteen, including instructors with masters degrees.
Special Notes: Several bedrooms are specially designed for people with disabilities. The building is identified as Class 1, according to the Northern Ireland Tourist Board. Courses can be booked online.
Nearby Attractions: Bellaghy Bawn, Church Island, Knockloughrim Windmill, St Lurach's Church, The Ulster Plantation Centre, Tirnoney dolmen, the market village of Draperstown and the town of Magherafelt.
Getting There: The centre is located five miles off the main Belfast-to-Derry road at the Tobermore turn-off.

MALIN HEAD HOSTEL

Malin Head
Inishowen

Tel: 077 703090

The Malin Head Hostel is set on Ireland's northernmost coastline along the scenic Inis Eoghain 100 Drive. Proprietor Mary Reynolds built the hostel on the land that her family has owned for generations. From the living room, one can sit comfortably in front of a large stone fireplace and look through windows that capture views of the west headlands of Donegal. Throughout the grounds are organic gardens and orchards, from which guests may harvest fruit and vegetables for purchase.

After completing diploma courses in reflexology and aromatherapy, Mary Reynolds recently began offering weekend introductory seminars in the hostel during the winter months. 'I believe sickness comes from stress,' she says. 'The experience of doing reflexology convinced me of the benefits, rather than being convinced before I started. As I go on, I learn more, and see how it affects different people for the better.'

The weekend often begins with guests sitting around an open fire and meeting and greeting each other. Instruction begins on Saturday morning after guests have had a chance to breakfast. The basic elements of reflexology are explained, along with its health benefits, and one or two lucky students receive a demonstration. After lunch, students practice their newly learned skills on each other. On Sunday there is an aromatherapy workshop, which includes a demonstration of a facial massage. Once again, students try out the techniques on each other. Plenty of time is left in the day to explore nearby stone circles and standing crosses, or to comb the beaches for semi-precious agate, cornelian and jasper stones.

Days and Hours of Operation: Weekend courses are offered throughout the year in the winter months, October to April. Therapeutic treatments are offered on Monday to Saturday from 11 am to 4 pm.

Accommodation: Four or five people in three dormitories. Three private rooms based on two people sharing.

Rates: Lodging for two nights and tuition cost €139.70, which includes coffee breaks. A typical reflexology treatment is €38.09 per one-hour session. A full-body aromatherapy massage is €44.44.

Credit Cards: None accepted.

Meal Plans: None provided. Two restaurants and a hotel serving tasty local fare are within a short drive.

Services: Weekend courses and treatments in reflexology and aromatherapy.

Recreational Activities: Hill walks, cycling and golf.

Facilities: Fully equipped dormitory-style hostel with kitchen, shower facilities, bicycle hire, organic garden and orchard.

Staff: Mary Reynolds is fully licensed and qualified in reflexology and aromatherapy.

Special Notes: No more than ten people at a time can participate in the weekend workshops.

Nearby Attractions: Raised beaches from the Ice Age with semi-precious stones, ninth-century ruined church, cave where a saint lived, wishing chair.

Getting There: The hostel is located 180 miles from Dublin, travelling northwest. From Derry or Letterkenny, bus goes directly to Malin Head. The bus company is Loch Swilly, tel: 04871 262017.

Suaimhneas Holistic Health Clinic

Main Street
Buncrana

Tel: 077 63550

Four years ago, Paul Brogan opened the Suaimhneas health-food shop in scenic Buncrana, Donegal. After two years, the shop evolved into a store-cum-holistic healing centre. 'One of the girls that works here full-time is a qualified aromatherapist and reflexologist,' says Paul. 'She had just done her courses and wanted to practise. I wanted to offer the treatments to customers and also use her skills as a qualified therapist.' Primarily for the benefit of the shop's loyal clientele, holistic therapies are now offered by two therapists throughout the week. Clients benefit from the homely, relaxing atmosphere in the small green therapy room, which has bright yellow curtains. 'The two people that I have here are very dedicated to what they do,' says Paul. 'There's no falseness there. They are very caring individuals.'

While all treatments are booked on an appointment-only basis, it is not uncommon for customers to request a service in the morning and be treated that afternoon. Future plans for the shop include a larger premises with more room for therapeutic treatments.

Days and Hours of Operation: The shop is open Monday to Saturday, 10 am to 6 pm. Therapeutic treatments are available on Wednesday and Saturday, from 10 am to 5 pm.

Rates: A typical hour-long session costs an average of €38.09. Fifteen-minute and half-hour treatments are also available, for €31.74 and €15.87 respectively.
Credit Cards: MasterCard, Visa and Laser.
Services: Reiki, spiritual healing, counselling, energy sessions, psychic readings, absent healing, relaxation sessions and colour therapy.
Facilities: A private treatment room is located at the back of the health-food shop.
Staff: At present, two therapists offer services from the shop.
Special Notes: Smoking is not allowed.
Nearby Attractions: The round fort of An Grianan Aileach, the stones of Kilcooney Dolmen, the Derryveagh Mountains, Glenveagh National Park, angling, salmon-fishing and golf.
Getting There: The centre is accessible by main roads directly from Dublin and Galway with links across Northern Ireland to Belfast. Bus Éireann offers a range of stops throughout the county. Flights from Donegal Airport to Dublin Airport take fifty minutes.

Yoga Therapy and Training Centre Ireland

Cnoc an Ri
16 Kinghill Road
Cabra BT34 5RB

Tel: 048 406 30686

Set in the beautiful hills of County Down, the Yoga Therapy and Training Centre Ireland (YTTC) was established in 1996 to meet the growing demand for quality professional yoga training for both Northern Ireland and the Republic. YTTC provides highly trained yoga teachers, of many disciplines, who are dedicated to practising, teaching and researching yoga. Emphasis is placed on the role of yoga in healing specific health-related problems. The centre also arranges group holidays in an old Spanish village. The yoga programme includes asanas (postures), pranayama (breath-work), meditation and discussion. Clients can also avail of holistic treatments, and a beauty therapist is available on request. Although it is listed as a yoga-therapy and yoga-training centre, the YTTC also offers a number of holistic therapies, including homoepathy, reflexology, aromatherapy and reiki.

Days and Hours of Operation: Weekend and week-long workshops. Yoga classes held daily.
Rates: Prices vary according to the course being taken. Weekend courses cost between £45 and £90 Stg. Early booking is essential.
Accommodation: Enquire for details; needs vary according to the nature of the course.
Rates: Therapies cost £30 Stg each. Yoga classes cost £30 Stg for a six-week course of evening classes, or £24 Stg for six weeks of morning classes, or £6 per class. Yoga weekends cost £90 Stg. Yoga holidays abroad cost £500 Stg, which includes flights, accommodation and tuition. The accommodation includes a swimming pool and gardens – and delicious vegetarian meals, with an ample supply of French wine!
Credit Cards: Cash or cheque only.
Meal Plans: A light vegetarian snack is provided on each day of the yoga weekend.
Services: Homoepathy, reflexology, aromatherapy and reiki. Yoga classes and yoga teacher-training course. This course embraces asanas, pranayama, anatomy, physiology, stress management and philosophy. The yoga teacher-training course costs £800 Stg and takes place over 15 months. Also available are an advanced yoga teacher-training course, yoga-therapy courses, yoga holidays abroad and yoga kits.
Staff: Dr Emmet Devlin is the course director. Emmet is a senior consultant physician at Daisyhill Hospital, Newry. He specialises in cardiology and diabetic medicine. He is a yoga teacher and a senior lecturer on the Yoga Therapy Diploma Course at the Yoga Therapy Centre's Yoga Bi-medical Trust in London. Dr John McGregor is a fellow of the Royal College of Physicians and Radiologists. He has practised as a consultant in diagnostic radiology since 1987 in Lancashire. Marie Quail has been involved in training yoga teachers and therapists for a number of years. She contributed to the yoga-therapy training course at the Royal Homeopathic Hospital in London. Dr Robin Monro

has gained worldwide recognition for his work in the field of yoga therapy. Guest tutors also teach on the training courses.
Facilities: Yoga-workshop areas, a shop selling items of yoga equipment, and therapy treatment rooms.
Getting there: From Belfast, take the M1 south to Sprucefield roundabout at Junction 7. Then take the A1 (the Dublin road) for twelve miles. Turn left onto the B10, signposted for Rathfriland (about nine miles). At the top of the hill in the town, turn left. Follow the A25 for two and a half miles, then turn right at a small crossroads onto Kingmill Road, and the centre is on the left.

Impact Health, Beauty & Aromatherapy

50A Main Street
Ballynahinch

Tel: 04897 563 222
Website: www.impactbeauty.Countyuk.

Soft music and subtle aromatic fragrances greet clients of the Impact centre, located in an old, white stone building in the market town of Ballynahinch. Staff at the salon, which has been open for more than ten years, offer a high level of personal attention – which explains the centre's many loyal clients.

All treatment rooms are soundproofed, so that any noise from the street or from other clients in the salon is completely muffled. 'I have gone to salons all over that were casual and noisy and you could hear the therapists running back and forth,' says owner Glynis Shilliday. 'I didn't like that. People that come here are getting away from children and work, so we try to limit conversation to the client. It is all very tranquil, quiet and calm. We even work in our bare feet.'

With the exception of the waxing area, all rooms are lit by candles. Essential oils burn and gentle music is piped in during the therapeutic body and beauty treatments. Shilliday cultivates a unique and comfortable atmosphere where each client is made to feel special. 'I want people to be treated as an individual and pampered,' she says. 'There is no rushing or anything like that. We do not schedule appointments back-to-back. When people walk in the door, we stop and see them as number one.'

Days and Hours of Operation: Open Tuesday, Wednesday and Thursday from 9 am to 9 pm, Friday from 9 am to 5 pm and Saturday from 9 am to 3 pm. Closed Sunday and Monday.
Rates: A one-hour massage typically costs £30 Stg.
Credit Cards: MasterCard, Visa and American Express.
Services: Aromatherapy, reflexology, reiki, colour therapy, Swedish massage, Indian head massage, seaweed body wraps, honey and almond body polish, firming and toning treatments, and a full range of beauty treatments.
Facilities: Semi-private entrance, nine treatment rooms, retail and reception area, and private waiting room.
Staff: Five fully licensed and qualified therapists, and one trainee.
Special Notes: Smoking is not permitted in the salon. Consultations and skin analysis are free of charge. New specials are available every quarter. No products are tested on animals. While children are welcome at the salon, they must be accompanied by parents into the treatment room.
Getting There: The salon is located twelve miles outside of Belfast, heading south.

FREEING THE ARTIST WITHIN

Black Sheep Arts Club
Dalkey

Tel: 01 284 0644

Valerie Coombes and Úna Balfe facilitate unique art workshops for beginners through to advanced levels. Classes commence with meditations to facilitate artistic flow and focus concentration. Body relaxation, movement, sound and stimulation of the imagination through the senses are all part of an effective process, specially designed to nurture the creativity of the participant. Emphasis is put on authenticity in the quest for one's personal artistic language and encouragement is given for people to be adventurous in terms of the way in which they express themselves. In addition to comprehensive technical tuition with relevant demonstrations, inspirational guidance is provided throughout the entire creative process. Individuals are brought through each stage from accessing and researching meaningful subject matter, and planning and developing an idea through to completion. Special art workshops for children are held in the summer months, with the same emphasis on encouragement and releasing natural ability. Residential workshops are held at Cedar Lodge in picturesque Rathdrum in County Wicklow, which retains all the charm of an old country village. No previous art experience is necessary.

Days and Hours of Operation: Tuesday, 9.40 am to 12.10pm and 3.45

pm to 6.15 pm. Thursday, 9.40 am to 12.10pm and 7.25 pm to 9.55 pm. Saturday workshops, 10 am to 6 pm. Also residential workshops, weekends and five-day courses.

Accommodation: Residential workshops are held at Cedar Lodge, Avondale House (Parnell Museum), Rathdrum, County Wicklow. Accomodation, in single rooms, is in a beautiful natural environment.

Rates: €57.11for five classes, €114.21 for ten. Day workshops, €57.11. Weekend residential courses, €190.36 each. Five-day courses, €444.16 each.

Credit Cards: Cash or cheque only.

Meal Plans: Gourmet vegetarian and non-vegetarian food. Extra charge for special diets.

Services: 'Freeing the Artist Within' workshops. Children's art workshops. Choice of residential or non-residential arrangement. Body relaxation and movement exercises, meditation, stimulation through sound and focusing-the-mind exercises.

Staff: Artist Valarie Coombes and course organiser Úna Balfe.

Special Notes: Included in the fee for the residential course are art materials, single-room accommodation and all meals. The extra time away from one's usual environment provides an ideal opportunity for the client to experience a powerful journey within and a truly satisfying creative experience.

Getting There: Take the N11 from Dublin towards Wexford and then the Dun Laoghaire coast road to Dalkey. For Rathdrum, take the N11 towards Wicklow. Rathdrum is signposted to the right, after Bray and the Sugar Loaf Mountain.

MACROBIOTIC ASSOCIATION

Teach Ban
6 Parnell Road
Harold's Cross Bridge
Dublin 12

Tel: 01 454 3943

The word 'macrobiotics' derives from the Greek for 'long life'. Today the term defines a method of eating and living in as natural a way as possible in order to become and remain well. While macrobiotic principles date back thousands of years, George Ohsawa is considered to be the modern-day father of the practice. Ohsawa's tenets promote nutrition and good health based on the idea that humans have an inherent capacity for well-being.

Ann Currie and Patrick Duggan have been involved with macrobiotics for more than twenty years. Ann first discovered it when she began to seek holistic treatment for migraine headaches. After Ann suffered an attack so severe it sent part of her body into temporary paralysis, a friend suggested she use yoga to combat the pain. Discovering that the yoga indeed helped, Ann began to examine her diet and eventually came across Ohsawa's teachings.

Today, the Macrobiotic Association offers year-round courses in healthy cooking, shiatsu and alternative medicine. Twice a year, about twenty participants travel with Ann and Pat to Templeboy, County Sligo, for a residential workshop in the principles of macrobiotics. The ever-popular weekends have been running for about fifteen years. Throughout their stay, participants enjoy meals made from locally grown, seasonal foods. 'We use our food as medicine, so what we take in on a daily basis is what keeps us going,' says Ann. 'You are what you eat.'

During the weekends, people are free to lie in, relax and enjoy themselves. There is no compulsion to adhere to a schedule, and participants are even free to wander up to the local pub if they so choose. Learning is, however, on the agenda. Both before and after sitting down to share healthy meals, guests are taught how to look after their health. Activities might include walking through the fields surrounding the large home where the workshops take place in order to harvest fresh seaweed at low tide. There also are expeditions to the seaweed baths at Enniscrone and to a Stone Age urn. 'The area is ideal,' says Ann. 'There is some beautiful energy there. It is totally surrounded by trees and there are even bats.'

The workshop appeals to young and old, male and female – with the common link being that all the participants want to learn how to live and eat in a more healthy way. 'Once we had seven children with us, and they played the whole time,' Ann says. 'There wasn't one cross word the whole time. It is a good time, especially for people who are trying to change their diet and maybe feel out on a limb and without family support. Really what we try to do is look after our health. Our health is our wealth.'

Days and Hours of Operation: The administrative office is open to address queries year-round, Monday to Friday from 10 am to 4 pm. Two residential workshops are held each year.

Accommodation: Between twelve and fourteen guests stay in one of four bedrooms. The single room has an en suite bathroom. All other guests share a bath and toilet. Local B&Bs house any overflow.

Rates: Weekend workshops cost an average of €190.50.

Credit Cards: None accepted.

Meal Plans: All meals are balanced and healthy, with organic produce used whenever possible.

Services: Weekend workshops involving healthy eating, shiatsu, seaweed-gathering and instruction in home remedies, and weekly courses in shiatsu, alternative medicine and healthy cooking.

Recreational Activities: Bicycling, swimming and surfing.

Facilities: Residential workshops are held in a large, old house in Templeboy, which has open fires and a spacious dining room.

Staff: Ann and Pat facilitate the workshops with the help of two assistants.

Special Notes: Guests are advised to bring raingear, plastic bags, a torch and wellingtons or good hiking boots.

Nearby Attractions: Enniscrone seaweed baths, Stone Age urn at Carrowkee, and beaches.

Getting There: Contact the Dublin office for details.

Jan de Vries Healthcare Clinic

464 North Circular Road
Dublin 1

Tel: 01 873 5052

World-renowned naturopath Jan de Vries has over forty years' experience in natural health care. He is probably best known for his herbal and flower-essence blends, which promote emotional and physical well-being. Jan has also written more than forty books and contributes regularly to television and radio programmes, health seminars, magazines and newspapers on the subject of natural health, offering natural solutions to modern ailments. The Dublin clinic is the latest addition to a string of six successful clinics offering complementary medical care. All the doctors, health-care practitioners and specialists at the clinic are trained in the use of natural health-promoting programmes that incorporate many multidisciplinary methods. They are also fully conversant with the latest concepts in healing, and the centre utilises the finest diagnostic equipment, treatments and therapies. Doctors in Jan de Vries clinics have been trained as conventional doctors before specialising in natural medical care.

The atmosphere in the centre is one of 'health care', where you genuinely feel your health is cared for. As the centre plays soft classical music, features wonderful interior décor and offers a beautiful view of the lush green garden, it is easy to forget you are in the reception area of a health-care centre. A program of therapies and remedies is tailored to every individual's needs. Any remedies that are required are available at the clinic. In addition, each client leaves with detailed advice and encouragement for health and lifestyle changes which aim to prevent illness and restore balance to the body.

Days and Hours of Operation: Monday to Friday, 9 am to 5 pm. Thursday, 9 am to 7 pm.
Rates: Consultation rates vary, according to the doctor the client sees. The average cost is €31.73 for a fifteen-minute consultation and €44.42 for thirty minutes.
Credit Cards: Visa, MasterCard, Laser and Ulster Bank.
Services: Health diagnosis, diet and nutrition advice, weight management, acupuncture, aromatherapy, chiropractic treatment, homeopathy, iridology, osteopathy, reflexology, reiki massage, electromagnetic therapy, Indian head massage and therapy lamps.
Facilities: The centre is situated in a traditional red-brick town house. The reception and waiting areas have been decorated with original antique furniture that adds to the comfort of the surroundings. The three treatment rooms are spacious, bright, airy and clean, with original rich wood furnishings. The latest equipment used in eye analysis and for light-treatment therapy is available in two of the therapy rooms.
Staff: Jan de Vries; Ann Harty, acupuncture, diet and nutrition; Síle Blount, reflexologist, Indian head massage, electromagnetic therapy; Sharon Buttimer, clinic manager; Dr Yvonne Majury, medical doctor, homeopath, osteopathy and phyto-

therapy; Dr Marcus Webb, osteopath, phytotherapy and acupuncture; Denise Hurley, cranial osteopath; and Gabrielle Macauley, reiki master, massage therapist and PR coordinator.

Getting There: Situated on the North Circular Road, at the junction of Lower Dorset Street and Drumcondra Road. The clinic is easily accessible by public transport or car, with ample parking space. It is also within easy walking distance of the city.

ACTIVE HEALTH

17 Rathfarnham Road
Terenure
Dublin 6

Mobile:	086 825 9888
E-mail:	info@active-health.org
Website:	www.active-health.org.

While working as the European sales manager for a successful UK company, James O'Sullivan travelled to Taiwan on business. It was there that he encountered traditional Chinese medicine, which changed the course of his life. After training under Dr Li Li, Dr Wu Jidong and Dr Lao Jin Huide in Ireland, James gained clinical experience in the Nanjing Hospital in China, where he specialised in acupuncture, tui na body-work, moxa cautery and cupping. Today he is one of the founders of Tui Na Ireland, which offers courses in Chinese medical massage up to practitioner level. He is also a teacher of complementary therapies in Senior College Dun Laoghaire.

Following what he believed to be his calling, James opened the Active Health clinic ten years ago in order to help people achieve better health, freedom, movement and well-being. 'People normally come to us with some form of a disharmony,' he says. 'I would like people to go away with a better understanding of what is happening in their body and feeling a lot better after treatments.'

Days and Hours of Operation: Monday to Friday, 10 am to 7 pm, Saturday mornings on occasion.
Rates: Services cost approximately €38.09 per hour.

Credit Cards: None accepted.
Services: Acupuncture, tui na acupressure massage, cranio-sacral therapy, reflexology, nutrition therapy, stress management, sports and remedial massage therapy, Swedish massage, t'ai chi and qi gung.
Facilities: One private treatment room, reception area.
Staff: One full-time and two part-time licensed and qualified therapists and practitioners.
Getting There: The centre is located within a ten-minute drive of Dublin's city centre.

ACUMEDIC

2 Talbot Place
Dublin 1

Tel: 01 856 1230

After studying traditional Chinese medicine in Ireland, Ali Asghar received a master's degree in this discipline at Xiang Ling College in China. In addition to offering healing therapies at the two-year-old Acumedic Clinic, he teaches courses in acupuncture at the weekend. Students who complete the one-year course are qualified to practise acupuncture. Ali continues to regularly travel to China to further his understanding of acupuncture.

Also affiliated with the clinic is Sarah's Beauty Room, where clients can treat themselves to facials, manicures, pedicures and other pampering treatments.

Days and Hours of Operation: Monday to Saturday, 9.30 am to 8 pm.
Rates: The average price of a treatment is €38.09.
Credit Cards: None accepted.
Services: Acupuncture, patent herbs, tui na massage, Indian head massage, reflexology, nutrition counselling and full range of beauty treatments.
Facilities: Four private treatment rooms on the ground floor.
Staff: Four full-time and two part-time qualified therapists.
Getting There: The centre is located in Dublin city centre, a two-minute walk from Connolly Train Station.

Acupuncture & Allergy Testing Clinic

564 Howth Road
Raheny
Dublin 5

Tel: 01 851 0285

Believing firmly that complementary medicine can work hand in hand with conventional Western medicine, Beverly McGovern treats everything from chronic ailments to stress relief at the Acupuncture & Allergy Testing Clinic. A number of the treatments are covered by several medical-insurance agencies and companies, including VHI, BUPA, HAS, the Prison Officers' Association and the Garda Medical Scheme.

Some of the conditions Beverly treats are migraines, smoking addiction, insomnia, heartburn, asthma and arthritis. The initial consultation generally begins with a comprehensive medical examination based on Chinese medicine. If special diets are introduced, clients are carefully guided throughout the process.

Beverly regularly lectures to various groups throughout Ireland on subjects such as food sensitivities, addictions, nutrition and acupuncture.

Days and Hours of Operation: Monday, Wednesday and Thursday, 9.30 am to 6 pm; Tuesday, 9.30 am to 9 pm.
Rates: While rates vary, initial consultations typically cost €25.39 for the first visit and €19.05 for subsequent visits.
Credit Cards: None accepted.
Services: Health and nutrition evaluation, allergy-testing, acupuncture, auricular acupuncture, Chinese herbal medicine, reflexology, homeopathy and tui na massage.
Facilities: Three private treatment rooms.
Staff: Beverly McGovern is a qualified reflexologist, nutrition advisor, Chinese herbalist, Chinese acupuncturist, allergy tester and massage therapist. She has studied in China, Germany, the United States, Russia, England, Northern Ireland and the Republic.
Special Notes: All treatments are strictly by appointment.
Getting There: The centre is within a ten-minute drive of Dublin's city centre.

Acupuncture & Sports Injury Clinic

68 Old Bawn Road
Dublin 24

Tel: 01 451 3207
Fax: 01 451 3207

Bringing thirty years of experience in alternative health to her interactions with clients, Phil Kelly has owned the Acupuncture & Sports Injury Clinic since 1988. She has trained in traditional Chinese medicine and yoga. When addressing the underlying cause of illness, Phil looks for what causes a body to get out of harmony. 'I start from that, rather than dealing with symptoms,' she says.

Clients at the clinic are encouraged to maintain telephone contact, whether it is a question about herbs, symptoms or a particular style of treatment. 'We pride ourselves on being very warm and friendly,' says Phil. 'We encourage people to ring us during treatments to keep us informed.'

Phil also trained as a focusing instructor in the United States and she currently serves as the coordinator for the Institute of Focusing in New York City. Focusing is a series of exercises designed to help individuals tap inner wisdom through gaining a better understanding of the body. Workshops in it are available through the clinic.

Days and Hours of Operation: Open Monday to Friday, 9 am to 5 pm.
Rates: Acupuncture treatments cost €50.79 per session, with follow-up treatments priced at €38.09. Herbal remedies cost an average of €12.70 for a three-week supply.
Credit Cards: None accepted.
Services: Acupuncture, Chinese herbal medicine, Vega allergy-testing, physiotherapy and non-surgical facelift CACI.
Facilities: Five private treatment rooms in a house which functions as a dedicated clinic.
Staff: Three fully licensed and qualified therapists.
Special Notes: The clinic is accessible for people with disabilities. Some treatments are covered by BUPA and VHI. Smoking is not allowed.
Getting There: The centre is within a five-minute drive of the M50.

Alara Beauty Salon

53 The Village
Ranelagh
Dublin 6

Tel: 01 497 0888

While Alara is neither a day spa nor a healing centre, the massage therapist on staff does offer some relaxing and health-promoting treatments, including reiki, aromatherapy and a back, neck and shoulder massage.

Days and Hours of Operation: Open 6 days: 10 am to 7 pm on Monday, 10 am to 8 pm Tuesday to Friday and 10 am to 3 pm on Saturday.
Rates: These vary according to services. A one-hour massage costs €44.44, while a series of ten toning body wraps costs €190.50.
Credit Cards: None accepted.
Staff: One fully licensed and qualified massage therapist and beautician.
Getting There: Located on the main Ranelagh Road, within a ten-minute drive of Dublin's city centre, the salon is easily accessible from major bus routes.

Amethyst Resource for Human Development

28 Beech Court
Killiney

Tel: 01 285 0976
or 01 285 0976
E-mail: amethyst@iol.ie
Website: www.holistic.ie/amethyst/

The therapies and courses developed at Amethyst combine the work and experience of founder and director Alison Hunter, who has twenty-five years' experience as a counsellor and regression therapist, and Shirley Ward, who has been a prenatal and perinatal therapist, healer and trainer for the past twenty years. Alison and Shirley provide psychotherapy with the added input of energy healing, in a discipline known as prenatal and perinatal psychology. As well as one-on-one therapy, they run courses and workshops, including a four-year counselling and psychotherapy training course, in which perinatal psychotherapy is introduced in the second year. According to Amethyst, the ethos of their training is humanistic. The core principle is growth and expansion – healing through the unfolding of each individual, by means of facilitation rather than seeking to provide a 'cure'. Techniques used include gestalt and regression therapy, with a special emphasis on body-oriented and energy work.

Days and Hours of Operation: Workshops and courses are held one weekend a month and for a week during the summer. Weekend workshops begin

on Fridays and end on Sundays and feature international trainers in the fields of perinatal psychotherapy and behavioural development.
Rates: Weekend workshops cost an average of €253 to €350. Fees for prenatal and perinatal psychotherapy and the primal-healing diploma course are €4,441, paid over two years.
Credit Cards: Cash or cheque only.
Services: The courses offered are 'Introduction to Counselling', various healing courses, 'Healing for the Twenty-first Century', 'Getting the Past out of the Present', 'Spirituality through Sacred Journeys', primal-integration and regression-therapy training courses, and 'Journey through Life' – a theoretical and experiential journey from conception to death.
Facilities: Therapy rooms, and a conference room for training.
Staff: Regression therapist, Alison Hunter. Prenatal and perinatal therapist, healer and trainer, Shirley Ward. Psychotherapist and teacher of peer counselling and body-work, Peter Labanyi. Professional child-care worker and teacher in play therapy and birth re-facilitation, Carmel Byrne.
Getting There: Beech Court is situated off Killiney Hill Road. The nearest DART station is Killiney.
Nearby Attractions: Killiney Bay and Killiney Hill.

Aqua, The Art of Beauty

No. 6, The Hill
Stillorgan

Tel: 01 278 1616

In November 1999, Michelle Casey opened the purpose-built Aqua day spa in order to offer a full range of revitalising therapies that subliminally engage the five senses. The cream and blue colour scheme provides a private, calm atmosphere in which men are just as comfortable as women, and a number of packages are designed specifically for male clients.

Feeling that Ireland was receptive to a new day spa, Michelle founded Aqua in order to combat the increasing levels of stress in society. Clients come in for anything from a basic one-hour reflexology treatment to an entire day of luxuriating in treatments provided by trained therapists. Day programmes may be tailored to suit individuals. By far the most popular treatment is the hour and a half hot-stone therapy, during which warm rocks are placed at particular points on the body.

Therapists are encouraged to limit conversation, as Michelle believes that people need a place to get away from chit-chat and simply relax. What conversation does ensue revolves around the therapies on offer, as individuals are told what to expect and are educated about how to take better care of themselves.

Particularly appealing features of Aqua are the hydrotherapy tub and steam shower, which are usually added on as part of the half-day or day-long package. Clients can sink into warm water scented with essential oils and position stiff limbs under high-powered jets for a controlled pressure massage. The steam shower also eases muscles and opens pores.

Days and Hours of Operation: Tuesday to Thursday, 9.30 am to 8 pm. Friday and Saturday, 9.30 am to 6 pm. Sunday, 10 am to 5 pm. The centre is closed on Monday.
Rates: One-hour therapeutic body treatments typically range from €38.09 to €57.14. A fifteen-minute steam shower or hydrotherapy soak costs approximately €19.05.
Credit Cards: Visa, MasterCard and Laser.
Services: Massage, ayurvedic shirodhara, aromatherapy, reflexology, hydrotherapy bath, body scrubs, body wraps, back facial, hot-stone therapy, steam shower, facials and full range of beauty treatments.
Facilities: Five purpose-built, modern private treatment rooms and calm reception area, all with cream decor.
Staff: Seven fully trained and qualified therapists.
Special Notes: Ample parking is available nearby. Mobile phones must be turned off during treatments. Customised day packages cannot be altered. Forty-eight hours' notice of cancellation is required. All courses must be paid for in advance.
Getting There: The day spa is located on many major bus routes.

ARDAGH MOBILE ACUPUNCTURE CLINIC

25 Ardagh Drive
Blackrock

Tel: 01 283 1328

Harmony equals good health, according to Peter Donnelly, owner of the Ardagh Mobile Acupuncture Clinic. Focusing on the physical, social, psychological and spiritual needs of each client, the clinic provides a balanced approach to overall health. Having trained as a psychiatric nurse and received an A level in psychology and child development, Peter brings a deep understanding and compassion to his work as an acupuncturist and reiki practitioner. He works as a mobile acupuncturist, visiting people in their homes in the south Dublin area.

Days and Hours of Operation: Treatments are available Monday to Friday on an appointment-only basis.
Rates: €44.42 per hourly session.
Credit Cards: Cash or cheque only.
Services: Acupuncture, counselling and reiki.
Facilities: Clients are treated in their homes in the south Dublin area.
Staff: Peter Donnelly, registered psychiatric nurse, acupuncturist and Level 2 reiki practitioner.
Getting there: From Dublin, take the N11 towards Wexford. At the Stillorgan dual carriageway, turn left onto Newtown Park Avenue. Ardagh Drive is the second left off this road.

The Beauty Parlour

23 Terenure Place
Terenure
Dublin 6W

Tel: 01 492 9977
Fax: 01 492 9280
E-mail: beautyparlour@eircom.net

Located in the calm and elegant surroundings of what was once a private home in Terenure, the Beauty Parlour offers an appealing mix of day spa packages. Owner Yvonne Laird, who opened the centre six years ago, still finds her work rewarding. 'It's very uplifting for people,' she says.

Yvonne notices that increasing numbers of people are interested in looking well; this development coincides with recent advances in scientific knowledge regarding skin therapies. The Beauty Parlour caters specifically to these people with enticing treatments that also help eliminate toxins from the body and promote relaxation. For example, the two-hour 'Heaven Scent' relaxation package begins with a consultation to determine what areas the client would like to tackle. A full-body aromatherapy massage is then followed by a reflexology treatment and body polish. Clients can then linger over refreshments before re-entering the daily grind.

Days and Hours of Operation: Monday to Friday, 8 am to 8 pm. Saturday, 9 am to 9 pm.
Rates: A typical two-hour package, including a variety of treatments, costs €127.

Credit Cards: Most major credit cards accepted.
Services: Aromatherapy, reflexology, scalp and back massage, fango mud wraps, facials and a full range of beauty treatments.
Facilities: Five private treatment rooms, shower facilities.
Staff: Three full-time therapists and aestheticians.
Special Notes: Gift vouchers valid for six months from the date of issue may be purchased at the cash desk. Twenty-four hours' notice is required on all appointments. A 50 per cent deposit is required for bookings of more than one hour.
Getting There: The centre is a ten-minute drive from Dublin city centre and is easily accessible from major bus routes.

Bellaza Clinic

27 Ranelagh Road
Dublin 6

Tel: 01 496 3484

Bellaza is primarily a beauty clinic, providing a wide range of beauty therapies and using products by G. M. Collin, Reparche and Academie. There is also a range of complementary treatments on offer.

Days and Hours of Operation:
Tuesday to Friday, 10 am to 8 pm.
Saturday, 9.30 am to 5 pm.
Rates: Therapies range from €19.04 to €38.07.
Services: In addition to beauty treatments, Bellaza offers aromatherapy massage, Swedish massage, full-body peel (to remove dead skin) and deep-cleansing back treatment for problem skin or acne.
Getting There: Situated at the canal end of Ranelagh Road. Easily accessible from Dublin city centre by bus or on foot (a fifteen-minute walk). Close to cafés and shops.

Bliss – Beauty and Massage

30 Sandycove Road
Sandycove

Tel: 01 280 8345
Fax: 01 285 2643
Website: www.bliss.ie
E-Mail: clare@bliss.ie

Well-known presenter and writer Clare McKeon understands the pressures of modern living. When she has deadlines to meet or feels under pressure, she always benefits from receiving a healing therapy or holistic beauty treatment. For this reason, she opened Bliss in 1998, providing a comforting, tranquil space to bring everything back into balance in body and mind. Wanting more than the usual salon experience, Clare employed an architect to create the atmospheric effect of the kind of place she wanted – which would offer an opportunity to unwind and ease away any stress in mind and body. The colours used in the salon were inspired by extensive travel to the Far East and Asia.

On arrival, clients experience the subtle aroma of organic oils mixed with gently scented candles, and relax in the waiting area, which is decorated in a soft cream colour, with curved furnishings and a flowing water feature. All treatments are hands-on and non-invasive. Using ingredients derived from nature has increased the popularity of the beauty treatments available, such as the lime and ginger scrub, the milk and almond pedicure, the coconut rub, the jasmine blossom float and the fennel wrap. Clare contends that her ongoing priority is to offer the best beauty treatments and holistic therapies at affordable prices, in a peaceful and relaxing environment.

Days and Hours of Operation: Open seven days a week. Also open late on Tuesday, Wednesday and Thursday evenings.
Rates: Back, neck and shoulder massage, €38. Deep-tissue massage, €57.14. Aromatherapy massage, €57.14. Bliss massage (in which two massage therapists work on the individual at the same time), €114.28. Reflexology, €50.79. Fennel cleansing wrap, €57.14. Lime and ginger scrub, €57.14. Body brushing, €44.44. Peppermint wrap, €69.84. Bliss facial (which includes a scalp massage and foot cleansing and massage), €57.14.
Credit Cards: Visa and Laser.
Services: Massage, reflexology, aromatherapy, wraps, body scrubs, facials, waxings, manicures, pedicures and false tans.
Facilities: Five beauty-treatment areas. Two manicure, pedicure and nail-treatment areas. Three specialist massage rooms, which are warm and quiet.
Staff: A full team of highly qualified beauticians and massage therapists.
Nearby Attractions: Dalkey, Glasthule and Sandycove villages, the seafront and the James Joyce Tower. Numerous restaurants and cafés nearby.
Getting There: Head south out of Dublin to Blackrock. After Blackrock, take the coast road to Dun Laoghaire. From Dun Laoghaire seafront, drive along the coast to the Joyce tower. Turn right there, and the centre is located beside the traffic lights. Alternatively, take the DART to the Glasthule or Sandycove stop, turn right, and the centre is a seven-minute walk away.

BLUE ERIU

7 South William Street
Dublin 2

Tel: 01 672 7818
Fax: 01 672 5778
E-mail: therapy@blueriu.com

In a fresh and modern city-centre locale, one of Dublin's newest day spa offers quick fixes for weary bodies and tired complexions. While the emphasis is on luxury pampering, many of the stress-reducing treatments are unquestionably health-promoting, such as the clay-earth mask with homeopathic preparations followed by a lymph stimulation of the face and neck in the Dr Hauschka cleansing facial.

Men particularly will be delighted with the three-and-a-half-hour 'God Bod' package designed exclusively for them. The treatment begins with an aromatherapy massage designed to balance the man out and bring him back to life. A cleansing and exfoliating Eve Lom facial follows.

There are plans to add more rooms at the day spa, so as to be able to accommodate a larger clientele.

Days and Hours of Operation: Monday to Friday, 9.30 am to 8 pm. Saturday, 9.30 am to 6 pm. Sunday, 2 pm to 6 pm.
Rates: Varying according to services. A one-hour massage with an additional fifteen-minute consultation typically costs €63.49.
Credit Cards: MasterCard and Visa
Services: Therapeutic massage, aromatherapy, algae and aromatherapy wraps, sea-salt exfoliation and body

brushing, facials and waxing treatments.
Staff: Nine fully licensed and qualified therapists and aestheticians.
Special Notes: Children under sixteen are not allowed. Clients arriving more than fifteen minutes late will either be charged for the missed service or will receive a shortened treatment for the full price. Gift vouchers are available at the cash desk.
Getting There: Blue Eriu is located in Dublin city centre, a few minutes' walk from Grafton Street.

The Body & Beauty Spa

Total Fitness Health and Fitness Club
River Road
Castleknock
Dublin 15

Tel: 01 822 4659

Tiffany Mulroy opened the Body & Beauty Spa three years ago in Dublin's Castleknock area as a natural extension of her interest in beauty and health. While the emphasis is on beauty treatments, men are made to feel comfortable as well and can even have a facial designed to reduce razor-burn sensitivity.

In addition to the standard salon treatments, guests can avail of some beneficial relaxing therapies, such as reflexology and massage. Particularly effective is the hour-long seaweed body treatment, during which seaweed is warmed to body temperature and spread across the skin and a deep-tissue massage is provided.

Days and Hours of Operation: Monday and Tuesday, 9 am to 7 pm. Wednesday to Friday, 9 am to 9 pm. Saturday, 9 am to 6 pm.
Rates: Prices vary. One hour-long reflexology treatment costs €38.09. For any course of six treatments, the sixth treatment is free.
Credit Cards: MasterCard, Visa and Laser.
Services: Massage, reflexology, seaweed body wraps, body scrubs, facials and a full range of beauty treatments.
Facilities: Five treatment rooms, shower facilities, retail area.
Staff: Six therapists and aestheticians.

Special Notes: Gift vouchers are available for purchase at the cash desk. Group discounts are also available.
Getting There: The centre is a ten-minute drive from Dublin city centre and is on many major bus routes.

Body Harmony Healing and Workshops

65 Park Lawn
Clontarf
Dublin 3

Tel: 01 833 0656
E-mail: rosemaryK@unison.ie

'Body harmony' is a hands-on healing technique designed to integrate the body, mind, emotions and spirit. After working as a beauty and massage therapist in New York, Rosemary Khelifia trained as an international body-harmony teacher. She has been involved in holistic health for twenty years and has worked in the field of body harmony for most of this time.

According to Rosemary, body harmony is an important way of healing that works by releasing stored cellular memories from the body in a non-threatening, gentle way. Left untreated, stored negativity and trauma in the body may lead to emotional and physical illness, Rosemary believes. Body harmony also works on the principle of freeing the restraints in the body, allowing it to move more freely. More movement leads to more 'aliveness', Rosemary says. As well as working with posture, body harmony includes hands-on work, moving body tissue intuitively and bringing about deep healing. Body harmony incorporates positive thinking with hands-on healing, allowing Rosemary to practise a truly holistic form of healing.

Days and Hours of Operation:
Monday to Friday, 10 am to 8pm.

Rates: Body-harmony treatments cost between €50.76 and €82.49. Weekend courses cost an average of €253.81.
Credit Cards: Cash or cheque only.
Services: Body-harmony treatments and training sessions, and weekend courses.
Facilities: Waiting room and healing room. Workshops are held in the conference room, which has access to the canteen.
Staff: Courses are usually facilitated by three members of staff. Body-harmony sessions are carried out on a one-to-one basis.
Nearby Attractions: Bull Island natural wildlife reserve, Howth Head and St Anne's Park.
Getting There: Turn left off the Clontarf road at St Anne's Park, and the second left is Park Lawn.

Castleknock Physiotherapy & Acupuncture Clinic

1 Auburn Green
Castleknock
Dublin 15

Tel: 01 820 1668

Staff at the Castleknock clinic find combining acupuncture and physiotherapy proves very effective in providing treatment for back and neck pain, muscle and joint pain and sports injuries and in managing stress. By effectively releasing muscle spasm and relaxing the nervous system, acupuncture is particularly effective in relieving stress.

Days and Hours of Operation: Open Monday to Thursday, 8 am to 7 pm, Friday, 8 am to 1 pm.
Rates: €35 per session.
Services: Acupuncture and physiotherapy.
Facilities: Three treatment rooms.
Staff: Four qualified in physiotherapy, two qualified in acupuncture.
Getting There: Take the 38 bus from Dublin's Abbey Street. By car, take the Dublin Road towards Blanchards-town. After the Halfway House pub, turn left at the roundabout onto Auburn Avenue. Turn left onto Auburn Drive 150 yards further on, and Auburn Green is at the end of the road.

Celtic Health Centre

117–119 Ranelagh Road
Dublin 6

Tel: 01 491 0689
E-mail: celtichealth@clubi.ie

This central Ranelagh centre is a hub for promoting a healthy lifestyle in a neighbourhood already boasting an organic grocery and a recently opened juice bar. Though the sound of traffic occasionally filters up and the waiting room sometimes resembles a busy family room, the place is overflowing with heart and good intent.

Clients walk upstairs to a small waiting area, where they are patiently directed toward the best therapy that suits their needs or ailments. People who sign up for a course in yoga instruction and discover that the instructor teaches at a pace that does not work for them can be redirected to another instructor or referred to a class offered outside the centre.

Originally working at the centre as a massage therapist, owner Jane Kennedy bought the centre just over four years ago. While she believes in the profound therapeutic benefits of massage, her goal is to enable clients to develop their own health-maintenance programme rather than depend on a massage therapist for pain relief. Referring to the hectic pace of today's society, Jane says, 'Things have gone from being fairly low-key to people working all hours. The traffic is chaotic and they're chasing their tails. People are getting sicker and you can see it. It is just a matter of whether or not they want to address it. We are just facilitators.'

Although a wide range of services is available through the centre, a referral service is in place for individuals who require treatments that are not on offer, such as homeopathy or Chinese medicine.

The centre offers ongoing ITEC diploma courses in massage and reflexology. There is also a short introductory course in massage for people who are considering it as a profession or couples who may simply want to learn to work on their partners. Future plans for the centre include a full-time two-year educational curriculum.

Days and Hours of Operation: Open Monday to Thursday from 10 am to 10 pm, and Friday and Saturday from 10 am to 6 pm.
Rates: Vary according to services. Treatments typically cost €38.09. A five-week course in Swedish massage costs €177.80.
Credit Cards: None accepted.
Services: Foot and aromatherapy, Thai, Swedish and Indian head massage. Also Hatha and Iyengar yoga, osteopathy, acupuncture, shiatsu, kinesiology, t'ai chi and courses in reflexology. A corporate chair-massage service is available through the centre.
Facilities: Four private treatment rooms and yoga-instruction room.
Staff: Two full-time and ten part-time therapists, teachers and counsellors.
Special Notes: Services are available strictly by appointment. As the centre gets busy, it is best to book treatments at least two days in advance. A range of health supplements, aloe vera products and yoga mats, blocks and belts are available for purchase. Gift vouchers may be purchased for Thai, Swedish, Indian

Head, foot and aromatherapy massage.
Getting There: The centre is located on Ranelagh Road, a ten-minute drive from Dublin city centre, and is easily accessible from major bus routes.

The Chinese Acupuncture Clinic

62 Dame Street
Dublin 2

Tel:	01 677 3591
Mobile:	087 247 6355

Su Pin Chen studied acupuncture at Shanghai Acupuncture, Channels and Collaterals Research Institute. When she moved to Ireland, she felt that her training would be very effective in helping relieve stress and physical illness. Su Pin has operated out of this central location in Dublin for over two years. Appointments are made on request and not on a drop-in basis.

Days and Hours of Operation: Monday to Friday, 11 am to 5 pm. Saturday, 11 am to 2 pm.
Rates: First visit costs €38.10, subsequent visits €31.75.
Credit Cards: Cash or cheque only.
Facilities: One treatment room, one reception area.
Staff: One qualified acupuncturist.

Chinese Medical Centre

47 Upper George's Street
Dun Laoghaire

Tel: 01 280 0268
Fax: 01 280 9160
Website: www.homepage.eircom.net/-cmcirl

Dr Beizheng Liu has been providing traditional Chinese medical care in her Dublin centre for three years. Although she notes that there is an ever-growing interest in traditional medicine, she also observes that first visits are usually by clients who have experienced no relief from illness using conventional medicine. She finds it more difficult to treat in this way, as the longer the illness is in place the more difficult it is to cure it.

When treating a patient, Dr Liu views the body as an integrated whole and incorporates the Chinese concept of yin and yang – two conflicting yet interdependent energies in the body. By looking at both physical symptoms and qi or 'life energy' imbalances within the body, she aims to restore balance and harmony, as well as alleviating pain and discomfort. This form of diagnosis and treatment, using traditional therapies, is available in all hospitals in China, where traditional and conventional forms of health care work together. Dr Liu hopes that, in time, this approach to health care will become more common in Ireland.

Days and Hours of Operation: Monday to Friday, 10 am to 7 pm. Saturday, 10 am to 5 pm.
Rates: An initial consultation costs €25.38, with follow-up consultations costing €6.35 each. Herbs cost €6.98 per dose, acupuncture €25.38 to €32.99, acupressure €31.73 for thirty minutes, and reflexology €27.92.
Credit Cards: Cash or cheque only.
Services: Chinese medical diagnosis treated with Chinese medicine, herbal therapy, acupuncture, acupressure, moxibustion, qi gung and t'ai chi.
Facilities: Four treatment rooms, one exercise room, one reception area and a herbs-purchasing area.
Staff: Three full-time Chinese medical doctors, one part-time practitioner qualified in herbs and moxibustion.
Local Attractions: People's Park, Dun Laoghaire Pier, cinemas and shopping.
Getting There: Located at Lower George's Street near People's Park. Serviced by the 45A bus from Dublin. The nearest DART stations are Sandycove and Glasthule.

Complementary Healing Therapies

136 New Cabra Road
Cabra
Dublin 7

Tel: 01 868 1110

Catherine Collins worked as a nurse for four years before deciding to train as a reflexologist. Her reflexology training opened up a whole new world for her, in which she began to deepen her understanding of treating and healing the individual as a whole. This, she explains, involved looking beyond the physical symptoms of an ailment, to find and treat any deeper physical, emotional or lifestyle causes of discomfort, stress or illness. To enhance her healing skills, Catherine decided to train as a holistic massage therapist, which she has been doing for ten years. When treating an individual, Catherine combines her skills as a reiki master with massage and reflexology, bringing a calmness and peace to her work, as well as remedying emotional ills and physical ailments.

Having seen the benefits of complementary therapies in individual clients, Catherine decided to bring these skills to others and now trains groups in ITEC holistic massage, reflexology and Indian head massage. She also uses her training as a counsellor to facilitate stress-management workshops and teaches reiki levels 1, 2 and 3. According to Catherine, complementary therapies can be enjoyed for pure relaxation purposes in order to release tension, or to connect to the deeper aspects of the self, allowing the receiver to grow to fulfil their true potential.

Days and Hours of Operation: Monday to Friday, 9 am to 5 pm. Later and earlier appointments are available by appointment. ITEC certificate training: one weekend a month for 8 months.
Rates: Reflexology, €25.39. Massage, €38.09. ITEC certificate in holistic massage, Indian head massage or reflexology, €888.82, payable in instalments.
Services: Holistic massage, Indian head massage and reflexology. Courses in ITEC holistic massage, Indian head massage and reiki levels 1, 2 and 3. Workshops in stress management.
Facilities: One treatment room and waiting area, For courses, one conference room and dining facilities.
Getting There: The 121 bus from O'Connell Street stops outside the centre, which is located on Cabra Road in the direction of Blanchardstown, just before the Statoil garage.

Complementary House

91 Terenure Road North
Dublin 6W

Tel: 01 492 9077
E-mail: courses@complementaryhouse.com
Website: www.complementaryhouse.com

Complementary House, also known as the Complementary Healing Centre, offers a warm and friendly atmosphere to clients and therapists, who have been attending the clinic since it opened in 1994. The aim of the centre, which is run by Marnie Cook, Michael Sheridan and Kay Deveroux, is to raise awareness through healing and to help individuals achieve a sense of balance and fulfilment in their lives. Marnie Cook's work involves channelling energy through what she describes as spirit guides. She gives readings and teaches others how to channel psychic communication and energy. Interpreting dreams and their hidden meanings is Michael Sheridan's area of interest. Hands-on therapies such as full-body massage, ki massage and reflexology are also available, and are taught in courses run from the centre. The interior is comfortable and gentle music helps alleviate the stresses and strains of the day. The planned gift shop for candles, oils, crystals, dream-catchers and books will provide holistic gifts and material for practitioners and clients.

Days and Hours of Operation: Monday to Friday, 10 am to 9 pm, and Saturday, 10 am to 3 pm.
Rates: Therapies cost from €22.84 for thirty minutes of Indian head massage to €57.11 for a sixty-minute bioenergy treatment. The average cost of a therapy is €50.76. Courses cost from €88.83 for reiki 1 to €253.81 for full-body massage, run over seven evenings.
Credit Cards: Cash or cheque only.
Services: Aura readings, tarot, hypnotherapy, present-life progression, spiritual healing, angel readings, psychic readings, zen shiatsu, Native American healer, tea-leaf reading, reiki, spiritual healing, reflexology, psychic/spiritual medium, acupuncture, Indian head massage, past-life regression, psychotherapy, ki massage, Swedish sports massage, hand analysis, bioenergy therapy, dream interpretation, life-coaching and counselling.
Facilities: Four spacious therapy rooms (available for hire by complementary practitioners), attic space and shop.
Staff: One aura-reader, one tarot, hypnotherapy and present-life progression practitioner, two spiritual healers, one medium, angel-readings practitioner and psychic counsellor, one zen shiatsu practitioner, one Native American Healer, one tea-leaf reader, one Chinese reflexologist, one psychic/spiritual medium, one ki and Indian head massage therapist, two psychic and tarot-card readers, one Swedish sports masseur, one bioenergy therapist, one dream interpreter, one qualified life-coach, one counsellor and one hand-analyser.
Special Notes: Courses available in full-body massage, Indian head massage, divining the tarot, reiki level 1, angel workshop, psychic awareness, dream interpretation and self-development.
Getting There: Located above the Spar shop in the centre of Terenure.

The Complementary Medicine Clinic

48 Drumcondra Road Upper
Dublin 9

Tel: 01 836 8201
Mobile: 088 620557

The goal of the Complementary Medicine Clinic is to restore and maintain good health without the use of drugs or medication. The proprietor, Rosemary Campbell, has thirty-eight years' experience in the teaching and practice of holistic medicine. Rosemary has travelled extensively in the United States and England to further her training in complementary therapies. She has used her extensive qualifications and the knowledge she has gained over the years through research, practice and observation in her practice. Rosemary is also director and principal tutor of the International Academy for Holistic Health Therapies.

Rates: The average cost of therapies is €31.75 per hour.
Credit cards: Cash or cheque only.
Services: Physical therapy, deep heat, G5, aromatherapy, reflexology, acupressure, Lazer magneto therapy, deep-tissue lymph-drainage massage and electro skin-brushing. Twenty-minute lunchtime appointments available: deep shoulder and neck massage for €15.23, hypnotherapy, counselling
Staff: Director Rosemary Campbell, therapist Deirdre Hanna and hynotherapist Rebecca Gibson.

Dan-Tien Complementary Health Studio

29 Bride Street
Dublin 8

Tel: 01 473 8845
E-mail: info@dan-tien.com
Website: www.dan-tien.com

Behind a small blue door on Bride Street lies the newly opened Dan-Tien Complementary Health Studio, which has already secured a steady and loyal clientele from the surrounding neighbourhood. Owners Dave Shipsey and Deirdre McDermot – both registered nurses – bring their combined backgrounds in traditional Chinese medicine to the services offered at the centre. Soon to be married, the two met while completing their studies at the Nanjing University of Traditional Chinese Medicine. Upon returning from China, they set about opening the small clinic, with its calming atmosphere, where clients receive private consultations and treatments in secure and comfortable surroundings.

Dave specialises in wrist and ankle therapy, as well as auto-immune dysfunction. Deirdre, who is particularly adept at working with children, maintains a strong interest in the role of diet and lifestyle as they pertain to overall well-being. Both continue to deepen their understanding of traditional Chinese medicine by regularly travelling to China for further intensive study.

Clients may also receive herbal prescriptions, which can be filled at the Chinese Natural Herbal Centre on nearby Aungier Street.

Days and Hours of Operation: Open Monday to Friday from 10 am to 6 pm, and Saturday from 10 am to 4 pm. Evening appointments are available.
Rates: The first treatment costs €38.09, with subsequent visits costing €31.74
Credit Cards: None accepted.
Services: A range of traditional Chinese medicine techniques, including acupuncture, auricular acupuncture, acupressure-heat and electromagnetic-wave treatment, cupping, electric-pulse stimulation and herbal medicine.
Facilities: One private treatment room.
Staff: Two full-time, qualified and licensed acupuncturists.
Special Notes: Dan-Tien is recognised by both VHI and BUPA. It is also registered with the Acupuncture Foundation of Ireland. Parking is available either on the street or in a nearby car park. Needles are disposed of immediately after use.
Getting There: The centre is located a five-minute walk from Dublin city centre, between Christ Church and St Patrick's Cathedrals.

ENDORPHIN RELEASE CLINIC

24 Errigal Road
Crumlin
Dublin 12

Tel:	01 455 8266
or	01 456 0480
Fax:	01 494 1600
E-mail:	lgcarty@iol.ie

Seven years ago, John Carty established the Endorphin Release Clinic, to counteract what he felt was a lack of drug-free pain-release services. With many people now seeking a more holistic or drug-free way of treating pain, the clinic, which takes a natural approach to pain relief, has gone from strength to strength. John originally tried his self-taught method of endorphin-release therapy for pain relief on his own children. Finding it extremely effective, he left his full-time job as a business executive to set up the Endorphin Release Clinic. Although he has no previous medical training, his approach has received a great deal of positive media coverage.

During endorphin-release treatment, fingertip pressure is applied around the area of discomfort, to ascertain which nerves are affected. Pressure is then applied from the fingertip directly onto the nerve, to release the patient's own endorphins. This initially anaesthetises the area being treated and helps the patient to begin the process of healing, using their own chemicals. The clinic also uses an orthopaedic mobility scanner to scan the initial restrictions of movement and measure how they are improving. The clinic claims to have a 90 per cent success rate; John contends that the treatment is particularly effective for whiplash injuries, lower-back problems, sciatica and frozen shoulder.

Days and Hours of Operation: Monday to Friday, 9.30 am to 5 pm. Saturday, 9.30 am to 12 noon.
Rates: €63.45 per visit
Credit Cards: Cash or cheque only.
Services: Endorphin-release therapy – drug-free, manipulation-free pain-relief treatment.
Facilities: Three cubicles on the ground floor and six on the upper floor.
Staff: Seven endorphin-release therapists.
Getting There: Take either the 121, 122 or 123 bus from O'Connell Street, heading South. The centre is located directly behind Our Lady's Hospital for Sick Children in Crumlin.

FAIRVIEW THERAPY CENTRE

10 Fairview Strand
Dublin 3

Tel: 01 856 1289

It is the aim of Fairview Therapy Centre to nurture the growth of wellness in mind, body and spirit. The counsellors and psychotherapists working at the centre use their expertise to help clients with a wide range of issues, such as anxiety, depression, bereavement, chronic illness, relationship difficulties, sexual abuse and trauma. Couples, family counselling, life coaching and neurolinguistic programming are also available. People also visit the centre to enjoy the many therapies on offer or to receive relief from physical pain, as well as stress reduction and deep relaxation. The centre acknowledges that optimum health is achieved by considering all aspects of emotional and physical well-being. Fairview offers facilities and therapies to assist and encourage people to achieve this.

Days and Hours of Operation: Operates an appointment-only system. Phone answered most weekdays between 3 pm and 5 pm. Outside these hours, callers can leave a message.
Rates: Vary between €31.73 and €57.11 for an hour-long session.
Credit Cards: Cash or cheque only.
Services: Counselling, psychotherapy, aromatherapy, massage, reiki, homeopathy, reflexology, sports massage, ki massage and shiatsu.
Facilities: Purpose-built therapy centre with counselling and treatment rooms and reception area.

Staff: Seventeen fully qualified and licensed counsellors, psychotherapist and therapists
Getting There: The centre is a ten-minute walk from Clontarf DART Station and is on numerous bus routes from Dublin city centre.

Harvest Moon Centre

24 Lower Baggot Street
Dublin 2

Tel: 01 662 7556
Website: www.harvestmoon.ie.

It is not uncommon to find fliers for the Harvest Moon Centre on the reception desks of Dublin city centre offices. Stacked in with the daily mail, the flier gets a few brief glances and then the passing comment, 'Ah well, I'm not that stressed yet.'

They don't know what they're missing. Something as simple as complete silence and floating in warm, salinated water is profoundly relaxing, and Harvest Moon offers this combination through its flotation tanks. Initially designed to prepare astronauts for total sensory deprivation in space, the unexpected and pleasant side effect of use of the tank was a state of deep relaxation. For those who would rather not get their feet wet, the many holistic therapies on offer at the centre also provide substantial benefits for the mind, body and spirit.

Walking along busy Baggot Street, it would be easy to miss the downstairs clinic, if it were not for the noticeboard on the footpath. Muted turquoise, burnt orange and sienna yellow coat the walls of the narrow waiting hall. The unique framed prints and close proximity of chairs and reading material create the feel of a family den. It is a small place all right, and clients walk out of the treatment rooms right into the waiting area. Sometimes footsteps from the office above can be heard, despite the use of soft music. Nonetheless, there is a certain appealing calm to the place, and local nine-to-fivers would be crazy not to take advantage of some of the therapies on offer.

Peter Kane founded the centre approximately five years ago, as a natural extension of his interest in holistic healing. After having contacted a healer to care for his sick mother, Peter became interested in holistic treatments. Soon he and his brother were offering spiritual healing sessions from their home in Blackrock. Although Peter had never intended to go into the healing profession, the people who visited him for treatment kept coming back. One of his regular clients was an estate agent who found the Baggot Street property.

Commenting on the general process of healing, Peter says, 'All holistic therapies basically do the same thing: they raise awareness by removing blocks. It is like taking away a cloud where there normally is light. I provide the space where people can take stock of their lives. I encourage them to take responsibility for themselves, their health and everything – and not take life too seriously.'

Days and Hours of Operation: Open seven days a week: Monday to Friday, 11 am to 9 pm, Saturday and Sunday, 11 am to 6 pm.
Rates: A full-body massage costs an average of €38.09, as does a one-hour flotation session. Special offers include three one-hour flotation sessions for €88.88 and a one-hour flotation session plus a full-body holistic massage for €63.49. Prices for corporate packages are available on request.
Credit Cards: MasterCard, Visa.
Services: Various types of massage, flotation, yoga, chiropractic, reiki and counselling.
Facilities: Two treatment rooms for massage, counselling or movement therapy and a separate room for flotation tanks, complete with private shower facilities.
Staff: Approximately twenty-five therapists are employed on a part-time basis at the centre. Inquire individually as to the accreditation and experience of each practitioner.
Special Notes: Crystals and other unique items are available for purchase either at the centre or via the website.
Getting There: Located within a 10-minute walk of Dublin's city centre.

The Healing House

24 O'Connell Avenue
Berkeley Road
Dublin 7

Tel:	01 830 6413
Fax:	01 830 6060
E-mail:	info@healinghouse.ie
Website:	www.healinghouse.ie

Healing House owner John Kenny opened this Mecca of healing spirituality and personal growth to provide a space where people can squarely face their lives in an atmosphere of peace and acceptance. 'The staff involved are also growing spiritually,' says spiritual healer and massage therapist Brenda McKenna. 'There is a sense of everyone growing together. No one is better than anyone else.'

Any number of treatments, courses and workshops are on offer at this terraced Victorian home, from cranio-sacral therapy treatments to morning yoga sessions. Each December, a 'ceremony of light' is held, during which participants drum, sing, talk and share supper. Also on offer is a 'holistic week' in a private Spanish villa in the small village of La Florida. During the week guests can wander through the spacious, scenic grounds, which are within a fifteen-minute walk of the sea, or lounge beside the private swimming pool. The house accommodates up to ten people, who enjoy a week of meditation, personal-growth workshops and reflexology and aromatherapy treatments. Further information is available on the centre's website.

Days and Hours of Operation: Therapeutic treatments, consultations and workshops are held seven days a week, by appointment.
Rates: Treatments typically cost between €6.35 and €50.79. A sliding scale is in place for those who cannot afford to pay the full rates.
Credit Cards: None accepted.
Services: Acupuncture, African drum and songs, aromatherapy, Australian bush-flower essences, psychotherapy, counselling, stress management, hypnotherapy, amatsu back-pain clinic and cranio-sacral therapy. ITEC diploma courses in aromatherapy, reflexology and healing massage. Weekend workshops in flower essences, essential oils, drumming, healing massage, numerology, tarot, awakening of the soul and healing of the body, mind and spirit. A year-long certificate course in gestalt therapy. A ten-week instructor course in spiritual healing, reflexology and Australian bush-flower essences. Drop-in support groups on Monday nights. Morning and evening yoga classes.
Facilities: Seven private treatment rooms, three group rooms, kitchenette and garden.
Staff: Approximately twenty-five therapists offer services that are available from the centre.
Special Notes: Smoking is not allowed inside the house.
Getting There: The centre is a fifteen-minute walk from Dublin city centre.

The Healing Place

61 St Assam's Park
Raheny
Dublin 5

Tel: 01 848 4270
Mobile: 087 246 1853

Having been greatly helped personally by complementary medicine, Joseph McGuire trained in shiatsu, stress management and cranio-sacral therapy to help others in their healing journeys. The Healing Place aims to provide a safe environment in which clients can benefit from treatments that stimulate the innate healing powers of body and mind which exist in all of us. It provides a unique blend of Western and Oriental approaches, working on the premise that the body is primarily a physical representation of a person's state of well-being. The natural-health therapies provided at the centre aim to restore health, prevent illness and clear energy blocks and imbalance caused by stress, grief, trauma, environmental pollution and other modern-day ailments.

Days and Hours of Operation: Monday to Friday, 10 am to 8 pm. Saturday, 9 am to 2 pm, by appointment only.
Rates: €44.45 for treatments, which last one hour. Counselling is €31.75 per session. There are concession prices for the unemployed and the low-paid.
Services: Cranio-sacral therapy, shiatsu, counselling, stress management, 'What the Face Reveals' courses, nine-star ki astrology and shen therapy.
Credit Cards: Cash or cheque only.
Staff: Marlies McGuire provides counselling and Joseph McGuire provides the therapies listed above.
Special Notes: Joseph McGuire also presents stress-management sessions on an in-house basis for companies and hospitals, and workshops, 'What the Face Reveals' courses and nine-star ki Oriental astrology at various locations around Ireland.

The Healing Room

326 Clontarf Road
Dublin 3

Tel: 01 833 9646.

Standing in the Healing Room, one can easily take in a view of the gulls and walkers dotting the Clontarf strand. Owner Margie Flynn founded the one-room centre four years ago in order to help people discover self-esteem, peace of mind and release from anger, guilt and fear. Clients seeking therapies at the Healing Room will probably sense her intention to create a safe and comfortable atmosphere. At present, four therapists offering a range of holistic therapies operate out of the room. Margie herself specialises in reiki and offers courses in its various stages.

Days and Hours of Operation: As appointments are booked with therapists, hours vary.
Rates: An hour-and-a-half treatment costs an average of €44.44.
Credit Cards: None accepted.
Services: Reflexology, reiki and Swedish, aromatherapy, Indian head and holistic massage.
Facilities: One private treatment room.
Staff: Four therapists currently work out of the Healing Room.
Special Notes: Smoking is not allowed. Clients must be capable of climbing one flight of stairs.
Getting There: The 130 bus stops right outside the entrance to the Healing Room.

Health and Harmony

Chinese Herbal Medicine and Acupuncture
41B South Richmond Street
Portobello
Dublin 2

Tel: 01 475 9648

Health and Harmony provides expertise on Chinese herbal medicine as well as acupuncture and moxibustion, which have successfully served the Chinese population for over 4,000 years. Dr Jane Li arrived in Dublin in 1998 after four years spent practising in London. She is a highly qualified and experienced herbalist and licensed acupuncturist, with fifteen years' work experience in hospitals and clinics in China, the UK and Ireland. Working with her friendly medical team, Dr Li is keen to help local people with her comprehensive traditional Chinese medicine skills, and provides clients with appropriate acupuncture, or selected herb mixtures to deal with their needs. They have over three hundred different herbs in stock. They are happy to work alongside GPs where possible. Their aim is to encourage a healthier life, leading to increased happiness. For those who have a fear of needles, the centre offers alternative treatments that involve electrical acupuncture, moxibustion and heat cupping.

Days and Hours of Operation: Monday to Friday, 10 am to 7 pm. Closed Thursdays. Saturday, 10 am to 5 pm.
Rates: Treatments cost an average of €35.55 each.

Credit Cards: Visa and MasterCard.
Facilities: Two treatment rooms and a waiting room.
Services: Acupuncture, moxibustion and herbal medicine.
Getting There: Richmond Street, a continuation of Camden Street, is served by numerous bus routes.

The Herbal & Iridology Clinic

11 Anglesea Street
Dublin 2

Tel: 01 672 5870
Mobile: 086 849 1849

When the mind and body work together in healthy balance, an individual's mental, spiritual and emotional status also functions at its optimum level. One system affects the other, and vice versa, says iridologist and herbalist Helen Begadon. Helen specialises in detoxification programmes at her three-year-old Dublin city centre clinic, where she works closely with her full-time assistant, a reflexologist. The clinic's unique detox programme is based on raw fruits and vegetables, as well as therapeutic treatments and herbal medicine. 'We get some amazing results and we are extremely busy,' says Helen. 'With herbs, it really works.' Future plans for the centre include hiring more therapists to offer a wider range of holistic treatments.

The clinic is also the headquarters of the Irish School of Natural Healing, which offers Ireland's first ever three-year course in herbal medicine. The school is founded in the tradition of well-known American herbalist Dr John Ray Christopher.

Days and Hours of Operation: Open Monday to Friday from 9 am to 6 pm. Educational seminars are held at weekends.
Rates: Iridology treatments cost €63.49 each, and an hour-long reflexology treatment costs €38.09.

Credit Cards: MasterCard and Visa.
Services: Iridology, herbal medicine and reflexology.
Facilities: Two private treatment rooms, and waiting area.
Staff: Two fully licensed and qualified therapists.
Special Notes: The centre is accessible for people with disabilities.
Getting There: The centre is located in Temple Bar in Dublin city centre.

The Holistic Healing Centre

38 Dame Street
Dublin 2

Tel:	01 671 0813
Fax:	01 679 0415
E-mail:	info@hhc.ie
Website:	www.hhc.ie

Situated in the heart of Dublin, the Holistic Healing Centre offers a comprehensive range of treatments, classes and diploma courses, all based on the holistic philosophy of well-being. All these courses work towards helping to restore a person's optimum level of health. Clients are encouraged to take responsibility for their own health by following individual programmes designed for them. All members of staff are completely committed to increasing awareness of healthy living and encouraging guests to progress in their personal journeys. Underlying all activities in the Holistic Healing Centre is the aim of helping clients to relax and reduce their stress levels. In addition to treatments, the staff provide advice and guidance on nutrition, exercise and relaxation. The centre provides a varied choice of yoga classes, which combine hatha and raja yoga: hatha yoga is a physical approach to yoga through postures and breathing; raja yoga features the use of numerous relaxation techniques designed to promote calm and ease in the mind.

The College of Holistic Therapies was founded in 1986 to provide professional training in the field of complementary therapies. The founders' aim was to produce highly skilled professional therapists who work with sensitivity and an awareness of the energy or life-force at work in each individual they treat. The graduates are invited to join the Association of Holistic Therapies, the professional body governing all therapies taught at the college. Whether you require purely relaxation and pampering or have a specific problem to be treated in the remedial or specialist clinic, the Holistic Centre provides a choice of treatments to suit your needs.

Days and Hours of Operation: Monday to Thursday, 9 am to 7.30 pm. Friday, 9 am to 6 pm. Saturday, 10 am to 6 pm.
Rates: Costs range from €35.53 for forty-five minutes of Indian head massage to €60.91 for ninety minutes of aromatherapy massage.
Credit Cards: MasterCard, Visa and Laser.
Services: Healing, Indian head, seated on-site and remedial massage. Healing therapy, aromatherapy, reflexology and beginners' and intermediate yoga classes. Diplomas in healing massage and aromatherapy.
Facilities: Two yoga studios, three treatment rooms, one healing clinic room for nutrition advice and healing, reception area, changing area.
Staff: Don Gowing, founder of holistic healing centre and qualified nutritionist. Marie Candon, qualified social worker, healing therapist and yoga instructor. Dr E. Rose-Marie Eno-Mark, ear, nose and throat doctor and research fellow in the combined management of various diseases. Alison Gowing, qualified massage therapist, yoga and Indian-head-massage teacher, healing therapist, reflexologist, aromatherapist and sports-massage therapist. Marguerite Hilliard, bioenergy healer, massage therapist, reflexologist, deep-tissue-massage therapist, yoga teacher and Indian-head-massage therapist. Aubrey Gowing, massage therapist, yoga instructor, reflexologist and practitioner in deep-tissue massage and healing therapy.
Getting There: Serviced by all city-centre bus routes and Tara and Pearse Street DART stations.

Holistic Sourcing Centre and Harmony Book Shop

67 Lower Camden Street
Dublin 2

Tel: 01-478-5022
E-mail: namaste@tinet.ie
Website: www.holisticsourcingcentre.com

In 1996, Earl Gallogly and Mary Rose Glennon decided to open the Holistic Sourcing Centre after their own profound experiences of the benefits of complementary therapies. Although they had no experience in the area of holistic health, they were clearly determined to create a warm and welcoming centre in which qualified therapists are genuinely committed to helping clients find their own path towards a vibrant, healthy life.

The therapies and services on offer represent Earl and Mary Rose's original intention to establish a compassionate environment that is sensitive to a diverse range of beliefs and orientations. Commenting on the unique atmosphere of the centre, shop manager Eamonn Perkins says, 'It's a heart connection. The bottom line is really about empowerment.'

Days and Hours of Operation: The Holistic Sourcing Centre is open Monday to Saturday, 10 am to 9 pm. Reception hours for the healing centre are Monday to Friday, 12.30 pm to 7.30 pm. The shop is open Monday to Saturday, 10 am to 6 pm.
Rates: A typical one-hour treatment costs ¤38.09.
Credit Cards: None accepted.
Services: Acupuncture, aromatherapy, art therapy, counselling, emotional-freedom techniques, hypnotherapy, therapeutic massage, occupational therapy, past-life regression, polarity therapy, psychotherapy, reflexology, reiki, shen therapy, spiritual healing, stress management, yoga, t'ai chi, and courses in personal development and on 'The Artist's Way', as well as 'A Course in Miracles'.
Facilities: Six private treatment rooms, large workshop space, kitchenette and shop.
Staff: Approximately twenty-five therapists and counsellors offer services through the centre. All staff are qualified and licensed.
Special Notes: Clients who have booked appointments after shop closing hours can enter the healing centre by climbing the stairs adjacent to the front entrance.
Getting There: The centre is located a ten-minute walk from Dublin city centre.

Ikebana Spirit Mind Body Centre & Sundanda House Residential Supportal

4 Wynnefield Road
Rathmines
Dublin 6

Tel: 01 496 0948
Mobile: 086 883 3440

Individuals waiting for a treatment or class at Ikebana can glance out of the window at the peaceful roof garden. The atmosphere is so calm that even the workmen take off their shoes when they enter the place. Ikebana, which opened more than eight years ago, is possibly one of the most authentic healing centres in Ireland in terms of intent. As part of Sunanda Charity Trust, it aims to establish a safe healing environment for anyone, irrespective of financial status. This does not mean that therapists work for free, rather that no one will be turned away due to lack of funds.

When it is established, the Sundanda House 'Supportal' will be a residential centre providing support to individuals wishing to take the necessary steps towards healing, whether the ailment is bereavement, fear, fatal disease or heart attack Anyone from a child to an elderly person will find a safe environment in which to receive the encouragement to listen to their inner spirit and gain a greater sense of being alive. 'The support is to help people make that step out of what looks like a never-ending black tunnel and come out the other end seeing the light,' says founding director Alana Corraí.

Sundanda guests and residents will have the opportunity to grow organic foods, maintain horses, participate in sweat lodges and dance workshops, learn from artists and receive treatments and consultations from massage therapists, osteopaths and counsellors. A nurse and medical doctor will be on call around the clock in the event of emergencies. Similar to the idea of an eco-village, Sunanda will be as self-sufficient as possible while integrating trade and exchange with people in local communities.

'The idea is that you stay until you just can't wait to get out there and share this with the rest of the world,' says Alana. 'It is not just a great holiday place, though. A person who comes to Sunanda House thinking that we will heal them will not be admitted. They must know that all healing is within and they just need the support to help themselves.'

Days and Hours of Operation: The centre is open seven days a week on an appointment-only basis.
Rates: Vary according to therapist; a sliding scale is in place.
Credit Cards: None accepted.
Services: Therapeutic massage, Thai massage, Indian head massage, psychotherapy, reflexology, counselling, transformational therapy, yoga, homeopathy, kinesiology, vortex healing, allergy-testing, trager, reiki, bioenergy, seichim, aura soma, rebirthing, breathwork and creative therapy.
Facilities: Two private treatment rooms and two workshop rooms on the first and second floors; also waiting room, reception and tea kitchen.
Staff: Eighteen fully qualified therapists and counsellors.

Special Notes: The centre is accessible for people with disabilities.
Getting There: The centre is located a fifteen-minute drive from Dublin city centre and is on numerous bus routes.

INNER ADVENTURE COMPANY

92D Foxrock Avenue
Deansgrange

Tel: 01 289 7154
E-mail: irjaf@gofree.indigo.ie.

When the rent was increased at her former Dublin 2 acupuncture clinic, Irja Karjalainen decided to form a new business with her spiritual counsellor and tantric teacher Siobhan Uí Mhurchú, with whom she had worked for four years. Excited about the opportunity to pool their more than twenty years' combined experience and resources, the two brought on board Martine Longum, a therapeutic body-worker specialising in rolfing, and Johanna Harmala, an aura soma specialist. The name of the new centre is inspired by the idea that it is an adventure to discover who we really are.

Non-denominational spiritual development is the focus at Inner Adventure, and clients are encouraged to connect with their own sources of strength and creativity. 'We are all very powerful, but sometimes we don't realise it,' says Irja. 'I often see my work as sculpture. We get a block of marble and we chip away everything that is not the person, then empower them to be themselves. It is all based on awareness and self-realisation. Basically, in the final analysis, there is nothing wrong with anyone. We just think there is.'

One-day courses are on offer, such as the 'I Am Woman' workshop, designed to empower women to reclaim their true identities. There are also plans to provide residential weekend workshops.

Days and Hours of Operation: Open six days a week. While opening hours are flexible, they typically range between 9 am and 8 pm.
Rates: Although prices vary, treatments typically range between €31.74 and €50.79.
Credit Cards: MasterCard, Visa
Services: Acupuncture, Chinese medicine, spiritual healing, aura soma, energy medicine, counselling, tantric workshops and healing workshops.
Facilities: Two private treatment rooms and workshop space.
Special Notes: Services are booked strictly by appointment. Meditation and relaxation tapes are available for purchase.
Getting There: The 46A bus from Dublin city centre and the 75 bus from Tallaght stop at Kill Lane. The centre is within a short walk of the bus stop, near Foxrock Church.

INNER CIRCLE HEALING CENTRE

1 Sutton Cross
Sutton
Dublin 13

Tel:	01 832 3777
Fax:	01 832 3809
Mobile:	087 237 4718

Three years ago, Magda Batista opened the Inner Circle Healing Centre to provide a space for both physical and inner healing. In a bright and peaceful atmosphere, clients receive a range of complementary therapies aimed at improving physical, emotional, mental and spiritual well-being.

In addition to a regular schedule of treatments, the centre offers two- and three-day workshops throughout the year. Out-of-town participants can receive referrals to nearby B&Bs and hotels. In between courses, participants can walk along the Howth and Baldoyle coast roads and take in stunning views of Dublin Bay.

Days and Hours of Operation: Open Monday to Friday from 10 am to 9 pm, with the last appointment taken at 8 pm. Open Saturday from 10 am to 3 pm, with later appointments available by arrangement.
Rates: Treatments typically cost €45 per hour.
Credit Cards: None accepted.
Services: Therapeutic massage, aromatherapy, lymphatic drainage, sports massage, Indian head massage, reflexology, chiropody, podiatry, acupuncture, reiki, energy medicine,

chakra-balancing, hypnotherapy, psychotherapy, stress management, rebirthing, pilates, Hopi ear-candle treatment, and workshops on meditation, reiki, pilates, integrated energy therapy and other topics.

Facilities: The clinic, which is located on the second floor, consists of three therapy rooms and a reception. There is a little garden at the top of the landing as you come in, and the centre sells Forever Living products.

Staff: Eight fully qualified, certified and insured therapists.

Special Notes: Smoking is not allowed. Gift vouchers are available for purchase at reception.

Getting There: The centre is a thirty-minute drive north of Dublin city centre. The Sutton DART station is a three-minute walk from the centre and the 30, 31A and 31B buses go to the clinic from Lower Abbey Street.

INNIÚ SCHOOL & HEALING CENTRE

11 Main Street
Lucan

Tel: 01 628 3467
E-mail: inniu@gofree.indigo.ie

After working as a nurse for many years, Inniú School & Healing Centre owner Martina Coyne realised the importance of caring for the whole person. 'In hospital it's very difficult to give people more attention than just the bare minimum,' she says. 'For twenty years I have been looking at a holistic approach and working with people who are challenged in their lives.'

After training in a variety of holistic disciplines abroad, Martina returned to Ireland with a mission to raise awareness of and standards for complementary therapies in Ireland. Although Inniú functions primarily as a school, individuals who come to the centre for therapeutic treatments will benefit from the emotional support and personal-growth work that Martina incorporates into all sessions at the quiet Lucan location.

As a registered member of the Guild of Complementary Practitioners in the United Kingdom, Martina holds her students to strict standards. 'For the reiki course, I require anatomy, physiology and first aid,' she says. 'You cannot just go through and be a reiki master in three courses.' After her reiki course was approved by the British College of Nursing, she decided that her next step would be to introduce reiki into hospitals in Ireland.

Future plans for Inniú include establishing a course in massage therapy that is at least twice as stringent as existing courses in Ireland. 'The Guild are preparing that course at the moment,' she says. 'Instead of just 120-hour requirements for massage, I want to provide training that is more extensive and that includes time for personal-growth work as well.'

Four evenings a week at the school are devoted to reiki and healing-work courses for children aged eight and above.

Days and Hours of Operation: All treatments are booked on an appointment basis only, from Monday to Friday. On Saturday and Sunday the centre is used for workshops and training.
Rates: Treatments cost from €57.14 per hour.
Credit Cards: None accepted.
Services: Therapeutic massage, intuitive massage, reiki, reflexology, multi-dimensional cellular healing, la stone therapy and hot-stone massage.
Facilities: One private treatment room on the first floor and one teaching room.
Staff: In addition to Martina, a naturopathic doctor is available one day a week. On Thursday evenings, students practise on members of the public at a reduced rate.
Special Notes: Smoking is not allowed.
Getting There: The centre, which is located on the main street in Lucan village, is easily accessed by buses 25, 66 and 67.

INSPIRATIONS

Unit 337
Third Floor
Dun Laoghaire Shopping Centre

Tel: 01 284 2662

The mind-body-spirit shop and healing centre known as Inspirations, which began life as the Sweet Earth Healing Centre, carries on the tradition of providing uplifting calm. Today, owner Máiréad Conlon stocks plenty of incense, eco-friendly products, spiritual books, and vitamin and minerals for vegans and vegetarians. An entire section of the shop is devoted to all things angels: pins, statues, cards, and other items. 'It's a very peaceful place to be in and you get a nice feeling of calm,' she says. 'It's only a small shop, but it's a place where I'd like people to feel inspired to be better people – to come in and think it's lovely and that it has good energy.'

Three therapists specialising in various holistic modalities operate out of the private treatment room in the shop. Máiréad particularly recommends the massage for women who are pregnant or have just given birth. Once a month, Dr Glen Smeade travels from his Body & Sole Centre clinic in Galway to offer cranio-sacral therapy treatments. Smeade is one of only a handful of people practising the ancient healing technique of jin shin jyutsu in Ireland, so it is well worth visiting him.

Days and Hours of Operation: Open Monday to Saturday from 9.30 am to 6 pm.
Rates: The average price of a treatment is €38.09.

Credit Cards: None accepted.
Services: Therapeutic massage, aromatherapy, Indian head massage, Bach flower remedies, reiki, cranio-sacral therapy and reflexology.
Facilities: One private treatment room.
Staff: Three fully licensed and qualified therapists.
Special Notes: Smoking is not allowed.
Getting There: The centre is located a three-minute walk from Dun Laoghaire DART Station.

The Irish Institute for Integrated Psychotherapy

26 Longford Terrace
Monkstown

Tel/Fax: 01 280 9313
E-mail: iiipnolan@eircom.net

Patrick and Inger Nolan, directors of the IIIP, have combined their vast and wide-ranging experience in order to provide psychological care that is more about enabling the individual to accept themselves and grow than it is about changing them. The Nolans have a very therapeutic approach to care, which includes psychoanalytic, body-oriented, systemic-psychotherapy and gestalt forms of healing. Body-oriented psychotherapy attempts to understand and work with the human personality through the body. Gestalt is concerned with the whole person, encouraging a lively balance between body, feelings, intellect and imagination. Patrick and Inger's work also incorporates methods like psychodrama, painting, dream-work, imagery and massage.

Patrick has received a great deal of training in integrative psychotherapy in London and Dublin and has also trained in psychoanalytic psychotherapy at St Vincent's Hospital in Dublin. He works extensively in facilitating training courses and supervision groups for educators, psychotherapists and other people in the caring professions. Inger worked as a psychologist for nineteen years in Sweden, where she trained in family and art therapy. She also trained at the Gestalt Institute of Scandinavia. Her work includes supervising and teaching people who work with families. She also specialises in early-bonding work with parents and children. Working with groups who want to explore painting, clay-work, imagery and movement as a personal language is particularly useful in raising self-esteem and encouraging creative self-expression. Yoga, belly dancing and movement classes are held throughout the week.

Days and Hours of Operation: Monday to Friday, 9 am to 10 pm.
Rates: The cost of treatments ranges from €31.74 to €57.14.
Credit Cards: Cash or cheque only.
Services: Psychotherapy and counselling for individuals, couples and families. Psychotherapeutic massage for individuals. Professional consultancy for business organisations, focusing on team-building, stressful work situations and advice on addressing management issues. Consultancy service to professionals in health and educational services. Exploring the symbolic language of art, imagery and movement. Holistic therapies such as shiatsu and homoeopathy. Regular classes are held throughout the week in yoga, belly dancing and movement. Rooms are available for groups and therapists to rent.
Facilities: Comfortable building, close to DART and bus services, with five consulting rooms and two large rooms for group seminars and art therapy.
Staff: Two psychotherapists and counsellors, one massage therapist.
Getting There: The centre is across the road from Seapoint DART Station and is on the 7 and 8 bus routes.

LALLOO'S MEDICAL CENTRE

Unit 6
Phibsboro Shopping Centre
Dublin 7

Tel: 01 860 0561
Fax: 01 830 9551

Ranjith Lalloo studied physiology, pharmacology and pharmacy at University College Dublin and also obtained a doctorate in comple-mentary medicine. His centre incorporates therapies such as acupunture, homeopathy and herbalism as a means to promote health naturally. Lalloo also provides allergy-testing and treatment for food and chemical allergies. His interest in this area developed as a result of his own children's allergies.

Days and Hours of Operation: Monday to Saturday, 9 am to 6 pm.
Rates: The cost of treatments ranges between €25 and €44.50, with concessions available for OAPs and children.
Services: Health and dietary consultations, food allergy-testing and treatment, acupuncture, reflexology, reiki and homeopathy.
Staff: One acupuncturist, reflexologist, allergist and reiki healer. One pharmacist, acupuncturist and homeopath.

Light Therapy Ireland

Unit 4
35 Main Street
Swords

Tel:	01 890 4133
Fax:	01 890 4143

Sabrina Smith opened Light Therapy Ireland in Swords as a haven away form the hustle and bustle of this hectic north-city suburb. The clinic is both centrally located and tranquil. Treatment rooms are decorated in sunny yellow and furnished in vibrant blue. They are situated behind an inner door, where the only sounds are those of relaxing music and the only movement is the flicker of candles burning essential oils. As the centre's name suggests, many of the holistic healing therapies offered use light therapy as part of the treatment.

Light therapy is a holistic health and beauty treatment that using different wavelengths of light, seen as colours, to treat various ailments of the mind and body. This type of therapy is non-invasive, painless and extremely relaxing. Light is also channelled through fibre-optics onto acupuncture points as a painless way to treat various conditions: it is used to cleanse and detoxify the colon and lymph system, de-stress, boost the immune system, and provide relief from muscle aches and tension and respite from eczema, acne and psoriasis.

After discovering the light-therapy system in London, Sabrina felt it perfectly matched her philosophy on holistic healing and welfare – literally bringing the light into people's lives. Innosol SAD lamps and bright-light therapy is also available at the clinic and, according to Sabrina, is extremely helpful in alleviating Seasonal Affective Disorder, symptoms of which include lethargy, sleep disorder, anxiety, sometimes depression, and an increase in appetite leading to weight gain. The lamp is used to flood individuals with bright light in order to stimulate the production of serotonin (the 'happy' hormone) and balance melatonin in the brain. The clinic also offers a full range of beauty treatments and is a perfect place to relax and emerge feeling de-stressed and renewed.

Days and Hours of Operation: Monday to Saturday, 9 am to 6 pm. Tuesday and Thursday, 9 am to 8.30 pm.
Rates: Beauty treatments begin at €6.35 and costs vary, up to €190.36 for more complex detox series of treatments. Holistic therapy costs €44.42 per session on average.
Credit Cards: Laser, MasterCard and Visa.
Services: Light-therapy treatment, aromatherapy massage, Indian head massage, acupuncture, weight-loss management, a full range of beauty therapies, and nutrition therapy with Richard Burton, a qualified nutritionist and lecturer. The centre is also an agent for SAD lamps and various ranges of skincare products.
Facilities: Four treatment rooms, a relaxing reception area and a bathroom.
Staff: Two full-time and four part-time beauty/light therapists.
Nearby Attractions: Malahide Castle and Portmarnock Golf Club.
Getting There: The clinic is situated in the middle of the main street in Swords opposite the Hawthorn Hotel.

MELT: TEMPLE BAR HEALING CENTRE

2 Temple Lane
Temple Bar
Dublin 2

Tel:	01 679 8786
E-mail:	info@2melt.com
Website:	www.2melt.com

Originally a sculptor by profession, Michelle Magill taught art to the blind and people in a remand centre for four years before opening the Melt healing centre. Shortly after leaving art college in the early 1990s, Michelle began suffering from anxiety attacks. As she researched how to cure herself of these attacks, she began to meditate and change her diet. She also took a course in massage therapy, although she did not feel comfortable working in the very few places that offered therapeutic massage at that time. She continued to sculpt and look for teaching jobs, which were scarce at the time. While holding an exhibition at the RDS, she realised she wanted to open a healing centre.

'I had seen this building and felt it had a real pulse. It takes on a calmness even in the chaotic city centre,' she says. 'My thinking was very focused. Nothing would stop me. I knew it had to be really strong and it could not be about money. Really what I was trying to do was create a place where I would feel safe.'

The chefs at the restaurant across the street were laughing when Michelle first hung up her sign. 'It seemed ridiculously embarrassing to the people that knew me,' she says. 'It was a very confident thing to put up at the time.' Today, upwards of thirty-five teachers and therapists work from the centre, and a referral service is in place for individuals who may require treatments that are not available there.

A palpable and pleasant buzz can be felt at Melt, which is reflected in the camaraderie students often feel during their movement-therapy classes. 'I was teaching here and I suggested we all go down for a weekend somewhere,' Michelle says. 'The class was enthusiastic about it. I could see they just wanted some mates to hang with. Maybe there will be painting holidays with yoga in the future. In a way, I am trying to do what my mum created with her farm: to have a place where people can bring in their art or even their baby and just have a naturalness. I am definitely not doing it for the money because I could have made a lot more.'

As for how the centre arrived at its most recent name, Michelle refers to a quote from a book of Chinese wisdom: 'When ice melts, it changes its name to water.' The title refers to the welcome softening which can occur as a result of the healing process.

Michelle plans to open a residential detoxification and Chinese medical centre, specifically for the chronically ill, in Trim. 'I see people that need more than an hour's treatment,' she says.

Days and Hours of Operation: Open Monday to Saturday, from 10 am to 8 pm, by appointment.
Rates: Therapies typically cost from €38.09 to €44.44 per hour. Certification training courses may range from €40.63 to €127.
Credit Cards: MasterCard and Visa.

Services: Various types of therapeutic massage, including Swedish, lymphatic, sports-injury, Chinese tui na, Thai, aromatherapy, reflexology, Indian head and ayurvedic. Yoga, cranio-sacral therapy, kinesiology, trager, shiatsu, aura soma, homeopathy, herbal medicine, polarity therapy, bioenergy, reiki and astrology. Certification training courses in t'ai chi, yoga, pilates, art therapy, reiki, massage, feldenkrais, reflexology and synergy dance yoga.
Facilities: Converted Temple Bar townhouse with six treatment rooms, two yoga rooms, modern art gallery and private rear balcony for relaxing between treatments.
Staff: Between twenty and twenty-five therapists and nine yoga teachers. All are fully licensed and have appropriate credentials.
Special Notes: Smoking is not allowed.
Getting There: Located in the Temple Bar district of Dublin city centre.

THE NATURAL THERAPY & BEAUTY CLINIC

Coolmine Sports Complex
Clonsilla
Dublin 15

Tel: 01 820 7172

For nine years, Tricia O'Reilly has offered massage, reiki, healing and beauty treatments from the Natural Therapy & Beauty Clinic. 'When I started, I wondered if anyone would come for massage,' she says. 'Then I saw that massage is what people wanted more and more of – so it worked really well in that way.'

Continually educating herself so as to offer fresh perspectives and techniques to her loyal clientele, Tricia has just completed a course in meditation and neurolinguistic programming. She offers a very personalised service and cultivates relationships. 'It is a small little place I have here,' she says, 'but I think people find it quite comfortable and enjoy it. The healing helps them to unwind and relax. Hopefully they'll go out feeling better than when they came in.'

Tricia has long had an interest in healing and firmly believes that people can heal themselves and achieve genuine well-being in some way or another. She aims to instil a sense of calm and relaxation in her clients. 'It is just a little lift to help them,' she says. 'Everyone has to make their own journey. Massage and reiki are just a little gee-up along the way. I don't see myself as this wonderful healer, because ultimately people have to heal themselves. Some people come in and say, 'I want you to sort me out.' That is not what healing is about. It is a helping hand along the way.'

Days and Hours of Operation: Tuesday and Thursday, 2 pm to 9 pm. Wednesday, 10 am to 6 pm. Friday and Saturday, 9 am to 6 pm.
Rates: Vary according to services. A one-and-a-half-hour combined reflexology and reiki treatment is €31.74.
Credit Cards: None accepted.
Services: Reiki, aromatherapy, reflexology, metamorphosis, Indian head massage, facials and beauty treatments.
Facilities: The Natural Therapy & Beauty Clinic is a one-room clinic on the ground floor of the Coolmine Sports Complex.
Staff: Tricia O'Reilly is a reiki master and a member of the Natural Federation of Spiritual Healers in the UK.
Special Notes: Twenty-four hours' notice is required for the cancellation of an appointment.
Getting There: Close to the M50 near Blanchardstown.

Nuala Woulfe

4c Glasthule Road
Sandycove

Tel: 01 230 0244
Fax: 01 230 4882
E-mail:
   nualawoulfebeautysalon@eircom.net
Website:
   www.nualawoulfebeautysalon.ie

Encouraged by a loyal clientele that began to demand a wider variety of treatments, Nuala Woulfe opened her eponymous salon seven years ago and is still enjoying what she does. In the course of her twenty years in the business, Nuala has gained an impressive list of qualifications in massage therapy, aromatherapy, reflexology, spa-therapy treatments and beauty therapy. She is particularly knowledgeable about skin and the problems associated with it, as well as diet, holistic therapy and ways to de-stress.

In the professional, relaxed atmosphere at the clinic, clients can receive any number of body and beauty treatments. One of the more tantalising treatments is the two-hour 'Ultimate Aromatherapy Experience', which begins with breathing exercises designed to promote deep relaxation. The body is then softly brushed to soften the skin and eliminate toxins. A full-body massage is followed by the application of an exfoliating and detoxifying mask. The treatment ends with a calm-inducing scalp-massage. After the treatment, the client can wander through the village of Glasthule for a breath of seaside air.

Days and Hours of Operation: Monday and Saturday, 9.30 am to 6 pm. Tuesday to Friday, 9.30 am to 8 pm.
Rates: Vary according to services. The 'Rescue Remedy' package, which consists of a Repocharge seaweed body treatment, an Aveda stress-recovery treatment, reflexology, luxury pedicure, back massage, lash- and brow-tint and light lunch, costs €253.95.
Credit Cards: Visa, MasterCard, Laser.
Services: A wide range of facial and body treatments, beauty and slimming treatments, light therapy, seaweed wraps, Dead Sea mud and seaweed treatments, external colonic cleansing, aromatherapy and reflexology.
Facilities: Five private treatment rooms and shower facilities.
Staff: Up to eight aestheticians and massage therapists on duty. All are fully qualified and affiliated to the Society of Applied Cosmetology.
Special Notes: Mobile phones must be turned off in the salon. Twenty-four hours' notice of cancellation must be given. A 50 per cent deposit is required for bookings of more than one hour. The deposit is fully refundable if at least twenty-four hours' cancellation notice is received. Gift vouchers valid for six months from the date of issue may be purchased at the cash desk.
Getting There: Located a thirty-minute drive from Dublin city centre, and served by the DART.

ODYSSEY HEALING CENTRE

15A Wicklow Street
Dublin 2

Tel: 01 677 1021

Waiting for a gentle body-harmony treatment in the Odyssey Healing Centre, located in Dublin city centre, one might look out of the third-floor window and see seagulls tending their nests. An atmosphere of calm pervades the centre, doubtless aided by the colourful painted dolphins on the ground floor, marking the entrance.

Brenda Doherty opened Odyssey when she moved her successful massage-therapy practice out of her home in Glasnevin five years ago. 'I had always dreamed of opening a healing centre in the city,' she says. 'I grew up in Dublin and I like it. You can reach people on a wide scale here because it is so easy to access. People come in during their lunch breaks or after work.'

All the therapists at the centre share the same ethos, which is fundamentally to provide a healing experience for the mind, body, spirit and emotions. A wide range of therapies is on offer; these therapies ultimately complement each other. The central theme throughout is that health is a journey, and clients are encouraged to become actively involved in this journey. Brenda believes that healing can occur gently and safely. 'I prefer people to go at the pace of the slowest part of themselves,' she says.

While Brenda's aim is one day to offer 'everything under one roof', at the moment a referral service is in place for clients who may require the services of a homeopath, naturopath or other holistic health practitioner who may not be available through Odyssey. Future plans for the centre include introductory days for anyone wanting to find out more about the various therapies on offer.

Days and Hours of Operation: Open Monday to Friday, 9.30 am to 8.30 pm. Saturday, 10.30 am to 6 pm.
Rates: Acupuncture costs €38.09 per one-hour session. All massage therapies are €38.09 for one hour; full-body massage is €50.79. A one-hour bioenergy session is €50.79. Rebirthing is €63.49 per session. Shiatsu is €50.79 per hour. Reflexology is €38.09 per session, as is aromatherapy. Chinese herbal medicine is €38.09 for the first session and €25.39 for each follow-up session. Body harmony treatment is €57.14 per session. Energy healing is €57.14 for two hours, and €25.39 per hour for additional sessions. Stress management is €50.79 for an initial consultation; subsequent sessions cost €44.44 each.
Credit Cards: None accepted.
Services: Acupuncture, aromatherapy massage, bioenergy healing, body-harmony treatment, Indian head massage, rebirthing, reflexology, Chinese herbal medicine, shiatsu and reiki. Chinese tui na, Swedish and Thai massage. Courses in bioenergy, rebirthing and personal development, and 'Embracing the Goddess' seminars.
Facilities: Spacious waiting room and six private treatment rooms.
Staff: Seven fully licensed and qualified therapists.
Special Notes: As treatments are booked strictly by appointment, walk-in clients are rarely accommodated. Gift vouchers and a wide range of oils are available for purchase.
Getting There: Odyssey is located a five-minute walk away from Grafton Street.

The Pat Henry Figure & Fitness Centre

14 Lower Pembroke Street
Dublin 2

Tel: 01 661 6195

As his business is primarily a figure-and-fitness centre, some may be surprised to learn that Pat Henry puts great emphasis on overall well-being. The centre, which opened more than fifteen years ago, specialises in offering a high level of personalised attention and provides some of the best service in the country. Pat guarantees that his staff will do everything they can to get clients in shape, even going so far as to phone them if they begin missing appointments. 'There is no one here I wouldn't know,' he says.

But the underlying philosophy at the centre goes beyond physical fitness. 'My idea in the beginning was to try and teach people to have more awareness, so that their lives would improve,' says Pat. 'It is not just about a gym for exercise, it is about an all-over wellness. The belief that we work towards is that there is something special inside everyone and we try to help people find it. We try to get people to come to some awareness that there is something more than them inside themselves. The whole purpose of exercise is lost if they don't realise this. We also try to break the conditioning people form that they are not worthy of success or health or wealth. You can have those things, but you have to believe it.'

Another facet of the centre is the Irish Academy of Body Sculpting, which offers professional-training certification courses that are officially sanctioned by the American government. Graduates of the course are qualified to teach in twenty-six countries throughout the world.

Days and Hours of Operation: Open Monday to Friday from 6 am to 9 pm, and on Saturday from 9 am to 5 pm.
Rates: Vary according to services.
Credit Cards: MasterCard and Visa.
Services: Ki massage, reflexology, deep-tissue massage, various fitness programmes, such as body sculpting and the 'Hollywood Legs' program, yoga, pilates and kai bo.
Facilities: Fully equipped gym, punchbag area, cardio equipment, sauna and showers.
Staff: Five fully qualified diet and yoga teachers, two massage therapists. All staff have received accreditation from the Irish Health Culture Association.
Special Notes: The centre is accessible for disabled people. Booking two weeks in advance is recommended for massage and personal training. Pat Henry's best-selling book *Hollywood Legs* and a complete exercise programme on video are also available.
Getting There: The clinic is a short walk from St Stephen's Green.

Pu Shan Chinese Medicine Centre

Suite 14
Dame House
24–26 Dame Street
Dublin 2

Tel: 01 679 9753

Roughly translated, 'pu-shan' is Chinese for 'spreading goodness'. After a few pain-relieving acupuncture sessions with Dr Wang, most of his clients would agree that the name fits. Situated behind door Number 14 on the third floor in Dame House is the unassuming centre where loyal clients go to find relief from any number of chronic conditions through the application of traditional Chinese medicine.

Dr Wang, an official doctor for the Chinese athletic team in Tianjin, specialises in promoting quick recovery from sports injuries. His credentials include being a member of a team of doctors chosen by the Chinese government to establish the Chinese Medical Centre in Bath, England. Dr Sun, who has combined her background in Western allopathic medicine with traditional Chinese medicine, now specialises in dermatology, as well as drug and tobacco addiction.

A translator accompanies Dr Wang's patients as he makes his insightful diagnoses. Depending on the individual's condition, acupuncture may be administered on the spot, and a three- or four-day supply of medicinal herbs is then provided. Careful verbal and written instructions on how to prepare the herbal remedy are given.

Days and Hours of Operation: Monday to Friday, 10.30 am to 6.30 pm. Saturday, 10.30 am to 4 pm.
Rates: Acupuncture treatments typically cost €31.74. Any accompanying herbal prescriptions cost an additional €19.05 each.
Credit Cards: None accepted.
Services: Traditional Chinese medicine, acupuncture, reflexology, massage and herbal medicine.
Staff: Dr Wang Zheng, an acupuncturist and massage therapist, is a graduate of the Tianjin College of Traditional Chinese Medicine. Dr Sun Yuhua, a herbalist and acupuncturist, was a senior doctor at the Tianjin Chest Hospital. Both doctors are members of the Acupuncture & Chinese Medicine Organisation. Many therapies offered at the centre are BUPA-approved.
Special Notes: While one session is often enough to provide immediate pain relief, patients are encouraged to schedule a series of at least three visits.
Getting There: The centre is located in Dublin's city centre, a five-minute walk from Grafton Street.

The Raja Yoga Centre

61 Morehampton Road
Dublin 4

Tel: 01 660 3967
Website: www.bkwsu.com

For more than twenty years, the Raja Yoga Centre has provided a place for individuals to take part in yoga, meditation and personal development. Nick Gent facilitates the ashram and also offers courses in hatha yoga, which emphasises postural work and breathing exercises. The centre is affiliated with the Brahma Kumaris, an organisation that was founded in India in the 1950s and currently has consultative status with UNICEF and the Economic and Social Council of the United Nations.

Daily classes in raja yoga are offered to people who have completed an introductory course. Meditation classes are held every Thursday evening. The centre's busiest time is in the spring. Consequently, individuals who want to book individual hatha-yoga sessions with Nick Gent should ring several days in advance during this time.

Days and Hours of Operation: The centre is open year-round on an appointment basis.
Rates: Raja yoga is free of charge. Hatha yoga costs approximately €12.70 per hour-and-a-half session.
Credit Cards: None accepted.
Services: Hatha yoga, raja yoga, meditation and spiritual development.
Facilities: A medium-sized room serves as both yoga and meditation space.
Staff: In addition to Nick Gent, volunteer staff help facilitate the centre. Guest visitors are often invited to give lectures.
Special Notes: The centre is strictly vegetarian, and alcohol and smoking are not allowed.
Getting There: The 10 and 46A buses go right past the door of the centre.

Re:fresh

WestWood Health Club
Leopardstown Race Course
Dublin 18

Tel: 01 289 1392

Also at

WestWood Health Club
Clontarf Road
Dublin 3

Tel: 01 853 0381

Whether you want to relax completely or just pamper yourself, Re:fresh offers the opportunity to do both, with its wide range of complementary therapies and beauty treatments. Based in WestWood, one of Dublin's largest and most stylish health clubs, Re:fresh is enjoyed by those who want to avail of a relaxing aromatherapy massage after a strenuous workout in the gym, or have a reiki to balance the energies after a hard day's work. Although the club is for use by paid members, the beauty and therapy centre is open to non-members. This includes use of an Olympic-size swimming pool and an excellent spa area with a spacious jacuzzi, sauna, Turkish bath and relaxation room, complete with heated terracotta tiles and mural. Therapies and beauty treatments are tailored to the guest's needs. There are specific therapies to help people detox, de-stress or catch up on beauty treatments.

The use of light therapy, a revolutionary new beauty and healing treatment, is particularly popular with visitors to the day spa. Using wavelengths of light that are applied to areas of the body, this gentle, safe and relaxing treatment is used to work with the body's natural systems and also controls cellular regeneration. In addition to its use in most of the listed beauty therapies, it can counteract jet lag by resetting the body's biological clock to a new cycle. It is also used to boost the immune system, thereby aiding recovery after illness, or to reduce stress and promote a feeling of well-being. Light therapy is also popular with some of the 10 per cent of Irish people who suffer from SAD, Seasonal Affective Disorder during the long winter months.

Combining beauty and complementary therapy is both therapeutic and revitalising. The full detox treatment, which lasts two and a half hours, incorporates massage, healing light therapy, a facial and the use of detoxifying herbs. This naturally speeds up and detoxifies the body and gets rid of waste material which may be lodged in the colon. There is also a follow-up treatment one week later. The treatment is non-intrusive yet extremely effective. I felt completely refreshed and reenergized after the experience. My skin had a new radiance and the massage left me feeling de-stressed and energised.

The staff are highly qualified, friendly and helpful, and guests are extremely well taken care of.

Days and Hours of Opening: Monday to Friday, 9 am to 10 pm. Saturday and Sunday, 9 am to 6pm.
Rates: Average cost per treatment is €50.80. Day packages vary in price. All packages include lunch and full use of WestWood's gym facilities, including classes and use of hydro-spa area. The

delux package is €318, men's grooming package is €204, and ladies' rejuvenating package is €204.
Therapies: Introductory, full-body, tension, back and facial, mother-care, Swedish and sports, and Indian head massage. Aromatherapy special, reflexology, full detox treatment, external colonic cleansing, de-stress treatment, immune-system booster, treatment for jet lag and SAD, homeopathy, physical therapy, acupuncture, reiki, shiatsu and nutrition counselling.
Credit Cards: Visa, MasterCard, Laser and Bonus Bonds.
Facilities: Ten treatment rooms, spa area (jacuzzi, sauna, Turkish bath and relaxation room), fifty- and twenty-five-metre swimming pools, tennis and squash courts, café and bar, health-food shop, hairdressers, and classes for pilates, spinning, step and toning.
Meal Plans: Café available for panini, coffee and fresh juices
Staff: All thirty staff have ITEC, CIDESCO and CIBTAC qualifications.
Getting There: For WestWood Leopardstown, take the N11 from Dublin towards Wexford. Three miles out from city, take the right turn for Leopardstown Racecourse. For WestWood Clontarf, take the Howth road from Dublin towards Clontarf. The health club is two miles from the city centre.

THE RHIANNON CLINIC

St Paul's Grounds
North King Street
Smithfield
Dublin 7

Tel: 01 670 4905
Mobile: 087 239 9571
E-mail: kward@iol.ie.

Taking its name from the Celtic goddess of healing and spirituality, the Rhiannon Clinic is a haven of calm in the busy modern world. Situated close to the burgeoning Smithfield neighbourhood, the clinic's soothing atmosphere is an oasis for visitors in need of recuperation after a long international flight.

Owner Karen Ward opened the clinic in 1998, and massage therapist Valerie Ward joined her in 2000 to help accommodate the growing clientele. Both Karen and Valerie strive to create a warm, holistic environment where clients are treated to an eclectic mix of soothing treatments.

Days and Hours of Operation: Monday and Wednesday, 10 am to 9 pm. Friday, 1 pm to 8 pm. Saturday, 10 am to 2 pm.
Rates: A one-hour therapy treatment typically costs €44.
Credit Cards: None accepted.
Services: Ki massage, diet consultation, private yoga, psychotherapy, and body-sculpting courses.
Facilities: Small Georgian house with private treatment rooms.
Staff: Two full-time staff are fully licensed and qualified. Karen Ward is a member of the Irish Association of Holistic Medicine.

Special Notes: Therapies are booked by appointment. Gift vouchers are available for purchase at the cash desk.
Getting There: Located in Dublin city centre, a ten-minute drive from Temple Bar.

ROSEANNA CROTHERS BEAUTY SALON AND COMPLEMENTARY THERAPIES

89 Morehampton Road
Donnybrook
Dublin 4

Tel: 01 660 8408

and

2 Railway Road
Dalkey

Tel: 01 285 0077

At Roseanna Crothers beauty salons, you can indulge yourself completely by enjoying one or more of the vast range of beauty treatments on offer. This can then be complemented by a deeply relaxing massage treatment or a detox treatment to rejuvenate the entire body.

Days and Hours of Operation: Monday and Tuesday, 9.30 am to 5.30 pm. Wednesday and Thursday, 9.30 am to 8 pm. Friday, 9.30 am to 8 pm. Saturday, 9 am to 5 pm.
Rates: Beauty treatments range in price from €10 to €190. Complementary therapies range from €38 for Indian head massage to €64 for full-body aromatherapy massage.
Credit Cards: Laser and Visa.
Services: Beauty therapies, agents for Guinot, Thalgo, Nailtiques, Tea Tree, Apilus and Royal make-up. Therapies include full-body, back and shoulders, face, head and shoulders, Swedish, and Indian head massage. Also aroma-

therapy and detox treatment, including steam, marine algae and frigi thalgo.
Facilities: Three treatment rooms, and reception area.
Staff: Qualified beauticians and massage therapists.
Getting There: Dalkey: Dalkey DART Station is two minutes' walk away.
Donnybrook: From Dublin, take the N11 towards Wexford. The salon is served by the 45 bus route from Dublin.

THE SANDYCOVE CLINIC

50 Sandycove Road
Sandycove

Tel: 01 280 3505

The Sandycove Clinic was established in 1990 by Nicholas Power, a qualified acupuncturist and practitioner in traditional Chinese medicine. The aim of the clinic is to provide a professional service in the area of complimentary health care and to develop a multidisciplinary practice, which would give a wider range of choice to people who wish to receive natural health care. The clinic provides a range of therapies in a clean, modern, bright environment, which is decorated in Oriental style. Nicholas believes the way forward for health care is to work closely with and appreciate other health-care professionals and what they have to offer. This relationship has meant that the clinic regularly receives referrals from other professionals in the area, such as GPs, psychologists and pharmacists.

Days and Hours of Operation: Monday to Friday, 9 am to 6 pm. Saturday, 10 am to 1 pm.
Rates: An initial consultation costs €63.45 and follow-up visits cost €38.07 each. Treatments cost an average of €44.42.
Credit Cards: Cash or cheque only.
Services: Traditional Chinese medicine, acupuncture, herbal medicine, therapeutic massage, qi gung (now covered by VHI and BUPA), Japanese osteopathy (amatsu), Japanese natural medicine, cranio-sacral therapy, cranial osteopathy, kinesiology, remedial

massage, shiatsu, homeopathy, psychoanalytic psychotherapy, 'Stop Smoking' programme, weight-loss programme with advice on nutrition and lifestyle changes, homeopathy, energy work, art work and guided-visualisation work.
Facilities: Two treatment rooms, and a waiting area.
Staff: Two traditional Chinese medical practitioners, one shiatsu therapist, one homeopath, one psychoanalytic psychotherapist, one practitioner in amatsu, Japanese osteopathy, neuro-muscular repatterning, kinesiology and remedial massage.
Nearby Attractions: Sandycove beach, Joyce Tower and Dalkey heritage town.**Getting There:** The centre is located opposite Fitzgerald's pub in Sandycove. The nearest DART stations are Sandycove and Glasthule: on exiting the station, turn right and walk for fifteen minutes.

Shamrock Health Clinic

12 Birchview Close
Tallaght
Dublin 24

Tel: 01 451 0212

When Robert Dowdall lost his sight twelve years ago, he decided to turn it to his advantage. He studied a variety of alternative therapies in England and trained with John Sharkey in Ireland as a sports-massage practitioner. After converting a building adjacent to his home into a healing centre, he opened the Shamrock Health Clinic just over two years ago. Robert, who is one of only a handful of blind people in the country who are practising sports-massage therapists, believes that his condition makes people feel uniquely at ease with him and consequently allows him to massage the tissues more deeply. Striving to offer a uniquely personal touch, he accepts no more than twenty clients a week, in order to spend ample time and energy with each one.

Days and Hours of Operation: Open Monday to Friday from 9 am to 9 pm and on Saturday from 9 am to 5 pm.
Rates: Treatments typically cost €25.39 per hour.
Credit Cards: None accepted.
Services: Sports massage, Indian head massage, reflexology and cranio-sacral therapy.
Facilities: One private treatment room.
Staff: Robert Dowdell is fully licensed and qualified in every therapeutic treatment he offers.
Getting There: Located just before the Green Hills in Kilnamanagh.

Skerries Healing Centre

85 Strand Street
Skerries

Tel: 01 849 4457
Mobile: 087 251 7345
or 086 316 6128

Gary Westby, founder of the Irish Yoga Association, set up what is now the Skerries Healing Centre approximately seven years ago. Throughout his more than twenty years' experience, Gary has taught remedial yoga, breathing techniques, meditation and relaxation. He also undertook his postgraduate clinical training at the First Affiliated Hospital in Nanjing and the China–Japanese Hospital in Bejing. His colleague David Cosgrave studied Chinese herbal medicine with him. David also worked as a massage therapist for the Irish Olympic team in Atlanta, Georgia. Both Gary and David have taught at the Acupuncture Foundation of Ireland.

Commenting on the philosophy behind the Skerries Healing Centre, Cosgrave says that he and Westby are motivated by a desire to allow people to live life to its fullest potential. 'We have good therapists, and although we specialise in dermatology, we treat everything,' he says. 'Quite a few athletes comes to us as well, as we practise physical therapy. People from the rugby and martial-arts clubs often come to us.'

Also associated with the centre is the Weston House Skin Clinic in Sligo, where traditional Chinese medicine is used to treat a wide range of skin conditions. After an initial assessment, clients are usually placed on a homeopathic detoxification programme. Skin creams and Chinese herbs are often prescribed to supplement the treatment.

Days and Hours of Operation: Open Monday from 11 am to 6 pm, Tuesday to Thursday from 10 am to 6 pm, and Friday from 7.30 am to 4 pm.
Rates: The average price of a treatment is €31.74.
Credit Cards: None accepted.
Services: Physical therapy, massage, reflexology, complex homeopathy, Vega allergy-testing, acupuncture, Chinese herbal medicine and auriculotherapy.
Facilities: Two private treatment rooms, a consultation room and a waiting room.
Staff: Three full-time therapists.
Special Notes: The centre is accessible for people with disabilities. It is also recognised by both VHI and BUPA.
Getting There: The centre is on the main street in Skerries, a short walk from the beach.

T'AI CHI IRELAND

P.O. Box 8726
Dublin 6

Tel: 01 402 2005 (2 to 5 pm only)
Mobile: 087 979 5042
Fax: 01 496 8342
E-mail: jang@indigo.ie
Website: www.taichi-ireland.com

Specialising in the gentle flow of movements known as t'ai chi, Jan Golden teaches what he refers to as body mechanics. 'I correct people's structural habitual misalignments, which they have learned from childhood,' he says. In the sessions, which are designed for people who have little time to practise the techniques of t'ai chi, students start off learning a basic standing posture and progress into what is known as a short form of the discipline. 'What I do is teach people from the inside out,' he says. 'T'ai chi has the person use multiple forms of exercise, to have a synthetic effect on the whole body, either on yourself or on somebody else.'

Days and Hours of Operation: Individual and group classes are offered throughout the week, by appointment.
Rates: Courses cost €88.88 for eight weeks. Clients who are repeating courses pay only €44.44. There are concession for students, the unemployed and OAPs.
Credit Cards: None accepted.
Services: T'ai chi short form, long form and martial application. Qi gung standing meditation and energy-gates qi gung. Taoist mediation and Taoist breathing.
Facilities: On average, about two hundred students are involved in classes.
Staff: Jan Golden studied with B. K. Francis and has trained in the wu and yang styles of t'ai chi.
Getting There: Contact Jan Golden for information on the location of courses.

Tethra Spa

The Merrion Hotel
Upper Merrion Street
Dublin 2

Tel: 01 603 0600
Fax: 01 603 0700
E-mail: info@merrionhotel.com
Website: www.merrionhotelcom

Tethra Spa takes its name from the promised land, mentioned in early Irish literature, where there is neither sickness nor death, where happiness is abundant and where those who wish for something at once possess it. While downtown Dublin's Merrion Hotel was hardly what the original storytellers had in mind, the spa located in its basement is a quiet place where people can relieve the stresses of everyday life.

In a relaxed and tranquil atmosphere, hotel guests and the general public alike can take advantage of enticing treatments such as the eighty-minute 'Restorative Mud Envelopment'. In this treatment, which is designed for people suffering from superficial skin problems and general aches and pains, the skin is gently brushed to exfoliate dead cells. This is followed by a rub-down of moisturising oils and finally a full-body application of warm marine mud.

As the timing of the busy season can vary, guests are advised to book treatments in advance. In addition to massage therapists and beauty aestheticians, a team of five personal trainers specialising in sports-injury recovery provide personal assessments designed to cater to individual needs.

Days and Hours of Operation: Open Saturday to Friday, 6.30 am to 9 pm, with treatments available between 9 am and 9 pm. Open seven days a week for treatments. On Saturday and Sunday, the spa is open for use from 8 am to 9 pm, with treatments available from 9 am.
Rates: Vary according to services. An hour-long massage typically costs €44.44.
Credit Cards: MasterCard and Visa.
Services: Full range of treatments in the treatment room. These include beauty treatments, body treatments, facials, pedicures, manicures and leg wax, body self-tanning and eye-care treatments.
Staff: Two massage therapists, five personal trainers and two beauty aestheticians.
Facilities: An eighteen-metre infinite-lap pool, ozone-treated to reduce chlorine. Other facilities include a steam room, a state-of-the-art gym and resistance-training equipment.
Special Notes: Membership, which is available to the general public, includes use of the swimming pool, steam room and gymnasium. No access without membership.
Children are not allowed to be members and are not allowed to use the gym, but children who are resident in the hotel can use the facility. Gift vouchers can be purchased in the hotel.
Getting There: Located off Dublin's Merrion Square.

Three Rock Institute

Quinn's Road
Shankill

Tel:	01 282 7331
Fax:	01 282 0237
E-mail:	tri@indigo.ie

The surroundings of the Three Rock Institute, with its mature redwoods, oak trees and lush green lawns, lend themselves to providing the 'close to nature' feeling essential for the many environmental courses run from the centre. Goff Lawlor established the institute to promote humanistic education and solution-based approaches to social, practical and economic human behaviour. Goff weaves these principles into his courses and aims to combine a practical approach to building and living while working with, rather than against, the environment. Each course is a step towards an environmentally sustainable society, based on the principle of fairness to all generations, contends Goff. In addition to the courses, the Three Rock Institute offers an eco-consultancy service, which covers energy, transport, construction, waste and water management, agriculture and forestry. The service is increasingly drawn upon by private individuals, state agencies and corporations. The centre intends to extend its educational facility in the future, to include a primary school based on the philosophy of the renowned Japanese philosopher Tsunesaburo Makiguchi. The school will aim to encourage trust, friendship and understanding through education.

Days and Hours of Operation: Courses are held at weekends. The office is open for telephone queries and bookings from 10 am to 5 pm, Monday to Friday. Booking in advance is required for courses.
Rates: Two-day courses cost an average of €152.28.
Credit Cards: Cash or cheque only.
Meal Plans: A substantial organic vegetarian lunch is provided on course days.
Services: Courses include: eco-renovation of old buildings; green building, design and construction; downshifting – living with less; sustainable forestry, renewable energy in the home, garden composting, reed-bed and wetland – natural sewage solutions; self-build house series (€1,269), with timber frames; learning from the wisdom of indigenous people; natural building for kids; organic gardening; organic willow-growing and basketmaking; permaculture design; and eco-consultancy.
Facilities: Large period Georgian house with dining room used for conferences. Straw-bale and timber-frame houses are built on the surrounding land.
Staff: Goff and Eunice Lawlor, and other support staff, as required for particular courses.
Nearby Attractions: Killiney Bay and Sugarloaf Mountain. The Wicklow Mountains are twenty minutes away by car.
Getting There: On the N11 towards Wexford, take the exit for Shankill (about ten miles from Dublin). Drive through Shankill, and Quinns Road is left off the mini-roundabout at the end of the village. The nearest DART station is Shankill.

Turning Point Positive Health Centre

23 Crofton Road
Dun Laoghaire

Tel:	01 280 7888
or	01 280 0626
Fax:	01 280 0643

From Turning Point, which faces the sea, students and clients can see boats headed towards Dun Laoghaire harbour. A registered charity, the clinic was the first centre in Ireland to pioneer a holistic approach to the psychological care of cancer patients. Founders Kay Conroy and Mary Paula Walsh invited author Elisabeth Kübler-Ross to Ireland in 1985 and have since organised several residential workshops and public lectures for her in Ireland. They also initiated the Safe Harbours workshops for survivors of abuse.

The services available at the centre are designed to provide an integrated approach to healing, whether from serious illness or a major life crisis. Individuals are encouraged to take charge of all aspects of their lives and thus restore their inner harmony. Clients at Turning Point are viewed in their complex entirety of body, mind, spirit and emotions, and as social beings. All therapies and activities on offer complement prescribed treatments by general practitioners and medical specialists. 'I suppose our approach is a bio-psycho-social approach and working with the immune system,' says Kay.

In recent years, Kay and Mary have increasingly emphasised training. 'You can only help a small number of people, but if you train other people, it's more energy-effective,' notes Kay. Turning Point runs a graduate diploma and MSc course in integrative counselling and psychotherapy, as well as continuing professional-development courses.

One of the more intriguing therapies on offer at the centre is autogenic training, a relaxation technique developed to counteract the physical 'fight-or-flight' mechanisms of stress. Used to treat a wide variety of chronic ailments, such as high blood pressure, diabetes, insomnia, eczema, irritable-bowel syndrome and even addiction to tobacco or tranquillisers, the technique involves a series of simple mental exercises under the guidance of an experienced instructor. Through the exercises, clients are able to access repressed emotions such as anger and fear. After further effort, a state of deep peace and tranquillity can be achieved on a prolonged basis.

Days and Hours of Operation: Open Monday to Friday from 9.30 am to 5.30 pm, as well as evenings by appointment. Training takes place over the weekends.
Rates: Costs for training are on a sliding scale from €12.70 to €63.49 per hour. The MSc course costs €4,000 per year.
Credit Cards: None accepted.
Services: Psychotherapy and counselling for individuals, couples, families and groups. Grief counselling and grief therapy, stress management, autogenic training, cancer and bereavement support groups, and professional training in integrative counselling and psychotherapy in conjunction with Dublin City University. Art and drama therapy for children, mediation, supervision, supervision training and

personal-development courses. Saturday specialist seminars for professionals, and one or two residential workshops per year.
Facilities: Student common room, kitchen, five workshop and therapy rooms, student library, and two computers with Internet access for students.
Staff: Six fully licensed and qualified therapists.
Special Notes: The centre will soon be accessible to people in wheelchairs. Smoking is not allowed.
Getting There: Three minutes' walk from Dun Laoghaire DART Station.

WALMER CLINIC & COLLEGE OF HEALING AND NATURAL THERAPIES

Tonlegee House
Millbrook Grove
Dublin 13

Tel: 01 847 5410
or 01 847 5338
Fax: 01 847 5363
E-mail: walmer@indigo.ie

The Walmer Clinic was founded in 1989 in response to the steadily growing public demand for professional training in comple-mentary medicine. It is based on the principle of balancing the mind, body and spirit in a safe and calm atmosphere. It is one of the largest complementary-health centres in Dublin, with a team of twenty-three therapists offering various treatments. Bridal parties and corporate days out are proving to be very popular, with a growing number of individuals choosing to de-stress and drift away to a happier place by listening to music that feeds the soul or to release tension by receiving a therapy in the warmth of a cosy treatment room. One-to-one time and care is rapidly becoming more popular than 'time out' in the pub for stressed workers. In addition to providing therapies, the centre offers training in all ITEC complementary therapies and holistic studies.

Days and Hours of Operation: Monday to Friday, 9 am to 10 pm. Saturday, 10 am to 6 pm.
Rates: Acupuncture costs €45, aromatherapy massage €48, aura soma

€38, counselling €45, Indian head massage €25, cranio-sacral therapy €46, holistic massage €42, hypnotherapy €45, McTimoney chiropractic €32, psychotherapy €45, polarity therapy €45, reflexology €38, colour therapy €38, stress management €38, spiritual healing €32, rolfing €70 and essence-drawing €45.

Credit Cards: Laser, Access and Visa

Services: Acupuncture, aromatherapy, chiropractic, cranio-sacral therapy, essence-drawing, healing clinic, holistic massage, hypnotherapy, kinesiology, McTimoney chiropractic, psycho-therapy and reflexology.

Facilities: Three main training rooms, seating eighteen, three treatment rooms, kitchen and bathroom.

Additional Notes: The centre runs ITEC diploma courses in holistic massage, anatomy and physiology, in aromatherapy, and in diet and nutrition. It also runs an ITEC and AOR-accredited course in reflexology, a diploma course in stress management, and courses leading to a graduate certificate in sports massage and certificates in Indian head massage and first aid.

Staff: The centre employs twenty-three therapists qualified in the above therapies.

Getting There: Take the 42A or 42B bus from Lower Abbey Street near the Irish Life building. By car, from the city centre take the Malahide road, then right turn onto Tonlegee road, pass Smurfits on the left and take the third turn on the left at the traffic lights. Turn left again immediately onto Millbrook Grove. Alternatively, from the M50, turn right at the Malahide exit onto the Malahide road. Take left for Donagh-mede, pass Ayrfield Church, at the roundabout turn right onto Millbrook road and then take the third right into Millbrook Grove. Finally, turn right into Walmer Drive.

Yoga Therapy Ireland

20 Auburn Drive
Killiney

Tel: 01 235 2120
Fax: 01 235 2120
E-mail: yti@eircom.net
Website: www.yogatherapyireland.com

Yoga therapy adapts classical yoga practices in order to address the individual needs of people with specific health problems. Carried out on a one-to-one basis with a yoga therapist, all the basic principles and aims of yoga, including basic postures, breathing techniques, relaxation and meditation, are taught during a session.

Yoga Therapy Ireland is a non-profit association servicing anyone with an interest in yoga. Formed by five yoga teachers and therapists, YTI aims to promote yoga throughout Ireland and increase unity among Irish yoga organisations. The association provides anyone who is interested with a free nationwide referral register of teachers and their qualifications, as well as dates and times of classes. Venues range from small studios in people's homes to health clubs and healing centres.

Prior knowledge of yoga is not required in order to attend a yoga-therapy session. During sessions, clients are initially given a confidential consultation, after which they receive a holistic yoga programme designed to suit their individual requirements. Throughout the session, clients are encouraged to increase their self-understanding and feeling of self-empowerment on all levels. They are also encouraged to take an active role in their own well-being. Techniques for pain management are taught through breathing- and body-awareness.

Yoga Therapy Ireland also has experience in providing workshops for stress management within the corporate sector. Seminars and workshops structured to heighten public awareness of yoga as an effective therapy for common ailments are planned.

A two-year part-time teaching course is available through the centre. Applicants must have actively practised yoga for two years. Aspects of yoga covered during the course are asana, pranayama, meditation, philosophy, relaxation, first aid, anatomy and physiology. The holistic course is fully accredited by the Guild of Complementary Practitioners in the United Kingdom, as no accreditation body exists yet for courses in Ireland. The association is also on the verge of university recognition by Queen Margaret University in Edinburgh and Middlesex University in England. As yet, no university in Ireland offers this type of recognition.

Days and Hours of Operation: Although dates and times vary, teachers are generally available throughout the year for morning, afternoon and evening appointments.
Rates: Costs of classes range from €7.62 to €11.43 for a class lasting an hour and a half.
Credit Cards: None accepted.
Services: Yoga consultations for pregnancy, arthritis, back pain, breathing difficulties, multiple sclerosis, asthma and other conditions.
Facilities: Vary according to instructor and location.

Staff: Five fully qualified therapists provide individual and group sessions.
Special Notes: YTI members receive a regular newsletter, as well as discounts on workshops, seminars and open days organised by the association.

INNISH BEG COTTAGES

Innish Beg
Blaney
Enniskillen BT93 7EP

Tel/Fax: 048 6864 1525
E-mail: gabriele@innishbegcottages.com
Website: www.innishbegcottages.com
and www.yogaholidayireland.com

Innish Beg is an oasis away from hectic modern living. The 170-acre farm has panoramic views over Lough Erne. The proprietor, Gabriele Tottenham, is a warm and welcoming person, ideally suited to this type of retreat. Originally from Germany, Gabriele came to Northern Ireland to learn English and fell in love with the beautiful countryside. Accom-modation at Innish Beg is in traditional-style cottages, with modern comforts. The therapies are given in a quaint, original two-storey cottage overlooking beautiful Fermanagh countryside. Gabrielle teaches yoga in a purpose-built room complete with wooden floor and imaginative yellow colour scheme. There is ample light from the small cottage windows.

If you are unsure of which therapies might suit you, Gabrielle will provide you with a personalised programme for your weekend. This can include an opportunity to release the artist within. Jill Mulligan is the centre's local artist in residence, interior designer and part-time art teacher. Under her guidance, guests are encouraged to experiment with watercolours, charcoal, pastels and mixed-media techniques. All levels of ability are welcome.

Within easy reach of the centre are forest walks in Ely Lodge and Navar forests and ancient historical sites. Guests have free use of bicycles to experience the great natural beauty in the surrounding area. They can also avail of rowing boats in order to spend a tranquil afternoon on the vast lakes, sharing the waters with wildlife such as swans, cranes, ducks and a host of other creatures. The lake is full of uninhabited islands, although I was not brave enough to set foot on any of them! One word of advice: if taking to the waters, don't forget your map. I was so moved by the tremendous beauty that I forgot where my journey started and spent much of the afternoon rowing in circles! Having said that, if you wish to experience a peaceful retreat close to lakes, Innish Beg is ideally located to provide the perfect break.

Days and Hours of Operation: 'Pamper days', week breaks and weekend breaks are available all year round.
Accommodation: The four-star, traditional-style cottages offer accommodation that is both homely and fully equipped. All the cottages have open fires in the living room. There is a large bright room used for group-work and treatments. Breakfast is self-service in your own cottage. All other meals are served in a communal dining area.
Rates: Pamper days cost from £70 Stg per day and include tea, yoga, lunch, walk and massage therapy (the centre caters for a maximum of ten people per day). Weekend breaks cost from £125 Stg per person sharing for two nights; there is a single supplement of £15 Stg per night. Week breaks cost from £400 Stg per person sharing for six nights, with a £15 Stg single supplement per night. Painting breaks cost £85 Stg per person sharing for two nights, including tutorial and half-board accommodation, with a £15 Stg single supplement. Therapies cost an average of £30 Stg each.
Credit Cards: Visa
Meal Plans: There is a wonderful selection of locally grown produce, organic where possible. Vegetarian food is the centre's speciality; special diets are catered for at a small additional cost.
Services: Yoga classes, aromatherapy, reflexology, ki massage, Indian head massage, reiki, body massage, remedial massage, dance, painting, beauty treatments and aerobics classes.
Recreational Activities: Quiet country walks. Guests have access to the lake and are welcome to use rowing boats and bicycles to enjoy the local scenery.
Facilities: Innish Beg is a 170-acre retreat centre with four cottages, ample room for camping, a cottage for holistic treatments, dining area, yoga and aerobic exercise hall.
Staff: One aromatherapist, one therapist in ki massage, one remedial massage therapist, three qualified therapists in Indian head massage, one reiki practitioner, one reflexologist and three qualified yoga teachers.
Nearby Attractions: The historic island town of Enniskillen is seven miles from Innish Beg. It is a busy market town, catering for all your retail therapy needs, with shops, pubs, cafés and a lively nightlife. Castle Hume Golf Club is just three miles away. Innish Beg is situated next to the incredible Fermanagh Lakeland and close to woodlands and various sites of historic interest.

Getting There: From Donegal, take the A46 towards Enniskillen. From, take the A32 to Enniskillen, then the A46. From Belfast, take the A4 to Enniskillin and then the A46. Innish Beg is situated beside lower Lough Erne.

Weekend Breaks at the Fisherman's Cottage

Inisheer
Aran Islands

Tel:	099 75073
Mobile:	086 283 6379
E-mail:	foodwise@eircom.net

Website:
www.foodwisecookerycentre.com

For ten years, Enda and Marie Coneely have run the award-winning Fisherman's Cottage restaurant on Inisheer, the smallest of the Aran Islands. Throughout the quiet winter seasons, the Coneelys diligently studied various disciplines of cooking and healing, which resulted in their opening the Organic Wholefood Cookery School. With the intention of creating a tranquil getaway far from the stresses of urban life, the Coneelys now offer residential weekend courses covering various aspects of cookery and health.

'People go to health-food stores and see loads of wholegrains, but they don't always know how to use them,' says Marie. 'We show the value of everything involved in using the local products that are here: the fish, the wild thyme, the seaweed, the garlic. We get people to take note of how they feel after eating certain foods, so they become more aware of how they are feeling. They notice the effects as soon as they start eating it. It is also about using the space here so you can come and relax and just really chill out. We have stunning views of the sea all around and a resident dolphin.'

Last year's course on the harvesting

and medicinal uses of herbs had guests drying plants gathered from the Coneelys' garden, preserving them for use during the winter, making medicinal decoctions and infusions, as well as discovering herbal remedies for minor ailments. Guests were also taught recipes for herb-flavoured oils and vinegars. During the ayurvedic healing foods course, instructors touched on the basic concepts of the ancient Indian system of healing. Various cooking styles and techniques for balancing the three body types, or *doshas*, were taught, together with unique ways to mix Indian spices. Developed for sugar addicts, the 'Healthy Breakfasts and Sugar-free Desserts' course had pupils learning to use natural flavours to produce enticing dessert and breakfast dishes. Biodynamic psychotherapist Brigid Daly also led a course entitled 'Gentle Explorations of Life's Journey', which aimed to help individuals take stock of their lives in peaceful, supportive surroundings.

Days and Hours of Operation: Weekend courses run throughout May, June, July, August and early September.
Accommodation: Guests stay in local B&Bs within walking distance of the school. A list of local accommodation can be supplied on request.
Rates: The average cost of courses is €247.65.
Credit Cards: MasterCard and Visa.
Meal Plans: Organic wholefood meals are included on macrobiotic courses. The fish-cookery weekend also includes lunch and dinner.
Services: Residential two- and three-day courses on topics such as healthy wholefood cookery, herbalism, shiatsu and feng shui.

Recreational Activities: Light exercise, bicycling, scenic walks, swimming, kayak rental and boat trips.
Facilities: Courses are taught in the kitchen of the Coneelys' restaurant, as well as in a conservatory area, which has views of the sea. There are plans to build a separate cooking school. The couple also maintain an organic garden.
Staff: Enda studied medicinal cooking, cooking for healing and five-element cooking at the International Hospitality Management Insitute in Switzerland. He is also a graduate of the Ballymaloe Cookery School and is a member of toques, the European Community of Chefs. Marie is a shiatsu therapist. The Coneelys both studied Taoist healing arts, including nutrition, with Master Mantak Chia in Zurich and at his centre in Thailand. In addition to Enda and Marie, guest lecturers also sometimes lead courses.
Special Notes: As the weather on Inisheer is often unpredictable, bring plenty of rain-gear and suitable outdoor clothing. Course fees must be paid at least four weeks in advance to guarantee a place. In the event of cancellation, a full refund less the deposit will be given, provided written notice of the cancellation is received at least four weeks prior to the start of the course. The Coneelys reserve the right to alter the timing and content of a course in the event of unavoidable circumstances, such as inclement weather.
Nearby Attractions: Monastic ruins, Bronze Age settlements, sixteen-acre inland lake, the remains of the *Plassy* shipwreck, and panoramic views of the Burren, Galway Bay and the Twelve Pins in Connemara.

Getting There: The school may be reached via ferries from Doolin, County Clare, or Rossaveel, County Galway. Aer Arann operates a direct flight from Connemara Airport.

The Burren Yoga & Meditation Centre

Lig do Scith
Cappaghmore
Kinvara

Tel:	091 637 680
E-mail:	burrenyoga@yahoo.com
Website:	www.burrenyoga.com

Situated in a magical, peaceful, tranquil environment, the Burren Yoga & Meditation Centre is a place where visitors can escape their busy lives and take time out. The centre sits on a beautiful, grassy two-acre site, surrounded by mature native trees and a recently built dolmen and stone circle. The main aim of the centre is to promote well-being, self-awareness and self-development on a physical, mental, emotional and spiritual level. The centre is designed especially for yoga workshops and can be hired out for weekend and evening courses. The building was designed using the principles of feng shui, with an emphasis on natural light, fresh air, minimalist décor and warm, comfortable surroundings. A variety of yoga courses, pilates courses and complementary therapies are available.

Satyananda, astanga and iyengar yoga are the main yoga types on offer. Satyanda yoga begins very gently and is suitable for everyone, whether fit or unfit, large or small. It is very relaxing and includes plenty of breathing practices. Iyengar requires a reasonable level of fitness and the postures are quite demanding. Astanga is a very dynamic strong form of yoga and requires a fairly high level of fitness and flexibility. It is increasing in popularity, especially since singing icon Madonna confirmed that she uses the form of yoga to keep her toned, flexible body in shape.

Days and Hours of Operation: Weekend workshops begin at 6 pm on Friday and end on Sunday at 2 pm. Midweek classes begin at 7 pm.
Accommodation: The dormitory, with bunk beds, sleeps eight people. There are also two double and two single rooms. The centre also includes a bright, spacious kitchen with organic, shaped wooden counters.
Rates: Weekend courses cost €203.05 and include tuition, accommodation and meals. Treatments cost €31.73 each.
Credit Cards: Visa and MasterCard.
Meal Plans: Breakfast, lunch and dinner are included in the cost of the weekend course. Superb vegetarian food is prepared by a gourmet vegetarian cook.
Services: Residential yoga and pilates courses and weekly yoga classes. Workshops in feng shui, detox and holistic health. Therapies include aromatherapy, reiki and Swedish and shiatsu massage.
Facilities: Yoga room with underfloor heated wooden workspace and large windows for natural light. Day room, which also features underfloor heating and large windows, offers spectacular views of the Burren. Treatment room, dormitory and kitchen area.
Staff: Varies according to course requirements. Ten yoga teachers and two pilates teachers are available for instruction. Therapists include three massage therapists. Also manager Dave Brocklebank and one gourmet cook.
Nearby Attractions: The Burren, Ailwee Caves, Cliffs of Moher, Dunguaire Castle, picturesque village of Kinvara, Poulnabrone dolmen and many other ancient sites.
Getting There: Situated at the foot of the Burren Hills, five miles from Galway Bay and twenty-five miles from both Galway city and Ennis.

Delphi Mountain Resort & Spa

Leenane

Tel:	095 42987
or	095 42208
Fax:	095 42303
E-mail:	delphigy@iol.ie
Website:	www.delphiescape.com

Past the mussel farms and glacier-swept Mweelrea Mountains lies the three-hundred-acre estate housing the four-star Delphi Mountain Resort and Spa. The spa, which has been open since April 2001, developed as a natural extension to the eighteen-year-old Delphi Adventure Centre. Now guests can get the best of both worlds – a full day of exciting activities, combined with relaxing spa therapies. Or they can simply content themselves with a relaxing sit in a swirling jacuzzi under twinkling fairy lights behind floor-to-ceiling curved glass that faces the mountains of Connaught.

As a member of the International Spa & Fitness Association, Delphi is based on the American model of health spas, which means the daily schedule of activities is more activity-based than in a typical European spa. At any time of year, guests can wake up in their chalet-style room and set out into the mountains or explore the woods, rivers and ocean. Those who choose the gentle option of an unguided walk along the road should be sure to stuff a few apples into their pockets to feed the donkeys. Whether the day involves surfing, rock-climbing or simply sitting comfortably on the patio with a good book, a relaxing afternoon wind-down can include anything from a seaweed body wrap to an Indian head massage. In between all the activity and spa treatments are the enticing meals. On request, the chef will make a delectable fresh batch of mint leaf, lemon, ginger and honey tea.

Owner Frank Noone plans to expand the spa, eventually bringing in medical staff to offer more comprehensive health programmes. People with specific health concerns will also be able to avail of programmes uniquely designed for them, such as a 'Healthy Heart' weekend and a course for diabetics. In addition, guest speakers will guide people through the organic garden as part of courses in low-fat cooking. 'It will be a place where you can escape into the wilderness and rejuvenate,' says director Pat Shaughnessy. 'Eventually, we'll be bringing in actual seaweed baths and peat paths. We are letting nature influences us.'

The organic garden will ultimately provide 60 per cent of the spa's food supply, and the recycling programme will be enlarged to include the composting and mulching of biodegradable waste. On a lighter note, a jazz pianist will be brought on board to enliven the evening's entertainment options. There are also plans to construct a helicopter pad, which will make getting to and from the spa from Knock and Galway Airports much easier.

Days and Hours of Operation: The spa is open year-round for one-day and residential programmes.
Accommodation: Up to sixty adults are housed in a combination of single, double and triple rooms and suites. All

rooms are en suite and centrally heated, and have direct-dial telephones, a hairdryer and hot-drink-making facilities. Also available is a cottage that sleeps up to seven and overlooks Killary Harbour.

Rates: Although prices vary, a typical fully inclusive health spa weekend costs €443.14 per single and €405.05 per double. A typical à la carte one-hour spa treatment costs between €38.09 and €57.14.

Credit Cards: MasterCard, Visa, American Express and Laser.

Meal Plans: Meals are included with most residential and day programmes. With advance notice, all special diets can be accommodated.

Services: Therapeutic massage, reflexology, aromatherapy, Indian head massage, balneotherapy, body wraps, body scrubs and a full range of beauty treatments. Delphi also offers corporate retreats and team-building programmes.

Recreational Activities: Surfing, sailing, fishing, boat tours, kayaking, canoeing, water-skiing, dolphin-watching, archery, tennis, horse-riding, golf, cycling, abseiling, rock-climbing, hill-walking, t'ai chi, yoga, aerobics, dancing, strength-training, star-gazing and Irish dancing.

Facilities: Eighty guest rooms; health suite (with steam room, sauna and Jacuzzi), relaxation room, library, aerobic-dance studio, yoga room, indoor sports hall, adventure centre with high-ropes course, organic garden, restaurant, bar and laundry/drying room.

Staff: The total staff of between seventy-five and a hundred people includes therapists, instructors, catering personnel, administration staff and other client-support employees.

Special Notes: Hill-walkers and other outdoor enthusiasts should bring hardy walking shoes and adequate rain gear. Swimming costumes must be worn in the health suite. To avoid disappointment upon arrival, please pre-book all spa treatments. Smoking allowed only in designated areas. Mobile phones are not allowed in any public areas.

Nearby Attractions: Kylemore Abbey, Inishturk, Inishbofin, annual curragh race, annual Famine Walk, Castlebar walking festivals, ogham stones, pollution-free Blue Flag beaches and bars, Irish music and dancing in Westport.

Getting There: Transfers may be arranged for individuals and groups arriving at Westport Train Station, as well as from Dublin, Shannon, Knock or Galway Airports.

Galway Bay Health Farm

Loughaunrone House
Oranmore

Tel: 091 790606
Fax: 091 790837
E-mail: lochan@iol.ie
Website: www.galwaybathealthfarm.ie

Situated in a graceful Georgian residence on a fifty-acre deer farm overlooking Galway Bay, the six-year-old Galway Bay Health Farm offers a personal approach for guests wanting to eliminate stress and regenerate the mind and body. 'We are small and focused,' says owner Margaret McNulty. 'I will always say to people that we offer a unique experience to a better life.'

Margaret, who has a background in nursing, also holds a diploma in nutrition advice and is a qualified fitness instructor. 'I am coming from the health side rather than beauty,' she says. Her experience is reflected in the health farm's ethos, which is to provide a kick-start to a healthy lifestyle. Programmes are geared towards inspiring people to look after themselves properly. The approach is holistic, with equal emphasis placed on relaxation, exercise, a balanced diet and having a positive attitude.

In a small, private and personalised setting, guests benefit from the down-to-earth and practical staff. 'We live the life,' says Margaret. 'It is not work for us. The people who do the work genuinely love doing what they do.'

A typical stay at the health farm begins with a private health consultation with a registered nurse on the night of arrival, followed by an evening meal. After a balanced breakfast the next morning, the day might include a full-body therapeutic massage, gym instruction, yoga, swimming, a guided walk, a reflexology treatment and a relaxing sit in the steam room or sauna. If that is not enough, guests are free to use the tennis court and bicycles. A resident psychotherapist also leads talks on sensible eating, behaviour modification and how to look one's best with minimum effort.

For those who want just to escape to the quiet, wild surrounds of the West, a self-catering cottage, accommodating up to nine people, is available. At the time of writing, a new pool and leisure centre accessible for people with disabilities are being built.

Days and Hours of Operation: Open for three-, four- and six-day residential programmes year-round, with the exception of two weeks at Christmas. Non-residential services and 'pamper days' are offered on Tuesday, Wednesday, Thursday and Saturday.
Accommodation: Ten people at a time are accommodated in single, twin or double en suite rooms.
Rates: The average price for a non-residential day is €125.73, which includes lunch, dinner, an hour-long body massage, use of all facilities, talks led by a psychotherapist, yoga instruction and various outdoor activities.
Credit Cards: MasterCard, Visa, American Express, Eurocard and Access.
Meal Plans: All meals are included in the residential programme. Menus follow 'Healthy Heart' guidelines, which include the reduced use of fats and sugars. The venison, chicken and turkey are free-range, and vegetables are purchased from local producers.

Services: Nutrition consultations, image consulting, psychotherapy, therapeutic massage, reiki, aromatherapy, daily gym instruction, full range of beauty treatments, reflexology, and Indian head, holistic and Swedish massage.
Recreational Activities: Swimming, guided walks and yoga.
Facilities: Fifty-acre deer farm, Georgian residence, two beauty-treatment rooms, gym, steam and sauna room, tennis court and bicycles, and self-catering cottage.
Staff: A professional staff of twenty-three includes several full- and part-time therapists and instructors.
Special Notes: Guests are advised to bring a tracksuit, sweatshirts, swimsuit, suitable footwear for walking, runners and gym shoes. All towels and robes are provided. Children under eighteen are not allowed. Smoking and alcohol are not permitted.
Nearby Attractions: One hundred acres of woodlands, Galway Bay Sailing and Golf Club, horse-riding, sixteenth-century castle in nearby Renville, Coole Park and Galway city.
Getting There: The health farm is a fifteen-minute drive away from Galway Airport.

GALWAY YOGA & MEDITATION CENTRE

Churchyard Street
Galway

Tel: 091 844 449
E-mail: info@galwayyoga.com
Website: www.galwayyoga.com

Shraddha and Chetan Murti have taught yoga in the satayanda tradition for fifteen years. Inspired by their yoga teacher while living in Denmark, the married couple began to train together and eventually met their instructor, Satayanda, while practising in India. The couple returned to Shraddha's home in Galway, where they began to teach classes. Although very few people were offering yoga at the time, one hundred people showed up for the Murtis' first-ever open day. Today the Murtis' courses are so popular that three months' advance booking is recommended. Among the offerings is a class specifically designed for senior citizens living in Galway.

As people who attended the daily classes wanted to do more intensive study, about ten years ago the Murtis developed a residential centre around ten miles from Oranmore beach in Athenry. Instruction takes place in a dedicated yoga structure built adjacent to the Murtis' home, which is surrounded by old trees on three acres in the silent, pastoral countryside. Guests have the option of participating in a digestive-cleansing programme, which consists of a detoxifying diet combined with specific yoga postures aimed at eliminating toxins. The ten-day courses, which take place during the summer, are intended to show people that they can 'switch off' completely away from telephones and TV. 'There are three whole days with no communication whatsoever,' says Shraddah. 'There are classes every day, and we work on chakras and do meditation. It's really a way to get to know yourself.'

Although the ten-day residential programme only takes place in July, various weekend courses are held throughout the year. Subjects include yoga in daily life, the chakras and working with breath.

Days and Hours of Operation: Yoga classes are held on Monday to Friday from 6 to 7.30 pm and from 8 to 9.30 pm. On Wednesday and Thursday, classes are held from 11 am to 12.30 pm and from 1 to 2 pm.

Accommodation: Up to fourteen people are housed in shared accommodation. In addition to two double rooms, one room sleeps six and another sleeps four.

Rates: A twelve-week course costs €76.18. The ten-day residential course costs €380.91, with full room and board.

Credit Cards: None accepted.

Meal Plans: All meals are vegetarian, with organic food used where possible. Guests help to make meals.

Services: Yoga, meditation and detoxification programmes.

Facilities: A well-lit yoga room on the second floor of a building in Galway city centre. For residential programmes, facilities include a dedicated yoga room, sitting room, dining room, kitchen and showers.

Staff: In addition to teaching yoga courses themselves, Shraddha and Chetan Murti also hire guest lecturers for various programmes.

Special Notes: To avoid disappointment, book classes three months in advance. Children under sixteen are not allowed.

Getting There: Taxis to the residential centre, which is seven miles from Galway Airport, are available from Athenry Train Station.

Slánú Cancer Help Centre

Uggool
Moycullen

Tel:	091 555 898
Fax:	091 555 894
E-mail:	info@slanu.ie

'*Slánú*', which is a hybrid of the words '*slán*' and '*sláinte*' that means 'to make whole', implies a journey away from oppression into freedom and fullness of life. The Slánú Cancer Help Centre, the only one of its kind in Ireland, offers a five-day residential programme for individuals living with cancer or any other life-threatening illness. The programme is also open to family members of cancer patients, as well as individuals experiencing a personal crisis.

During their stay in the centre, which is surrounded by peaceful countryside, people are encouraged to take stock of their lives, to find focus through looking within from a holistic perspective and to participate in their own healing and well-being. The chief aims of the centre are to provide a means for people to come to terms with their illness, to explore their own inner processes and transformation, to learn healthy attitudes and skills for living life as fully as possible, and to enhance an awareness of the value of the present moment.

Sister Bridget Tuohy from County Clare originally founded the centre in 1987 as a result of her frustration and feelings of isolation after being diagnosed with cancer. Although Sister Tuohy died the following year, she received great comfort while staying at the Bristol Cancer Help Clinic in England. The Sisters of Mercy undertook the running of the centre up to 1995, when psychotherapist Eileen Joyce-Henelly became the director. While spirituality is an underlying theme throughout the programme, the centre claims no religious affiliation. Guests freely adhere to and express their own unique belief systems.

While the centre is still small and has limited resources, an ever-widening circle of friends offers support services such as bread-making and hairdressing. A large amount of funding comes through donations.

Days and Hours of Operation: The centre is open seven days a week, from 10 am to 5 pm. Residential programmes are available from January to November.
Accommodation: Guests stay in one of three bedrooms in the home.
Rates: The cost of the five-day programme at the centre is €888.89, though guests are only asked to pay half that amount. Those who cannot afford the cost may pay whatever they can afford.
Credit Cards: None accepted.
Meal Plans: All meals are fresh and from organic sources where possible.
Services: Five-day residential programme of supportive therapies, such as counselling, journalling, art therapy, relaxation/visualisation, medical consultation, nutrition advice, massage, healing prayer and meditation. Drop-in centre and helpline for crisis counselling, support groups, advice and information regarding cancer, counselling services, information services, and educational courses on a variety of subjects, such as vegetarian cookery, nutrition, art therapy, environmental awareness and complementary therapies.

Facilities: Five bedrooms, three bathrooms, kitchen, and sitting room with an open fire and television.
Staff: Eileen Joyce-Hennelly, director of services and biodynamic psychotherapist; Miriam Byrnee, coordinator; Anna King, massage therapist; Annette Joyce, nutrition advisor and massage therapist; and Corina McCarthy, reiki practitioner. Also kitchen support staff and volunteers.
Special Notes: Smoking is not allowed.
Nearby Attractions: Galway city, the Aran Islands, golf courses, equestrian centres and boat tours.
Getting There: The centre is located approximately five miles from Galway city, towards Moycullen.

ANAM CARA

Loughrea
(also in Dublin)

Tel: 091 634591
(Dublin tel: 087 827 4508)
E-mail: yourmystar@ireland.com

Marguerite Brady brings a wealth of experience to Anam Cara, in terms of both conventional medical sense and holistic healing. Marguerite worked as a nurse for years before training in African reflexology and foot-reading; she has since trained in many areas of complementary health. With her naturally caring and friendly attitude, she provides healing care which is truly holistic in nature. The roof of the treatment room is painted sky blue, complete with white fluffy clouds, to help you float away to a peaceful place while enjoying your therapy. As Marguerite works with aromatherapy, the scent of orange and lavender or other sweet aromas wafts through the air. This, combined with soft relaxation music, enhances the mood and relaxes the mind. Marguerite is director of the Anam Cara International Academy of Reflexology, which is a member of the National Register of Reflexologists in Ireland. She runs fourteen-month courses in reflexology and three-month postgraduate courses in African reflexology.

Days and Hours of Operation: Monday to Saturday, 9 am to 9 pm.
Rates: €44.42 per hour, €57.11 for an hour and a half, or €76.14 for two hours. The fourteen-month reflexology course costs €1903.55 per student.

Credit Cards: Cash or cheque only.
Services: African reflexology and foot-reading, Western reflexology and teacher, aromatherapy, ki massage, homeopathy, reiki master and teacher, Indian head massage, colour therapy, bush- and Bach flower consultant.
Facilities: Two clinics, one in Dublin and the other in Galway. One treatment room, one waiting area, one toilet.
Staff: Two qualified therapists.
Nearby Attractions: The Dublin clinic is situated on a quiet road, close to the city centre. The Galway clinic is located close to the sea and to peaceful country walks.

ANNAGHDOWN SEAWEED SPA

Corrandulla

Tel: 091 791 918

Annaghdown Seaweed Spa owners Michael and Ann Joyce are good at what they do. For more than twenty years, they owned and operated a residential health farm where they used products from the Dead Sea to induce a healthy glow in the skin of satisfied clients. As customers increasingly enquired about day-spa services, the Joyces decided to open a strictly day facility specialising in the treatment of psoriasis, eczema, general aches and pains, and giving slimming body wraps, through the use of natural seaweed and Dead Sea mud and mineral crystals. 'People always say they feel great after the treatments,' says Ann.

One of the more interesting packages on offer is the half-day 'Pampering Package', which consists of a Turkish bath, a hydrotherapy spa bath and a detoxifying full-body wrap. The Joyces also offer a selection of vitamin and mineral supplements and skincare products which they believe uniquely complement and support the spa treatments.

Days and Hours of Operation: Open Monday to Friday, 10 am to 7 pm, and Saturday, 10 am to 4 pm.
Accommodation: Clients may enquire at the desk about referrals to nearby B&Bs.
Rates: Prices vary. Seaweed baths cost €12.70, while a full-body Dead Sea psoriasis and eczema treatment costs €57.14.

Credit Cards: MasterCard, Visa and Laser.
Services: Dead Sea mud and seaweed baths, mineral crystal baths, body wraps, salt scrubs and facials.
Facilities: Turkish bath, sauna, three hydrotherapy baths and three treatment rooms with showers.
Staff: Four full-time and three part-time therapists.
Special Notes: Ample parking is available. Clients receive free black-mud soap with prepaid courses costing €95.23 or more.
Nearby Attractions: Annaghdown Pier, St Brendan's Monastery and scenic walks. The beach is ten miles away.
Getting There: The spa is located nine miles from Galway city.

THE BODY & SOLE CENTRE FOR HEALTH EDUCATION & RELAXATION

Frenchville Lane
Eyre Square
Galway

Tel: 091 539 622
Fax: 091 539 633

Down a quiet lane, a short walk from Eyre Square, lies the Body & Sole Centre. Walking in, one instantly notices the gentle arrangement of healing stones and plants. 'You invite nature in and see it on the way out to calm you and balance you,' says owner Mary Irwin. 'That's where healing should start – at the door. We try to include a sense of colour, sound and smell as much as possible, then the touch of the therapies. It is really important for me that it is not just cream walls. This is a special space.'

A professional nurse and midwife with many years' experience, Mary became frustrated at the lack of time she had to spend with each patient. Finding her calling through natural medicine, Mary drew together a team of therapists whose specialities complemented each other, and opened the centre just over five years ago. 'We work a lot with education and helping people help themselves,' she says. 'They do their own healing – we just give them the space and time. We try to bridge the gap between sickness and health. A red light will come on in the car and we take care of it, but a pain comes along in the body and we just drive on. We wouldn't do it to the car, but we do it to our bodies. We have got to learn that we create a lot of healing in our body – mentally, physically and spiritually.'

A wide array of profoundly beneficial therapeutic treatments are available at the centre. 'Body Talk', for example, is used to repair the network of circuitry that is impaired by the accumulation of mental, emotional and physical stress. This painless, hands-on form of healing incorporates advanced yoga, kinesiology and the energy dynamics of acupuncture. During sessions, trigger points are held by the therapist while the client takes a series of deep breaths. The skull and sternum are then gently tapped. Studies have shown 'Body Talk' to help in more than 70 per cent of cases of dyslexia, chronic viruses, infections, allergies and back pain.

Structural Maintenance and Rehabilitation Therapy, or SMART, is another interesting therapy offered at the centre. This therapy is derived from applied physiology, chiropractic, cranio-sacral therapy, jin shin jyutsu, sacro-occipital technique, nutrition and herbology. The various disciplines combine to relieve pain and facilitate the body's inherent healing power. During treatments, therapists are concerned specifically with the structure of the body, the balance of the life energy in the chakras and meridian, and the emotional, nutritional and physical causes of the particular ailment.

Clients typically find that on their first visit to the centre, the appointment lasts an hour and a half in order to give the therapist time to record a brief health history and discuss the various healing techniques that will be used during the session. A personal support system may be developed for the client to assist with the healing process at home.

Days and Hours of Operation: Open Monday to Saturday from 10 am to 6 pm, with earlier or later appointments by arrangement. The centre is open during the weekend for workshops.

Rates: On average, the cost of treatments ranges from €25.39 to €44.44 per hour.

Credit Cards: None accepted at present.

Services: Acupuncture, Chinese herbal medicine, aromatherapy massage, aura soma, 'Body Talk', chakra-balancing, cranio-sacral therapy, crystal healing, vortex healing, family therapy and counselling, energy-work, flower and gemstone remedies, holistic massage, Indian head massage, magnified healing, natural vision improvement, reflexology, reiki, shiatsu, sports massage and 'Stop Smoking' programme. Day-long and weekend workshops in ITEC certification for Indian head massage, and Irish Institute of Reflexology accreditation in reflexology, feng shui and space-clearing, Alexander Technique, 'Body Talk' training and natural vision improvement.

Facilities: Four private treatment rooms and teaching room.

Staff: Seven full-time licensed and qualified therapists.

Special Notes: The centre is wheelchair-accessible with a wheelchair-accessible toilet located in the building next door. Gift vouchers are available for purchase at the cash desk. A 10 per cent discount is offered on appointments before 2 pm. Twenty-four hours' notice of cancellation is required on all appointments.

Getting There: The centre is within walking distance of Galway train and bus stations.

Clinic of Alternative Medicine

33 Shantalla Road
Galway

Tel: 091 522631

This recently established clinic was opened by Alan Brannelly, who has qualified in acupuncture, osteopathy and Vega testing (for allergies). He has trained for more than fourteen years in Ireland, England and Sri Lanka. Over the past decade, he has built up a very successful practice and offers expert advice on drug-free therapies and medicine using only natural methods. The clinic of alternative medicine specialises in spine and joint disorders, sports injuries, allergy/food-intolerance testing and complex homeopathy.

Alan has introduced the Power Assisted Micro-Manipulator, the newest tool in the treatment of back pain, to his practice. According to Alan, successful results are now possible on chronic back-pain sufferers who have longstanding spinal disorders. Alan has been using this machine, the first of its kind in Ireland, to treat clients with scoliosis, whiplash, postural problems and chronic back pain.

Days and Hours of Operation: Monday to Friday, 9.30 am to 5.30 pm. Thursday, 9.30 am to 10 pm.
Rates: Average cost of treatment is €38.07, with specialist treatments costing €57.11.
Credit cards: Cash or cheque only.
Therapies: Acupuncture, osteopathy, Vega testing (for allergies), complex homeopathy, herbal medicine and Chinese herbal medicine.
Facilities: Two treatment rooms, reception and waiting area.
Special Notes: The clinic is wheelchair-accessible and off-street parking is available.
Nearby Attractions: Lough Corrib and Galway Bay.
Getting there: Next to University College Hospital.

Galway Rolfing Clinic

Pollnaclough
Moycullen

Tel: 091 555 025

In the 1980s, Barry O'Brien suffered from severe back pain. Seeking help through all the normal medical channels, as well as many alternative ones, he eventually found his way to the only certified Rolfer in Ireland. It was under the care of this Rolfer that Barry's back problem was cured. So enthusiastic was he about this experience that he flew to Munich to train as a Rolfer himself.

At that time, Barry and his wife Helen had just received their PhDs in marine biology. As work was difficult to come by, Helen began to train as a fitness instructor. It was during this training that she developed a keen interest in holistic therapies. Together, the two opened the Galway Rolfing Clinic in 1990, with the primary goal of educating people about their own healing abilities. Clients also receive a great deal of individual attention. 'We take a lot of time with the patients,' says Helen. 'They can call us up any time for phone support and follow-up.'

Helen qualified as a skenar therapist. The doctors who invented this therapy, which was developed in Russia for cosmonauts who could not tolerate drugs in space, received the equivalent of the Russian Nobel Peace Prize for their work in this area. The treatment involves the application of a small remote-control-sized device to the skin to realign the body's energy and trigger therapeutic processes. Primarily used for relief from pain caused by arthritis and back problems, skenar can be used to good effect no matter what the symptoms, says Helen.

Days and Hours of Operation: Open Monday to Saturday, 9 am to 8.30 pm.
Rates: Rolfing costs €63.49 per session, allergy-testing costs €50.79, and skenar therapy costs €38.09 per session.
Credit Cards: None accepted.
Services: Rolfing, allergy-testing and skenar therapy.
Facilities: Two private treatment rooms.
Staff: Barry O'Brien is a certified Rolfer, and Helen O'Brien is a qualified skenar therapist and allergy tester.
Special Notes: Appointments are booked strictly by telephone.
Getting There: About five miles from Galway city centre, off the N59 towards Clifden.

Harmony Acupuncture & Angel Aromatherapy Clinic

Kilcolgan & Flood Street
Galway

Tel: 091 568 871

After training with the Acupuncture Foundation of Ireland for three years, Linda Lyons attended the International School of Chinese Medicine in Nanjing to receive further training in traditional Chinese medicine. Soon afterwards, she established the Harmony Acupuncture Clinic, which functions alongside and in conjunction with the Angel Aromatherapy Clinic.

Linda, who is still an active member of the Acupuncture Foundation, ensures that confidentiality is upheld and that all equipment and methods of treatment meet the society's guidelines. During treatments, she aims to instil in each client a feeling that they have been not only listened to but heard. 'I would like them to feel that their particular ailment has been relieved and that they understand a little more about how it came to be,' she says.

Understanding that it is sometimes difficult to get a good massage at a beauty salon, Martina Lyons runs the Angel Aromatherapy Clinic, which offers a range of holistic health and beauty services in a relaxing atmosphere.

Days and Hours of Operation: Monday to Friday, 10 am to 7 pm. Open late and on Saturday by appointment.
Rates: Treatments typically cost around €38.09.
Credit Cards: MasterCard and Visa.

Services: Acupuncture, herbal medicine, moxibustion, cupping, aromatherapy, deep-tissue and Swedish massage, reiki, reflexology, facials, body scrubs and full range of beauty treatments.
Facilities: Two private treatments rooms on the ground floor, tanning bed.
Staff: Two full-time and three part-time licensed and qualified therapists and aestheticians.
Special Notes: As Linda Lyons is VHI- and BUPA-approved, certain treatment costs are refundable. Smoking is not allowed.
Getting There: The clinic is located within a five-minute walk of Eyre Square, close to the Spanish Arch.

Eskine House of Silence

Eskine
Tahilla
Sneem

Tel: 064 89212
E-mail: dunsdroogers@eircom.net

While working as a general practitioner in a Dutch hospital, Mark Droogers realised that many processes, such as diagnosis and therapy, had to be dealt with before he could actually speak with a patient about what their disease might mean to them and how they could cope with it. Believing that there must be a better way to approach well-being, Mark and his wife Babette purchased the comfortable County Kerry chalet overlooking an ancient stone circle in order to open the Eskine House of Silence. 'We felt the urge to do this kind of work, and we couldn't find it in our jobs or studies,' Mark says. 'What I really wanted was contact with people and to be able to know what lives inside them, in their hearts.'

A typical stay at Eskine involves not only yoga but also breathing exercises and a well-balanced diet. Guests are gently encouraged to realise a profound awareness of the here and now. Mark and Babette believe that, if people learn calmly to connect to the present, they will lead a more fulfilling life. 'We believe everybody has a right to live a happy life – a life full of inner prosperity,' Mark notes. 'The techniques we use here are intended to bring people to a well of inner wisdom that they can take home with them and keep in contact with.'

An understated and yet appealing part of a stay at Eskine is the level of personal care each guest receives. 'People really feel at home when they are here,' says Mark. Days typically start with yoga and meditation at 7 am, followed by a breakfast of fresh fruits and grains. From 12.30 until lunch at 1 pm, guests find an inspiring, comfortable location for thirty minutes of complete silence. More meditation follows the 4 pm tea and coffee, and after dinner at 7 pm guests have the option of taking part in intuitive painting, clay-moulding, or simply curling up on the couch for a relaxed chat.

Mark says that Irish guests often ask whether massage and saunas are available during the stay. For the moment, there are no plans to include them in the programme offered at the centre. 'We try to make people self-sufficient and give them something they can do themselves,' Mark notes. 'We find that working with yoga, meditation and so on provides people with tools that they can always use.'

Days and Hours of Operation: Weekend and week-long packages offered year-round.
Accommodation: Guests stay in one of two spacious guest rooms. Hardy guests who want to connect with nature can stay in a 'beehive' hut on the property.
Rates: The weekend package costs €146.05, and the week-long package costs €476.25. Both programmes include room and board.
Credit Cards: None accepted.
Meal Plans: Healthy, balanced meals using organic wholefoods where possible are included in the price of the programme.

Services: Weekend and week-long yoga, meditation and creative counselling packages.
Facilities: Picturesque country house with two spacious guest rooms, complete with open fire and central heating. Rustic 'beehive' huts also available.
Staff: Babette Duns, yoga instructor and creative counsellor, and Mark Droogers, medical doctor and meditation coach.
Special Notes: No smoking. No massage services available.
Nearby Attractions: The Ring of Kerry, Sneem Sculpture Park and nearby hill-walking trails.
Getting There: From Dublin, take the train to Killarney. From Killarney, catch a bus to Sneem and a taxi to the centre. With prior arrangement, the Droogers will pick up guests for a fee of €25.39.

LIOS DANA HOLISTIC CENTRE

Inch
Anascaul

Tel: 066 915 8189
Fax: 066 915 8223
E-mail: liosdana@gofree.indigo.ie
Websites:
  www.liosdana.foundmark.com
  www.holistic.ie/liosdana/index.htm

Anne Drechsler and partner Michael Travers met while taking an aikido course in Dublin more than twenty years ago. At the time, the two had a dream to build a community for healing work and wanted to open a centre. In 1985, that dream came true when they discovered the location of what is now Lios Dana, where guests can take in a view of MacGillycuddy's Reeks and Dingle Bay while having breakfast. The purpose-built centre is set in ten acres of wild, exposed coastal headlands. Anne is a shiatsu practitioner and macrobiotic counsellor and Michael is a talented painter. 'Partly because of my love of cooking, I wanted to create an environment where people could share food and relax,' says Anne.

Residential programmes held throughout the year offer instruction in yoga, aikido, meditation, the Alexander technique, shiatsu massage, morning exercise and vegetarian wholefood meals. Up to eighteen people at a time stay in double rooms in the modern house, which has central heating and a hearty solid-fuel stove. The average day might begin with some light morning stretches and non-denominational meditation. Yoga or shiatsu instruction may follow. Between lunch and dinner, guests can explore the wind-carved beaches, wander through the miles of fuchsia hedgerows or settle in comfortably with one of the many books on self-healing techniques from the centre's library. For those wanting to celebrate the New Year in a quiet retreat space, the annual New Year Break is held from December 29 to January 2.

Days and Hours of Operation: Open for residential workshops throughout the year.
Accommodation: Eight bedrooms capable of housing up to eighteen people. Two of the rooms are en suite.
Rates: Daily rates vary between €50.79 and €76.18. A three-day holiday break costs €82.53 per person per day for food, lodging and sessions. The B&B price is €25.39 per person per day.
Credit Cards: None accepted.
Meal Plans: Macrobiotic, vegetarian meals are offered with B&B or full-board accommodation. Occasionally, fish is served.
Services: Workshops in Alexander technique, yoga, meditation, shiatsu, t'ai chi, dream-work, writing, aikido and macrobiotics.
Recreational Activities: Windsurfing, swimming, fishing, boat trips, horse-riding and hill-walking.
Facilities: Large recreation room for activities such as yoga, meditation and t'ai chi, reading room, library, conservatory room and dining area.
Staff: While Anne and Michael run the centre and offer workshops, various facilitators lead courses.
Special Notes: Services offered in the workshops are not available to individuals outside of arranged programmes. Lios Dana offers B&B or full-board accommodation throughout most of the year. Smoking is not allowed in the house.
Nearby Attractions: Town of Dingle, Fungi the dolphin, Slea Head, Dúnbeg Fort, beehive huts, Slieve Mish mountain range and the Blasket Islands.
Getting There: From Dublin take the train to Tralee and from there take a bus to Anascaul. A pick-up service is available from Lios Dana by prior arrangement.

The Ashe Street Clinic

Tralee

Tel: 066 712 2626
Fax: 066 712 2626
Mobile: 087 254 1000

As with many of the newly established health centres in Ireland, the Ashe Street Clinic benefits from combining a conventional approach to medicine with a choice of complementary healing therapies. Dr David Buckley established the clinic in 1992 and believes that having orthodox medicine, counselling and homeopathy under the same roof provides the patient with complete health care to suit their individual requirements. The aim of the centre is to provide high-quality patient care in a courteous and efficient manner.

Days and Hours of Operation: Monday to Friday, 9 am to 5.45 pm; Saturday, 10 am to 1 pm.
Rates: Average €38.07 per session. Vary according to treatment required. VHI and BUPA cover accepted.
Services: The Ashe Street Clinic diagnoses, investigates and treats all common allergy problems, including food allergies, asthma, hay fever and eczema. Services offered include skin-prick testing, blood allergy-testing, skin-patch testing and exclusion diets. Also clinical, complex and classical homeopathy, counselling, women's health, surgical clinic, dental clinic, skin clinic, general practice, physiotherapy and sports-injury centre.
Facilities: Treatment rooms and reception area.
Staff: Medical practitioner, practice nurse, chartered physiotherapist, psychologist, dental surgeon, consultant ophthalmologist, homeopath, office manager, secretary and receptionist.
Getting There: Situated opposite the courthouse in the centre of Tralee.

Coiscéim Natural Therapy Centre

8 Church Street
Tralee

Tel/Fax: 066 718 1855

Coiscéim is the Irish word for 'footstep'; the centre was established as a place of peace, quiet and relaxation, to enable people to take steps towards restoring balance and harmony in their lives. Anne O'Donnell has been a complementary-health practitioner for five years, offering a wide variety of therapies in a relaxed and supportive environment. The second therapist, Juliana Murphy, previously worked as a child-care worker and with women's groups at home and abroad. She worked in Africa for six years before returning to Ireland and training as a massage therapist and reiki practitioner. She offers the compassion required to facilitate a profound level of healing.

Days and Hours of Operation: Tuesday to Saturday, 10 am to 5 pm.
Rates: €31.73 for an hour-long session of treatment.
Credit Cards: Cash or cheque only.
Therapies: Massage, reflexology, polarity therapy, reiki, bereavement support, Bach flower remedies, bioresonance testing, and colour psychoanalysis.
Workshops: A nine-week programme in personal development includes sessions on examining behaviour patterns, coping with stress, characteristics of birth signs, diet, exercise and relaxation. Pamper days for firms and businesses are also run at the centre.
Facilities: Two therapy rooms, reception area, office, three group rooms and kitchen. The centre also has a mobile home twenty miles from Tralee. The mobile home, which is surrounded by golden sandy beaches, is used for group days of relaxation and reflection.
Staff: Two therapists and one receptionist.
Getting there: Located in the centre of Tralee, opposite the Abbey Gate Hotel on Church Street.

Dingle's Natural Therapy Centre

Lámh Iomlán Teo
The Coastguard Cottage
Cooleen
Dingle

Tel: 066 915 2474

Dingle's Natural Therapy Centre, overlooking Dingle Bay, provides a nurturing environment for healing. The modern, purpose-built centre is an addition to the historic coastguard cottage, built in 1850. It offers first-rate complementary health care designed to promote relaxation and aid recovery from a wide range of ailments. Most of the clients attending the clinic benefit from relief of symptoms such as back problems, stiff neck, painful shoulders, sports injuries, migraines, stress and fatigue, depression, menstrual irregu-larities, skin complaints and sore joints, muscles and tendons.

The therapists work in an integrated way with conventional medicine, and referral to a medical doctor is made if such a course of action is deemed appropriate. If you are unsure which therapy would suit you best, you can avail of a free initial consultation to help you choose an appropriate course of treatment. After enjoying a massage or other treatment, you can relax in the sauna, or rest in the comfortable waiting room or on the terrace and watch the boats go by in the harbour.

Days and Hours of Operation: In wintertime: Tuesday to Saturday, 11 am to 5 pm. In summertime: Monday to Saturday, 10 am to 5 pm.
Rates: The cost of treatment varies between €38.10 and €50.80 for each one-hour session.
Therapies: Massage, acupuncture, reflexology, shiatsu, Indian head massage, chiropractic, cranio-sacral therapy, Bowen technique, lymphatic drainage, aromatherapy facials, Dr Hauschka facials, natural manicures, natural pedicures and reiki. Also individual classes in yoga, as well as psychotherapy and counselling.
Facilities: Four treatment rooms, a sauna, showers and a large waiting room.
Staff: Ten qualified therapists, one manager, one receptionist.
Nearby Attractions: Dingle is best known for Fungi the dolphin, who has remained in the harbour for years. It is also famous for its *craic:* although it is a small village, it contains fifty-two pubs, which host great Irish music and other entertainment. It is situated in a beautiful part of Ireland, close to long sandy beaches, golf clubs and horse-riding facilities.
Getting There: Drive into Dingle and turn down the lane opposite Moran's Esso garage, on the Tralee road, near the roundabout in Dingle. The cottage is on the right-hand side, before the end of the lane.

Oasis Alternative Medical and Flotation Centre

5 Gas Terrace
Tralee

Tel: 066 714 4998
E-mail: oasiscentre@eircom.net

Oasis is one of only six flotation centres in Ireland, and is the only one in Kerry. Flotation therapy was developed as a way of isolating the mind and body from external stimuli in order to gain a deep feeling of calm. It is also used to treat conditions such as high blood pressure, arthritis and back problems and to help alleviate depression. Under-floor heating in the float room adds to the comfort of the experience, and the room also benefits from natural light coming in through a large circular stained-glass window, enhanced with mosaic tiles. Before being rejuvenated in the flotation tank or receiving a therapy, guests can enjoy the special ambiance of the reception area, with its tropical aquarium and views of the scenic garden to the rear of the building. The centre offers over fifteen therapies and provides a free initial consultation, to ensure the client receives the therapy most suited to their needs. With the perfect balance of subtle decor, privacy and location, the centre has the ideal surroundings to relax and unwind.

Days and Hours of Operation: Monday to Friday, 10 am to 7 pm (last appointment). Saturday, 10 am to 6 pm (last appointment).
Rates: The average cost of a treatment is €44.50.
Credit Cards: Laser and Visa.
Services: Flotation therapy, shiatsu massage, reiki, cranio-sacral therapy, allergy-testing, Bach flower remedies, body talk, tui na Chinese massage, energetic massage, Indian head massage, reflexology, kinesiology, nutrition, acupuncture, traditional Chinese medicine, bioenergy and medical herbalism.
Facilities: Flotation room, including shower; four treatment rooms, in which six practitioners and therapists provide therapies; reception area and outdoor garden.
Staff: Manager Jacqueline Dennehy, six fully qualified therapists in above therapies, Chinese medical practitioner, nutritionist and medical herbalist.
Nearby Attractions: Oasis is situated in Tralee town centre, two minutes' walk from the main shopping area. It is close to the Dingle Steam Railway, Siamsa Tíre folk theatre, the *Jeanie Johnson*, Blennerville Windmill and Visitor Centre, and Fenit Seaworld.
Getting There: Tralee is fifty minutes' drive from Killarney and thirty-five minutes from Kerry Airport, on the main N22 Killarney-to-Tralee road, and is accessible by both mainline train and bus. The centre is a twenty-minute walk from Tralee railway station.

The Celbridge Physiotherapy & Acupuncture Clinic

Main Street
Celbridge

Tel: 01 627 5628

There are three chartered physiotherapists currently working in the Celbridge Physiotherapy & Acupuncture Clinic. Two of the physiotherapists, having completed four-year degree courses in Trinity College and University College Dublin respectively, also undertook a three-year course with the British College of Acupuncture. The four members of staff have found physiotherapy to be particularly effective in the treatment of sports injuries, back and neck pain, limb pain and biomechanical problems such as orthotics, foot pain, heel spurs, repetitive-strain injuries and incontinence. They use the ancient Chinese art of acupuncture to treat ailments such as arthritis, asthma, hypertension, insomnia, irritable-bowel syndrome, premenstrual tension, skin conditions and stress-related tiredness. The aim of the clinic is to facilitate healing and promote well-being using both Western and Eastern knowledge of conventional and complementary healing.

Days and Hours of Operation: Morning, afternoon and evening sessions on Monday to Friday, by appointment.
Rates: €32 per session.
Credit Cards: Cash or cheque only.

Services: Physiotherapy, acupuncture, sports medicine, manual therapy and biomechanical and orthotic assessment.
Facilities: Two treatment rooms, one waiting room.
Staff: Óisín Hannan, Sheenagh Sexton and John Donovan.
Getting There: Celbridge is situated beyond Leixlip on the N4 road.
Nearby Attractions: Castletown House, a period Georgian house with gardens, is open to the public. Maynooth College is five kilometres away.

The Complementary Treatment Clinic

Crookstown Lower
Ballytore
Athy

Tel: 0507 23231
Mobile: 086 240 6770

The Complementary Treatment Clinic offers a range of therapies to treat illness, stress, injury and disease naturally. They also offer consultations and house-calls by appointment. At the moment, the Midlands is underserved by practitioners of complementary health care, but this purpose-built clinic goes a long way towards remedying this situation, given the comprehensive choice of therapies that is available there.

Days and Hours of Operation: Monday to Saturday, 9.30 am to 6 pm.
Accommodation: Two rooms with en suite bathroom at €32 per person sharing, per night.
Rates: Therapies cost an average of €40 per session.
Credit Cards: Cash or cheque only.
Meal Plans: B&B. Breakfast includes home-made traditional Irish bread, fresh fruit and yogurt, or full cooked Irish breakfast, for non-vegetarians.
Therapies: Ki, sports, aromatherapy and Indian head massage. Eurowave, acupuncture and healing-herbs reflexology.
Facilities: Two treatment rooms, waiting room.
Staff: One nurse, reiki practitioner and physical therapist, one massage therapist and reiki practitioner, and one practitioner in aromatherapy, Indian head massage, reflexology, advanced healing therapy, acupuncture and sports massage.
Nearby Attractions: Quaker village with museum and mill, Drummond Boy's Well, Punchestown Racecourse and the Curragh Racecourse are twenty minutes away by car. The nearest shopping town is Naas or Athy.
Getting There: Take the M9 from Dublin; at Kilcullen, take the N9 towards Carlow. The Complementary Treatment Clinic is between Narraghmore and Crookstown on the Carlow road.

Fairgreen Holistic Clinic

Fairgreen
Naas

Tel: 045 898 243

The Fairgreen Holistic Clinic, on the main street of Naas, officially opened its doors in April 1999, as the fruit of a longstanding dream of Kate Curtis and Heidi Winston. Many different complementary therapies are being offered under the same roof, so people can pick which one is best able to help them. Kate and Heidi, both former specialist nurses, were drawn into the field of natural medicine when they realised that there was more to healing a person than tackling their physical condition. Discovering that the mind, body and spirit have to be dealt with in unison for real progress to be made, they decided to open a clinic. Here, they provide therapies and encourage people to take responsibility for their own healing and health. They also run various workshops on various subjects, including stress management, from the centre. In this workshop, participants are taught to alleviate stress by relaxing deeply, which allows the nervous system to calm down and leads to an overall sense of well-being.

Days and Hours of Operation: Monday to Saturday, 9 am to 8 pm.
Rates: The cost of treatments ranges from €31.73 to €50.76 per session.
Credit Cards: Cash or cheques only.
Services: Acupuncture (VHI- and BUPA-approved), aromatherapy, bio-energy healing, colour therapy, counselling, emotional-release body-work, homeopathy, hypnotherapy, personal-life coaching, magnified healing and use of a medical practitioner. Sports-injury, deep-tissue and Indian head massage. Neurolinguistic programming, psychotherapy, reiki, psychic surgery, spiritual healing, shiatsu, reflexology, transformational cellular healing, trager therapy, use of transpersonal therapist, and tarot-card readings.
Facilities: Four treatment rooms, small workshop room, kitchen and reception area. Relaxation CDs available. T'ai chi and yoga classes organised in local hall. Reiki workshops for adults and children are held regularly throughout the month. There are additional classes in colour therapy and magnified healing. Special antenatal classes also held.
Staff: Two acupuncturists, two massage therapists, two aromatherapists, two reflexologists, three reiki practitioners, two reiki masters (one teaching), two spiritual healers, one psychic healer, one transpersonal therapist, one trager therapist, two shiatsu therapists, two homeopaths, one magnified healer, one colour therapist, three psychotherapists, one family therapist, one personal-life coach, one neurolinguistic programming practitioner, one hypnotherapist, one medical practitioner, one emotional-release body-work therapist and one transformational cellular healer.
Nearby Attractions: Naas is a very busy rural town in the heart of horse-racing country, with Punchestown Racecourse and the Curragh nearby. The town is surrounded by rich farmland and has wonderful walks along the canal. It is close to the Japanese Gardens in Kildare town, and Blessington Lakes are a ten-minute drive away.

Getting There: From Dublin, take the Kildare bus from Bus Áras, or take the train from Heuston Station to Sallins. Then take the feeder bus to Naas (a two-mile journey). Car parking is available at the rear of the clinic.

The Blue Room Meditation & Healing Centre

Bennettsbridge

Tel:	056 27004
Mobile:	087 697 6395
E-mail:	judithashton@unison.ie

Judith Ashton, president of the Irish Massage Therapy Association, has brought her more than twenty years' experience as a complementary healer to the two-year-old Blue Room. 'I feel that I have a really deep understanding of the mind-body-spirit connection from having worked for so many years on the physical level,' she says. 'I am also a trained psychotherapist, so I have an understanding of how stress affects the body. Having worked with many spiritual people who are into meditation and so on over the years, I really try to help people get in touch with their deeper soul self.'

A wide range of holistic therapies are available at the centre, as well as a new two-year creative-arts training course in therapy and music. Judith will work with Daniel Perret, who has practised for more than twenty-five years as a music therapist and healer. The curriculum includes a study of human-energy fields, and the elements and impact of sound and music for healing and harmonisation.

At present, guests stay in nearby B&Bs for the occasional weekend workshop. However, at the time of writing, Judith is moving into a house that will accommodate residential guests for one weekend each month. Directly associated with the Blue Room, the new centre will be a quiet haven for people to get away from the city for a weekend of massage, healthy food and refreshing outdoor air. 'I think the key to all healing is relaxation,' says Judith. 'Everybody needs to learn how to relax. This has been a long-time dream. I have had the idea for twenty-something years. The house is in the most beautiful scenic area with panoramic views – definitely bring the wellies.'

A typical package might include one or two holistic massages, hill-walking, the use of Mount Juliet's swimming, golf, tennis and horse-riding facilities, and daily excursions to local art colleges and glass-blowers. Although breakfast will be included, guests will have the option of dining in or out. All food will be organic and vegetarian.

Days and Hours of Operation: Open Monday Friday, from 10 am to 7 pm, and some Saturdays. Workshops are held at various times throughout the year.
Accommodation: At present, guests are referred to local B&Bs for residential workshops.
Rates: The average price of a treatment is €38.09 per session.
Credit Cards: None accepted.
Meal Plans: Organic vegetarian meals are included with some residential packages.
Services: Counselling, psychotherapy, massage, yoga, homeopathy, kinesiology, allergy-testing, reiki, dream analysis, spiritual-journey work, relaxation therapy, meditation, weekend workshops, and training courses in therapy and music.
Recreational Activities: Hill-walking, cycling, horse-riding, golf and fishing.

Facilities: The centre consists of a large, spacious room in an old renovated shop.
Staff: In addition to Judith, four part-time therapists work at the centre. All are fully licensed and qualified.
Special Notes: The centre can be hired for meetings. Smoking is not allowed.
Nearby Attractions: Kilkenny Castle, Kilkenny Design Centre, St Canice's Cathedral, the Black Abbey and St Francis' Abbey.
Getting There: Centrally located in Bennetsbridge, the Blue Room is opposite the cemetery, next to a car park and over the Bridge Pottery. Lifts may be arranged from the train station in Kilkenny or Thomastown.

Holistic Healing Centre

High Street
Graiguenamanagh

Tel: 0503 24298

The gentle River Duiske meanders past the Holistic Healing Centre, which is situated deep in the Barrow Valley and offers an ideal setting to move on in one's journey. Much of the surrounding flora and fauna has not been touched since the Cistercian monks practised their own form of healing nearby approximately eight hundred years ago.

In 1998, Joe Fox, a qualified ki massage therapist, opened the centre to assist people in their spiritual journey, as well as to relieve pain, both physical and emotional. 'My purpose in life is to inspire people,' he says. 'I do that in a subtle sort of a way while people are in for massage. Within the three years we have been open, people's consciousness of all this type of thing has changed. People are just crying out for healing of all types. Very often with massage they will want something extra beyond the physical to help them.'

Full-time staff member Noeleen Mahon practises reiki, while Joe specialises in remedial deep-tissue massage. If a client has a particularly bad injury, Joe combines this massage with 'Quantum Touch', a form of hands-off energy healing.

Believing there is only so much he can do for people on a one-on-one basis, Joe has launched an ongoing 'Crossroad of Life' seminar to accommodate large groups. Long-term plans for the future include the introduction of residential healing programmes.

Days and Hours of Operation: Open Monday to Saturday, 9 am to 8 pm.
Accommodation: Three guest flats are currently under construction. Once they are built, the centre will offer residential programmes.
Rates: A thirty-minute, full-body treatment costs €38.09, while an hour-long treatment costs €63.49.
Credit Cards: None accepted.
Meal Plans: Meals will be included in the residential programmes once these programmes are up and running.
Services: Ki massage, reiki, Indian head massage, reflexology, aromatherapy, psychotherapy, counselling, and around half a dozen other disciplines provided by part-time therapists.
Facilities: Three treatments rooms, seminar workshop area and adjoining kitchen.
Staff: The centre employs two full-time, fully licensed and qualified therapists.
Nearby Attractions: Scenic walks, Duiske Abbey, Kilkenny Castle, Kilkenny Design Centre, St Canice's Cathedral and the Black Abbey.
Getting There: The centre is approximately twenty minutes by car from Kilkenny town.

Namaste

Rossleaghan
Portlaoise

Tel: 0502 61691
E-mail: gohan@iol.ie

The lush green laneway to Michael Rice's home is alive with the sounds of birdsong, and nestled at the end is a tastefully designed three-bedroomed house and centre for courses. Built with an indigenous sandstone and limestone mix, combined with red deal wood painted in smoky blue, the house and centre blends organically into the surrounding landscape.

The workspace room is spacious and inviting, with subtle colours and soft curves. Feng shui principles have been applied to the structure and layout of the area – an indication of the fact that a deeper consciousness was at work in the design of the building. As an architect, Michael designs using his in-depth knowledge of feng shui to create a more harmonious environment that positively affects those living and working in the space provided.

According to Michael, being in rhythm with natural universal energies when designing is essential. To help him with this, Michael has travelled to Tibet, China, Amsterdam and America to gain a comprehensive understanding of feng shui. He runs weekend seminars in sacred geometry, feng shui and meditation, in which participants learn how to create a home using ancient Eastern philosophies.

Days and Hours of Operation: Courses are run over weekends. E-mail for information on upcoming courses.
Rates: €254 for sacred-geometry course, €571 for feng shui workshop.
Credit Cards: Cash or cheque only.
Meal Plans: Home-baked wholesome vegetarian lunch provided on both days.
Services: Feng shui, sacred-geometry and meditation workshops.
Facilities: A five-hundred-foot domed workshop and meditation space with kitchen and toilet and a stone labyrinth situated in tranquil and secluded woodlands and orchards.
Staff: Michael and Heather Rice and invited guest facilitators.
Special Notes: The centre is accessible for people with disabilities. Smoking is not allowed.
Nearby Attractions: Slieve Bloom Mountains, golf courses and Portlaoise town.
Getting There: The centre is located one mile from Portlaoise on the Tullamore road, the N80.

Limerick Healing Centre of Colour & Light

65 Catherine Street
Limerick

Tel: 061 400 431

John Quinlivan began studying relaxation and yoga in 1981. Shortly afterwards, he learned transcendental meditation while continuing to pursue his keen interest in self-healing. In 1994, he opened the Limerick Healing Centre of Colour & Light, where he now offers a variety of healing therapies.

John primarily focuses on spiritual counselling and healing. He aims to unite his client's body, mind and spirit in order to restore harmony between the individual and the world at large. Believing himself to be a channel of universal love and light, he typically closes a consultation by laying his hands over his client to promote healing. 'Empowering the individual that comes here to do a lot of the work themselves – that's the idea,' he says.

Days and Hours of Operation: Open Monday to Friday, and some Saturdays, from 9.30 am to 9.30 pm.
Rates: An hour-and-fifteen-minute treatment costs €50.79.
Credit Cards: MasterCard and Visa.
Services: Aura-sketching, aura soma colour-readings, dream-work, meditation, relaxation, reiki, yoga, regression therapy, seichem, spiritual healing, counselling, angel therapy and courses in reiki and seichem.
Facilities: Two private treatment rooms.
Staff: At present, John Quinlivan employs no other staff.
Special Notes: Walk-in appointments are welcome. John will travel to facilitate group-work.
Getting There: The centre is located in Limerick city centre.

Acorn Counselling and Therapy Centre

Wellington Quay
Drogheda

Tel: 041 984 4277

The Acorn Counselling and Therapy Centre, which combines professional psychological counselling with complementary therapies, enables clients to benefit from healing on both an emotional and physical level. The professional, confidential counselling provided is designed to help individuals and couples to understand and tackle anxiety, depression, trauma abuse, addictions, eating disorders, bereavement, losses, phobias and low self-esteem. The centre also provides counselling for marital breakdown and relationship difficulties. The holistic approach to these things is that they also affect our physical well-being. As a result, Acorn offers a wide range of treatments to de-stress and uplift the mood. As nutrition is also important for optimum overall health, they provide advice on diet and nutrition. This initiative – relatively new in Ireland – of providing such an all-encompassing support system is a welcome and much needed approach to overall health.

Days and Hours of operation: Monday to Saturday, 9.30 am to 5.30 pm.
Rates: €31.73 per hour.
Therapies: Acupuncture, aromatherapy, ki massage, reiki, hypnotherapy, reflexology, bioenergy, metamorphosis, stress management, personal development, yoga, sports massage, and diet and nutrition.
Counselling Available: General counselling, addiction counselling, family and relationship counselling, psychotherapy, counselling for eating disorders, cellular healing and astrology.
Facilities: Yoga classes. Talks and courses are held regularly. Rooms are available to rent by the hour, day or part-day.
Staff: All therapists have professional qualifications and are full members of professional bodies.
Getting There: Near the Dominican church in Drogheda.

Cloona Health Centre

Westport

Tel:	098 25251
E-mail:	info@cloona.ie
Website:	www.cloona.ie

In 1973, what is now Cloona Health Centre opened as a haven for Tibetan lamas who had fled their country after it was invaded by the Chinese. The parents of the current owner, Dhara Kelly, had nearly finished a complete restoration and conversion of the two-hundred-year-old corn mill into a comfortable home for the lamas when the Irish government refused to grant them visas. With a refurbished building on their hands, the couple opened Cloona, originally as a venue for healing programmes such as meditation and yoga. 'People were mostly coming from Britain then, because there wasn't much of that going on in Ireland at that time and there were only a few venues,' says Dhara.

It was not long before former guests began calling Cloona to ask whether they could stay in between arranged bookings. Dhara's mother then devised the original health programme, which has since been revised by Dhara and his wife.

The centre's exclusively residential programmes were developed to cleanse and relax the body and spirit. As there is only one programme on offer, guests should be well-informed of the day-to-day routine and meal plans before arriving.

What the Kellys would like guests to take from a stay at Cloona is a heightened awareness of their body and increased clarity when approaching decisions and opportunities. Individuals are encouraged to take responsibility for their lives, to gain a strong sense of what they can and cannot do, and to develop an enhanced sensitivity to their own responses to activities, diet, energy and relationships.

'The cleansing takes place not just on a literal biochemical level, but also emotionally, spiritually and mentally,' says Dhara. 'That is what makes it more expansive than just a plain detox programme. It is about attunement with all of the interests in life.'

A typical day begins with a breakfast of fresh citrus fruit. At 10.45 am, a two-hour hatha yoga course gets under way. This type of yoga is the embodiment of the ethos at Cloona. At 1 pm, the main meal of the day, consisting of a hearty soup and organic salad, is served. At 2.15, Dhara leads a daily walk, taking guests on a different route each day. Free time follows; this may include a stroll along the garden labyrinth or optional shiatsu, massage and reflexology treatments. Cycling, horse-riding and golf are available locally. At 6 pm, an evening meal of assorted sweet and semi-sweet fruits is served, followed by a sauna and massage at 7 pm.

While the diet may sound stark, the Kellys believe it gently assists guests in taking the initiative and developing a sensitivity to how individuals respond to various foods or energies in their day-to-day lives. 'The course wouldn't work if guests experienced hunger,' Dhara says. 'There is plenty of food – it is just light, so the body can digest it easily and efficiently and get on with the other things we are focusing on. We look at the poetics of cleansing – where things need to be cleared out: emotional baggage, baggage from the future in the form of apprehension and fear of change. The programme works in a subtle, discreet way. These things are addressed indirectly, and there is no group psychotherapy whatsoever. They occur throughout the process. The overall effect is a sort of *je ne sais quoi.*'

Evidence of Cloona's success is its 70 per cent rate of clients returning. In this visually stunning corner of Ireland, people come away feeling good about themselves, lighter energetically and physically, and more empowered.

Days and Hours of Operation: From March to September, programmes are offered each week from Sunday to Friday. From October to February, weekend programmes are offered from Thursday evening to Sunday afternoon.
Accommodation: All guests are accommodated in comfortable, individual rooms with custom-made oak furniture.
Rates: The current price for the Sunday-to-Friday programme is €450, and for the Thursday to Sunday programme, €300. Both include room, board and full programme.
Credit Cards: MasterCard and Visa.
Meal Plans: All meals are included in the programme price. The centre provides a strictly vegetarian diet.
Services: Yoga, walking (guided walking with an emphasis on movement and posture awareness), massage, detoxification, reflexology and shiatsu.
Recreational Activities: Walking, yoga and cycling.
Facilities: Converted two-hundred-year-old corn mill, with ten single bedrooms with hot and cold water in each room, shared bathrooms, sauna, treatment rooms, garden with labyrinth, bicycles, and hill-walking paths.
Staff: Massage therapists operate on a part-time, self-employed basis. Full-time reflexologist, shiatsu practitioner and yoga teacher.
Special Notes: Bring loose, comfortable clothing and walking shoes or runners, house shoes or slippers, rainwear, and a large towel, for use in the sauna. The centre has no television. Children under sixteen are not allowed. Smoking is not allowed. Tea and coffee are not served. Guests are encouraged to avoid newspapers and the radio during their stay. Book two to three weeks in advance.
Nearby Attractions: Croagh Patrick, Clew Bay, Clare and Achill Island, Nephin Beg Mountains, Sheefry Hills, standing stones, fulachta fiadh (Bronze Age cooking sites), ring forts, ruined abbeys and churches, the town of Westport, golf courses, fishing, horse-riding and cycling.
Getting There: The nearest train station is Westport. People flying into Shannon can catch a bus from Limerick. Horan International Airport (Knock) is forty-five miles away from the centre. A taxi will cost €57.14 each way.

Rosmoney Spa

Rosmoney
Westport

Tel:	098 28899
Fax:	098 28974
E-mail:	aqua@anu.ie
Website:	www.rosmoneyspa.ie

In July 2000, Dee and Steve Mooney opened the Rosmoney Spa on eleven acres of land on the coast of County Mayo. The Mooneys aimed to create a dedicated thalassotherapy centre similar to those they had visited in Europe. 'We wanted to make these type of spa treatments more accessible and we felt that the marriage of the two great Irish traditions of the B&B-style accommodation and seaweed baths combined well with the European Thallaso Spa model,' says Dee.

Guests at Rosmoney Spa, which is one of only a handful of thalasso centres in the United Kingdom and Ireland, benefit from fresh seawater drawn daily for use in the hydro pool and in therapeutic treatments. Upon arrival, clients are asked to fill in a consultation form, and treatments are prescribed based on the individual's personal goals while staying at the centre. Any existing medical conditions are taken into account. Programmes range from detoxification and slimming to special programmes for cellulite, fluid retention and giving up smoking. Especially popular are the 'Vitality Day' and 'Beauty Day' pampering packages.

The residential programmes have grown out of the success of the day-spa packages. The Bord Fáilte-approved guest-house-style accommodation is both affordable and comfortable. The Mooneys are currently constructing eight self-contained cottage units, which will be ready towards the end of 2002.

A typical day at Rosmoney depends on whether or not you are a resident. Day packages, which begin at 10 am and finish at 5 pm, can include a pampering Vichy shower, an individual sauna known as the Vibrosaun, sea-mist therapy, a facial, stimulating pressotherapy, a seaweed bath, access to the hydrotherapy pool, steam-room and jacuzzi, and a hair-wash and blow-dry. Lunch, served between 1 and 2 pm, is also included.

Spa residents start the day at 10 am after a low-fat, high-nutrition breakfast. One hour of t'ai chi or relaxation exercises is followed by thalasso treatments until lunch at 1 pm. Further treatments follow until 5 pm, when dinner is served. Evenings include time in the hydro pool, hot tub and steam-room. Guests are encouraged to relax between treatments. 'Clients are very often surprised at just how tired they feel,' says Dee. 'Most of the treatments kick-start the lymphatic system and are very tiring.'

The spa itself is located in a designated area of outstanding natural beauty and special scientific interest. Seals, otters and a myriad of native birds can be seen while walking along the quiet shore. The natural harbour at Rosmoney also affords views of Croagh Patrick, an impressive two-thousand-foot peak. The modern, purpose-built facility is set amidst an ancient monument known locally as 'the Dane hole'. Listed at the Office of Public Works in Dublin, it consists of two room chambers and an intricate network of tunnels dating from 600 AD.

Days and Hours of Operation: While residential spa packages are on offer all year round, these times reflect current day-spa opening hours. Open seven days a week from 10 am to 6 pm, with late opening on Thursday, until 9pm. On Sundays and bank holidays, hours are 12 pm to 6 pm. Residential guests can use the facilities until 10 pm.

Accommodation: Guests stay either in standard en suite rooms or mini-suites.

Rates: Residential breaks start from €215.90 for two nights' accommodation, breakfast and lunch, as well as four thalasso spa treatments, through to €800.10 for a seven-night break with treatments.

Credit Cards: MasterCard and Visa.

Recreational Activities: T'ai chi and yoga.

Services: Full range of thalassotherapy treatments, including balneotherapy, brumisation, Vichy marine showers, algotherapy, seaweed baths, pressotherapy and cryotherapy. Also offered are reflexology, reiki and a full range of beauty treatments.

Facilities: Heated hydrotherapy pool with underwater and back massage stations, fountains, whirlpool, volcano, and counterswim jets. Steam room, jacuzzi, sauna, twelve dedicated state-of-the-art treatment rooms. and relaxation suite with view of ocean and mountains. Private slipway and jetty, moorings and tender service available for private sailing boats.

Staff: The centre employs a resident qualified massage therapist, as well as a fully licensed and qualified reflexologist, t'ai chi instructor and several beauty aestheticians.

Special Notes: Smoking is not allowed. The spa is closed during November for annual maintenance. Children under sixteen are not allowed.

Nearby Attractions: Scuba-diving facilities, horse-riding, seal- and otter-watching, sailing, sea and freshwater angling, eighteen-hole championship golf course, walking trails, town of Westport, excursions to Clare Island, Inishbofin and Inishturk, powerboat tours around Clew Bay, Tourmakeady Forest Trail, Nephin Beg Forest and Tochar Phadraig (the ancient pilgrim path from Ballintubber Abbey through Aughagower to Croagh Patrick).

Getting There: Transfers can be arranged from Knock, Galway and Shannon airports, as well as from Westport train station.

Casement Centre of Complementary Therapies

Casement Street
Ballina

Tel: 096 72900

The Casement Centre is a Spiritual Healing Clinic which focuses on energy healing in order to maximise health and release self-limiting feelings such as fear, nervousness and anger. The purpose of the therapies is to heal and release the individual's full potential. To help people incorporate this sense of harmony into their daily life, the centre also offers yoga classes. The goal of the centre is to help people master stress and make better choices through a heightened sense of awareness, once energy blocks are released.

Days and Hours of Operation: Monday to Friday, 10 am to 6 pm. Outside these hours, by appointment only.
Rates: Each therapy costs an average of €38.10.
Credit Cards: Cash or cheque only.
Therapies: Reflexology, massage therapy, remedial and sports-injury massage, relaxation, ear-coning, energy-balancing, reiki, metamorphosis, magnified healing, seichim, tarot-counselling, hypnotherapy and yoga.
Staff: A reflexologist and massage therapist, a massage therapist, a hypnotist and a practitioner in reiki, metamorphonis, magnified healing and holistic massage.

Castlebar Health Care Clinic

Linenhall Street
Castlebar

Tel: 094 25655
Mobile: 087 631 7063

Soothing music and the smell of fragrant essential oils greet clients who climb the stairs to the small Castlebar Health Care Clinic. Grace O'Malley opened the clinic four years ago with the intention of creating a sacred and sane place for people to heal themselves. The ultimate aim of the therapies on offer is to help individuals discover a sense of balance and gain focus so that they can take responsibility for their health.

Grace initially became interested in holistic health after completing a bioenergy course. 'It introduced me to a totally new philosophy of life,' she says. 'Doing that course, I was opened to so many avenues of thinking. I was really kind of amazed.' Following on from bioenergy, she began to study aromatherapy, holistic massage and a number of other therapies before opening the clinic. 'Different therapies are appropriate for different people,' Grace says. 'Each therapy opens you up to an even newer approach and way of looking at health.'

Days and Hours of Operation: Open Monday to Saturday from 10 am to 6 pm.
Credit Cards: None accepted.
Rates: Treatments range from €19.05 to €38.09.
Services: Therapeutic massage, aromatherapy, reiki, seichim, reflexology,

Indian head massage, bioenergy healing and metamorphosis.
Facilities: Two private treatment rooms.
Staff: Grace O'Malley owns and operates the centre on her own.
Special Notes: Smoking is not allowed.
Getting There: The centre is a few minutes' walk away from Castlebar's main street.

His 'n' Hers Hair & Beauty Day Spa

Upper Charles Street
Castlebar

Tel: 094 21967

For twenty-three years, Mary Gannon has owned and operated this County Mayo salon, which in the last five years became a day spa catering to both male and female clients. 'It is just a place where you can come in, relax and pamper yourself all under one roof,' says Mary. 'I really wanted to complete the whole thing.'

Particularly soothing is the 'Peppermint Sea Twist' treatment, which is recommended for people with dry skin, eczema, psoriasis or dermatitis. The treatment also helps to improve circulation and reduce swelling. The body is first exfoliated with sea salt, and then a combination of peppermint essential oil and seaweed and sea algae is spread over the skin.

Days and Hours of Operation: Open Monday to Thursday and Saturday from 9 am to 6 pm, Friday from 9 am to 7 pm. Late appointments are available by prior arrangement from Monday to Saturday.
Rates: Treatments typically cost between €31.74 and €50.79.
Credit Cards: MasterCard and Visa.
Services: Massage, body wraps, facials, muscle stimulation, and full range of beauty and hair salon services.
Facilities: Located on the ground floor, the day spa has three private treatment rooms, a sunbed, a separate area for hair-

salon services, and a coffee room.
Staff: Seven fully qualified and licensed therapists and aestheticians.
Special Notes: Smoking is allowed only in designated areas. Gift vouchers are available for purchase at reception. Students receive a 10 per cent discount.
Getting There: The day spa is located beside FBD Insurance in the centre of Castlebar.

The Natural Healing Centre

Corclough West
Belmullet

Tel: 097 82065

Belmullet is situated on the rugged coast of County Mayo in the picturesque west of Ireland. The Natural Healing Centre was established by Gisela Jurgen in 1992 to heal the mind, body and spirit of clients. The centre offers treatments, instruction, resource materials and follow-up support to encourage individuals to continue making positive and lasting changes in their life. Gisela combines her twelve years' experience working as a qualified nurse in Germany with her training in natural health care as a reiki practitioner and instructor, and kinesiologist, to provide the best overall health care to clients. The centre also offers natural vision improvement, which, according to Gisella, was responsible for her own improved sight, resulting in her discarding her thick-lensed glasses. The philosophy of the centre is to empower the individual to restore, promote and maintain vitality, as well as clarity of vision, both inside and outside.

Days and Hours of Operation: Seven days a week, all year around. Appointments essential.
Rates: The average rate per treatment is €32 for a one-hour session.
Credit Cards: Cash or cheque only.
Accommodation: Self-catering, solid-fuel centrally heated mobile home for rent, on the premises. The daily rate is

€19.04, the weekly rate €120.56. The mobile home is suitable for up to four people. Holistic weekends are available; these include accommodation in the mobile home for two nights, and two relaxation sessions daily. The cost for the weekend is €114.21 per person or €215.74 for a full week.

Therapies: Indian head massage, reflexology, reiki, kinesiology, full-body massage, allergy balance, magnet therapy, past-life regression, emotional healing, pranic healing, natural vision improvement and group meditation.

Staff: One reiki master and natural vision improvement teacher, one kinesiologist. one massage and reflexology practitioner, and one Reiki practitioner, Indian head massage therapist and qualified allergy tester.

Recreational Activities: Walking, golfing, fishing and cycling.

Nearby attractions: The Céide Fields form a unique neolithic landscape of world importance which has changed our perception of our Stone Age ancestors. Belderrig prehistoric farm site, at the western limit of the Céide Fields, dates from 1500 BC. A nearby sculpture trail, the largest public arts project ever undertaken in Ireland, is also worth a visit.

Getting There: By train: From Dublin, get a connection to Ballina. The latest arrival should be 6 pm, to catch the 6.10 pm bus from Ballina. Arrive in Belmullet at 7.30 pm. Collection can be arranged. By car: From Belmullet square, take the main road towards the hospital. Turn left at Coreclough Frenchport pier. The Natural Healing Centre is just past the church on the left.

Tír na nÓg Holistic Beauty Centre

The Square
Claremorris

Tel: 094 62678

Clients of Tír na nÓg Holistic Beauty Centre, which is conveniently located in the centre of town, walk up one flight of stairs into the calm and quiet atmosphere of the clinic. 'You feel like you are away from everything,' says owner Donna Flatley-Toughey.

Wanting to offer natural, hands-on beauty therapies, Donna opened the centre five years ago. Also available at the centre are therapeutic treatments such as sports-injury massage, reflexology and reiki. Before receiving massages or facials, clients receive an in-depth initial consultation, which includes a record of diet and lifestyle habits.

Days and Hours of Operation: Open Tuesday to Saturday, from 10 am to 6.30 pm.

Rates: A full-body massage typically costs €38.09.

Credit Cards: Cash or cheque only.

Services: Reflexology, aromatherapy, sports-injury massage, holistic massage, relaxation massage, reiki, Dr Hauschka holistic facials and full range of beauty treatments.

Facilities: Two private treatment rooms, reception area and retail space.

Staff: Two full-time and two part-time therapists and aestheticians.

Special Notes: Smoking is not allowed.

Getting There: Seven miles from Knock.

Johnstown House Hotel & Spa

Enfield

Tel:	0405 40000
Fax:	0405 40001
E-mail:	info@johnstownhouse.com
Website:	www.johnstownhouse.com

Creating a sanctuary of personal space in which to relax, unwind and enjoy ultimate luxury is the promise of the new Johnstown House Spa. It is a perfect addition to the magnificent seventeenth-century Georgian hotel, set in eighty acres of stunning parkland. Whether you want to achieve a sense of vitality and zest or to have a sense of solitude, personal space and well-being, the spa provides the perfect environment. The gym overlooks the lush Meath countryside and is equipped with visual entertainment and a radio system, encouraging the individual to enjoy their workout. Personal fitness instructors will design a programme to suit every level of fitness.

Aromatherapy essences are diffused in the treatments area to help purify, re-energise and sooth aching muscles, while fibre-optic light therapy prepares the body and mind for ultimate relaxation. There is a wide-ranging choice of holistic therapies on offer, many which are unique to the spa, such as the 'Holistic Stressbuster with Hot Stone Therapy', an all-encompassing treatment commencing with a full-body skin brushing and exfoliation to prepare the skin, leaving it soft and smooth. This is then followed by a deep body, face and scalp massage using hot and cold stones on vital energy points and a blend of essential oils chosen to suit individual requirements. This truly holistic experience will bring harmony to both mind and body.

Holistic treatments are tailored to harness the best of aromatherapy, hydrotherapy and phytotherapy. Robes, slippers and towels are provided during your spa visit and can also be worn in the Spa Café, where you can relax after your workout. Those who need to put a spring in their step can avail of high-energy classes such as spinning, step aerobics and boxercise or slow down the pace with yoga, meditation, pilates and t'ai chi. Swimming is made even more enjoyable with the addition of an open-air hydro pool with geyser jets of warm water, gently massaging different areas of the body. Showers infused with a mist of aromatherapy oils can invigorate with the power-jet setting or sooth with tropical rain, completing a unique spa-therapy experience.

Days and Hours of Operation: Due to open in late spring 2002. Opening hours: Monday to Saturday, 8 am to 10 pm, Sunday, 10 am to 8 pm.
Rates: The following full-day packages will be offered. The Espa Total Indulge (€233) includes marine-hydrotherapy bath, aromatherapy body and scalp massage, rebalancing aromatherapy facial, and holistic hand and nail treatment or holistic foot and nail treatment. The Espa Purifying (€190) includes 'jet blitz', detoxifying aromatherapy massage, and detoxifying 'sea of senses', incorporating full-body exfoliation and Indian head massage. The Espa Complete Luxury (€172) includes luxury aromatherapy facial,

manicure or pedicure and Vincent Longo make-up. The Espa Fitness Programme (€190) includes personal-wellness profile, one-to-one personal training session, marine hydrotherapy bath and sports-and-fitness massage. The Espa Taster (€125) includes Espa back massage and Espa aromatherapy facial. The Spa Time (€51) includes participation in any of the scheduled classes, use of the gymnasium, swimming and hydro pools, aroma steam room, sauna, laconium, and relaxation area, and lunch in the Spa Café. Half-day spa programmes also include the use of all facilities. They range in price from €91 for the Espa Energising Programme, which includes a marine hydrotherapy bath and sports-and-fitness massage, to €132 for the Espa Programme for New Beginnings. This package is designed for pregnant and nursing mothers. It includes a massage with advanced massage techniques, using nourishing muds, creams and calendula oil, and a holistic foot and nail treatment.

Credit Cards: American Express, Laser and Visa.

Services: Holistic stress-buster with hot-stone therapy, jet-lag reviver massage, traditional full-body massage, aromatherapy body massage, Indian head massage, salt and oil scrub, marine hydrotherapy bath, jet blitz, reflexology, 'Prenatal for New Beginnings', holistic hand and nail treatment with hot-stone therapy, and holistic foot and nail treatment with hot-stone therapy. Full range of beauty treatments available, including Vincent Longo make-up, bridal make-up, day and evening make-up, waxing and facials.

Facilities: A twenty-metre lap pool leading through into a heated outdoor multijet hydro pool. State-of-the-art gymnasium with audio-visual entertainment system, unisex and separate-sex relaxation areas, saunas, aroma steam room, laconiums, lifestyle showers, twelve beautifully designed treatment rooms, two hydrotherapy rooms, one jet blitz, fitness studio, chi studio, hair salon, Spa Café, crèche, retail-therapy shop, outdoor tennis courts, and manicure, pedicure and make-up studio.

Staff: Forty full-time staff, including holistic practitioners, beauty therapists, hairstylists and café staff.

Additional Notes: Spa will be open to hotel guests and clients on day and half-day spa programmes. A variety of membership packages are available.

Nearby Attractions: Trim heritage town and castle, Maynooth Castle, Belvedere House and gardens in Mullingar, the Royal Canal, equestrian centres and golf facilities.

Getting There: From Dublin, take the M50, turning off at the Galway (M4) exit. Take the M4 in the direction of Maynooth. Enfield is just past Maynooth. From Galway, take the N4 towards Dublin. From Sligo and Mayo, take the N6. From Derry, take the N2, from Navan the N3 and Belfast the N1, then travel to Dublin and follow the directions above.

The Transpersonal Centre

Dunderry Park
Navan

Tel: 046 74455
Fax: 046 74455
E-mail: marduffy@hotmail.com

The Transpersonal Centre is situated in the heart of historic County Meath, close to the ancient sacred sites of Tara, Newgrange and Loughcrew. It is surrounded by twenty-four acres of mature wooded parkland. The two-hundred-year-old Georgian residence has been completely restored in keeping with the original style. Each room is furnished in antique and solid oak or pine furnishings. These furnishings, together with the pine floors and open fireplace, provide a comforting, peaceful setting for meditation retreats and workshops. The centre is available for rent to groups for days or weekends. Established by Lorna St Aubyn, an author of several books on transpersonal healing, and Martin Duffy, a counsellor and psychotherapist, the centre is a welcome environment for healing courses and seminars. It can hold a hundred people seated for conferences or workshops of various sizes. It has also been used for weddings and special blessings. Martin intends to convert the original old servants' quarters in the courtyard into artists' studios and individual retreats. Given the surrounding environment, it is an ideal space for creative talent to be nurtured.

Days and Hours of Operation: The centre, including accommodation, healing rooms and seminar area, is available for rent to groups for days, weekends or longer.
Rates: Rental of the centre costs €55 per person per day for food, accommodation and use of the centre's facilities and grounds. Courses cost an average of €184 per weekend, including accommodation and food.
Credit Cards: Cash or cheque only.
Accommodation: There is shared accommodation for thirty people. The rooms are decorated in period style to a very high standard. The four en suite rooms and bedrooms sleep between two and four people each.
Meal Plans: Quality vegetarian wholefood meals with vegetables and herbs from the centre's organic garden. Special diets are catered for. Please give advance notice of your requirements.
Services: Shamanic workshops, shamanic counselling and healing on a one-to-one basis, weekend stress-management courses, dance and movement workshops and holotropic breath-work, 'Dancing the Rainbow', 'Five Rhythms', and voice-work courses – singing and sacred chanting.
Facilities: Workroom (forty-one by nineteen feet) available to hold a maximum of hundred people. Two healing rooms. Two lecture or meeting rooms.
Staff: Lorna St Aubyn is the author of several books and ran a similar centre in France for eleven years. Martin Duffy is an accredited counsellor and psychotherapist with a Jungian/transpersonal orientation. He is the former director and head of training at the Dundalk Counselling Centre. Martin is also the Irish regional coordinator for the Spiritual Emergence Network. He runs several shamanic workshops and sees

individuals for shamanic counselling and healing. Other staff are employed as required for workshops.

Nearby Attractions: Close to the sacred ancient sites of Tara, Newgrange and Loughcrew.

Getting There: From Navan town, take the road towards Trim. Turn right at the sign for Athboy, towards Dunderry. Past Klondyke pub, take the next right into Dunderry Park.

Abbey House Physiotherapy Clinic

Abbey Road
Navan

Tel:	046 27254
or	046 22126

Abbey House, which has been in operation since 1992, is primarily a physiotherapy clinic, but owners Miriam Cremin and Frances Lee also practise acupuncture in combination with physiotherapy. Each woman holds a licence in acupuncture from the British Acupuncture Association. Although the majority of clients at the clinic suffer from musculo-skeletal conditions, therapists at the clinic treat a wide range of conditions that respond well to acupuncture, including sinusitis, migraines and certain gynecological conditions. Each patient undergoes a thorough assessment within a physical, mental and social framework. Acupuncture and physiotherapy are offered as an alternative to drug therapy. Particular emphasis is placed on educating patients about the cause of their problems and an effort is made to teach them how to prevent and/or manage them at home.

Days and Hours of Operation: Open Monday to Friday from 8.30 am to 8 pm.
Rates: An initial assessment and treatment costs €38, with subsequent treatments priced at €30.
Credit Cards: None accepted.
Services: Physiotherapy and acupuncture.

Facilities: Reception, physiotheraypy room, chiropody and surgery.
Staff: Three chartered physiotherapists, two of whom are licensed acupuncturists.
Special Notes: Combines conventional medical treatment with complementary health care.
Getting There: The clinic is located beside Navan Shopping Centre.

NAVAN HOLISTIC THERAPY CENTRE

26 Railway Street
Navan

Tel: 046 75781

After spending thirteen years in Sydney, Australia, studying various aspects of natural health, John Brown recently returned to his native country to open the Navan Holistic Therapy Centre. He is currently a member of the Australian Traditional Medicine Society, the National Herbalists Association of Australia and the British Naturopathic Association. Individuals seeking treatment receive a personalised programme of care designed to foster physical well-being, mental and emotional balance and spiritual wholeness. John uses a variety of diagnostic tools and therapies to address a broad range of chronic conditions, including allergies, asthma, bronchitis, digestive problems, impotency, menopause, skin disorders and stress.

One of John's primary aims is to determine the root cause of an ailment, rather than just cure symptoms. 'People come to me feeling sick or with some sort of health condition and it's my job to make them feel better and give them an idea as to how to stay healthy,' he says.

Days and Hours of Operation: Monday to Saturday, 10 am to 8 pm.
Rates: A typical hour-long treatments costs an average of €44.44.
Credit Cards: None accepted.
Services: Naturopathy, herbal medicine,

iridology, live blood analysis, Swedish and remedial massage, lymphatic drainage, reflexology and ear-candling.
Facilities: Three private treatment rooms located up one flight of stairs.
Staff: John Byrne holds an advanced diploma in naturopathy, as well as diplomas in botanical medicine, nutrition, remedial massage and lymphatic drainage. He received a degree in health science from the University of New England. A number of therapists also provide other therapies on a part-time basis: acupuncture; reiki; clairvoyance; and Indian head, aromatherapy and reflexology massage. The centre also runs ITEC diploma courses in reflexology and holistic massage.
Special Notes: Treatments are by appointment only. Gift vouchers are available for purchase.
Getting There: The clinic is located in the centre of Navan, a short walk away from the Loreto Convent.

Niamh's Beauty Salon

Connaught Street
Athboy

Tel: 046 30855

A beauty salon first and foremost, Niamh's Beauty Salon does however offer rejuvenating day spa treatments, which help counteract the stresses of daily life. Owner Niamh Higgins trained as a massage therapist, choosing to specialise in Swedish and aromatherapy massage. While her clientele consists of people with back injuries, she also caters to busy mothers and workaholics who choose aromatherapy for relaxation purposes. Niamh also works with people who are trying to lose weight, and uses a special blend of aromatherapy citrus oils to aid the lymphatic flow.

Days and Hours of Operation: Open six days a week: Monday, Tuesday, Wednesday and Friday from 10 am to 5.30 pm; Thursday, 10 am to 8 pm; and Saturday, 10 am to 5 pm.
Rates: Vary according to services. A one-hour, full-body aromatherapy massage costs €44.44.
Credit Cards: MasterCard and Visa
Staff: Niamh Higgins employs one licensed and qualified massage therapist.
Special Notes: It is best to book appointments one week in advance. Late appointments are available by prior arrangement.
Getting There: The centre is twenty miles from Dublin and ten miles from Navan.

Pine Lodge

Ross Road
Screggan
Tullamore

Tel:	0506 51927
Fax:	0506 51927

Since 1990, Claudia Krygel has operated a B&B from her award-winning country home situated on two acres of woodland overlooking the Slieve Bloom mountains. After taking a massage-therapy course in 1994, she began to offer healthy weekend pamper breaks. Basing her programme on the belief that complete relaxation should include a bit of pampering and getting away from everyday life, Claudia has earned the loyalty of her clients, who return year after year.

Guests arrive on a Friday for a weekend of reflexology and therapeutic massage treatments, yoga instruction and quiet time to relax in the sauna, steam room or gentle country air. 'Normally people come to the door and don't know what to expect,' says Claudia. 'They settle down in the room, come in for tea and say what a beautiful house it is. I can see them already starting to relax. When they leave, their faces are completely smoothed out.'

Days and Hours of Operation: Weekend pamper breaks are run from April to October.
Accommodation: Two double and two twin en-suite bedrooms.
Rates: A weekend pamper package costs €200.
Credit Cards: None accepted.
Meal Plans: Breakfast is included in the package price, as is dinner in town at a local restaurant on Saturday night. Fruit, coffee, tea, hot chocolate and water are available throughout the day.
Services: Massage, reflexology, reiki and kinesiology.
Recreational Activities: Golf, fishing, boating, hill-walking, horse-riding and sailing.
Facilities: Country home with sauna, steam bath, private indoor pool, sunbed, and private room for therapeutic treatments.
Staff: A part-time reflexologist, a massage therapist and a yoga instructor are available on an as-required basis.
Special Notes: Hill-walkers and other outdoor enthusiasts should bring sturdy walking shoes and adequate rain gear. Swimming costumes must be worn in the health suite. To avoid disappointment upon arrival, all spa treatments should be pre-booked. Smoking is allowed only in designated areas. Mobile phones are not allowed in any public areas.
Nearby Attractions: Slieve Bloom mountains, Bog Train, monastic settlements, the Country Show, Tullamore Golf Club, Charleville Castle, Lough Derg, Lough Ree, Lough Ennell and Lough Owel.
Getting There: The centre is located four miles from Tullamore town off the N52.

The Midas Touch Clinic

High Street
Tullamore

Tel: 0506 22236

Patricia Hoedt first became interested in complementary therapies when her chronic back pain was healed. This experience gave her a new lease of energy, and she decided to train in complementary therapies, with a view to bringing the healing she had received to others. Eleven years later, she has never looked back, and thoroughly enjoys working as a therapist specialising in ki massage, aromatherapy and spine-works in the form of non-force realignment. Patricia contends that most back pain is caused by injuries which may have occurred in childhood or even at birth. She also works with energy in reiki healing. Combining both disciplines enables Patricia to heal the physical and emotional disharmony in the body. Her son Stephen also works with her. He is a reiki master and psychic who uses the crystal ball and tarot-card readings. Most of the centre's clients come from personal referrals.

Days and Hours of Operation: Monday to Friday, 10 am to 6 pm.
Rates: Between €38.10 and €50.80 for a one-hour session.
Credit Cards: Cash or cheque only.
Services: Ki massage, reiki, aromatherapy, spine-works (non-force realignment), chakra-balancing, aura-cleansing and tarot-card reading.
Facilities: Two treatment rooms, one reception area.

Staff: One qualified therapist in ki massage, aromatherapy, spine-works and healing through cellular memory. One reiki master and tarot-card reader.

The Little House of Avalon Holistic Health Farm

Taughmaconnell
Ballinasloe

Tel: 0905 83002
Website: www.littlehouseofavalon.com

Taking its name from author Marion Zimmer Bradley's tale *The Mists of Avalon*, this midlands holistic health farm draws everyone from local farmers and housewives to Dublin builders, doctors and dentists. After studying complementary therapies in South Africa, the Far East and Europe, Anthony and Bernadette Smith-McGowan opened the retreat three years ago to provide an oasis from the rush of the outside world and to help people restore balance, calm and energy to their lives.

No more than six guests at a time stay in the 120-year-old cottage. Bernadette and Anthony sit down with each guest on arrival to develop a personalised programme. Both day-long and residential packages are available. Days typically begin with a cosy sleep-in. Breakfast stays on the table as long as it takes for guests to get up. Any variation of treatments may follow, including Thai massage, reiki, African aromatherapy massage, counselling and iridology. There follows an organic, vegetarian lunch, which may be accompanied by organic wine or tea. If the weather holds, guests may want to head out along the Green Heartlands route on one of the centre's two bicycles. After dinner, another treatment may follow, or guests can simply flop in the tea room with a good book. Fruit baskets and herbal teas are available throughout the day.

One particularly appealing package is the half-day 'Stress-buster', which begins with a one-hour facial, followed by a gentle foot-reflexology treatment and a full-body aromatherapy massage. To get even more chilled out, guests can then take a sauna or sit in the Hammam, which is set in one of two small chalets in the garden.

The McGowens aim to look after each guest. 'We try to allow people to understand what goes on within their body,' says Bernadette. 'We are in a very peaceful environment within a farmer's community. It is absolutely quiet, there is clean air, and the spring water comes from our own well. If their journey to relax takes them into the mind and soul, then this is the place to come to, because relaxation starts in the mind. Everything is absolutely confidential.'

Days and Hours of Operation: Open Monday to Wednesday and Friday to Sunday, from 11 am to 7.30 pm. The centre is closed on Thursday.
Rates: While prices vary according to treatment and meal options, the average stay costs between €127 and €228.60 for a two-night, two-day stay. Body and beauty treatments cost an average of between €38.09 and €57.14. Most treatments cost €38.09 each.
Credit Cards: None accepted.
Accommodation: Two en suite rooms for single or double use and one double room.
Meal Plans: Three organic, vegetarian meals are included in the price of package programmes.

Staff: In addition to Bernadette and Anthony, there is a part-time therapist on the staff.
Services: Reflexology, aromatherapy, Indian head massage, shiatsu, Thai body-work, reiki, holistic beauty treatments, foot-reading, foot and joint mobilisation, patented 'Back Smith' treatments involving gentle movement and manipulation, crystal healing, crystal reiki, kinesiology, and counselling – personal motivation, personal empowerment, nutrition and herbalism.
Recreational Activities: Fishing in the River Suck, riding and pony-trekking, pitch and putt, golf, fishing, museums and boat cruises.
Facilities: Tea room and library, meditation room, sauna, Hammam bath house, Inipi sweat lodge, two bicycles available for use, and board games.
Nearby Attractions: The 270-kilometre Green Heartlands Bicycle Route, historical sites.
Special Notes: Smoking is not allowed. Workshops and packages may be tailored to suit particular groups.
Getting There: Pick-up may be arranged from the Ballinasloe bus station. Taxis are also available. From Dublin, take the N6 towards Galway.

Rainbowhill Healing Centre

Evikeens
Boyle

Tel/Fax: 079 62114

Drawing on a diverse background of psychology, shamanic counselling and massage, Henry Schwab opened the Rainbowhill Healing Centre in August 2001 at the base of the sloping Curlew Mountains. Henry's approach to healing involves looking at the uniqueness of each individual and offering whatever he or she needs in order to get better. 'It is a client-focused philosophy and I approach things in a holistic way,' he says.

At present, Henry is only able to accommodate small groups, but he plans to set up facilities outside the centre to handle larger gatherings. Although he offers courses and workshops, Henry's main emphasis is on healing. Rather than confining individuals to one method of treatment, he incorporates a variety of disciplines to promote and encourage good health.

Days and Hours of Operation: The clinic is open by appointment, Monday to Saturday.
Rates: Treatments typically range from €44.44 to €50.79 per one-hour session.
Credit Cards: None accepted.
Services: Reiki, seikim, Indian head massage, aura- and chakra-balancing, psychic readings, group and individual hypnotherapy, hypno-analysis, psychotherapy, self-development and shamanic journeying.

Facilities: The centre houses two private treatment rooms and a small waiting room.
Staff: Henry Schwab is a trained psychologist, psychotherapist, and Indian head massage, reiki and seikim practitioner. He holds an advanced diploma in hypnotherapy and is a sakara master.
Special Notes: The centre is accessible for people with disabilities, but the bathroom is not designed to accommodate wheelchairs. Smoking is not allowed.
Getting There: The nearest train station is in Boyle, which is only a five-minute drive from the centre.

Sligo Natural Health & Yoga Centre

Collinsfort
Drumcliffe

Tel: 071 46171

After nine years of working as a residential social worker in Galway, Helen Gillan changed tack and began to study shiatsu and do-in at London's Kushi Institute. She also enrolled in a yoga course at London's Iyengar Institute. Diplomas in hand, she returned to her native Sligo in 1994 to open a natural health centre with her partner and fellow yoga instructor, John Callinan.

'When we came back, there wasn't anything like this here,' says Helen. 'It started off with friends, friends of friends and friends of family literally in a spare bedroom of the house we rented. It just took off from there.'

Today the Sligo Natural Health Centre is located on the first floor of a brightly lit building in the centre of Drumcliffe. In addition to John and Helen's services, a t'ai chi instructor offers regular courses and individual sessions. Special classes are available for children, active-retirement groups, teenagers and men. The centre also has yoga equipment, which John has either made or imported from India. While she will still offer individual treatments, Helen is gradually reducing her emphasis on shiatsu and moving increasingly towards yoga instruction. 'Yoga helps people work out their own long-term programme of health,' she says.

As the centre gradually expanded, so did the demand for residential workshops. 'Since we opened and put our number in the phone book, people have been asking all over the country and even from England if they can come and stay with us,' says Helen. The idea took hold, and now visitors can attend workshops in John and Helen's secluded stone cottage on three acres of private land just two minutes from the Drumcliffe river. The couple modernised the cottage, which is more than a century old, with firm flooring, extra light and heat. A new detached yoga room accommodates up to thirty students.

As Helen is one of the senior yoga instructors in Ireland, she endeavours to keep her own skills refreshed by inviting more experienced teachers over from England to lead residential teachers' workshops. In November 2001, the couple launched a yoga school with a two-year curriculum.

Weekend workshops for yoga beginners are available throughout the year as well. Participants enjoy daily yoga sessions, healthy food from the couple's organic garden, shiatsu treatments, and walks, horse-riding and cycling throughout the vast, scenic countryside.

Days and Hours of Operation: Open Monday to Saturday by appointment.
Accommodation: Helen and John can accommodate up to six guests in their home for residential weekend workshops. As many as eight can stay in purpose-built apartments, complete with en suite bathrooms and kitchenette, adjacent to the house. Local B&Bs house the overflow from the workshops.
Rates: An hour-and-fifteen-minute class costs €6.35. Individual sessions cost €39.36 each. A teachers' weekend costs €82.53 for tuition and €19.05 for room and board. Residential workshops for yoga beginners cost an average of €222.25 for tuition, room and board.
Credit Cards: None accepted.
Meal Plans: A breakfast of wholegrain breads, cereals and fruit is supplied for workshop participants. All other meals are self-catering. There are plans to employ a cook for future workshops.
Services: Shiatsu, individual tuition in yoga, t'ai chi, women's writers groups, residential workshops in yoga, and teacher-training courses in yoga.
Recreational Activities: Local bike companies will deliver bicycles. Climbing, walking, swimming, horse-riding and golf can also be done locally.
Facilities: A well-lit private treatment room, a fully-equipped yoga room and a changing area.
Special Notes: As the centre is on the first floor and therefore difficult to access for people with disabilities, Helen and John will make home visits to people with mobility problems.
Nearby Attractions: Yeats's grave, Lissadell House, Sligo Arts Festival, Ben Bulben, Carramoore Tombs, and Glencar lake and waterfall.
Getting There: From Dublin, take the N4 towards Sligo. Flights are also available into Sligo Airport.

Celtic Seaweed Baths

Strandhill

Tel: 071 68686
Fax: 071 68686
Website: www.celticseaweedbaths.com

Celtic Seaweed Baths owner Neil Walton had the idea of bringing seaweed baths back to Strandhill, County Sligo, after using the baths in Enniscrone to recover from the muscular aches and pains brought on by competing internationally for the Irish triathlon team. Working closely with Sligo County Council, the County Sligo Surf Club and the Strandhill Development Association, Walton opened the baths in July 2000.

Bathers are guided to their own private treatment room, complete with Victorian cast-iron bath and steam unit. All staff are well versed in how to use the baths, and patiently guide guests through the routine. A five- to ten-minute steam shower is recommended before bathing. Individuals can then immerse themselves in a warm seaweed bath, followed by another steam shower and an invigorating cold shower. All rooms are hygienically cleaned, and fresh seaweed is added to the bath after each session. Guests may follow their bath with an aromatherapy massage.

Days and Hours of Operation: From May to September, the centre is open from 10 am to 9.30 pm, Monday to Friday and from 10 am to 8.30 pm on Saturday and Sunday.
Accommodation: Two hotels, hostels and an abundance of B&Bs accommodate guests at the Celtic Seaweed Baths.
Rates: Adults pay €12.70 per hour. Two adults sharing costs €19.05 per hour. A concession rate of €10.16 per hour is available to senior citizens and students during off-peak times.
Credit Cards: MasterCard, Visa, American Express and Laser.
Meal Plans: None provided.
Services: Seaweed bath, steam bath and aromatherapy massage.
Facilities: Ten private rooms containing seaweed bath and shower and steam unit, as well as a private treatment room for massage.
Staff: In addition to the staff who facilitate clients' use of the baths, there is a full-time licensed and qualified massage therapist.
Special Notes: Towels are provided. The last booking is taken one hour before closing time. Gift vouchers are available for purchase at the cash desk.
Nearby Attractions: The Carrowmore tombs, Knocknarea Mountain and the Atlantic coastline.
Getting There: Strandhill is located eight kilometres west of Sligo town.

Kilcullen's Seaweed Baths & Tea Rooms

Enniscrone

Tel: 096 36238
Mobile: 087 230 8020
Fax: 096 36895

Edward and Christine Kilcullen own and operate their own bathhouse, which has been open since 1912. Built on a site acquired by the Kilcullen family in 1898, the Edwardian building features private bathing rooms complete with original glazed porcelain baths, solid brass taps and panelled wooden shower cisterns. The actual experience of the therapeutic baths involve a luxurious soak in silky oils extracted from fresh seaweed mixed with seawater that is pumped in from the nearby Atlantic Ocean. The amber tinge in the warm brew indicates that it has a high iodine content. Steam baths are taken in an enclosed cedarwood cabinet in which the client sits with his or head exposed in order to breathe cool air as the moist vapour extracts toxins from the body. The treatment is followed by a seaweed bath and refreshing cold sea-water shower.

Days and Hours of Operation: From 1 November to 1 May, the centre is open on Saturdays, Sundays and bank holidays from 10 am to 8 pm. From 1 May to 30 October, the centre is open daily from 10 am to 9 pm. In July and August, opening hours are 10 am to 10 pm.
Rates: The average price of a seaweed bath is €15.24. All other therapies cost an average of ¤40.
Credit Cards: MasterCard and Visa.
Services: Steam and seaweed baths; also ki massage, Swedish massage and aromatherapy massage.
Facilities: Two therapy rooms, one steam box and sixteen seaweed bathrooms.
Staff: Two massage therapists, one qualified physiotherapist, one receptionist and four attendants.
Special Notes: Towels are supplied. Bookings are not accepted.
Nearby Attractions: Waterpoint Swimming and Fitness Centre, an eighteen-hole championship golf course and Eniscrone Beach are all nearby.
Getting There: Kilcullen's is located thirty miles from Sligo Airport and forty miles from Knock Airport.

The Sanctuary Health & Holistic Centre

An Tearmann Beag
Mooresfort
Kilross

Tel:	062 55102
Fax:	062 55102
Website:	www.thesanctuary.ie

Set amidst the Golden Vale of Tipperary is the Sanctuary/An Tearmann Beag Holistic Healing Centre. This pastoral retreat was founded by qualified therapists Mary Condren and Sally McCormack in 1992 as a realisation of their dream to create a regenerative oasis of peace. A relaxing atmosphere pervades the centre, to which guests are free to bring their own wine if they wish. Mary and Sally have designed a variety of programmes to address specific chronic ailments, such as stress, back pain, digestive disorders, migraine headaches, insomnia and allergies. 'Healing can actually happen in the quietness and in the space provided,' says Mary. 'We try to encourage people towards a lifestyle change, and that becomes self-empowering for them.'

Although programme schedules vary, a stay at the Sanctuary typically begins with a home-cooked organic meal on Friday evening. Guests then sit down with Mary or Sally to develop a treatment programme that suits their specific needs. An aromatherapy massage might then follow, before guests settle in for a restful night's sleep. As there is no specific wake-up time, a self-catering breakfast remains on the table as long as necessary. The only set times at the centre are for lunch and dinner: 1 pm and 6 pm respectively. In between meals and treatments, guests are free to explore the nine acres of grounds, go on a guided walk through the pine forest of Slievenamuck or, if it is raining, curl up on the couch in the sitting room with a good book.

Days and Hours of Operation: Open Wednesday to Sunday for four-day, three-day and weekend programmes. Hourly sessions are available by appointment between Wednesday and Saturday, from 9.30 am to 6 pm. Later appointments are available with prior arrangement.

Accommodation: Three twin rooms and two doubles, all en suite. Accommodation for two is also available in the old-style cottage, which has a log fire and central heating.

Rates: The four-day programme costs €635 for a single person or €558.80 per person in the twin room for room, board and treatments. The three-day programme costs €508 for single and €444.50 for twin. A weekend break costs €292.10 single and €254 twin.

Credit Cards: MasterCard and Visa.

Meal Plans: Three healthy, balanced meals a day are included in the programme price. Organic food is used when possible. Guests are asked in advance of their stay whether they prefer meat-based or vegetarian meals.

Services: Aromatherapy, reflexology, biodynamic massage, allergy-testing, homeopathy, back massage, holistic massage and bioresonance testing.

Recreational Activities: Golf, horse-riding, guided walking tours and fishing.

Facilities: The purpose-built bungalow has a sitting room with a library of books, videos and tapes. There are also two private treatments rooms and a garden.

Staff: Two full-time and one part-time licensed and qualified therapists.

Special Notes: Children under eighteen are not allowed. The centre is able to accommodate pets. Smoking is not allowed.

Nearby Attractions: Tipperary Races, nature park and the Galtee, Knockmealdown and Comeragh Mountains, the pine forest of Slievenamuck and the scenic Glen of Aherlow.

Getting There: By car, take the main road from Dublin to Cork and towards Tipperary at Cashel. The centre is half a mile from Kilross village. Limerick Junction is the nearest train station. A taxi from the train station costs approximately €12.70.

An Solas Healing Centre

The Hermitage
Mountanglesby
Clogheen

Tel: 052 65566
E-mail: info@an-solas.com
Website: www.an-solas.com

Located in the foothills of the Knockmealbown Downs and Galtee Mountains in County Tipperary, An Solas is located in a peaceful and tranquil setting. The house dates from 1866 and was formerly a convent. This has given the centre a serene energy and makes it ideal as a place for healing, according to owners Phil Maloney and Anne Boyle. An Solas offers teaching in massage and polarity therapy and rents out healing rooms. They also run various workshops at the weekends. The house, situated in an idyllic valley, is positioned on the pilgrim route from Holy Cross to Mount Melleray, further emphasising its sacred location. It is now a listed building.

Before the Hermitage was opened, a significant restoration project was carried out on it. The house was totally refurbished, with particular emphasis placed on the former chapel. The room is now one of the focal healing and teaching spaces in the centre. Another feature is the meditation room, which includes a wonderful stained-glass window of the Catholic saint Bridget, also considered by many to be a Celtic goddess. The grounds also mirror the serenity of the house and help to induce a mood of complete relaxation. Two recent additions to the centre – a labyrinth and a sweat lodge – are now used as part of healing courses.

Days and Hours of Operation: Open every day except Wednesday, from 9 am to 6 pm, all year round.
Rates: Residential workshops cost an average of €190.36 to €254, including accommodation and food.
Credit Cards: Cash or cheque only.
Meal Plans: Organic, wholesome, home-cooked food. The centre caters for vegetarians and people with special diets on request.
Accommodation: Twin and three-bedroomed en suite rooms decorated in soft, subtle colours.
Staff: Phil Maloney and Anne Boyle are both qualified massage therapists and energy healers. Additional trainers are employed to facilitate courses, as required.
Services: An Solas runs ITEC diploma courses in anatomy and physiology and in polarity therapy. There are weekend workshops in meditation, acupuncture, aromatherapy, astrology, aura soma, cognitive therapy, corporate workshops, creative writing, dream interpretation, enneagram, feng shui, kinesiology, rebirthing, reiki healing, relaxation, sound therapy, shamanic workshops, St Bridget's four directions, sacred dance, sweat-lodge ceremonies, t'ai chi, vegetarian-cookery classes and yoga.
Facilities: Twelve en suite bedrooms, one meditation room, one seminar room, one additional kitchen for students, dining room and sitting room.
Recreational Activities: Yoga, creative-dance classes, hill-walking, golf, gym and horse-riding are all available nearby.
Nearby Attractions: Mount Melleray Cistercian monastery, Clare Castle and the Swiss cottage in Cahir.

Getting There: The centre is located off the main Dublin-to-Cork road. Coming from Dublin, turn left in the outskirts of Cahir. Take the road to Clogheen for twelve miles. In Clogheen, take a left after the Spar supermarket. An Solas is situated next door to St Teresa's Hospital and Day Centre.

Monaincha Health & Fitness

Monaincha
Roscrea

Tel: 0505 23757

During her last two years at university, Niamh Moore began working in a health and fitness club. It was there that she was inspired to open the first health and fitness club in Roscrea, the Monaincha Health & Fitness Centre. Membership entails the standard access to gym, sunbeds and aerobics classes. Also available to members and the general public are holistic treatments such as sports-injury therapy, Swedish massage, yoga classes and aromatherapy.

All members of the club receive an initial consultation, during which they are screened for heart conditions or serious ailments before commencing an exercise programme. The consultation also includes suggestions for improving eating habits and developing practical habits for healthy living.

A qualified massage and sports therapist, Niamh intends to offer health and relaxation weekend and midweek breaks consisting of healthy meals, holistic treatments and daily yoga sessions. Guests would stay at a purpose-built facility near Niamh's family home in the Tipperary countryside. 'So many people are stressed out at the moment,' she says. 'This would be a good way of getting away from it all – for local people or even those from as far away as Limerick and Dublin.'

Days and Hours of Operation: Open Monday to Friday, 9 am to 9.30 pm, and Saturday, 10 am to 6 pm.
Rates: Vary according to services. A one-year membership costs €381.
Credit Cards: None accepted.
Services: Massage, reflexology, yoga, facials and a range of beauty treatments.
Facilities: Fully equipped gym, aerobics room, sauna, tanning bed and yoga room.
Staff: In addition to Niamh, the centre employs a personal trainer, an aerobics instructor and a beauty therapist.
Special Notes: Children under eighteen are not allowed.
Getting There: The centre is on the main N7 between Dublin and Limerick.

Shoselish Holistic Healing Centre & Crystal School of Reflexology and Massage

Blenheim Cross
Dunmore Road
Waterford

Tel: 051 875 444

Set in a quiet, hill-surrounded valley on the boundary of Waterford city is the Shoselish Holistic Healing Centre. A stream runs through the acre and a quarter of private land, which also contains abundant greenery and a dolmen within the perimeter. Visitors to the centre cross over a stone bridge and enter the dedicated building, which has been constructed with wood floors and ceilings to create a natural feel. Three of the four main rooms in the centre, as well as the corridor, have now been finished entirely in natural wood.

Proprietor Joseph McCormack spent several years working both as a psychiatric counsellor for drug addicts and as a nursing instructor. Eventually he became head of a nearby regional hospital. Joseph had originally planned to use his degree in health economics to open a management-consultancy service in health and safety, but when the hospital closed down he began to pursue his interest in complementary medicine. Today he is qualified to teach both ITEC-accredited courses in massage and reflexology courses recognised by the National Register of Reflexologists in Ireland and the Association of Reflexologists in England. A combination of courses and therapeutic treatments is on offer throughout the year.

As for his thinking behind opening the five-year-old centre, Joseph believes that people today need more than mere prescriptions. 'I have seen the effects of drugs, prescribed and otherwise, on the system,' he says. 'Doctors would believe in the orthodox approach, and I felt differently, even twenty years ago. Obviously we clashed. I saw people – rather than patients, as I don't like the word – receiving tranquillisers for anxiety, which affect only the symptoms rather than the problem. Fighting the system in those days was sheer heresy.'

Clients ranging in age from young babies to people in their eighties visit the centre to address various health concerns, whether mental, physical or emotional. Joseph particularly emphasises the role of nutrition in achieving and maintaining overall well-being. 'I have always believed in people being able to heal themselves,' he says. 'It is just a matter of finding the right way to educate the public in ways to take responsibility for their own health.'

Days and Hours of Operation: Open Monday to Friday for treatments, with hours of opening based on appointments. The centre is open at weekends for various courses on holistic-health subjects.
Accommodation: For residential courses, guests stay in one of three double en suite bedrooms.
Rates: An hour-long session typically costs €38.09. There are concessions for students, the unemployed and OAPs.
Credit Cards: None accepted.
Meal Plans: A B&B-style breakfast is provided during residential courses.

Services: Reflexology, aromatherapy, kinesiology, reiki, energetic massage and 'Touch for Health'.
Facilities: The two-storey, dedicated building houses a lecture room, three private treatment rooms, a kitchenette and shower facilities.
Staff: At present, Joseph McCormack employs no other staff.
Special Notes: The centre has a private car park for sixteen cars. Smoking is not allowed.
Getting There: From Dublin, take the N7 towards Waterford. Bus Éireann and Iarnród Éireann also service the city of Waterford.

Temple Country House and Health Spa

Horseleap
Moate

Tel: 0506 35118
Fax: 0506 35008
E-mail: templespa@spiders.ie
Website: www.spiders.ie/templespa

Lining the country laneway of Temple House are towering mature oak trees, which lead to a beautifully maintained manor house. Although the signs of the ancient monastery site on which the house was built are long gone, the two-hundred-and-fifty-year-old house has retained all of its rustic charm and has been tastefully extended to include a health farm which provides comfort, relaxation and the chance to experience a wide choice of therapies and beauty treatments in incredible surroundings. The first recorded guest to Temple House was John Wesley in 1748; no doubt he was received into the same dining room in which guests are now welcomed to have their candlelit meals by a crackling open fire. This adds to the warmth of the experience, as guests sit together around three large dining tables and share stories and laughter over delicious wholesome meals.

The programmes on offer give you the opportunity to participate as much as you choose in group events or take time out on your own. Organised guided walks and cycling tours give the guest the opportunity to take in some of the magnificent surrounding countryside, with its peat bogs, lakes, natural wildlife and historical sites. There are yoga and Do-in sessions and light-exercise classes available, in a purpose-built exercise room with views of the farm and a grassy hill which formed part of the early network of trade routes which ran throughout Ireland. Visits begin with yoga or light-exercise sessions. These are followed by a choice of full-body massage, aromatherapy, reflexology and hydrotherapy. A sauna, steam room and full beauty treatments are also available. After experiencing one of the best deep-tissue massages I had had for some time, I drifted off to the sound of Chopin while enjoying the aromas in the creams used for my exquisite facial. Pure luxury!

Each of the bedrooms is furnished in rich, solid mahogany, and the en suite bathrooms overlook the hundred acres of farmland which surrounds Temple House. The bedrooms and treatment rooms are decorated in soft pastel colours to help relax the mind. This theme of relaxation runs through everything that is on offer in Temple House.

Days and Hours of Operation: Open year-round, with pamper days, midweek breaks, mini-weekend specials and weekend breaks. Guest arrival time is 6.30 pm on Friday evening, and departure time is 3 pm on Sunday.

Accommodation: Eight stylish and comfortable en suite guest bedrooms with solid dark-wood furnishings.

Rates: The 'Relaxing Day' – a full day, including massage or reflexology – costs €95.23 midweek, and €107.93 for Saturdays. The 'À La Carte Weekend' – two days and nights full-board accommodation (from dinner on Friday evening to lunch on Sunday), daily yoga and relaxation classes, guided walks, use of facilities and one spa treatment – is €340 per person sharing, and €375 for a single room. The 'Pamper Weekend' – Yonka Aroma plus facial, eyelash tint and body wrap – costs €476.15 sharing or €501.55 single. Overnight full board, including yoga class and one spa treatment, is €184.11 per person sharing, and €196.81 single. The 'Therapeutic Midweek Spa Break', from Tuesday to Friday, includes three spa treatments and one balneotherapy session and costs €565 per person sharing or €605 single. The 'Midweek Spa Break' is €480 per person sharing or €510 single.

Credit Cards: Visa, MasterCard, American Express or Laser.

Meal Plans: The cuisine is generous and health-conscious and uses fresh ingredients. Special dietary needs are catered for, if the centre is informed of them in advance.

Services: Massage, reflexology, Indian head massage, shiatsu, kinesiology, cranio-sacral therapy, reiki, hydrotherapy bath with seaweed, yoga, Do-in, walking workout, 'Breathing for Relaxation', deep detoxifying herbal wrap, body-firming treatments, choice of beauty treatments and facials using Yonka products.

Facilities: Nine treatment rooms, sauna, steam room, relaxation room with views of surrounding countryside, eight en suite guest rooms, dining room and sitting room with open fires, exercise and yoga room, and gardens.

Staff: The centre is owned and managed by Declan and Bernadette Fagan. There are ten full-time qualified massage therapists, four full-time beauty therapists, one person qualified in

shiatsu, three qualified in reflexology, one Reiki master, and one qualified in kinesiology and cranio-sacral therapy.
Recreational Activities: Yoga, cycling and scheduled walks.
Nearby Attractions: Golf, horse-riding, angling, sailing and hill-walking. Clonmacnoise, and Lockes Distillery and Museum.
Getting There: Horseleap is just off the N6, midway between Dublin and Galway. The turn for Temple House is on the right, 500 yards after the village from the direction of Dublin, or left just before the village from the direction of Galway. There is an hourly bus service from Bus Áras in Dublin to Horseleap, and Declan or Bernadette will meet you from the bus.

Dungarvan Alternative Health Clinic

Pookeen Lane
Main Street
Dungarvan

Tel: 058 44299
E-mail: dahc@cablesurf.com

Within the heart of bustling Dungarvan town is a beautifully and sensitively restored eighteenth-century house, which is now home to the local alternative health clinic. The clinic was established as a place of healing and support for anyone with health problems, be they spiritual, emotional or physical. When receiving therapies, it is important to do so in a relaxed environment, and this health clinic provides a peaceful and inviting atmosphere in which to enjoy receiving the many treatments on offer, or to balance the mind and body by participating in t'ai chi and qi gung classes.

The t'ai chi instructor, Jon Donovan, has practised the discipline for more than thirteen years. He qualified as an instructor with the Raising Dragon T'ai Chi School in 1990. After studying the teachings of Dr Chi Chang Tao, he is now studying and teaching the Grand Master Huang Sheng Shuan system. Jon is also a qualified teacher of the Michael Mann Universal Healing Charts, which are helpful for self-healing and for people who are working with qi: laughter, love and light.

Days and Hours of Operation: Tuesday to Saturday, 10 am to 6 pm.

Rates: Treatments cost between €19.04 and €38.10.
Credit Cards: Cash or cheque only.
Services: Aromatherapy, traditional Chinese medicine, acupuncture, chiropractic, Indian head massage, reflexology, massage, and t'ai chi and qi gung classes.
Facilities: The centre is housed in a converted eighteenth-century stone building which has been beautifully restored and has a calm and relaxing ambience.
Staff: Seven fully qualified and registered practitioners in the above treatments. The general manager is Orla Casey.
Nearby Attractions: Dungarvan town and its environs is a beautiful, scenic area, surrounded by the sea, mountains, rivers and lakes. It is popular with tourists, particularly in summertime, as it has wonderful beaches, such as those at Clonea and Ardmore.
Getting There: On the main street in Dungarvan.

HEALTH THERAPIES CLINIC

13 Gladstone Street
Waterford

Tel: 051 858 584

Rose McDonald abandoned the nursing profession in order to open the Health Therapies Clinic in the centre of Waterford ten years ago. 'I have a lot of knowledge as a foundation,' she says. 'I am always building on it and always learning more.'

A therapeutic practitioner and teacher, Rose aims to help people secure a better quality of life through gaining better overall health and a sense of balance. 'I try to help people enjoy their life and live it accordingly,' she says.

Rose, who combines various therapies to treat a variety of physical, emotional and spiritual ailments, says that the majority of her clients notice a change during their first consultation. 'Most people find that when they come to the end of the treatment, they feel relieved and very relaxed,' she says. 'It doesn't matter whether it is an acute or a chronic condition.'

Days and Hours of Operation. Open Monday to Thursday, from 10 am to 8 pm. Weekend courses are occasionally offered.
Rates: Hour-long sessions cost between €25.39 and €44.44.
Credit Cards: None accepted.
Services: Reflexology, reiki treatments and courses, Indian head massage, polarity therapy, energy healing and on-site massage.
Facilities: Waiting area and two private treatment rooms.

Staff: Rose McDonald owns and operates the centre alone.
Special Notes: Rose will travel to the home of disabled people should they request treatments.
Getting There: The centre is located in the centre of Waterford city.

Anvil House & Therapeutic Centre

Newbawn
Foulksmills

Tel:	051 565 609
Fax:	051 565 991
E-mail:	wallts@indigo.ie

Anvil House is a purpose-built therapeutic centre consisting of two therapy rooms, a sauna, a steam room and an exercise room. Accommodation is in the family-run bed and breakfast, in a two-storey modern 1970s house adjacent to the centre. The food is traditional Irish in nature, and the host, Siobhan Wall, is welcoming and friendly. Siobhan, a qualified nurse, opened the centre after training in therapeutic and holistic massage and reflexology. She also runs yoga-for-beginners classes midweek. If you want to stay in a B&B in the Wexford area, with the additional benefits of on-site massage or reflexology, Anvil House provides this service.

Days and Hours of Operation: Open seven days a week, all year round.
Accommodation: Three en suite bedrooms.
Rate: Weekend: two days' B&B, two lunches and two therapies for €189.09 or €214.47 per person sharing. Weekend: full board and two therapies for €227.16 or €252.54 per person sharing. Midweek: three days' B&B, two lunches and two therapies for €239.85 per person sharing. Midweek: full board, three therapies and use of facilities for €328.68. 'Holistic health and pamper

day': one therapy, steam, sauna and lunch for €74.87 per person.
Credit Cards: Visa.
Services: Therapeutic and holistic massage, nikken magnetic therapy, reflexology, yoga and stress-management courses.
Recreational Activities: Given its rural location, walkers will enjoy wandering around in the local area.
Staff: One full-time massage and reflexology therapist, and two part-time massage and beauty therapists.
Special Notes: If interested in yoga classes, check in advance for class timetable. Gift vouchers available.
Nearby Attractions: Johnstown Castle Gardens, Wexford, Irish National Heritage Park and Tintern Abbey are all worth a visit and are within driving distance of Anvil House.
Getting There: From Dublin, take the N11 to Wexford and join the N25 after Ferrycarrig to Ballinaboola. Turn left there to the Campus station. The journey takes approximately two hours. From Cork, take the N24 to Waterford and join the N24 to Waterford, then the N25 to New Ross and on to Ballinaboola. Turn right onto the R736. Approximately two hours.

BALLYCOURSEY LODGE HEALTH SPA

Enniscorthy

Tel: 054 37736
E-mail: info@ballycoursey.com
Website: www.BallycourseyLodgeHealthSpa.com

'A host of golden daffodils' complements the driveway to Ballycoursey Lodge Health Spa. These, together with the surrounding woodland and immaculately kept mature gardens, make the visitor instantly feel that they have discovered a peaceful haven, away from it all. The golden hue continues to the interior of the lodge, which is tastefully decorated in yellows, soft turquoise, peach and cream colours. The philosophy of Ballycoursey lodge is to meet the unique needs of each individual. For this reason, proprietor Margaret Bourke keeps the maximum number of guests to just six. This, she says, allows a very personalised service for each client, while also giving individuals space to relax, either on their own or as part of a small group of guests. There is a wide range of specialised therapeutic treatments to choose from, leaving the client feeling refreshed and revitalised. Those who enjoy outdoor exercise can avail of the tennis courts. I spent my time relaxing in a hammock in the garden while listening to the birds compete in song.

The staff are very professional and their good humour is a reflection of the harmonious environment in which they work. Meals are held in the dining area and give you an opportunity to meet the other guests. The food is delicious, with plenty of choice. If you prefer to spend time on your own, the rooms are very spacious and comfortable. In addition, given the small number of people being catered for, the relaxation area, which includes a conservatory with a water feature, overlooking the garden, is also an ideal space to while away the hours.

Days and Hours of Operation: Open seven days a week, 10 am to 6 pm.
Accommodation: Three beautiful en suite twin/double bedrooms.
Rates: The 'Pamper Day', which includes a choice of four treatments and a delicious lunch, costs €114.21. A 'Breakaway Weekend' costs €260 for a single person or €304.57 for a twin or double per person sharing, including accommodation on Friday and Saturday night with delicious breakfast, lunch and four treatments on Saturday and Sunday. The 'Midweek Break' costs €291.88 single or €266.50 for a twin or double per person sharing. Additional treatments cost between €31.75 and €57.11.
Credit Cards: Visa and MasterCard
Meal Plans: Overnight guests enjoy gourmet meals. Pamper days include lunch. There is an excellent choice of vegetarian dishes.
Services: Aromatherapy massage, holistic massage, lymphatic massage, salt-scrub exfoliation, enzymatic sea-mud pack, body-therapy hydro pack, therapeutic spa bath, thermal mud treatment, full or express facial, seaweed body wrap, beauty treatments, yoga classes and personal-development workshops.

Facilities: Therapy rooms, sauna, steam room, tennis courts and beautiful gardens. Yoga room. Relaxation room with water feature. Dining room.
Staff: Two full-time and two part-time massage and beauty therapists.
Recreational Activities: Nature walks, hiking and biking in the surrounding area. The centre is located close to facilties for horse-riding and fishing.
Nearby Attractions: Ballycoursey Lodge is a ten-mile scenic drive from the beautiful sandy beaches of Curracloe. Also situated near the national 1798 visitor centre and the Irish National Heritage Park.

Therapeutic Spa & Beauty Centre at Kelly's Resort Hotel

Rosslare

Tel:	053 32114
Fax:	053 32222
E-mail:	kellyhot@iol.ie
Website:	www.kellys.ie

Kelly's renowned four-star hotel has been a family-run establishment for four generations since it was founded by William J. Kelly in 1895. It boasts many well-known guests, including George Bernard Shaw, who was a regular visitor in the 1920s. During my stay there, I noticed that it is a very family-friendly hotel, with children really enjoying the landscaped gardens and parents and grandparents relaxing and enjoying the sea views in the dining area or in the leisure and beauty complex. The food is delicious and there is a huge selection, whether the guest is eating in the elegant dining room or in the buffet-lunch area. There is a superb collection of modern and contemporary art on display throughout the hotel. This collection includes works by Howard Hodgkin, David Hockney, Stephen McKenna, Josef Herman, Picasso, Miró and Irish artists Jack Yeats, Felim Egan, Michael Mulcahy and Louis le Broquy.

The Therapeutic Spa & Beauty Centre is part of the Aqua Club area. The pool area has a terracotta-tiled Orangerie Terrace and is an excellent place for guests to relax, observing the panoramic views across the sea and along the beach, or rejuvenate with the scent of lemon and orange trees surrounding the pool. There are two separate pools for adults and children. There is also a sauna, steam room, jacuzzi and outdoor Canadian hot tub. The two large, energetic free-standing sculptured pieces by Benedict Byrne really add to the innovative design of the pool area. The spa and beauty area has a wide choice of treatments on offer and the therapists are extremely helpful. If you suffer from back pain or tight muscles, I would highly recommend that you receive a full-body sports massage, which did wonders in completely relieving my lower-back pain.

Days and Hours of Operation: The hotel is open all year round, with the Therapeutic Spa & Beauty Centre open Monday to Saturday, from 10 am to 7 pm.
Accommodation: Choice of en suite single, double or family rooms.
Rates: Vary from season to season. The average summer tariff for a six-day stay is €634.52 per person for a double en suite room. A four-day stay in springtime costs €418.78 per person sharing a double, en suite room. Two-night weekends (Friday to Sunday) €247.46 price per person sharing a double or en suite room. The average cost of treatments is €38.07 to €50.76.
Credit Cards: Visa, Access and American Express.
Meal Plans: Three gourmet or buffet-style meals a day. Excellent choice of food. Vegetarians are well catered for.
Services in Therapeutic Spa Area: E'Spa aromatherapy facial, E'spa luxury eye treatment, E'spa aromatherapy total body care, holistic massage, E'spa body polish, detoxifying algae wrap, mud envelopment, E'spa pre-natal treatment,

E'spa luxury foot and leg treatment, E'spa luxury hand and nail treatment, E'spa stress-buster, sports-therapy massage, reflexology. Detoxifying spa day treatments also available. Throughout the year, Kelly's offers a choice of interesting workshops, which are included in the overnight stay. These include gardening and cookery demonstrations, interior design and feng shui workshops, ballroom dancing and golf-techniques classes.

Facilities: Two swimming pools, jacuzzi, outdoor Canadian hot tub, sauna and steam room, yoga and aerobics studio, gymnasium, crazy golf, jogging track, table tennis, badminton, bowls and croquet lawns, children's playground, holistic therapy rooms, beauty salon and hair salon.

Recreational Activities: Outdoor tennis, and golf packages, including free use of Kelly's indoor golf-training centre.

Staff: Two massage therapists, one sports-therapy massage therapist, three reflexologists, two reiki practitioners, two Indian head massage and four scalp massage therapists.

Nearby Attractions: Johnstown Castle Gardens, Wexford, Irish National Heritage Park and Tintern Abbey are all worth a visit and within driving distance of Anvil House.

Getting There: From Dublin take the N11 (the centre is 95 miles away). From Cork take the N25 (124 miles). From Belfast take the A1/N1 to Dublin and the N11 to Rosslare (197 miles).

ATAR COMPLEMENTARY THERAPY CLINIC

Centre for Natural Therapies
George Street
Wexford

Tel:
Catherine George: 086 813 8528
Nikk George: 086 617 9994

Run by Catherine and Nikk George, the Atar Complementary Therapy Clinic offers a wide range of therapies which are all reasonably priced. They recommend a course of weekly treatments as the most effective way to achieve overall well-being. The first session includes a free confidential consultation to ascertain details of lifestyle, diet, exercise and emotional health. This ensures that the most appropriate oils are selected for any aromatherapy treatment and that individual needs are catered for. During the treatment, the focus is on relaxing the client; background music is used to help attain this. All oils used are 100 per cent pure and manufactured in Ireland. A therapist – and shop discount – is available on request.

Days and Hours of operation: Monday to Saturday, 10 am to 6 pm.
Rates: Each treatment costs an average of €31.73.
Services: Swedish massage, sports massage and biotriggernetics. Aromatherapy treatments: whole-body massage; back, neck and shoulders massage; back, upper chest, face and scalp massage; foot and leg massage; neck, face and scalp massage; and anti-cellulite treatment.

Facilities: Two treatment rooms.
Staff: Two full-time massage therapists.
Getting there: Situated in the heart of Wexford town.

Centre for Natural Therapies

16 Lower George Street
Wexford

Tel: 053 21363

The Centre for Natural Therapies is one of the largest practices of complementary therapists in the south-east. Located in the centre of Wexford town, the clinic offers a wide variety of natural therapies, which are based on the principle of working with the body, mind and spirit to heal the whole person. Anna Skrine and Heike Wiehagen established the centre in the heart of Wexford to allow complementary therapies to be more freely accessed by the general public there.

The centre offers body treatments, counselling and stress management, which is very popular with clients, given the pace of modern life. Many physical health problems arise from having a poor diet, and with a qualified in-house nutritionist, each aspect of health, including diet, is catered for. The centre offers a complete range of therapies for optimum physical, emotional and spiritual health.

Rates: The cost of treatments varies from €25.40 to €50.80. (In cases of genuine financial hardship, concessions are available.)
Days and Hours of Operation: Monday to Friday, 9 am to 6 pm.
Services: Acupuncture, aromatherapy, 'cutting the ties that bind', homeopathy, hypnotherapy, iridology, nutrition, professional counselling, reflexology,

reiki and seichem, spinal healing, stress management and therapeutic massage.
Additional Services: Belly-dancing classes, t'ai chi, qi gung, yoga, relaxation techniques and introductory homeopathic classes.
Facilities: Two treatment rooms, reception area and office.
Staff: Nine full-time therapists: one homeopath, one osteopath, one professional counsellor and reiki master, one osteopath, one reflexologist and practitioner in guided visualisation, one massage therapist and stress-management consultant, one spinal healer and consultant in iridology and nutrition and one qualified aromatherapist, hypnotherapist and practitioner in acupuncture.
Special Notes: The centre is a non-profit-making organisation.
Nearby Attractions: The National Heritage Park and Johnstown Castle Gardens. The centre is also close to beautiful sandy beaches, nature walks, a wildlife reserve, fishing, pony-riding, boating and two golf courses. Local festivals of interest include the Wexford Opera Festival, the Strawberry Fair and the Kilmore Seafood Festival.
Getting There: The centre is located in the centre of Wexford town.

CHRYSALIS HOLISTIC CENTRE

Donard

Tel/Fax:	045 404 713
E-mail:	peace@chrysalis.ie
Website:	www.chrysalis.ie

Founded in 1989, Chrysalis offers a place for time out, personal growth and spiritual renewal. Situated one hour from Dublin, in the tranquil surroundings of the Wicklow countryside, the centre is an oasis within easy reach of the city. An extensive, varied range of workshops is available for clients. This house of healing is surrounded by mature, beautifully landscaped grounds, and fresh food is sourced from the centre's organic garden. The staff are welcoming and friendly and the mainly wooden interior and decor of soft pastel colours helps to put the mind at ease on arrival. This nurturing space is ideal for guests to unwind and learn from the many facilitators on the courses provided.

The centre caters for groups of around twenty at any one time. Daily and weekend courses are available. The vegetarian food is delicious and the smiling faces in the dining room were testament to the benefit the guests were deriving from the course. Chrysalis operates a volunteer programme for people interested in stepping off the treadmill for some respite. In exchange for kitchen and dining-room duties, they provide full board and lodging. There is also an opportunity to still the mind by staying in one of the two hermitage buildings set in a tranquil zen-meditation garden. Members of all faiths and traditions are welcome at the centre.

Days and Hours of Operation: Courses are held every day. The office is open for telephone queries and bookings between 10 and 1 pm and again between 2 and 5 pm, Monday to Friday. Booking in advance is required. The craft shop is open between 1.30 and 2.15 pm at weekends.

Rates: Daily courses cost an average of €63; weekend courses average €222. The latter are fully residential and include bed linens and all meals. Bring your own towels. Hermitage self-catering units cost €38 per day, or €63 per day based on two people sharing.

Credit Cards: Visa, MasterCard, Laser.

Accommodation: A mixture of clean single, twin and dorm rooms. Also two self-catering hermitage units. Minimum stay is two days. Central heating and bed linen are included. For the hermitage, you need to bring your own food, towels, torch and fuel.

Meal Plans: Home-baked dishes and irresistible vegetarian food are served in the intimate dining room. Each table seats up to eight guests and provides an ideal environment for people to get to know their fellow course participants.

Services: Holistic healing group workshops and lectures covering a wide range of subjects, including hom-eopathy for home use, creative writing, Anthony De Mello workshops, 'You Can Heal Your Life' sessions, intuitive massage, healing with herbs, aromatherapy for family and friends, holistic gardening, stress management and 'Experiencing Joy'. Weekend workshops are run on relationships ('The Dynamics of Intimacy, Career Change and Life Planning'), reiki, the Alexander technique, codependency ('Rediscovering Your True Self') and meditation.

Facilities: The complex consists of a converted eighteenth-century chalet situated in beautifully landscaped gardens. The complex also includes two hermitage units, a sauna and a gift shop.

Staff: In addition to the support staff, trained facilitators are booked for each course.

Nearby Attractions: Chrysalis is ideally located in the rural Wicklow countryside, and there are many excellent walks nearby.

Getting There: From Dublin, take the N81 past the Square shopping centre in Tallaght. Drive through Blessington. After ten miles, turn left at the Olde Tollhouse pub, signposted for Donard and Chrysalis. Bear right through the village of Donard. Outside the village, take the right fork, and Chrysalis is two miles further on, on the right-hand side of the road. From the south, make for Carlow, then Baltinglass. From the west, make for Kildare and then cross the Curragh to Kilcullen and Dunlavin. Exit Dunlavin on the main road, signposted for Baltinglass and Donard. After five miles, turn right at the N81 junction, then first left for Chrysalis. From the north, take the first exit after Dublin Airport for the M50 southbound. Drive to Tallaght on the N81 and follow the directions from Dublin (see above).

Using public transport: Buses leave from Bus Áras central bus station in Dublin at 9 am. The evening bus departs at 5 pm. Your destination is Annalecky Cross on the Waterford express bus. You need to order a taxi in advance to pick you up at the Olde Tollhouse Pub and take you the last four miles to Chrysalis. Book taxis direct with Dermot Allen on 0508 82222. Check with Chrysalis for more details.

Powerscourt Springs

Coolakay
Enniskerry

Tel: 01 276 1000
Fax: 01 276 1626
E-mail: info@powerscourtsprings.iol.ie
Website: www.powerscourtsprings.ie

Nestled in the heart of the Wicklow hills is the Powerscourt Springs, a beauty, health and fitness centre rolled into one. Relaxation and rejuvenation is the philosophy of this tranquil haven, which was established by Patricia Kinsella and Fiona Hanby. From the moment you arrive at the centre, you will find yourself immersed in an environment that allows you to forget your worries completely. When booking accommodation, ask for a room with a view of the Wicklow Mountains, which will add to the overall experience. The rooms are tastefully decorated and comfortable. Overnight guests may wish to relax in their room between treatments, or, if you enjoy company, the comfortable lounge area is a wonderful place to meet other guests.

There are many excellent treatments to choose from, and staff are attentive and experienced. The fact that it is situated only thirty minutes' drive from Dublin means that Powerscourt is extremely popular with people from the city who want to de-stress while remaining close to home. Although the centre is busy, it is managed very efficiently and each individual's needs are catered for. Fiona Hanby's background is in health and fitness, so there are plenty of optional extras to help people keep fit, such as aerobics classes, a fitness gym, aqua aerobics in the swimming pool and organised walks in the Wicklow Mountains and surrounding countryside. Whatever calories you lose in this way you may wish to regain by enjoying some of the delicious cooking on offer. Those who are calorie-conscious can choose from the light-diet menu.

Days and Hours of Operation: Open year-round for pamper days, midweek breaks, mini-weekend specials and weekend breaks. Guest-arrival time is 9 am and departure time is 5 pm.

Accommodation: All rooms are en suite and are fully equipped with remote-control television, hairdryers and direct-dial telephones.

Rates: 'Top to Toe Day' costs €145.94 from Monday to Thursday or €158.63 from Friday to Sunday. The day includes body exfoliant or hot-towel shave, personal steam-cabinet session, back massage, refresher facial, eyebrow shape, sunbed, unlimited use of classes and facilities, and a three-course lunch. 'Health Farm Day', which costs €95.18, includes steam-cabinet session, back massage, unlimited use of classes and facilities, and a three-course lunch. A midweek break for one night costs €177.66 for a single room or €158.63 per person sharing for a twin room from Monday to Thursday. Treatments available are as above, with a four-course gourmet dinner in the evening. The mini-weekend special costs €247.46 for a single room or €228.43 per person sharing for a twin room. This break features the same treatments as for the midweek break, as well as a manicure. The weekend break costs €379.44 for a single room and €341.34 per person sharing for a twin room. The treatments available are the same as for the mini-weekend special. Additional complementary therapies or beauty treatments cost an average of €44.45.

Credit Cards: Visa, MasterCard, American Express, Laser and Diners Club.

Meal Plans: A wide choice of fine cuisine for both vegetarians and non-vegetarians. Special diets are catered for. Three meals daily are provided for overnight guests.

Services: Massage: aromatherapy, full-body, ki, reflexology and Indian head. Cellulite treatments: G5 massage, Pannicocyt cellulite treatment, Aromazone and hydro bath. Also Clarins facials, body-firming treatments, detoxing body treatments and beauty treatments.

Facilities: Health farm situated in Wicklow hills, aqua-aerobic pool, jacuzzi, sauna, fully equipped gym, steam cabinets, sunbeds, tranquillity room, lounge area and, for day visitors, day room with lockers, showers, hairdryers and make-up area.

Recreational Activities: Aerobics, aqua aerobics, yoga, tennis, cycling and scheduled walks.

Staff: A hundred and eighty-three staff with eighty-three qualifed as massage therapists, hydrotherapy specialists and beauticians. One yoga teacher. Also reception staff and resident gourmet chefs.

Nearby Attractions: The Wicklow Mountains, known as the garden of Ireland, are ideal walking grounds for nature lovers. There are many idyllic villages in Wicklow, from which you can purchase Irish art and crafts.

SACRED JOURNEYS IRELAND

20 Temple Square
Dartry

Tel: 01 496 3637
Mobile: 086 829 6956

Set on four acres of land beside the Wicklow Way in the Glenmalure Valley, Sacred Journeys Ireland is where people come once a month to take part in a Celtic sweat-lodge ceremony. Founder Margaret Lawlor facilitates the monthly event, which she believes enables people to get in touch with a deeper part of themselves. 'People go away feeling better about their lives,' says Margaret.

Following the Lakota Sioux model known as the 'inipi', up to fifteen participants enter a small, dome-like structure covered with canvas. The group sits in a circle around heated stones, over which the facilitator pours water to generate steam. The ceremony, which begins with a salutation of peace to the earth, includes chanting and sharing experiences. The entire ritual lasts nine hours.

A residential programme is also offered throughout the year. During this programme, participants have the opportunity to address more deeply various issues of a physical, mental, emotional or spiritual nature.

Margaret also founded Life Management Solutions, which offers on-site chair massage and corporate health awareness and stress-management programmes.

Days and Hours of Operation: Monthly sweat-lodge ceremonies and healthy retreats held throughout the year.

Accommodation: Five twin en suite bedrooms.
Rates: Participation in sweat lodges typically costs €38.09 per session. Residential retreats generally cost €285.68.
Credit Cards: None accepted.
Meal Plans: Vegetarian meals are included with residential programmes.
Services: Monthly sweat-lodge ceremonies, health and well-being retreats, corporate-health programmes, on-site chair massage, and stop-smoking programmes.
Facilities: The outdoor sweat lodge is located on four acres of countryside. Also on the property is a farmhouse with a large kitchen, bedrooms, a large facility room and a private treatment room.
Staff: In addition to Margaret Lawlor, guest facilitators lead the sweat-lodge ceremonies.
Special Notes: Pregnant women and people with certain ailments should not participate in the sweat-lodge ceremony. Contact Margaret for instructions on the ceremony before arriving. Smoking is not allowed.
Getting There: Contact Margaret Lawlor for details.

SLÍ NA BANDE

Kilmurry
Newtownmountkennedy

Tel: 01 281 9990
Fax: 01 281 0551
E-mail: slinabande@eircom.net
Website: www.homepage.eircom.net/~yogaireland/index.html

With her solar- and wind-powered home nestled in the Wicklow hills and her Volkswagen Golf run on vegetable oil, Marlene French-Mullen radiates the message of harmony, which she teaches in her hatha-yoga classes. She runs weekly yoga classes, residential yoga weekends and yoga teacher training in a purpose-built wooden chalet complete with a wood-burning stove. This chalet has a very homely, comfortable atmosphere. Marlene ascertains each individual's emotional well-being and physical capabilities before each class or workshop and adapts the class to suit the needs of the group. Having had very little experience of yoga previously, I found the poses challenging though achievable, stretching and awakening areas of my body that I didn't know existed! Marlene's tone is gentle and encouraging. She enlivens the class with interesting conversation and insights.

As well as yoga classes and training, Marlene runs a sweat-lodge ceremony at Slí na Bande. This ceremony is a healing, purification and prayer ceremony. It follows spiritual traditions drawn from Celtic and Native American cultures. Participants can expect to be expertly guided through a unique healing experience which, according to Marlene, will bring them in close contact with their true selves, opening their consciousness – as far as they wish to open it – to themselves and the power of the elements. The sweat-lodge sessions are held on important days of the year, such as the solstices or equinoxes and St Bridget's Day. They are preceded by a qi gung practice.

Slí na Bande is used by people to take time out and reflect, to expose themselves to the healing power of the earth and to contemplate different ways of living and relating to themselves and loved ones. For those who wish to learn the postures of hatha yoga or to attain a deeper understanding of the philosophy of yoga, Slí na Bande offers an opportunity to discover this and much more.

Days and Hours of Operation: Yoga classes held on Tuesdays, 8 to 9.30 pm, and Wednesdays, 10.30 am to 12.15 pm, all year round. Dates for yoga weekends, yoga training and yoga holiday week are advertised on the centre's website.
Rates: Yoga classes, €8.88 each. Yoga weekends, held once a month, including meals and shared accommodation, €185. Yoga holiday week, €412.44 all-inclusive. Sweat lodge, €50.76.
Credit Cards: Cash or cheque only.
Meal Plans: All meals are vegetarian and prepared from organically produced food.
Services: Hatha yoga classes and residential yoga weekends are facilitated by Marlene French Mullen and include meditation, breathing practice, journalling, hatha yoga, partner-work and a sweat-lodge ceremony. Claire Haugh, a shiatsu practitioner, assists with the weekends. Yoga holiday week is run once a year and is open to all levels of practice and ability. Yoga training consists of eight residential weekends and one full week. The programme includes hatha yoga, pranayama, meditation, philosophy and anatomy, and provides an understanding of the subtle movement of energy through the body. The aim of the course is to assist the participants in their personal development through yoga and a deepening of their personal understanding and practice. Relationship training, which emphasises physical cleansing and the clearing of the emotional body, includes exercises to develop intimacy, such as yoga, rebirthing, qi gung, meditation and process-work. One-to-one counselling is also available.
Facilities: The main chalet group room, which overlooks the sea, contains a bathroom, a kitchen and a wood-burning stove. It is built entirely from wood and environmentally friendly materials. The Patio Room has three single beds and a wood-burning stove. The Sea-view Room sleeps four, the Courtyard Room sleeps three, the Forest Room sleeps two and the loft sleeps nine.
Staff: Marlene French-Mullen is a qualified yoga teacher and counsellor. Douglas French Mullen is a leading authority and adviser on renewable energy and building in an environmentally friendly and practical way. He also converts diesel cars to run on vegetable oil. Stephen Gregory is a qualified yoga teacher, massage therapist and rebirthing trainer. Claire Haugh is a shiatsu practitioner. Mark Kinghan is a practitioner of traditional Chinese medicine and teaches qi gung,

meditation and breathing exercises.
Recreational Activities: Organised hiking trips and walks in the Wicklow Mountains.
Local Attractions: Slí na Bande is situated approximately twenty miles from Glendalough, twenty miles from Brittas Bay, five miles from Lough Daan and three miles from Kilcoole beach, with its wild life sanctuary. Also golf, horse-riding and fishing.
Getting There: From Dublin, take the N11 towards Wexford. Take theh exit for Newtown Mount Kennedy. Turn right at the Catholic church in the village, follow the road to left and take the first right at the fork. Travel up this narrow road for one mile. The entrance to the centre is just past a small white cottage and a granite stone wall.

BRAY HOLISTIC HEALTH CLINIC

St George's
Herbert Road
Bray

Tel: 01 286 6611

Linda Ronayne and Fiona Shepherd met and became friends when they both turned to holistic health to resolve chronic ailments that allopathic doctors could not successfully cure. Once Linda's children were old enough to allow her to branch out, she and Fiona teamed up to open the Bray Holistic Health Clinic in 1993, with the aim of providing the community with a clinic dedicated to offering individualised, caring treatment to the whole person. Linda, a classical homeopath and full-time lecturer at the Irish School of Homeopathy, runs workshops at the clinic to teach people how to treat common ailments such as sore throats and upset stomachs in both children and adults. Shepherd trained to become a McTimoney chiropractor, a method which involves a gentle and straightforward adjustment of the bones to relieve pain and increase mobility.

Other staff include John Kelly, an acupuncturist and Chinese medical herbalist, Terry Thorpe and James Jameson, psychologists and hypnotherapists, and Catherine Chambers, a reflexologist and aromatherapist. Linda and Fiona admit that they set high standards. Consequently, all staff must be fully registered and have at least four years' experience before joining the team. Future plans for the clinic include employing a number of massage therapists.

The clinic is often busy and patients may have to wait up to a month for an appointment with Linda or Fiona. In crisis situations, however, Linda will offer telephone consultations with former patients and will treat them during lunch hour.

Days and Hours of Operation: Open Monday through Friday from 8.30 am to 6.30 pm, by appointment.
Rates: Vary according to services. Treatments typically range from €31.74 to €50.79.
Credit Cards: None accepted.
Services: Homeopathy, chiropractic, acupuncture, Chinese medicine, hypnotherapy, psychology, reflexology and massage.
Staff: Six fully licensed and qualified therapists.
Special Notes: The minimum wait for an initial appointment with Linda or Fiona is one month.
Getting There: The centre is located twenty minutes south of Dublin by car.

Greystones Physical Therapy Clinic

'Tullan'
Trafalgar Road
Greystones

Tel: 01 201 7908
Fax: 01 201 7909

After working in a physical-therapy clinic for six years, Ruth Stewart wanted to set up her own centre to provide a variety of healing therapies under one roof. When the opportunity to do this arose in April 2000, Ruth made the leap.

While the clinic primarily offers physical therapy, clients can also avail of holistic treatments, such as aromatherapy, reflexology and bioenergy therapy. Ruth is particularly adept at treating disorders of the musculoskeletal system, such as sports injury, whiplash and postural aches and pains. Individuals wanting to book appointments should be aware that certain therapies are available only on certain days.

Days and Hours of Operation: The clinic is open by appointment, Monday to Saturday.
Credit Cards: None accepted.
Rates: A one-hour treatment costs an average of €38.09.
Services: Physical therapy, bioenergy therapy, remedial massage, acupuncture, aromatherapy, reflexology and osteopathy.
Facilities: Three private treatment rooms.
Staff: One physical therapist, one acupuncturist, one osteopath and two

aromatherapists. All staff are fully licensed and qualified.

Special Notes: Free parking is available in a car park directly opposite the clinic. Smoking is not allowed. While the clinic itself is accessible for people with disabilities, the bathroom is too small to accommodate a wheelchair.

Getting There: The clinic is about thirty minutes south of Dublin by car and is accessible by train.

Glossary

Acupressure Based on the same ideas as acupuncture, acupressure is actually the older of the two methods. Also known as 'contact healing', the practice seeks to restore the flow of 'chi' or life energy through the application of finger and hand pressure along the body's meridians, or energy points. This pressure releases neurotransmitters that inhibit the delivery of painful sensations. During treatments, the individual lies fully clothed while pressure is applied with thumbs, palms, the heels of the hands and elbows, the knees and feet, roller-balls or bars along the body. While this non-invasive, simple technique may be performed by a skilled practitioner, it is not difficult for individuals to learn how to treat themselves using acupressure. One trick that dieters may appreciate, for example, is gently to squeeze the earlobes between the thumb and forefinger for one minute when the person is feeling hungry.

Acupuncture A branch of traditional Chinese medicine that originated more than three thousand years ago, acupuncture involves pressing small sterilised needles into various meridians, or energy points, located throughout the body. The discipline is based on the idea that energy flows throughout the body like so many small rivers and that obstructions in this flow have the same effect as a dam, restricting energy in some parts of the body and causing back-ups in others. By stimulating the energy points with needles, obstructions are dissolved and the proper flow of 'chi' is restored. Some studies indicate that acupuncture may cause the release of pain-killing endorphins. Acupuncture has been shown to be an effective treatment for a wide variety of chronic ailments, including stress, fatigue, addictions, backaches, asthma and migraines. A traditional Chinese doctor may also prescribe various herbs, dietary changes and exercise. While some individuals experience relief after only one session, a series of treatments may be required for more serious illnesses.

Alexander technique In the late 1800s, Shakespearean actor F. M. Alexander discovered that he could change his muscular responses through a combination of conscious changes to his posture and specific breathing exercises. As a result, he developed the Alexander technique, which involves non-invasive, gentle touch to increase the client's awareness of their own posture and body movements. Sessions typically begin with the practitioner observing the client's movements to discern whether or not any areas of the body are being put under undue strain. The practitioner then places their hands on those parts of the body that need adjusting and teaches the client how to move correctly. Individuals may be asked to lie on a plinth while adjustments are made to their shoulders or limbs. The Alexander technique has proved particularly effective for people with back pain, shoulder strain and stiff muscles. Other symptoms related to back pain, such as menstrual problems, asthma, fatigue and rheumatism, are often relieved by this therapy as well.

Aromatherapy Based on the research of French chemist Rene-Maurice Gattefosse, aromatherapy attributes physical and emotional healing aspects to various plants. In the 1930s, Gattefosse burnt his hand while conducting an experiment in his laboratory. Instinctively, he plunged his hand into a nearby container of pure lavender oil. Finding that the pain and redness lessened immediately and the burn healed within a matter of hours, the chemist later embarked on the study of plant oils. Aromatherapists use distilled, aromatic essential oils drawn from the flowers, roots, stalks, leaves and bark of trees and plants. Therapeutic treatments can range from simply unscrewing the cap of the bottle and inhaling its essence to adding a few drops of an oil to a diffuser or bath. The oils are also mixed into a carrier oil for the purpose of massage. Aromatherapy does not attribute the healing capacity of the oil strictly to its scent. The chemical properties of various oils often promote health through antiviral action or other means. It is therefore important to understand the characteristics of the various plants before beginning to use them. For example, people should refrain from putting orange-oil drops directly into bath oil, as this combination is very likely to burn the skin.

Aura soma Aura soma is a form of colour therapy developed by Englishwoman Vicky Wall in the 1980s. Wall, a seventh child of a seventh child, was able to discern auras around people at an early age. After losing her sight, her clairvoyant abilities greatly increased. Shortly afterwards, she was inspired to develop the first set of bottled colours while meditating. She later discovered that the clear oils and plant extracts she chose could be used to energise and balance the human aura. Today there are ninety-six bottles in all; each one consists of two sections containing different or similar colours. Individuals receiving aura soma are asked to choose four bottles; the reader interprets various meanings from the choices. The first bottle represents the soul and the particular path it is on, the second indicates various difficulties that the person has had to overcome in order to grow as a human being, the third stands for what the individual is experiencing in the present moment and the fourth shows how the three previous readings may play out in the future.

Auriculotherapy An integral facet of Chinese acupuncture, auriculotherapy is a system of diagnosing and treating illness throughout the body by examining the ear. This practice is based on the idea that the ear represents the body in microcosm. Practitioners believe that almost every area of the body has a correlating stimulus point within the ear. During treatments, specific points on the auricle, or outer ear, are stimulated either with an electric pulse, gold and silver pellets, a blunt probe, finger pressure or seed treatment to provide relief from a wide range of conditions. Auriculotherapy is particularly effective as a method of controlling pain, as it is believed to adjust neurotransmitters levels. The skin is not necessarily punctured during the process, which is non-invasive and safe. As with acupuncture, individuals may experience relief after only one session, although subsequent treatments may be required for more stubborn ailments.

Ayurveda Developed in India more than a thousand years ago, ayurvedic medicine is a natural system of healing that addresses physical, mental, emotional and spiritual health. According to its principles, each person contains varying combinations of the earth's five basic elements: earth, air, fire, water and ether. These combinations are divided into three categories of vital energy compositions or *doshas*, which govern all bodily functions. These categories are *vata* or wind, *pitta* or bile and *kappa* or phlegm. *Vata*-type energy represents a combination of air and ether, *pitta* is a mix of fire and earth, and *kappa* is a blend of water and ether. According to ayurvedic theory, disturbances among any of these three results in illness. Ayurveda aims to restore and maintain the balance of the these *doshas* through changes in lifestyle, therapeutic body-work and various natural therapies. Treatments, which typically begin with a pulse diagnosis, may include any combination of herbal or mineral supplements, marma-point therapy, detoxification treatments, meditation, herbal-steam therapy, body scrubs, oil massage and modification to diet.

Bach flower remedies In the 1930s, Edward Bach – a medical doctor, bacteriologist and homeopathic physician – developed a system of healing based on the essences from wild plants, trees and bushes. Dr Bach considered a positive state of mind to be essential in order for the body to heal itself. Consequently, the flower remedies – thirty-eight in all – that he devised are intended to transform negative emotions such as hopelessness, fear and worry into positive ones such as confidence, calm and joy. While the remedies are not designed to be used in isolation, they can help individuals gain emotional calm, empowerment and resolution and thereby improve their physical well-being. Several remedies may be taken at once, with a typical dosage being four drops, four times a day. While specialist advice may be sought as to which plants are most appropriate to the individual's needs, over-the-counter Bach flower remedies can be purchased from local pharmacies.

Balneotherapy Balneotherapy is a generic term relating to the practice of massaging the body with or submerging any part of it in water for therapeutic purposes. The practice is one of the oldest-known medical procedures. Various types of water may be used, including mineral water, sea water and water from natural hot springs. The most common technique is for individuals to lie in a specially constructed bathtub equipped with underwater jets. The therapist uses the jets in combination with a hand-held high-powered hose for the purpose of massage. The health benefits of this technique include improved circulation, a strengthened immune system and reduced muscle pain and stress. The American National Institute of Health recently published a report that found that balneotherapy soothed the pain of rheumatoid and osteoarthritis among people suffering from these diseases.

Bioenergetics The practice of bioenergetics is based on teacher Wilhelm Reich's study of the relationship between a person's character and their posture or 'muscular armouring'. This 'armouring' relates to the patterns of chronic muscle tension that develop as a protective response to painful emotional experiences. Psychologist Alexander Lowen, author of *Language of the Body*, adapted Reich's work into a series of basic positions and exercises that are known today as bioenergetics. The technique involves breathing exercises, massage and movements intended to revive life-energy, or 'chi'. While treatments may vary from therapist to therapist, sessions typically focus on enabling individuals to understand their character structure and learning to cultivate a sense of being grounded in the moment. Ultimately, the goal is to release the body's armour and allow people to feel sufficiently empowered to handle any emotional stresses. Patients are also encouraged to develop self-awareness and restore physical, mental and emotional vitality.

Biofeedback Biofeedback is a non-invasive form of treatment during which a therapist attaches sensors or electrodes to the body in order to obtain a variety of readings, or feedback. Even putting a thermometer under the tongue to take a temperature or stepping on a weighing scales to assess weight gain is a form of biofeedback, as both of these things give individuals 'feedback' about their body. Based on this feedback, a person may then decide what action to take – whether to see a doctor about a fever or embark on a weight-reduction programme. Similarly, biofeedback therapists use non-invasive equipment to gauge a client's overall health. Sensors attached to the skin typically measure temperature, pulse, blood pressure, muscle tension and brainwave activity. The measurements are intended to help individuals regulate various autonomic functions, such as heart rate and blood pressure, which were previously thought to be involuntary. With this information, clients can learn to make subtle changes in their responses and behaviours that can result in an improvement in a wide variety of disorders – particularly stress-related ones.

Body harmony 'Body harmony' is a gentle and non-invasive form of hands-on therapy based on the idea that the body remembers and retains all of a person's experiences. During sessions, the therapist carefully 'listens' to the individual's physical and emotional needs and seeks to help them remove and unblock tension and redundant thought patterns. Techniques represent a combination of both traditional and esoteric body-work methods used throughout the world, with the common thread being an emphasis on soft, sensitive touch. The client is viewed as the practitioner and facilitator of his or her own healing responses. Health benefits include pain relief, reduced stress and tension, restored movement, improved posture and enhanced interpersonal relationships. The practice was founded by American massage therapist, behavioural counsellor, chiropractor and shaman Don MacFarland. MacFarland teaches the elements of body harmony and related healing techniques to individuals, families, businesses and governmental agencies in twenty-seven countries.

Boxercise As a recently developed form of primarily aerobic exercise, boxercise can involve anything from a workout modelled on that of Olympic boxers to a combination of kick-boxing and dance techniques. As the health benefits of a boxer's training programme became more widely known, health clubs were soon designing programmes for the general public. Local boxing clubs also began offering recreational or 'fitness' boxing courses. As boxing focuses on optimum cardiovascular fitness, beginners soon notice a reduction in body fat and improved muscle tone, as well as a greater sense of overall well-being. Techniques are meant to promote physical fitness rather than serve as a means of self-defence. Workouts typically involve 70 percent aerobic exercise and 30 percent anaerobic exercise. Often taught by certified boxing coaches, classes typically involve punching bags, one-on-one boxing instruction, rope-skipping, steps, weight-training, abdominal work and callisthenics. Some courses are structured as circuit-training classes and include various activities that increase endurance and strength.

Breema The name 'Breema' is derived from the village of Breemava, which is located in a remote mountainous region in Kurdistan. Breema is a combination of body-work and exercises that is intended to enhance and increase the flow of life-energy while bringing the client's attention to the present moment. Nine 'Principles of Harmony' govern the practice: 'Body Comfortable', 'Full Participation', 'No Extra', 'No Force', 'Non-Judgement', 'Mutual Support', 'Single Moment – Single Activity', 'Gentleness and Firmness' and 'No Hurry – No Pause'. These principles are intended to put the client completely at ease and allow them to reconnect with a shared universal consciousness. Techniques represent a gentle and abbreviated blending of shiatsu and Thai massage, using comfortably supported movements including stretches, leans, brushes, holds and gentle rhythmic movements. Treatments, which are intended to create balance in the individual's life and help them to support others, typically take place on a comfortable padded floor, on which the recipient is either lying or sitting fully clothed. The health benefits of this approach include relief from emotional or physical tension and restored unity between the mind, body and spirit.

Centropic integration Centropic integration is a form of psychotherapy that integrates therapeutic body-work, breathing exercises and other healing modalities such as acupressure and evocative music. The word 'centropic', which refers to the physics principle of 'movement towards the centre', is used to describe the natural tendency of individuals to return to unresolved emotional experiences for the purpose of completion. The therapy is based on the science of psychoneuroimmunology (PNI), which is the biology of memory storage via the neuropeptide system. Practitioners aim to apply the principles of PNI directly to human experience, as well as to provide loving support either individually or in groups to facilitate desired change rapidly. Sessions generally begin with the therapist asking open-ended questions that are related to the client's personal and medical history. Queries then shift towards any emotionally charged areas, such as: 'What are you aware of right now in your body as you talk about your mother?' The client's disclosures often reveal childhood conclusions linked to current struggles with self-esteem, lack of trust and relationship difficulties.

Chakra-balancing The chakras are the human body's seven major energy centres, which vibrate at various frequencies. The chakra system is extremely complex when taken in its entirety: it consists of three master, four major and more than three hundred minor chakras throughout the body. In addition, a number of non-physical chakras are situated outside of the body. Detailed maps demonstrating the complete chakra system, with its many meridians and pathways, have been used since ancient times by Eastern mystics and healers. Each chakra represents a different aspect of human experience, such as spirituality, sexuality, love and creativity. Every thought, word and action is stored in the energy that permeates and surrounds the physical body. When the frequencies are in tune with each other, individuals are internally empowered to deal with specific life challenges and are consequently able to live more meaningful and fulfilling lives. Chakra-balancing consists of gentle hands-on work intended to release stored trauma, thus providing the individual with the energy to address and heal unresolved issues.

Chelation therapy Chelation therapy is used to cleanse the body of toxicity, particularly that caused by heavy metals. Chelating agents can be purchased at pharmacies and consumed orally at home, or they can be administered intravenously under the supervision of a doctor. Patients typically receive an injection of the antioxidant ethylenediamine tetra-acetic acid (EDTA), which binds metals, allowing them to pass through the body via the urinary tract. EDTA is believed to improve circulation, as it reduces abnormal blood-clotting and inflammation. Chelating agents work by binding with toxic heavy metals such as mercury and lead that have entered the body through water, food or other means. The body then naturally excretes the metals. Once the metals have been eliminated, essential nutrients are better able to be absorbed and utilised by the body. The treatment has been shown to be particularly successful as a way of dealing with Parkinson's disease, Alzheimer's disease, multiple sclerosis and arthritis.

Chi nei tsang With roots in the breathing exercises of qi gung used by Chinese Taoist monks, chi nei tsang is a form of massage therapy that integrates the physical, mental, emotional and spiritual aspects of the individual. Literally translated, 'chi nei tsang' means 'working the energy of the internal organs' or 'internal-organs chi transformation'. During sessions, practitioners focus mainly on the abdomen, using deep, soft and gentle touch to train the internal organs to work more efficiently and also address unprocessed emotional responses. During treatments, the body's main vital systems are tackled: digestion, urinary, reproductive, muscular, respiration, lymph, nervous and endocrine, as well as skin and energy meridians, as defined in acupuncture. The technique, which is particularly helpful for people who are overcoming addictions, activates the immune system and helps detoxify the body. It is also used to enhance the absorption of nutrients and to stimulate elimination of toxins.

Chinese medicine Chinese medicine, which has a written history dating back some two and a half thousand years, is a complex system used to promote the body's unique ability to heal itself. Chinese cosmology states that all creation arises from the union of two opposing forces, known as yin and yang, as represented by, among other things, night and day, cold and hot, and wet and dry. The two forces are interdependent: neither one of them can exist without the other. An individual's good health results from the two forces being in harmony. Blockages in this balance result in disease. Practitioners in Chinese medicine emphasise prevention and seek to generate optimum health through restoring a balanced flow of yin and yang, also known as 'chi' or life-energy, as it courses along hundreds of meridians that run throughout the body. Therapies include, but are not limited to, acupuncture, herbs, diet, massage and therapeutic exercise.

Chiropractic Chiropractic involves 'hands-on' spinal manipulation for the relief of temporary lower-back pain. Practitioners believe that when the spinal vertebrae are properly aligned, impulses travelling from the brain to the rest of the body via the spinal cord are able to move freely to various organs, promoting healthy body processes. Aligning the spine also allows the nervous system to return to normal functioning, resulting in the elimination of pain and the activation of the body's innate healing responses. Although the back is the primary focus of chiropractic, manipulations can also be applied to any muscle or joint in the body. Techniques vary according to the practitioner and the method of chiropractic chosen. In some cases, chiropractic is used to relieve acute and chronic pain in the neck, joints and middle back, as well as to combat headaches, muscle spasms and nerve inflammation.

Colonics Many of today's common health problems can be traced to the colon, also known as the large intestine. A high-fat, low-fibre diet can clog the intestines, causing remaining waste to become toxic and pollute the entire body, thus damaging the immune system. The resulting toxaemia can result in constipation, allergies, chronic-fatigue syndrome, migraine headaches and immune-related illnesses such as the common cold. Some researchers and nutritionists believe that this toxaemia can in time lead to more serious illnesses. A colonic performed under the guidance of a trained professional typically involves a diet of whole foods in combination with a series of warm-water or herbal enemas, known as colonic hydrotherapy. Individuals can also remove waste from their bodies through fasting – taking only fruit and vegetable juices – followed by a cleansing enema. Various herbal supplements can also aid in cleansing the colon.

Cranio-sacral therapy This therapy is based on the idea that healthy, living tissues move subtly, producing rhythmic impulses which can be manipulated by sensitive therapists. Around a century ago, osteopath Dr William Garner Sutherland discovered that cranial bones affected by the body's inherent life-force actually move. This motion, which Sutherland terms the 'primary respiratory motion', is connected to an intricate network of tissues and fluids, including the cerebrospinal fluid, the brain and spinal cord, and the membranes surrounding the sacrum and central nervous system. The ability of tissues to express this natural movement is a key factor in assessing their state of health. When emotional or physical trauma occurs, this natural expression may be hindered. Practitioners aim to sense the patterns and qualities of the primary respiratory motion in order to free any areas of inertia and allow the tissues to find healthy expression once again. Treatments are gentle and non-invasive. The client lies fully clothed while a therapist lightly manipulates their skull and pelvic bones. Breathing exercises help facilitate this hands-on work.

Crystals In what is sometimes referred to as gemstone therapy, crystals are used to assist in the healing of the body, mind and spirit. Crystals emit vibrations which are said to improve an individual's aura through realigning the chakras. The vibrations, it is argued, represent universal life-force, which was infused into the stones as the Earth was forming. Each crystal issues a different frequency, thereby addressing different types of energy blockages. The practice of gemstone therapy can be as easy as wearing a necklace made of crystals – although metal is said to inhibit the process. Other methods include 'clearing the crystal' by carefully washing it, then simply holding it while visualising a positive image. A crystal-healer may ask clients to lie down on a plinth while crystals are placed either on or around them. This is done to aid in the release of stress and to facilitate the expression of deeply suppressed emotions.

Cupping A traditional Chinese medicine, cupping involves the application, usually to the back, of one or more small cups made of glass, metal or wood, in order to produce a partial vacuum that has been created in them through heat. The cups may also be moved along the skin without removing the vacuum. The length of time that the cup is held in place varies according to the illness. The method is based on the theory that pain of any type is caused by a lack of oxygen to the cells due to an excess of toxins in the system. The technique, which is intended to stimulate chi, or life-force, is used to draw blood to the surface to create a counterirritant. Practitioners aim to produce a reddish or purple colour in the treated area. Despite its appearance, this result is painless, and it soon disappears. Afterwards, the skin feels warm and may become temporarily rough and bumpy. Benefits of this treatment include improved circulation, diminished swelling, and relief from stomach-ache, vomiting, diarrhoea, coughs and asthma.

Detoxification This is the process of ridding the body of excess toxins. Toxins are caused by poor digestion, poor excretion of waste products, excess alcohol intake, smoking cigarettes and pollution. Toxins in the body disrupt the flow of energy, causing lethargy and poor health. According to Ayurvedic and naturopathic beliefs, excess toxins in the body are a major source of illness. In Ayurvedic tradition, a practitioner may suggest cleansing or detoxifying by taking laxatives, washing out the nasal passages and even therapeutic vomiting. A gentler approach is offered in many health spas of combining a lymph draining massage, healing light therapy and Chinese herbs. Nutritionists advise a diet of fruit, raw vegetables, yoghurt and water to purge toxins from the body. Traditional Chinese Medicine recommends acupuncture and herbal detox. All treatments naturally speed up and detoxify the system and get rid of waste material, which may be lodged in the colon. Detoxification is recommended to increase energy levels, alleviate digestive disorders and help with headaches, allergies, heart conditions and hormonal problems.

Electro-acuscope therapy The electro-acuscope is an electronic instrument that is used in the treatment of a wide range of neuromuscular conditions and has met with particular success in the field of veterinary medicine. It has also been used extensively in veterinary medicine. The device measures tissue conductivity, which is generally very low in an area where the client is experiencing pain. It then introduces a gentle current in electronic waveforms similar to those found in the patient. This increase in electrical activity in the tissues is believed to activate a self-healing response among the cells. The acuscope is commonly used by professional athletic teams and sports-medicine practitioners.

Energy medicine Also known as vibrational healing, energy medicine is based on the idea that the human body is composed of numerous energy fields. Energy medicine is intended to allow a person to regain their holistic balance through detecting and removing any blockages in these fields. The concept of chi, as identified by traditional Chinese medicine, is often utilised by energy healers who typically rely on hands-on healing techniques. Some therapists aim to align a client's energy with that of their own in order to promote harmony, while others may use inanimate objects such as crystals to channel or restore energy. Other practitioners believe that the body's cells vibrate at certain frequencies when healthy, and abnormalities may be determined and corrected using an electronic device. What most methods have in common is the idea that positive thinking and relaxation are essential elements to any individual's overall well-being. Some of the more common forms of energy medicine include acupuncture, bioenergy, body harmony, resonance healing, aura soma and shen, which is used to release repressed feelings and help restore emotional balance.

Fango Heated volcanic mud, otherwise known as fango, is used in therapeutic spa treatments to detoxify the body and enhance skin tone. When applied to specific parts of the body, it can help to alleviate sore joints, muscle pains, arthritis and rheumatism. Although treatments may vary widely from spa to spa, a fango application typically involves a therapist brushing warm mud over the client's body, after which the client rests for twenty to thirty minutes. Some therapists may wrap the client in heated towels to contain the heat. A hot shower follows, after which the client is immersed in a thermal bath. Ozone may be added to the water to stimulate the circulation. After the bath and a short rest, the client receives a massage to stimulate the immune system and tone the muscles. Clients are advised to drink lots of water and eat plenty of fruits and vegetables following a fango treatment.

Fasting Even if one were to eat a balanced, nutritious diet and refrain from alcohol and cigarettes, toxins would still accumulate in the body through the air we breathe. Every so often, the body attempts to eliminate these toxins and consequently releases them from the tissues. From there, they enter the bloodstream, causing feelings of sluggishness or depression, or headaches. Fasting assists the body in detoxifying itself faster and with fewer unpleasant symptoms. Initially, fasts are best undertaken under the supervision of a trained professional at a health farm or residential spa. For those who fast at home on their own, it is important to research fully the various procedures and recommendations involved. The length of time of the fast depends on what the individual would like to accomplish. Three-day fasts are useful for eliminating toxins and cleansing the blood. Five-day fasts encourage the body's healing processes and rebuild the immune system. Although there are many different types of fast, the most common is a diet of fresh vegetable and fruit juices.

Feldenkrais After studying postural re-education therapy, Russian-born Israeli physicist Moshe Feldenkrais developed his namesake system of body-work in the 1940s. The method is based on the idea that the way a person carries him- or herself is directly linked to the way they perceive themselves. Through a series of gentle movements and directed attention, a Feldenkrais therapist aims to improve a person's posture, flexibility, breathing and movement. During sessions, practitioners guide clients through a series of exercises known as 'Awareness Through Movement'. These exercises are intended to help the client recognise poor posture and movement habits. Once these habits are identified, practitioners then educate the client on how to replace them with new patterns that enhance breathing and circulation – a process which is referred to as functional integration. The practice is useful for people who want to break unhealthy postural habits, such as persistent slouching.

Feng shui Feng shui is the ancient Chinese art governing the organization of space and the placement of objects, rooms and buildings to utilise energy, or 'chi', for optimum health, wealth, fulfilment and harmony in life. It originated with villagers and metalsmiths observed the cycles of nature and devising ways of working with them to improve their lives. These cycles consisted of a high and low point, night and day, winter and summer, up and down, and male and female; within the polarity of these opposites they perceived the oneness found in everything. The literal translation of 'feng shui' is 'wind and water', the two main sources of energy in the universe. 'Feng', meaning wind, is utilised to bring in positive energy by means of rivers, rows, avenues and the use of colour, light and music. 'Shui', meaning 'water', is the method by which this energy is contained, to prevent it from moving on too quickly. Feng shui teaches how best to take advantage of 'chi' and improve our lives by working with this energy. An imbalance in the yin or yang – or opposites – of a space is believed to cause an imbalance in the aspects of our lives which correspond with the particular area. Practitioners use a 'ba gua', or map, to read and improve the 'chi' movement of the area it represents; this in turn improves various aspects of our lives.

Focusing Focusing is a series of specific steps designed to enable people to gain a deeper understanding of how their bodies react to various situations. More than being simply about getting in touch with one's feelings, however, the practice is based on the idea that tapping into this innate wisdom allows people to view issues from a much deeper perspective and consequently arrive at new solutions. While it is possible to learn the techniques through reading about them, it is often easier to receive individual instruction in the early stages. Although the process itself is not rigid and allows for various differences and interpretations, six basic steps serve as a loose guide and are used as needed during focusing sessions. The steps, similar to meditative exercises, are known as: 'Clearing a Space', 'Felt Sense', 'Handle', 'Resonating', and 'Asking and Receiving'. Further information about focusing can be had from the Focusing Institute's website at www.focusing.org.

Flotation therapy Flotation therapy is used deeply to relax the mind by excluding external stimulation. Dr John Lilly, a neurophysiologist and psychoanalyst, developed it in the 1970s. Flotation takes place in complete darkness in highly salted water, for reasons of hygiene. The water is kept at skin temperature. During flotation, the body and mind experience a deep sense of relaxation and the brain releases endorphins, which uplift the mood. It is used to treat a range of conditions including stress, depression, high blood pressure, arthritis, painful joints or muscles, back problems or to simply unwind.

Fomentation This is a traditional form of healing which involves applying hot, moist substances such as herbs onto a linen or muslin cloth and applying them to specific area of the body in order to ease pain.

Gestalt therapy Meaning 'organized whole', this therapy was developed by German psychoanalyst Fritz Perls in the 1960s. In one-to-one or group sessions, the individual uses role-play and sometimes dream-recall to become aware of their own behaviour by experiencing their reactions to certain situations. By understanding behaviour patterns and body language, the individual learns to modify their destructive and self-sabotaging behaviour.

Green tea The rich nutritional content of green tea includes Vitamins C, B1, B2, D and K, as well as beta carotene, manganese, potassium, folic acid and selenium. Also found in green tea are molecular particles known as polyphenols. Polyphenols, which are collectively referred to as catechins, have been shown to contain powerful antioxidants that have long-term curative effects on the body. A few of the many health benefits of drinking green tea include strengthening the immune system, hardening tooth enamel, reducing cholesterol and blood fats, strengthening blood vessels, aiding the digestive process and reducing the risks of cancer, arthritis, heart disease and gum disease. Scientific research conducted in China and Japan demonstrated that people who drink three or more cups of green tea every day are less likely to develop various types of cancer, including stomach, lung, prostate and colon cancers. The tea must be drunk without milk, however, as otherwise the milk blocks the body's absorption of polyphenols.

Guided imagery Guided imagery, a technique which has grown in popularity over the last several years, draws on the mind-body connection to help individuals cope with a variety of ailments. Research has demonstrated that certain bodily functions once thought to be beyond the conscious control of a person may be improved through the use of various psychological techniques. Studies have also shown that a definitive link exists between negative emotions and lowered immune function, while positive emotions boost the immune system. For example, one test involves a group of fifty-five women in a neonatal intensive-care unit. The women were played a twenty-minute audiotape of progressive-relaxation exercises, and then descriptions of pleasant surroundings, milk flowing within their breasts and the infant's warm skin against theirs. The women produced twice as much milk as those receiving standard care. Guided imagery is a means of consciously replacing negative thoughts with positive ones. For example, exercises typically involve successively relaxing isolated muscles, doing concentrated breathing exercises and visualising positive scenarios. Health benefits include pain control, a lowered heart rate and reduced stress. Guided imagery has been particularly effective in the treatment of asthma, eating disorders and the symptoms of cancer and AIDS.

Harmonics A form of healing in which particular sounds resonate with specific physical energy centres, or 'chakras', and give the individual a sense of balance, insightfulness and well-being. This practice is used in Buddhist chanting and by monks in Gregorian chant.

Hellerwork Born in Poland in 1940, Joseph Heller emigrated to the United States to escape the threat of Nazism. Heller settled in Los Angeles and embarked on a career in aerospace engineering. After receiving a rolfing treatment, he was so impressed that he began to study under Ida Rolf. Within three years, Heller had been appointed director of the Rolfing Institute. Believing that simply restructuring the body was not enough, Heller eventually developed his namesake system of bodywork. Central to the method is the interweaving of body, mind and emotions. A complete Hellerwork treatment involves eleven sessions, each of which lasts approximately ninety minutes and deals with a different aspect of the body. Treatments involve verbal dialogue, breathing exercises and deep-tissue massage, which is intended to relieve tension in connective tissue. Another important element of Hellerwork is movement re-education, which includes video feedback of the client performing everyday movements such as sitting, standing, walking and bending. Anyone interested in receiving Hellerwork sessions directly from its founder can travel to Heller's Mount Shasta Clinic in northern California for a five- to six-day programme.

Herbalism Herbalism or herbal medicine is used in ayurvedic tradition, traditional Chinese medicine and Western herbal medicine to heal physical and emotional illness. The entire plant is used, although each part of it may have a different healing function. Given that the herbs are derived from plants, the body easily absorbs their molecular make-up and, if administered correctly, they produce no contra-indications. They are prescribed to support the body's natural healing powers. As with many other forms of holistic therapy, the underlying cause of the illness is also treated by the practitioner.

Holoenergetics This is a form of psychotherapeutic energy healing developed by the author of *Healing With Love,* Dr Leonard Laskow. During sessions, clients are encouraged to go to the root or source of their illness with absolute honesty and release it. According to the principles of holoenergetics, it is through releasing the root cause and coming to terms with the problem that people's bodies will be aligned with the positive energy of the universe and their illness, whether physical or mental, will be healed. During holoenergetic sessions the client is encouraged to release themselves from illusion and in doing so replace dysfunctional patterns with healthy ones.

Holotropic breath-work The use of breath-work to release emotional suffering and difficult physical experiences originated in the 1970s from the work of Stanislav and Christina Grof. In a breathing session, the individual will be encouraged to use breath to manifest, amplify and release blockages in the mind and body. The purpose of holotropic breath-work is to work at a level far deeper than that of our conscious understanding. Work is usually done in groups, with those attending alternating in the role of 'sitter' or 'breather'. Experienced holotropic breath-work trainers facilitate and oversee the sessions. The therapy is often used to help individuals overcome depression, premenstrual tension, migraine, muscular tension, backache and a wide range of psychosomatic pain.

Homeopathy An accepted medical discipline in many countries throughout the world, homeopathy is used to treat a wide variety of illnesses. Around the turn of the nineteenth century, German physician Samuel Hahnemann discovered that a malaria remedy caused healthy volunteers to develop symptoms of the disease. This led him to explore the converse effects of the phenomenon, eventually leading to his theory of 'like cures like'. Although this theory by no means a new one, Hahnemann took it a step further by integrating the 'Law of Infinitesimals', which states that the more diluted a remedy is, the more powerful is its ability to heal. During sessions, practitioners will undertake a thorough initial consultation, during which they record anything the patient might wish to discuss. In addition to physical, mental and emotional symptoms, patients might also mention such things as family relationships, nuances of thought, dreams and recurring ideas. Through understanding the patient's history, the homeopath aims to treat the root of the ailment rather than its symptoms. Practitioners can then avail solely of homeopathic remedies, or use them in combination with other holistic therapies. A homeopathic physician may prescribe conventional medicines as well as homeopathic treatments.

Hydrotherapy The therapeutic properties of water have been valued and used by many societies, from the Ancient Greeks to Native Americans. In hydrotherapy, water is used in a variety of ways – hot and cold, in liquid or steam form, and internally and externally – to energize and cleanse the body and to promote good health. Although spas have been popular since Roman times, they are enjoying renewed interest as individuals benefit from additional treatments such as whirlpool baths, Sitz baths, seaweed baths, Turkish baths, steam rooms and cabinets, and saunas and wraps as part of their overall spa experience. Hydrotherapy is said to improve blood circulation, stimulate circulation in the internal organs and be particularly effective for conditions such as anaemia, angina, arthritis and asthma. Dead Sea salts, seawater and seaweed are often used in hydrotherapy to nourish the skin and increase mineral intake. It is also used to relieve swollen joints, relax the muscles or simply promote a sense of well-being and inner peace.

Hypnotherapy Hynotherapists induce trance-like states in their clients for psychosomatic and psychoneurotic healing. The therapy is commonly used to release the individual from addiction such as cigarette smoking, or to help them overcome phobias and fears. Hypnotherapists expound on its safety, stating that no individual can be hypnotised against their will, as the subconscious mind is extremely unlikely to be open to unreasonable suggestions. During hypnosis the practitioner may delve into the past to understand the reasons for current behaviour. They may also feed the individual's subconscious various suggestions to change their views on a particular aspect of their lives, such as the reasons for their smoking or lack of self-esteem.

Indian head massage As the name suggests, Indian head massage originated in India, where it was used in ayurvedic tradition to improve blood flow, nourish the hair follicles and alleviate anxiety. Sessions usually last thirty minutes and involve an ancient form of massage used on the head, neck and shoulders.

Iridology Iridology is a diagnostic tool used to study the delicate structures of the eye's iris in order to analyse the body's biochemistry and any accompanying emotional and circumstantial factors. According to iridologists, the colouring, condition and markings in the eye act like a viewfinder in a camera, giving an overall picture of the patient's health. They claim that each of the nerve endings in the iris correspond to the linked body organ and tissue. Iridologists use a map, devised by American doctor Bernard Jensen, to relate a particular part of the iris with a particular body organ or area and treat this part of the body accordingly.

Jin shin jitsu This form of body-work was developed in Japan by Jiro Murai. It is similar to shiatsu and jin shin acupressure in that the practitioner uses his or her fingers, thumbs, elbows and knees to exert pressure on meridian points throughout the body. This is to promote 'chi' flow and release any blockages in energy flow. In jin shin jitsu, combinations of energy points are held for a minute or longer. According to the principles of this type of body-work, stimulating energy flow and releasing blockages restores health to individual organs and rebalances the mind and body.

Journaling Psychologists and counsellors often advise clients to write their thoughts and feelings into a daily journal to give coherency to their life events and release disturbing emotions derived from painful experiences. The practice is also sometimes used in creative-writing workshops to increase creativity.

Juicing The World Health Organisation recommends a daily intake of five portions of fruit and vegetables for optimal health. Juicing is an easy and enjoyable way to include the vitamins and minerals required for a healthy diet.

As the juices use raw vegetables and fruit, the body benefits from maximum nutrition. Juicing is also used to cleanse the digestive system and detoxify the liver. These health benefits are felt more quickly than would be the case with solid foods as the juice is rapidly assimilated into the body. Naturopaths often recommend juicing particular fruits and vegetables as a treatment for specific conditions or to benefit various organs.

Ki massage Also known as kiatsu massage, ki massage draws on the principles of the martial art of aikido to help facilitate the healing of injuries. Relaxed and gentle techniques are intended to relieve stiffness and restore the flow of 'ki', or energy, throughout the body. Ki massage practitioners follow the lines of the body, rather than the various acupoints used in acupressure. The client lies, fully clothed, in a comfortable position while the therapist places gentle and steady pressure along the muscle and limbs.

Kinesiology Through stimulating or relaxing specific muscle groups, kinesiology practitioners determine health imbalances in the organs and muscles and seek to correct them through gentle manipulation and massage. The technique is based on principles similar to those used in acupuncture – specifically, that energy coursing through the body affects health. Essentially, this energy becomes a valuable tool that can improve the connection between the body and the mind. Through restoring a balanced flow of this energy, the body's natural health-enhancing processes are activated. While methods vary, therapists typically manipulate or massage various points throughout the body that correspond with the energy meridians defined by traditional Chinese medicine. Practitioners also offer advice on diet, exercise and lifestyle. The technique was originally known as 'applied kinesiology', which had its roots in chiropractic traditions. 'Touch for Health' (TFH), a synthesis of naturopathy, osteopathy, modern chiropractic and acupuncture that developed as a branch of kinesiology, is a system of training designed for the general public to learn the basic principles of the method.

Kneipp Father Sebastian Kneipp established the first health farms in Europe based on nature being the natural cure for illness. He used fasting, nutrition, hydrotherapy (hot- and cold-water cures), herbs and exercise for healing. Naturopathy later developed on the principles laid down by Kneipp.

Kombucha tea Advocates of kombucha list up to a hundred benefits it offers, including relief from arthritis pain, insomnia, headaches, menopausal hot flushes and muscular aches and pain. Some also claim it is the ultimate hangover cure! It is believed to have been introduced to Japan in 414 by a Korean doctor known as Kombu. The tea is made by placing the kombucha culture of friendly bacteria and yeast in a solution of black or green tea and sugar. This is left to ferment for up to fifteen days and is then filtered for drinking. Kombucha tea tastes like a lightly sparkling apple cider with a slightly bitter tang. It is available from supermarkets, although many kombucha fans, who attest to its benefits, brew their own.

Kur Kur is a series of spa treatments combined with cultural activities such as seminars in natural health, meditation, cultural history and fine arts. The spa treatments use organic and natural ingredients in thermal baths. The combination of spa treatments and seminars is designed to develop good health, awareness and growth in body and mind.

La stone therapy This is a deeply centring massage therapy used to promote an intense feeling of calm and inner tranquillity. During the massage, heated basaltic rocks are glided over the body using essential oils. The therapy is also used to promote toxin-clearing and gentle energy-balancing.

Light therapy Sunlight contains the full-wavelength light spectrum, which is absent in many artificial forms of lighting. Insufficient exposure to the complete spectrum can result in seasonal affective disorder (SAD), suppressed immune function, fatigue, hair loss, hyperactivity and other chronic illnesses. The pineal gland, which is affected by the presence of light, regulates various bodily functions, such as the production of hormones, body temperature and sleep intervals. Disturbances in these functions can lead to insomnia and other sleep disorders, overeating and loss of libido. Light therapy is the use of light, natural and otherwise, to re-establish normal body rhythms. It is particularly helpful for people who live in regions that receive particularly low amounts of sunlight in the winter months, or shift workers who may have to get up in the middle of the night. Some of the more common forms of this treatment include bright-light, ultraviolet, cold-laser and full-spectrum light therapy. Each of these forms involves controlled exposure to varying intensities of light. A dawn simulator, for example, is a com-puterised device programmed to wake sleepers with gradually brightening light.

Lymphatic stimulation Lymph in the lymphatic system nourishes the tissue cells and takes away the body's waste products. The lymph nodes filter the lymph as it passes through and thus help prevent infection passing into the bloodstream. Stimulating the lymphatic system with massage improves the elimination of chemical wastes, such as lactic acid, from the body. A build-up of lactic acid leads to pain and stiffness in the joints and muscles.

Macrobiotics The macrobiotic lifestyle includes a diet that is low in fat and sugar and high in fibre. It utilizes food to provide nutrition and balance and to heal ailments. According to the macrobiotic approach, diet is linked to mood and so stimulants such as coffee, tea and sugar are avoided as they cause fluctuations in mood and cause cravings. People who follow a macrobiotic diet seek health, happiness and serenity by eating healthily. They aim to live according to the natural laws of life. Food is generally eaten when in season and is located locally where possible. The macrobiotic diet contains organic foods rather than processed foods, which may contain additives and colourings.

Magnets Magnets used in magnetic therapy are placed on the client's body to enhance blood flow. According to practitioners, iron atoms in the red corpuscles of the blood respond to the magnets. It is said to improve the supply of oxygen to the cells, stimulate the body's metabolism and help remove waste products. Magnetic therapy is also used in orthodox medicine, with electrical equipment generating electromagnetic fields that affect the body's natural electrical currents, thereby aiding the healing process. Magnets are often used for bone problems, particularly osteoporosis and fractures, magnetic wristbands are used for arthritis and inflamed joints and sprains, and fatigue, insomnia, hormonal imbalance and circulation problems are also treated with magnetic therapy. Magnetized water is used to aid digestion and magnetic insoles are used to improve blood circulation and increase energy levels.

Marma-point therapy An ayurvedic healing method that involves a massage with oils given by two masseurs, who work together on either side of you, stimulating the body's marma points. Ayurveda is a holistic system of healthcare which originated in India and is now a way of life for millions in both the East and the West. Marma points are similar to acupoints in shiatsu and acupressure. The technique is intended to improve the flow of 'prana', or life-energy, taken in through food and breath and to eliminate 'ama', or impurities, from the body.

Meditation While there are many different forms of meditation, spanning religions and cultures from Africa to Asia to the Americas, some methods are part of a religious practice and others are not. Similarly, although many disciplines cost nothing to participate in, teachers of some forms of meditation charge fees. The aim of meditation is to focus on the present moment and help people attain the wisdom to revitalise their lives and take positive action to improve themselves and the world at large. Research has shown that meditation can increase blood flow and reduce blood pressure, the heart rate and the respiratory rate. This practice also helps relieve stress, depression, chronic pain, insomnia, tension headaches and even heart disease. A typical meditation session may involve sitting in a comfortable position in the home and focusing on the breath or reciting a mantra – a phrase or word that helps a person slow their busy mind and counteract stress and unease. Some well-known mantras are said to have profoundly transformative effects. Examples include: *'Nam myoho renge kyo'* (the essence of the Lotus Sutra in Buddhism), 'Hail Mary, full of grace . . . ' (the Roman Catholic prayer) and *'Shema Yisroel, adonai elohenu, adonai ehod . . . '* (Jewish praise of God).

Moor mud Mud has been used since the time of the Pharaohs for its purifying qualities. The Ancient Greeks used bands of plaster hardened with a coating of clay mud in the treatment of fractures. Its medicinal properties have been rediscovered and advocated by world-renowned naturopaths such as Kneipp, Kuhn and Felke. Moor mud, renowned for its healing properties, is taken from the two-thousand-year-old Neyhardting Moor in Austria and used in health spas throughout the world. The mud contains more than seven hundred herbs and plants and is used in masks, soaps, baths, compresses and mud drinks. Mud is taken externally or internally to treat conditions such as arthritis, rheumatism, sciatica, fractures, bruises, sprains, bumps, migraines and shingles, and to aid digestion.

Moxibustion Used in conjunction with acupuncture and herbs, moxa sticks or moxa cones are used to create heat and stimulate acupoints. Although the cones are placed on the skin and the stick is positioned near to it, the heat is kept at a comfortable level. This treatment is mainly used in conditions where there is an energy or yang deficiency. The herb moxa is derived the dried leaves of the mugwort or wormwood tree.

Music therapy The controlled use of music or certain environmental sounds in the treatment of various mental, physical or emotional disorders is known as music therapy or sound therapy. Research has demonstrated the therapeutic capabilities of music and it is currently used to treat a range of chronic conditions, such as depression, asthma, high blood pressure, ulcers and migraines. The actual therapy can involve anything from listening to specific pieces of music or sound, participating in individual or group music lessons, singing, or engaging in physical activity that is accompanied by music. One particularly interesting method of sound therapy is known as the Tomatis method. This discipline was developed by French physician Alfred A. Tomatis in the 1970s. The method, which is based on the idea that the ear plays an essential role in healthy brain functioning, is used to treat people with conditions such as attention deficit disorder, autism, dyslexia and Down's syndrome. Dr Tomatis developed the method after he was consulted in relation to a case of depression and fatigue among an order of Benedictine monks – a condition that medical experts had failed to alleviate. When he learned that the monks had removed Gregorian chants from their daily schedule, Dr Tomatis recommended that they resume them. Shortly afterwards, their symptoms disappeared. Treatments involve enrolling in a sixty-hour listening programme, which includes listening each day to filtered Mozart, Gregorian chants or the client's mother's voice, and enjoying art, games or social interactions.

Myotherapy This form of therapy, devised by fitness and health pioneer Bonnie Prudden, is used to relieve muscle spasms, improve circulation and alleviate pain. Practitioners view pain as a manifestation of emotional stress. Clients are shown how to seek out and defuse trigger points within the muscles and, in doing so, release trapped pain, aches and other ailments. Exercise plays a part in the treatment, to restore health to all areas of the body.

Naturopathic medicine Naturopathic medicine has its origins in European medicine and was influenced by Hippocrates, Galen, Paracelsus and modern day nature doctor Alfred Vogel. Naturopaths use natural therapies and healing practices such as fasting, good nutrition, exercise, homeopathy, acupuncture, herbal medicine and water to heal illness. They may also use modern methods such as bioresonance, ozone therapy and colon hydrotherapy. Giving individual time and care to each patient, naturopaths view the person as a holistic unity of body, mind and spirit and consider lifestyle and environmental issues and emotional and physical health when treating patients. It is a wide-ranging discipline that is used to heal a variety of ailments and help maintain good health.

Neurolinguistic programming Developed by John Grinder and Richard Bandler in the 1970s, neurolinguistic programming (NLP) examines how we process external experiences through the five senses of seeing, hearing, feeling, smelling and tasting. This information is processed by the senses and then represented internally in the *holos* of mind and body. We also interpret and express our beliefs through language, and an awareness of our linguistic approach is crucial to our success, according to NLP practitioners. NLP programming involves the installation of a plan or procedure, used in our neurological systems, to achieve a specific outcome. By directing the individual towards something they want, rather than away from something they wish to avoid, NLP encourages the individual to have a goal to work towards and to focus on this goal in a positive way.

Neuromuscular therapy see **Trigger-point therapy**

Nutrition therapy What we eat has a profound effect on our health. A healthy diet, in addition to giving the body its basic requirements of nutrients, also reduces the risks of disease and enhances the body's ability to heal from illness. It can also increase energy levels and influence the way we feel. A nutrition therapist will advise the client on how to maintain a healthy, balanced and enjoyable diet based on understanding the purpose and healing properties of all the foods mentioned. This nutrition advice will be tailored to the individual's needs. Moving away from the typical Western diet of refined carbohydrates and sugar, saturated fats and processed foods, which have little nutritional value, a nutrition therapist will give advice on following a nourishing diet which provides all the essential proteins, vitamins and minerals. They will also provide advice on cooking methods and give menu suggestions.

Osteopathy Developed by US Army physician Dr Andrew Taylor Still in the 1870s, osteopathic medicine involves structural diagnosis and manipulative techniques intended to correct problems in the musculoskeletal system and promote the body's innate healing processes. The practice focuses on the importance of the musculoskeletal system as it relates to the proper functioning of all body systems and internal organs. Today, osteopathic physicians receive training as medical doctors and often utilise conventional medical therapies in combination with Osteopathic Manipulative Therapy (OMT). During treatments, the whole person rather than just the physical ailment is taken into account. A physical examination may include traditional diagnostic methods such as X-rays and laboratory tests. Issues that may be causing the illness, such as lifestyle, nutrition, environment and psychological or emotional factors, are also addressed. Techniques used during sessions include massage, muscle pressure and instruction in body mechanics, nutrition, stress reduction and exercise.

Par course A walking trail equipped with several stations providing equipment and instructions for exercise at various points.

Permaculture Permaculture, from the words 'permanent' and 'agriculture', is the design and maintenance of an agricultural system based on ecological principles. Natural waste material from one system is used for the growth of the next system, by means of recycling. The primary aim of permaculture, which can be used in buildings, gardens, orchards and woodlands, is to contribute to a more wholesome approach to land and building use, minimising damage to the natural environment and available resources. Bill Mollison expands on his theory of permaculture in his book *An Introduction to Permaculture*.

Pilates Pilates first came to prominence in New York in the 1940s, when Joseph Pilates developed his unique approach to teaching dance and choreography. Although there are varying forms of pilates, the basic principles are the same. The exercises aim to develop a longer, leaner body and improve overall flexibility and posture through slow, controlled and mind-focused exercises. The discipline is usually taught in groups with soft background music, although many people benefit from one-to-one instruction using specific pilates equipment. Many physiotherapists are recommending that their patients learn these gentle exercises, in order to alleviate pain from recurring back problems, repetitive-strain injury or muscular tension.

Polarity therapy Developed in the late nineteenth century by naturopath Dr Randolph Stone, polarity therapy draws on the principles of traditional Chinese medicine and ayurvedic principles. In this form of body-work, pressure is applied to particular points in the body to locate and relieve stagnation and encourage the free flow of energy around the body. Illness is perceived as being a direct result of stagnation and reduced energy currents. Practitioners may use a number of therapies to restore balance in the body; these include manipulation of pressure points, breathing exercises, reflexology and nutrition advice.

Pressotherapy Used primarily in rehabilitation, pressotherapy is a form of body-work designed gradually and progressively to drain metabolic waste and encourage cell regeneration. It involves a hand massage using varying degrees of pressure.

Psychosynthesis Italian psychiatrist Dr Roberto Assagioli developed psychosynthesis in the early twentieth century. It is referred to as the 'psychology of the soul', as it guides the clients to realise and experience a level of consciousness in which thoughts and emotions are merged with a higher or spiritual level of awareness. This is encouraged through creative expression in the form of painting, movement and writing. By connecting to the individual's highest potential, the client naturally realises solutions to their problems and finds it easier to make decisions which are ultimately right for them.

Qi gung Pronounced *'chee gung'*, qi gung is an ancient Chinese system of movement, meditation and breathing designed to enhance the flow of life-energy through the body in order to maintain good health. As a facet of traditional Chinese medicine, qi gung recognises the body's inherent ability to heal itself. Great emphasis is placed on the connection between mind and body. Simultaneous physical and mental exercises are intended to promote health and vitality. Mental exercises are primarily meditative, while physical practices involve graceful, low-impact movement. Benefits of the practice can include improved circulation and digestion, bolstering of the immune system, increased physical strength and more efficient functioning of bodily systems. The techniques can be easily learned and practised by people of all ages. The best way to learn qi gung is through individual or group instruction. Beginners generally start out with two thirty-minute sessions per week and build up to daily practice of the discipline. There are many qi gung exercises in lying, sitting, standing and walking positions. Specific exercises may be recommended for certain ailments.

Rebirthing Rebirthing is a type of psychotherapy which claims to release emotional and physical traumas experienced during birth. Practitioners contend that the newborn's experiences at childbirth have a fundamental impact on future relationships, creating feelings of separation or fear later in life. During a session, a combination of breathing techniques and therapeutic body-work is used to allow the individual back, to re-experience difficult emotions in a safe environment. Many people remember details about their birth and understand how these experiences may have negatively affected decisions they took later in life. It is through this awareness that they replace negative decisions with positive ones for the future.

Reflexology Although it is a contemporary form of body-work, the principles of reflexology have been practised for thousands of years. The term itself implies that a reflexive response may be triggered by stimulating specific points in the feet. These points correspond to ten zones, mapped out originally by the American Dr William Fitzgerald in the 1900s, then further researched by his protégée, physiologist Eunice Ingham. On the basis of ten years of research, Ingham mapped out the relationships between an individual's feet and the functions of the various organs, gland and body parts with which they correlate. While pressure is primarily applied to the feet, specific points along the hands and ears can also create change in other areas of the body. Research demonstrates that reflexology helps to alleviate a number of chronic ailments, including arthritis, muscle pain, insomnia, anxiety, diarrhoea and headaches. Proponents believe that regular reflexology treatments prevent illness. Treatments, which can last anything from twenty to sixty minutes, are gentle and relaxing.

Reiki Translated from the Japanese as 'universal life energy', reiki is a form of healing developed by Japanese theologian Dr Mikao Usui in the late-nineteenth century. Usui endeavoured to recover a Buddhist system of healing that was thought to have been lost. After intensive study in the United States and Japan, Usui discovered the system in ancient Buddhist texts written in Sanskrit. He then undertook a twenty-one-day fast and meditation on top of a holy mountain, where he received a vision that revealed the method of activating and transmitting universal life energy that is now taught as reiki. Practitioners place their hands either on or just above specific energy centres throughout the client's body. These centres correspond to chakras, which affect the internal organs and glands of the recipient. Through this energy transmission, the client's energy pathways are cleared, allowing renewed life-force to flow unimpeded. Sessions, which take place in total silence, may last anything from thirty to sixty minutes. The practitioner often relies on intuition as to which areas need attention. Research has demonstrated that the health benefits of reiki include accelerated healing, a strengthened immune system, relief from stress and depression, the elimination of toxins, and a reduced sense of helplessness when facing trauma.

Relaxation skills/stress-management techniques These techniques are used to promote a sense of calm in stressful situations. They may include breathwork, positive daydreams such as remembering a happy moment, or self-hypnosis to achieve a restorative state of relaxation. Self-hypnosis is usually performed by visualising a scene of tranquillity and accompanying this with the sounds of soft music or imagining soothing sounds, such as the sound of the sea. Positive affirmations like 'I am completely at peace and trust the best outcome will happen for me' can also be used. Aromatherapy oils such as camomile, lavender, neroli and sage are also used to relieve tension. The client is encouraged to meditate or walk for five minutes to escape from stress and clear their head for positive decision-making. Exercise and complementary therapies are increasingly used to relax the mind and alleviate stress.

Rolfing Also referred to as structural integration, rolfing is a massage technique that focuses primarily on the connective tissue holding the muscles and bones in place. Created by American biochemist Dr Ida Rolf in the 1950s, the method is based on the idea that, as tissues lose elasticity, they shorten and eventually harden. As this happens, the body becomes locked into an unhealthy holding pattern, which results in a limited range of normal physical movement, and misalignment with gravity. Dr Rolf asserted that physical and mental problems result from this misalignment. During sessions, practitioners apply sliding pressure using fingers, thumbs, knuckles and elbows to stretch the connective tissue, making it supple and pliable, thus bringing the body back into alignment. While some may find the therapy uncomfortable, the desired result of loosening adhesions and improving body alignment is often achieved. A series of ten one-on-one therapy sessions lasting approximately sixty minutes each is the recommended treatment, with a particular area of the body being focused on during each session. Rolfing is particularly effective with chronic pain and stiffness caused by poor posture, carpal-tunnel syndrome, stress and athletic injuries.

Rosen method Gentle touch is used to facilitate a process of self-discovery in the Rosen method. American physical therapist Marion Rosen created this therapy, which is based on the idea that when individuals suppress painful emotions and memories, they prevent themselves from living fully. The practice, although relaxing, is technically not a massage. Practitioners aim to detect areas in the body where individuals are 'holding' the muscles as a means of protection against experiencing distressing feelings. The client is guided through the safe release of both emotional and muscular barriers in order to facilitate the blossoming of the person. During treatments, traditional massage strokes are not used and there is no application of strong pressure or force. Observing the client's breath is also an important element of the method: for instance, the diaphragm is carefully observed for shallow breathing or holding patterns. Practitioners may hold the client's hand for a moment or two while placing another hand on the diaphragm or abdomen to encourage awareness and release. If a particular area appears too hard or lacking in movement, practitioners may ask questions intended to help clients understand what he or she may be holding back.

Rubenfeld synergy Ilana Rubenfeld developed this technique of healing and listening touch by integrating the principles of Alexander and Feldenkrais body-work, with the philosophical teachings of gestalt and Ericksonian hypnotherapy teachings. It uses body and mind exercises to relax, stretch and enhance awareness. The technique is based on the understanding that disturbing memories, emotions and deep yearnings are stored in the body and cause emotional pain. By combining body- and mind-work, uncomfortable memories of the past are released on both a physical and emotional level.

Salt glow This treatment, which is used in spa treatments to cleanse and exfoliate the skin, involves lathering the body with moist salt grains and may be followed by a seaweed mud wrap and aromatherapy massage.

Seichim Similar to reiki, seichim (pronounced *'say kim'*) is a form of energy healing. While working as a Peace Corps volunteer in Yemen in 1978, Patrick Zeigler visited the Great Pyramids in Egypt. Intuitively believing that he must spend the night inside one of the pyramids, he entered a small tunnel which led to the King's Chamber and spent the day meditating. When evening came, Zeigler lay down inside the sarcophagus. A few hours later, he began to hear a deep sound coming towards him and noticed a figure-eight pattern hovering over him. After this experience, Zeigler spent time studying with both a Sufi master and a reiki master, each of whom helped him understand and interpret his experience. The result is the method of energy healing practised today. Zeigler is careful to assert that he did not invent the technique but that it has been around for thousands of years, as evidenced by mention of it in *The Egyptian Book of the Dead* and other sacred Egyptian texts. A number of variations in the practice have developed since Zeigler began teaching the techniques; these variations include seichim, sekhem, SKHM, Isis seichim and kaun yin seichim.

Shamanism Shamanism was commonly used by indigenous people in America, Africa and Australia and was also an important part of ancient Celtic and Siberian culture. Shamanism involves 'journeying' to and realising a heightened state of consciousness. Many shamanic healers claim that this experience actually involves communicating with the spirit world. It is a form of healing by seeking spiritual guidance relating to the meaning of life and decision-making. A trance-like state of altered consciousness is induced using dancing and repetitive chanting and drumming. During this state, knowledge is said to be imparted indicating the cause of illness or suffering and how to heal it. This practice is also used by shamans to heal the soul. Most shamanic workshops take place over a weekend.

Shen therapy Richard Pavek created this form of therapy in the 1970s to release energy blocks and direct energy through the client's key emotion centres, releasing repressed emotions which, if not dealt with, would cause illness. He associated various emotional centres throughout the body with particular feelings, such as the heart and chest area with love, sadness and grief, the digestive tract with excitement and anger, and the genital area with inadequacy and confidence. When emotions are repressed in these areas, illness may result. Each session lasts between an hour and an hour and a half; the client remains clothed on the plinth while the practitioner uses his or her hands to balance energy in the body. This technique is commonly used to tackle emotional ailments like eating disorders and may also be used for premenstrual tension or stress.

Shiatsu Translated from the Japanese, shiatsu means 'finger pressure'. This ancient technique, which has roots in traditional Chinese medicine, is used to prevent disease by maintaining an internal bodily environment that is conducive to good health. The therapy is used to open communication between the body and the mind in order to enable a sufficient flow of dynamic life-energy – or chi – throughout the internal organs and systems. Practitioners aim to feel and interpret the flow of chi along the client's energy channels, or meridians. Treatments normally last between sixty and ninety minutes, during which the client sits or lies fully clothed on either the floor or a plinth. After an initial assessment, distinct pressure – of varying duration and depth – is applied to different points along the body's meridians. Although this pressure is normally applied with the thumbs, the practitioner also may apply it with the palms, elbows, feet and knees. The client may then be instructed in certain stretches and corrective exercises, followed by recommendations for changes in diet and lifestyle that are appropriate to the client's condition.

Sitz baths Used as part of hydrotherapy treatments, sitz baths are a set of two hip baths, one of which is filled with hot water, the other with cold water. It is a bath with two halves. The client sits in the hot section for three minutes, with their feet immersed in the cold half of the bath. They then sit in the cold half for one minute, with their feet in heated water on the other side. This treatment is believed to be particularly effective in improving poor blood circulation.

Somato-emotional release Expanding on the principles of cranio-sacral therapy, somato-emotional release (SER) is used to rid the body and mind of the residual effects of physical or emotional trauma. This mind-body technique was developed by Dr John Upledger during his work with autistic children at Michigan State University in the 1970s. Upledger observed the children spontaneously moving into positions that would allow the release of withheld memories and patterns with an emotional basis. He eventually dis-covered that dialogue could be used to help facilitate this release. Through 'speaking' with various parts of the body in a respectful and appropriate manner, an individual's 'inner physician' could be accessed to help resolve old conflicts which may have been hindering a return to overall well-being. Upledger developed the practice of therapeutic imagery and dialogue, which is an important element of SER. This gentle and non-invasive process occurs only at the invitation of the client, making it an effective and safe means of releasing various issues that may have been holding up the individual's healing process for many years.

Soul retrieval For more than forty thousand years, shamanic healers have practised the ritual of soul retrieval from throughout Africa, the Americas, Asia and Europe. Traditionally, the function of the shaman is to bridge the gap between ordinary and non-ordinary reality, or between humans and the spirit world. Shamans have 'travelled' to this ethereal realm to access help for their clients in the wake of emotional, physical or mental trauma. Such traumatic experiences can sometimes hurt so deeply that individuals are unable to heal the wounds or overcome their own denial mechanisms. Consequently, a part of the soul splinters off, resulting in disease and loss of power. Psychologists refer to this phenomenon as 'dis-association'. According to shamanism, this part of the soul may be located in other realities. A healer journeys to these realities to obtain guidance for the client with the help of power animals, as well as to remove any blockages in the individual's energy field, or aura. While techniques vary from culture to culture, ceremonies normally involve percussive instruments such as drums and rattles, which enable the shaman to enter into an altered state and communicate with spirits.

Sound therapy See **Music therapy**

Stress-management techniques See **Relaxation skills**

Sweat-lodge ceremony Native American sweat-lodge ceremonies are communal cleansing and purifying events. They aim to bring people into contact with deeper elements within themselves by voicing their own fears, concerns, prayers, wishes or intentions within a supportive and safe environment. The participants are involved in building the sweatlodge, which is made from bamboo shoots and heated blankets. Within the lodge, heated stones and sage create a warm, cleansed atmosphere, in which individuals sit and then share and discard unwanted thoughts and emotions, becoming renewed in their hopes for the future.

T'ai chi T'ai chi, which is also known as t'ai ji, is a major part of the traditional Chinese martial art of wu shu. It was first mentioned in *The Book of Changes*, written anonymously during the Zhou Dynasty in 221 BC. 'In all changes exists t'ai ji, which causes the two opposites, which cause the four seasons, and the four seasons cause the eight natural phenomena.' There are many different styles of t'ai chi, although they commonly involve slow and even movements. This graceful form of exercise combines a unique, gentle series of exercises that combine grace with strength, and concentration with constant flow. In addition to improving the body's physique, t'ai chi is said to reduce cholesterol levels, improve spinal suppleness and induce a feeling of spiritual well-being.

Tantra Tantra is an Indian spiritual tradition that promotes a mystical union with all life; sexual union is only a small subset of the discipline. Many schools of tantra have developed over time, with viewpoints ranging from the extremely heterodox to the orthodox. Although it is not a religious philosophy, tantra's techniques embrace a deeply spiritual understanding of life. In general, tantric practices are used to heal feelings of separation, as well as to develop an awareness of – and eventually to command the natural flow of – energy between one person and another. Sexual energy is viewed as a loving friend rather than something which must be suppressed. The philosophy asserts that individuals can celebrate life when the idea of separation, or 'otherness', disappears from the body and mind, allowing people to meet on various levels of consciousness, including the physical, mental, intellectual and spiritual. Practitioners aim to liberate the consciousness and connect the individual with planes of existence beyond the material world.

Thalassotherapy For centuries, sea water has been used in the treatment of disease. The Greek physician Hippocrates prescribed the internal and external use of it to preserve and restore good health. The word 'thalassa' is Greek for 'sea water'. Although theories about the roots of thalossotherapy differ, many credit its creation to French cyclist Louison Bobet, who used sea-water treatments to recover from a sports injury in the 1960s. The French Medical Academy defines thalassotherapy as 'The use of sea water, seaweed, sea mud or other sea resources and/or the marine climate for the purpose of medical treatment or treatment with a medicinal effect.' Medical doctors in France today prescribe thalassotherapy treatments, as they have been shown to relieve arthritis, asthma, stress, insomnia, inflammation and menopause and to aid recovery from surgery. It is also a particularly effective treatment for chronic skin ailments such as atopic dermatitis, psoriasis and eczema. Although various claims abound, anything that is bottled and sold off the shelf is not an authentic thalassotherapeutic treatment. The official definition of such a treatment is one that is received at a spa in a seaside environment which is free of pollution. Fresh ocean water, seaweed, mud and sand must be pumped into the centre daily. The spa must also employ a permanent medical supervisor, who is accompanied by a qualified team of trained therapists. Treatments include underwater massage, warm soaks with heated jets targeting sore muscles, steam inhalation, diet, relaxation and exercise. Simply walking on the sand next to ocean waves is considered to be an element of thalassotherapy, as it allows individuals to breathe in healthy ocean elements.

Therapeutic touch Despite its name, therapeutic touch does not involve a practitioner actually touching a client. This gentle, energy-based therapy was developed in the 1970s by registered nurse and professor Dr Dolores Krieger and Dora Kunz, a fifth-generation clairvoyant and natural healer. Kunz was president of the Theosophical Society of America from 1975 to 1987. The method is based on the idea that an electromagnetic energy field extends beyond the skin and surrounds the human body. This energy flows through the body along an intricate system of networks similar to those depicted in traditional Chinese medicine. Practitioners aim to identify and clear any areas of obstructed energy in the patient, after which they transmit a universal healing force into various areas that, it is determined, are deficient or blocked. Sessions typically last between fifteen and thirty minutes and take place with the client sitting up, fully clothed. Therapeutic touch is now part of the graduate-programme curriculum at New York University's nursing school.

Trager A form of movement education, Trager body-work involves gentle, rhythmic rocking and stroking motions designed to trigger an internal-relaxation response in the client's muscles and fascia – the tissues that enclose muscles and other organs. Former boxer, acrobat and physical therapist Dr Milton Trager developed the technique after studying transcendental meditation. Improving mental processes is central to the aim of Trager work. The underlying philosophy of the discipline is that chronic muscle pain and inhibited movement originate in the mind's neurological circuits and chemistry. When individuals repeatedly respond to traumatic life experiences by holding tightly to the muscles, over time blockages occur and eventually become habitual. Eventually, the habits become deeply entrenched in the mind-body response, resulting in chronic discomfort. Trager practitioners aim to help clients release their mental hold on the muscles in order to free them of contractions and pain. Sessions, which typically last between sixty and ninety minutes, involve the non-intrusive rolling, stretching, rocking and light compression of different parts of the body as the client sits or reclines on a table. Practitioners enter into a mild state of meditation in order to become more instinctively attuned to the client's responses and to transmit healing, positive energy. The session finishes with instruction in 'Mentastics', a system of creative-movement exercises designed to enhance the client's range of movement.

Trigger-point therapy This technique, which is used to relieve pain and dysfunction in the muscles and connective tissue, represents the lifelong work of Drs Janet Travell and David Simons. After working with patients at New York Hospital, Cornell Medical College Centre, Dr Travell provided personal care for Senator John F. Kennedy, eventually becoming the first woman to serve as physician to the president. For four decades, she studied pain management, resulting in the trigger-point myotherapy techniques practised today. Dr Simons began working with Travell, and eventually the two published the definitive reference text on the subject: *Myofascial Pain and Dysfunction: The Trigger-Point Manual*. Trigger points are small, ultrasensitive knots or wiry bands found throughout the body tissue, usually where nerves and muscles join. The points, which form as a result of injury or overwork, can lead to muscular aches and pains, pins-and-needles sensations, nausea, earache, blurred vision, headaches, stiffness, carpal-tunnel syndrome and back pain. Although the triggers are not visible using conventional medical testing, their location correlates with acupuncture points as defined by traditional Chinese medicine. After locating the points, practitioners briefly apply pressure, then release it and reapply it again with a pumping motion that corresponds to the client's breath. While it is common to experience significant relief after one session, repeated treatments may be required, depending on the severity of the client's condition. Stretching exercises are often recommended, and suggestions for correcting nutritional deficiencies may be made. Neuromuscular therapy is a form of trigger-point therapy.

Tui na Chinese body-work A facet of traditional Chinese medicine, tui na is a form of massage and manipulation technique used to restore the harmonious flow of chi throughout the body. Various methods emphasise different techniques: for instance, the nei gung school focuses on energy-generation exercises and specific types of massage for reviving depleted chi. In general, treatments include the massage of muscles and tendons, the stimulation of acupressure points, the manipulation of the musculoskeletal and ligamentous relationships and the application of external herbal poultices, compresses and salves. Sessions typically last between thirty and sixty minutes and take place while the client lies fully clothed on a table or floor-mat. Practitioners carefully examine the specific ailment of the client, after which they focus on correlating acupressure points, energy meridians, muscles and joints. Depending on the illness, additional treatments may be required. Treatments usually leave individuals feeling both relaxed and energised.

Vega testing This practice, which originated in the 1950s with the work of German doctor Reinholdt Voll, is often used in allergy-testing. Allergies are said to cause headaches, poor memory, lack of concentration, respiratory diseases such as asthma, cardiovascular diseases and emotional imbalance. In Vega testing, a low-voltage current is placed over acupuncture points, and changes in the resistance of the flow of electricity over these points are measured. Glass tubes are placed in a Vega machine with suspect substances inside and are introduced to the client's circuit. A tiny voltage of electricity is administered via a small electrode. The client holds a silver-plated cylinder to complete the circuit. Any food allergies, or intolerance or sensitivity to irritants, will register on the machine. These factors are then removed from the client's environment or diet in order to encourage optimal health. Homeopathic remedies are administered to heal the illness which resulted from the allergy. Vega testing is completely painless and lasts up to two hours.

Vichy shower Originating in France, a Vichy shower is a hydrotherapy spa treatment during which the client lies under a warm stream of water emitted from a bar of shower heads suspended over a massage table in a specially designed wet room. Also known as a rain bath, the treatment may be offered on its own as a relaxing water therapy or may be used to remove mud or algae after a body wrap. Anything from six to thirty-two spray jets are targeted at various parts of the body. A session typically begins with a full-body scrub to slough away dead skin cells. Natural, detoxifying ingredients such as pulverised seaweed or mineral-rich clay are then applied to the body during a head, neck and massage. After sea sponges are used to remove the ingredients, the client lies under the Vichy shower for a hydro-massage and rinse. The treatment typically finishes with the application of body lotion or dry oil.

Vision quest Originally an ancient wilderness rite of passage, modern-day vision quests have evolved as cross-cultural experiences that recognise the individual's need to access and integrate the internal changes required during times of transition. Ritual and ceremony is used to enhance the connection between people and the land, as well as to acknowledge and celebrate the individual's unique contribution to life and the community. Programmes typically last between eight and ten days, with the first few days spent acclimatising to the wilderness environment in the comfortable surroundings of a cabin. From there, the group will camp in the outdoors, gradually preparing each individual for the important element of the quest, which is one to three days' spent fasting in solitude with minimal shelter. After the fast, a period of one to two days is spent sharing experiences. People who may benefit from a vision quest include people who are ready to move to a new level after undergoing or emerging from a major life crisis or transition. Others may have successfully completed a process of significant mental, physical or emotional healing and simply be seeking clarity with regard to the purpose and meaning of life.

Watsu Watsu is a form of underwater zen shiatsu developed by Harold Dull, founder of the School of Shiatsu and Massage at Harbin Hot Springs in

California. After studying zen shiatsu in Japan in the 1970s, Dull returned to Harbin Hot Springs, where he discovered that, when floating horizontally, individuals were easily supported by a therapist's arms, freeing the spine from the force of gravity. This freedom is central to each watsu session, as it allows for the release of chronic physical and emotional tension. Treatments take place in a pool of warm water at chest level. Clients are supported by the head and hips while a combination of massage and flowing, dance-like movements is administered to their body. Practitioners carefully watch the client's breath patterns throughout a series of gentle rocking movements and stretches, while making sure that air is never obstructed. The nurturing support of the practitioner is intended to convey a sense of peace, simplicity and unconditional love reminiscent of early-childhood and womb states. A development from watsu is Waterdance, which draws on similar movements, with the main difference being that the practitioner gently applies a nose-clip to the client at brief intervals in order entirely to submerge the body in water.

Wheatgrass juice Similar to barley, oats and rye, wheatgrass belongs to a family of blade-bearing grasses. One pound of raw wheatgrass sprouts is said to be the nutritional equivalent of 25 pounds of raw vegetables. One ounce of the juice squeezed from its infant sprouts contains beta carotene, ninety different minerals, nineteen amino acids, calcium, magnesium, potassium, phosphorus, the trace minerals zinc and selenium, and vitamins B, C, E, H and K. When freshly cut, the sprouts also contain substantial amounts of chlorophyll. Scientific research has demonstrated that chlorophyll benefits the gastrointestinal tract, and further studies may show that it enhances the immune system. While not intended to replace the consumption of fruits and vegetables, the convenience of drinking wheatgrass juice makes it an easy way to supplement the diet. It is also believed that the juice stimulates the metabolism, curbs the appetite, neutralises toxins and slows the ageing process.

Yoga Yoga, which originated as part of the traditional Ayurvedic system for health and fitness, is a combination of body postures with breathing techniques to enhance physical and mental strength and awareness. It is known to relieve stress and increase suppleness and vitality. There are many schools of yoga, although the most popular in the West are hatha yoga and astanga yoga. (Madonna and Cher both expound the benefits of practising the energetic astanga yoga.) Yoga uses 'asanas', or postures, and breathing techniques to improve muscle tone and circulation and encourage the flow of 'prana', or life-energy, through the body. The mind is calmed using breathing techniques, which bring the body and mind into harmony. Some schools of yoga include a specific chant, which is used to raise the life-state by resonating with the seven chakras. Each of the chakras is an energy centre associated with various emotions and feelings.

Zero-balancing Taking its name from the 'balanced to zero' feeling with which it leaves clients, zero-balancing is a hands-on system of body-work developed by American osteopath and acupuncturist Dr Fritz Frederick Smith in 1973. This gentle, non-invasive technique, which integrates Eastern views of energy with Western views of science, includes both structural and energetic balancing. Practitioners always focus on the whole person, even when addressing specific needs. Sessions involve a combination of gentle holding and applied traction to stimulate the flow of energy through the body's structure and to enable the client to feel relaxed, open, alert and centred. What distinguishes zero-balancing from similar methods is a form of touch known as 'interface', during which practitioners evaluate the client's energy fields. Particular attention is paid to the skeleton, as Smith believes it contains the strongest energy currents. This therapy is particularly effective in alleviating stress and preventing illness.

Directory of Resources

Associations

Acupuncture & Chinese Medicine Organisation, 2–5 Johnson's Place, South King Street, Dublin 2, 01 679 4216

Acupuncture Foundation of Ireland, Dominick Court, 41 Lower Dominick Street, Dublin 1, 01 662 3525

Association of Rebirther Trainers, Rere No. 4, Crofton Terrace, Dun Laoghaire, County Dublin, 01 284 1660

Association of Reflexologists, 5 Robart House, Lodge Lane, London N12 8JN, UK, 0044 208 445 0154, aor@reflexology.org

Association of Systematic Kinesiology, 48 Percy Place, Ballsbridge, Dublin 4, 01 660 2806

Bioenergy Healing Association of Ireland, Bailieboro, County Cavan, 042 966 6779 or 087 231 7984

Chiropractic Association of Ireland, 126 Clontarf Road, Dublin 3, 01 833 4026, www.chiropractic.ie

Dublin Food Co-op, 12A North King Street, Dublin 7, 01 873 0451 or 01 873 0452, dfc@clubi.ie, www.clubi.ie/dfc

Holistic Sourcing Centre, 67 Lower Camden Street, Dublin 2, 01 478 5022

International Therapy Examination Council, 10–11 Heathfield Terrace, Chiswick, London W4 4JE, UK, 0044 020 8994 4141 or 0044 020 8994 7880, info@itecworld.co.uk, www.itecworld.co.uk

Irish & International Aromatherapy Association, Roscore, Blue Ball, Tullamore, County Offaly

Irish Association of Health Food Stores, Unit 2D, Kylemore Industrial Estate, Killeen Road, Dublin 10, 0903 29981

Irish Association of Holistic Medicine, 9–11 Grafton Street, Dublin 2, 01 671 2788

Irish Association of Hypnotherapists, 38 Park View, Castleknock, Dublin 15, 01 821 2897, www.hypnosiseire.com

Irish Association of Medical Herbalists, MIAMH, Derrynagittah, Gaher, County Clare, 061 924 268 or 061 924 182

Irish Association of Rebirthers, 33 Inchicore Road, Dublin 8, 01 453 3166 or 01 453 3166

Irish Health Culture Assocation, 66–67 Eccles Street, Dublin 7, 01 830 4211

Irish Massage Therapists Association, Ard

Lynn, Mount Rice, Monasterevin, County Kildare, 045 525 579

Irish Medical Homeopathic Association, 115 Morehampton Road, Donnybrook, Dublin 4, 01 269 7768 or 01 668 9242

Irish Nutrition & Dieticians Institute, 17 Rathfarnham Road, Dublin 6W, 01 490 3237

Irish Organic Farmers & Growers Association, Harbour Building, Harbour Road, Kilbeggan, County Westmeath, 0506 32563 or 0506 32063, iofga@eircom.net, www.irishorganic.ie

The Irish Osteopathic Association, c/o 17 Windsor Terrace, Portobello, Dublin 8, 01 473 0828

Irish Reflexologists Institute, 15 Chatsworth Road, Bangor, County Down BT19 7WA, 0801 247 466995, www.avcweb.com/reflexology

Irish Shen Therapy Association, 73 Claremount Road, Circular Road, Galway, 091 525941 or 091 529807, faherty@iol.ie

Irish Society of Homeopaths, 35–37 Dominick Street, Galway, 091 565 040 or 091 565 040, ishom@eircom.net

Irish Yoga Association, 108 Lower Kimmage Road, Harolds Cross, Dublin 6W, 01 492 9213, www.indigo.ie/~cmouze/yoga.htm

National Register of Reflexologists Irl., Unit 13, Upper Mall, Terryland Retail Park, Galway, 091 547 688

Professional Register of Acupuncture & TCM Practitioners of Ireland, 2–5 Johnson's Place, South King Street, Dublin 2, 01 838 8196

Professional Register of Traditional Chinese Medicine, 100 Marlborough Road, Dublin 4, 01496 7830

Register of Qualified Aromatherapists (Ireland), 111 Cliftonville Road, Belfast, County Antrim, 0801 232 753658 or 087 243 6496 or 0801 232 748236, aromatonem@fsbdial.co.uk

The Reiki Association, 8 Kilmoney Heights, Carrigaline, County Cork, 021 372 519

Shen Tao Practitioners Association, Room for Healing, Inver, County Donegal, 073 36406

Shiatsu Society of Ireland, 12 The Cove, Malahide, County Dublin, 01 845 3647

T'ai Chi Chuan Association, St. Andrew's Resource Centre, 114–116 Pearse Street, Dublin 2, 01 677 1930

Veterinary Homeopaths Association of Ireland, Inisglas, Crossabeg, County Wexford, 053 28226

Yoga Fellowship of Northern Ireland, 19 Elsemere Park, Belfast, County Antrim, 028 9070 5913

CONFERENCES

International Feng Shui Conference, PO Box 259, Zurich CH 8053, Switzerland, 0041 1 383 7364 or 0041 1 383 7364, rogergreen@fenshuiseminars.com, www.fengshuiseminars.com

COURSES

Academy International, 48 Upper Drumcondra Road, Dublin 9, 01 836 8201

Academy of Reflexology, 2 County View Terrace, Ballinacurra, County Limerick, 061 228860

American Holistic Institute of Ireland, 73 Claremount, Circular Road, Galway, 091 525941 or 091 529807, faherty@iol.ie

An Tain, Mount Avenue, Dundalk, County Louth, 042 932 6841

The Anam Cara International Academy of Reflexology, 48 Garville Avenue, Rathgar, Dublin 6, 01 496 4103

Annapurna Natural Healthcare, 6 Sidney Place, Wellington Road, Cork, 087 225 5831

As Solas Healing Centre, 'The Hermitage', Mount Anglesby, Clogheen, County Tipperary, 052 65566

Beams Holistic Therapy College, 20 Pontoon Drive, Castlebar, County Mayo, 042 26841

Beaumont School of Complementary Therapies, Beaumont Convent, Beaumont Road, Dublin 9, 01 857 1327

The Better Health School of Reflexology, Mill Street, Callan, County Kilkenny, 056 25575

Breath Move & Meditate, 26 Lein Gardens, Raheny, Dublin 5, 01 851 0943 (after 6 pm), rhaada@hotmail.com, www.spiralconnections.com

Brookfield Physiotherapy Clinic, Ardmanning Avenue, Togher, County Cork, 021 962 268 or 021 312 488, brookfieldphysio@tinet.ie

Celtic College of Holistic Therapy, Kilfrush, County Limerick, 062 53104

Celtic College of Holistic Therapies, Main Street, Newmarket, County Cork, 029 61115 or 029 60441

Clondalkin Holistic Healing Centre, Desmond House, Main Street, Clondalkin, Dublin 22, 01 464 0628

Coach House Courses, Easkey, County Sligo, 096 49181 or 096 49181, www.homepage.eircom.net/~forrestereaskey/index.htm

College of Integrative Acupuncture, 6 St Brendan's Road, Woodquay, Galway, 091 561 676

Cork Institute of Natural Therapy, Bishopstown, County Cork, 021 733 1096

Cork School of Shiatsu, 61 Westcourt Heights, Ballincollig, County Cork, 021 487 2324

The Crystal School of Reflexology, Shoselish Holistic Healing Centre, Blenheim Cross, Dunmore Road, Waterford, 051 875 444

The Divine Chalice School of Reiki Healing & Angelic Invocations, 'Hamilton Lodge', Turvey Avenue, Donabate, County Dublin, 01 840 7904 or 087 244 8545, gwendolinemcgowan@tinet.ie, www.avcweb.com/gwendoline

Donnybrook Medical Centre (ITEC), 6 Main Street, Donnybrook, Dublin 4, 01 269 6588

Dublin Meditation Centre, 23 South Frederick Street, Dublin 2, 01 671 3187

Dundrum Family Recreation Centre, Meadowbrook, Dundrum, Dublin 16, 01 298 4654

The European Institute of Classical Reflexology, 41 Parkfield, New Ross, County Wexford, 051 422 209

The European Institute of Complementary Medicine, Maryville, Murgasty Road, Tipperary, 062 51707

Evergreen Clinic of Natural Medicine, 79 Evergreen Road, Cork, 021 966 209

Georgina's International College of Therapy, 37 Shop Street, Galway, 091-564796

Golden Energy Arts, Flat 2, 76 Frankfurt Avenue, Rathgar, Dublin 6, 01 496 8342 or 01 496 8342, jang@indigo.ie, www.goldenenergyarts.com

Hahnemann School of Natural Therapeutics & Complementary Medicine, St Peter's Clinic, 143 St Peter's Road, Walkinstown, Dublin 12, 01 460 3474 or 086 253 5934

Harmony Holistic College, Dunsamney House, Desertmartin, Magherafelt, Derry BT45 5LA, 08 01 648 42590

Healing Arts College of Holistic Therapies, 10 Dungannon Road, Coalisland, County Tyrone, 0801 868 747 394

The Healing House, 24 O'Connell Avenue, Berkeley Road, Dublin 7, 01 830 6413 or 01 830 6060, info@healinghouse.ie, www.healinghouse.ie

Holistic Energy Healing Centre, Corsillagh, Newtownmountkennedy, County Wicklow, 01 281 0143 or 087 2611167

Holistic School of Reflexology & Massage, 2 Laurel Park, Clondalkin, Dublin 22, 01 459 2460

Inniú School & Healing Centre, 11 Main Street, Lucan, County Dublin, 01 628 3467 or 086 921 3808

Institute of Alternative Medicine, 6 Martello Terrace, Sandycove, County Dublin, 01 284 3275

International Institute of Reflexology (Irl), MIIR MIRI, Portmarnock, County Dublin, 01 846 1514

Irish Association of Holistic Medicine, 9–11 Grafton Street, Dublin 2, 01 671 2788

Irish College of Complementary Medicine, 6 Main Street, Donnybrook, Dublin 4, 01 269 6588

Irish College of Traditional Chinese Medicine, 100 Marlborough Road, Dublin 4, 01 496 7830

Irish Institute of Counselling & Hypnotherapy, 118 Stillorgan Road, Dublin 4, 01 260 0118

Irish Institute of Health & Healing, Unit 13, Upper Mall, Terryland Retail Park, Galway, 091 568 844

Irish Institute of Natural Therapy, Croaghta Park, Glasheen Road, Cork, 021 496 4313

Irish School of Feng Shui, Milltownpark, Ranelagh, Dublin 6, 01 492 1534

Irish School of Homeopathy, Declan Hammond, 47 Ratoath Estate, Cabra, Dublin 7, 01 868 2581

Irish School of Shiatsu, 22 Vernon Drive, Dublin 3, 01 833 7735 or 066 915 8223, shiatsu@eircom.net

Kinesiology Institute, 84 Cappaghmore, Clondalkin, Dublin 22, 01 457 1183

Lansdowne College of Acupuncture & Complementary Medicine, Fairfield House, Newbridge Avenue, Sandymount, 01 660 1487

Lifespring Centre, 111 Cliftonville Road, Belfast BT14 6JQ, 0801 232 753 658

Limerick Institute of Massage & Sports Therapy, Ballyhane, Birdhill, County Tipperary, 061 379 079, www.limst.20m.com

Living Earth Apprenticeships, Room for Healing, Inver, County Donegal, 073 36406

Mary Anderson Healing Centre, Hamilton House, 13 Trafalgar Terrace, Monkstown, County Dublin, 01 280 3635

Mid-West School of Reflexology, 2 County View Terrace, Ballinacurra, County Limerick, 061 228860

Moytura Healing Centre, 2 Lower Glenageary Road, Dun Laoghaire, County Dublin, 01 285 4005

National College of Exercise & Health Studies, 16A St Joseph's Parade (off Dorset Street), Dublin 7, 01 830 7063

Natural Health Training Centre, 1 Parklane East, Pearse Street, Dublin 2, 01 671 8454

Natural Living Centre, Walmer House, Station Road, Raheny, Dublin 5, 01 832 7859 or 01 832 7861

The Organic Centre, Rossinver, County Leitrim, 072 54338 or 072 54343, organiccentre@eircom.net, www.theorganiccentre.ie

Portobello School, Rere 40 Lower Dominick Street, Dublin 1, 01 872 1277

Pranic Healing Workshops, contact Lulu Hayes, 094 23255 or 087 637 6401

R & R School of Reflexology, Wheatfield, School Lane, Dunleer, County Louth, 042 51375

Robert Mechan College of Beauty, 17 Castle Arcade, Belfast BT1 5DG, 0801 232 664 960

School of Homeopathic Medicine, 30 Dame Street, Dublin 2, 01 679 4208

School of T'ai Chi Chuan, 10 Winton Avenue, Rathgar, Dublin 6, 01 269 5281

Shiatsu Ireland, 67 Wilfield Road, Ballsbridge, Dublin 4, 01 260 4669, enquiries@shiatsuireland.com

Suaimhneas Reflexology, 74 The Dunes, Portmarnock, County Dublin, 01 846 2574 or 087 684 9790, easyfeet@hotmail.com

Sunyata Retreat Centre, Snata, Sixmilebridge, County Clare, 061 36707, sunyata_ireland@hotmail.com

Tao School of T'ai Chi, 52 Monastery Gate Avenue, Clondalkin, Dublin 24, 01 459 1990, 01 459 1155, lgc@clubi.ie

The Tara School of Integrative Therapy, Tateetra, Dundalk, County Louth, 042 39815 or 042 30204

Teach Bán, 6 Parnell Road, Harold's Cross, Dublin 6, 01 454 3943

Three Rock Institute, Rosedale, Quinns Road, Shankill, County Dublin, 01 282 7331 or 01 282 0237, tri@indigo.ie

Yellow Brick Road, 8 Bachelors Walk, Dublin 1, 01 873 0177 or 01 873 0177, bobn@iol.ie

ENVIRONMENT

Conservation Volunteers Ireland, The Green, Griffith College, South Circular Road, Dublin 8, 01 454 7185 or 01 454 6935, info@cvi.ie, www.cvi.ie

Enfo, 17 St Andrew's Street, Dublin 2, 01 888 2001 or 01 888 3946, info@enfo.ie, www.enfo.ie

Irish Women's Environmental Network, Carmichael House, Brunswick Street North, Dublin 7, 01 873 2660 or 01 873 5737

Sustainable Communities Ireland, 159 Lower Rathmines Road, Dublin 6, 01 491 2327

Voice of Irish Concern for the Environment, 7 Upper Camden Street, Dublin 2, 01 661 8123 or 01 661 8114, avoice@iol.ie, www.voice.buz.org

MISCELLANEOUS

Alternative Animal Care, Allswell, Barley Hill, Ross Carbery, County Cork, 023 48811 or 087 249 4059, alternanimalcare@eircom.net

Nelson's Homeopathic Pharmacy, 15 Duke Street, Dublin 2, 01 679 0451 or 01 679 0457

Directory of Practitioners

Aromatherapy

County Antrim

Mary Grant
Lifespring, 111 Cliftonville Road, Belfast
Tel: 0801 232 753 658 or 0801 232 748 236
Website: aromatonem@fsbdial.co.uk

Jean Sage
Therapy Matters, 'The Trees', 31 Fortwilliam Park, Belfast BT15 4AP
Tel: 02890 777830

Dublin City

Anne Corcoran
The Aromatherapy & Reflexology Centre, Camden Court Hotel, Camden Street, Dublin 2
Tel: 01 475 9666

Marie Carton
Beauty Days, Francis Street, Dublin 8
Tel: 01 454 9349

Siobhán Kennedy
WestWood Club, Leopardstown Racecourse, Foxrock, Dublin 18
Tel: 01 289 5665

Maeve Macken
11 Sion Hill Road, Drumcondra, Dublin 9
Tel: 01 837 8310

Anne McDevitt
13 Wicklow Street, Dublin 2
Tel: 01 677 7962

Patricia McWilliams
Donnybrook Medical Centre, 6 Main Street, Donnybrook, Dublin 4
Tel: 01 269 6588

Therese O'Brien
45 Bulfin Road, Inchicore, Dublin 8
Tel: 01 454 0709

Audrey Ross
Donnybrook Medical Centre, 6 Main Street, Donnybrook, Dublin 4
Tel: 01 269 6588

Patricia Sheridan
62 Maple Drive, Castleknock, Dublin 15
Tel: 01 820 6554

COUNTY DUBLIN
Nuala Woulfe
Nuala Woulfe, 4c Glasthule Road, Sandycove
Tel: 01 230 0244

COUNTY GALWAY
Marie Smart
Kinvara
Tel: 091 637058

COUNTY WESTMEATH
Britta Stewart
Unit 17, Mullingar Enterprise Centre, Mullingar
Tel: 044 43444

AURA SOMA PRACTITIONERS
John Quinlivan, Limerick Natural Healing Centre, 64 Catherine Street, Limerick
Tel: 061 400431

BI-AURA THERAPISTS
COUNTY CARLOW
Patricia Lacey
52 Dalmin Gardens, Pollerton
Tel: 0503 42613

Carmel Nolan
Brookvilla, Friartown
Tel: 0503 63637

COUNTY CORK
Dr Anthony Walsh
Roberstown, Carrigaline
Tel: 087 647 9202

DUBLIN CITY
Joe Connolly
40 The Paddock, Navan Road, Dublin 7
Tel: 01 868 2516

Elaine Davis
54 Abbey Field, Killester, Dublin 5
Tel: 01 851 1569
Brenda Doherty

Odyssey Healing Centre, 15A Wicklow Street, Dublin 2
Tel: 01 677 1021

Orla McGrath
19 Tyrconnell Road, Inchicore, Dublin 8
Tel: 087 649 0278

Ann O'Brien
26 Lein Gardens, Raheny, Dublin 5
Tel: 0851 0943 (after 6 pm)
E-mail: rhaada@hotmail.com
Website: www.spiralconnections.com

COUNTY DUBLIN
Colm De Buitlear
177 Hampton Cove, Balbriggan
Tel: 01 841 2878

Peter McCulloch
Clonswords, Ballyboughal
Tel: 01 843 3166 or 01 843 3139

CHINESE MEDICINE
COUNTY CAVAN
Thomas F. Rehill
The Sonara Centre, 13 Town Hall Street
Tel: 043 24356

COUNTY CORK
Sile Hennigan
The Natural Health Centre, Stoneview, Blarney
Tel: 021 438 2151

Eoin Marshall
'Airedale', Ballyhooly Road, Ballyvolans
Tel: 021 551620

Kathleen McAuliffe Meaney
Acupuncture and TCM Clinic, Dooneen, Millstreet
Tel: 029 70498 or 086 2670068

also:
Acupuncture and TCM Clinic
15–16 West End, Mallow
Tel: 029 70498

Peter Sheriff
The Natural Healing Centre, Thompson House, McCurtain Street, Cork
Tel: 021 509903 or 087 6869071

DUBLIN CITY

Karen Costin
63 Haddington Road, Dublin 4
Tel: 01 285 0874 or 087 262 3287

Neil D. J. Austin
The Raheny TCM Clinic, 463 Howth Road, Raheny, Dublin 5
Tel: 01 832 8491

Peter Gaines
The Marlborough Clinic, 100 Marlborough Road, Donnybrook, Dublin 4
Tel: 086 826 2876

Frank Gleeson
17 Waterloo Road, Dublin 4
Tel: 086 603 940

Roisin Goodman
2 Pembroke Park, Donnybrook, Dublin 4
Tel: 087 295 6441

Kathryn Kelly
4 Station Road Cottages, Sutton, Dublin 3
Tel: 01 8394149

Thomas Kelly
3 Lower Mount Street, Dublin 2
Tel: 01 6788010

Josephine Lynch
Odyssey Healing Centre, 15A Wicklow Street, Dublin 2
Tel: 01 467 0116 or 087 237 2130
E-mail: josephinelynch@eircom.net

Ailish Malone
84 Meadow Copse, Hartstown, Clonsilla, Dublin 15
Tel: 01 8211919 or 01 820 6444 Extn 6823

Kerry McBride
The Marlborough Clinic, 100 Marlborough Road, Donnybrook, Dublin 4
Tel: 01 496 3857

Anne-Marie McClorey
The Marlborough Clinic, 100 Marlborough Road, Donnybrook, Dublin 4
Tel: 087 617 7958

Deirdre McDermot and Dave Shipsey
Dan-Tien, 29 Bride Street, Dublin 8
Tel: 01 473 8845
E-mail: info@dan-tien.com
Website: www.dan-tien.com

Michael McElroy
71 Roselawn Road, Castleknock, Dublin 15
Tel: 01 8215377 or 088 2154119

Emily Miggin
The Basement Clinic, 5 Morehampton Road, Donnybrook, Dublin 4
Tel: 01 6683132 or 087 2703119

Mary O'Dywer
17 Riverwood Copse, Castleknock, Dublin 15
Tel: 01 820 9138

Rhoda O'Reilly
10 The Crescent, Griffith Downs, Drumcondra, Dublin 9
Tel: 01 8360882

Leslie Proudfoot
15 Spireview, Riverston Abbey, Navan Road, Dublin 7
Tel: 01 868 4511

Gerry Rothwell
The Raheny TCM and Acupuncture Clinic, 436 Howth Road, Raheny, Dublin 5
Tel: 01 832 8491

Thomas Shanahan
The Marlborough Clinic, 100 Marlborough Road, Donnybrook, Dublin 4
Tel: 01 496 7830

Dr Sun
Pu Shan Chinese Medicine Centre, Suite 14, Dame House, 24–26 Dame Street, Dublin 2
Tel: 01 679 9753

Stephen Vaughan
Odyssey Healing Centre, 15A Wicklow Street, Dublin 2
Tel: 01 677 1021 or 087 235 6377

Sinead Woods
48 Castlerose View, Baldoyle, Dublin 13
Tel: 087 979 3369

COUNTY DUBLIN

Gary Westby
Skerries Healing Centre, 85 Strand Street, Skerries
Tel: 01 849 1741

David Cosgrave
Skerries Healing Centre, 85 Strand Street, Skerries
Tel: 01 849 1741 or 086 316 6128

John Fagan
4 Mont Alto, Sorrento, Dalkey
Tel: 01 285 2191

David McCartney
16 Church Road, Swords
Tel: 087 293 7280

COUNTY GALWAY

Paul Maloney
Upper Dublin Road, Tuam
Tel: 093 25148

Thomas Shanahan
The Acupuncture Clinic, The Crescent, Galway
Tel: 091 581 575

COUNTY KERRY

Gerald Culhane
74 Main Street, Castleisland
Tel: 066 714 2774

Janice Tucker
Dunmaniheen, Killorglin
Tel: 066 976 1066

Alan Sheehy
TCM Clinic, Upper Bridge Street, Killorglin
Tel: 066 976 2344

also:
TCM Clinic, Dunmaniheen, Killorglin
Tel: 066 976 1066

COUNTY KILDARE

John Donnelly, 199 Kingbury, Maynooth
Tel: 087 283 8141

Theresa Donnelly
199 Kingsbury, Maynooth
Tel: 01 628 5670

Keith Kelly
147 Riverforest, Leixlip
Tel: 01 6247300 or 087 2934356

Ann Prendergast
Betaghstown Cottage, Betaghstown, Clane
Tel: 045 861892 or 087 2069642

COUNTY KILKENNY

Irene Broderick
5 The Dell, Dukesmeadow
Tel: 056 64390

COUNTY LAOIS

Anne Keenan-Buckley
54 Beladd Upper, Portlaoise
Tel: 0502 61470

COUNTY LIMERICK

Eugene Coveney
25 Aylesbury, Clonmacken, Ennis Road, Limerick
Tel: 061 453277

Gerald Culhane
Hillview House Healing Centre, Castlemahon Road, Newcastlewest
Tel: 087 6210669

COUNTY LONGFORD

Thomas F. Rehill
Chinese Medicine Clinic, 6 New Street, Longford
Tel: 043 24356

Gerard Ward
Chinese Medicine Clinic, 6 New Street, Longford
Tel: 043 46993

COUNTY LOUTH

Evelyn Kilcullen
Acorn Centre, Wellington Quay, Drogheda
Tel: 041 685 2133 (Tuesdays only: 041 984 4277)

COUNTY MEATH

Ailish Malone
Acupuncture Clinic, Market Square, Trim
Tel: 046 31118

Christine Sheeran McCaffrey
Oriel Road, Collon
Tel: 087 632 5098 or 041 982 6847

Anne Marie McClorey
The Holistic Therapy Centre, Railway Street, Navan
Tel: 087 6177958 or 046 75781

Pauline McDermott
65 Balreask village, Trim Road, Navan
Tel: 046 73549

Michael McElroy
Dunshaughlin Holistic Centre, Main Street, Dunshaughlin
Tel: 01 8215377 or 088 2154119

Thomas F. Rehill
The Sonara Centre, 18 Market Street, Monaghan
Tel: 043 24356

Maria Donegan
Whiteford, Crinkill, Birr, County Offaly
Tel: 0509 21410

COUNTY OFFALY

Betty Meyler
Spa, Boyle
Tel: 029 62844

COUNTY ROSCOMMON

Siobhan Meehan
Acupuncture Clinic, Church Street, Athlone
Tel: 0902 374 541

also:
Lisdillure, Cornafulla, Athlone
Tel: 0902 37454 or 086 2670037

COUNTY SLIGO

Louise Farren
Tully, Strand Hill Road, Sligo
Tel: 071 68804

Marie McKeone
Rosses Point
Tel: 0717 7447

COUNTY TIPPERARY

Raymond O'Brien
The Acupuncture and TCM Clinic, Templemore Road, Cloughjordan
Tel: 0505 42270

Lucy Townsley
Acupuncture and Chinese Medicine Clinic, Cashel Beauty Clinic, Friar's Street, Cashel
Tel: 052 32414 or 087 2273084

also:
Acupuncture and Chinese Medicine Clinic, Dr Lonergan's Surgery, Kickham Street, Thurles
Tel: 052 32414 or 087 2273084

COUNTY TYRONE

Michelle Campbell
22 Tattykeel Road, Omagh BT78 5DA
Tel: 048 8224 4687

Anne Dolan
28 Botera Upper Road, Tattykeel, Omagh
Tel: 048 8224 7459

Cynthia Hamilton
104 Tirquin Road, Omagh BT79 7PB
Tel: 048 8224 1984

Elsie Johnson
Tara Centre, Holmview Terrace, Omagh
Tel: 048 822 46657

Aileen McCallan
4 Carraig Drive, Omagh
Tel: 048 8076 1096

Kate McCanney
Clanatogan Road, Omagh
Tel: 079 8069 7172

Bronagh Quinne
27 Gleannan Park, Omagh
Tel: 048 8224 5330

COUNTY WATERFORD
Nigel Begadon
'Fernhollow', Ballineesha, Cork Road, Waterford
Tel: 051 358128 or 051 73863

Pat Lee
Natra-Med, 19 Thomas Street, Waterford
Tel: 051 304678 or 051 851530

COUNTY WESTMEATH
Gerry Ward
Traditional Chinese Medicine, Austin Friars Street, Mullingar
Tel: 044 47944

COUNTY WICKLOW
Anne Burke
41 Ashton Wood, Herbert Road, Bray
Tel: 01 286 0416

Richard Burton
'The Aske', Dublin Road, Bray
Tel: 086 8520060 or 01 276 0949

Kevin Carey
The Annex, McGrealy Pharmacy, Main Street, Blessington
Tel: 0508 81030

COLOUR THERAPY
COUNTY LIMERICK
Aileen O'Connor
2 County View Terrace, Ballincarra
Tel: 061 228 860

John Quinlivan
Limerick Natural Healing Centre, 64 Catherine Street, Limerick
Tel: 061 400 431

CRANIO-SACRAL THERAPY
Joseph McGuire
The Healing Place, 61 St Assam's Park, Raheny, Dublin 5
Tel: 01 848 4270 or 087 246 1853
E-mail: josmcg@adent.ie

ENERGY HEALING
John Quinlivan
Limerick Natural Healing Centre, 64 Catherine Street, Limerick
Tel: 061 400 431

FLOWER REMEDIES
Aileen O'Connor
2 County View Terrace, Ballincarra, Limerick
Tel: 061 228 860

HERBALISM
COUNTY CLARE
Carole Guyett
Derrynagittah, Caher
Tel: 061 924268

COUNTY CORK
Nicola Darrell
Evergreen Clinic of Herbal Medicine, 79 Evergreen Road, Cork
Tel: 021 496 6209
E-mail: nikkidarrell@eircom.net

Stephen Gascoign
The Clinic of Chinese Medicine, O'Rahilly Street, Clonakilty
Tel: 023 33323; E-mail: gasco@eircom.nct

Jackie Kilbryde
Cooragurteen, Ballydehob
Tel: 028 37549 or 028 37019
E-mail: coora@tinet.ie

Rosari Kingston
Tragumna Road, Skibbereen
Tel: 028 22803; E-mail: herbfarm@iol.ie

Kevin Orbell-McSean
Evergreen Clinic of Natural Medicine, 79 Evergreen Road, Cork
Tel: 021 496 6209
E-mail: docbob@gofree.indigo.ie

Susan O'Toole
'Five Crosses', Croagh Bay, Gubbeen, Schull Road, Ballydehob
Tel: 028 28960; E-mail: sot@eircom.net

County Derry

David Foley
Derry City Clinic of Herbal Medicine, 7 London Street, Derry BT48 6RQ
Tel: 04871 271 500
E-mail: dmfoley@indigo.ie

Mimm Patterson
Derry City Clinic of Herbal Medicine, 7 London Street, Derry BT48 6RQ
Tel: 02871 271500

County Donegal

Murrough Birmingham
'Invarie', Ramelton Road, Ballyraine, Letterkenny
Tel: 074 24559

Jamshid Hashemi-Zadeh
23 Whitehorn Park, Gortlee Road, Letterkenny
Tel: 074 27164; E-mail: jhz@iolfree.ie

Dublin City

Noelle Cullinane
59 Hermitage Park, Rathfarnham, Dublin 16
Tel: 01 494 5628; E-mail: jsadlier@iol.ie

Bernadette Jewell
Clondalkin Acupuncture & Herbal Clinic, Boot Road, Clondalkin, Dublin 22
Tel: 01 464 0050

Celine Leonard
24 Hamilton Street, Dublin 8
Tel: 01 454 2140 or 01 416 9666
E-mail: leoferr@indigo.ie

Josephine Lynch
35 Westbourne Drive, Clondalkin, Dublin 22
Tel: 01 467 0116
E-mail: josephinelynch@eircom.net

Michael McCarthy
65 Kenilworth Square, Dublin 6
Tel: 01 497 8958; E-mail: tcm@iol.ie

Helen McCormack
186 Philpsburgh Avenue, Marino, Dublin 3
Tel: 01 836 8965
E-mail: helenmccormack@hotmail.com

Claire McGreevy
153 Howth Road, Clontarf, Dublin 3
Tel: 01 853 3043
E-mail: clairemcgreevy@iol.ie

County Dublin

Deirdre Courtney
The Priory Clinic, 18 Priory Hall, Stillorgan
Tel: 087 8178561; E-mail: deirdrec@indigo.ie

Christopher Davala
12 Clarinda Park North, Dun Laoghaire
Tel: 01 280 1740 or 071 61796

Margaret Hennessy
15 The Old Rectory, Lucan
Tel: 01 628 3795

Anna-Maria Keaveney
5 Cherbury Park Avenue, Lucan
Tel: 01 628 1362
E-mail: akherbal@hotmail.com

Paul McCarthy
Sunnyside, Seafield Avenue, Monkstown
Tel: 01 280 1950

Nicole Treacy
6 Sandycove Avenue East, Sandycove
Tel: 01 230 1841 or 01 280 5284
E-mail: nicoletreacy@eircom.net

County Galway

Marian Brady
'Kilrainy', Moycullen
Tel: 091 555 706

Margaret Brehany
The Acupuncture Clinic, 2 Churchyard Street, Galway
Tel: 091 567 576
E-mail: mercedes1@eircom.net

Dilis Clare
Alternative Health & Herbs, 11 William Street West, Galway
Tel: 091 583 260
E-mail: clareherbs@eircom.net

Dympna Kennan
Knockakilleen, Doorus, Kinvara
Tel: 091 638 183; E-mail: pmar@iol.ie

Mercedes Varona
The Acupuncture Clinic, 2 Churchyard Street, Galway
Tel: 091 567 576
E-mail: mercedes1@eircom.net

County Kerry

Gilbert De Meester
Mega Herb Stores, Old Market Lane, Killarney
Tel: 064 35761 or 064 35995
E-mail: gdm@megaherbstores.com

Dean Moriarty
Tig Admaid, Killaha, Kenmare
Tel: 064 42721
E-mail: deanpmoriarty@hotmail.com

County Mayo

Maggie Deffely
Glenside, Castlebar
Tel: 094 22940

County Meath

Marian Shanley
Lisanisk House, Athlumney, Navan
Tel: 046 73697 or 046 78148 or 046 29537

County Roscommon

Juliet Fishbourne
Mount Druid House, Mount Druid, Ballangare, Castlerea
Tel: 0907 70763 or 086 606 5173

County Sligo

Áine Molloy
Sligo Natural Health Centre, 42 Castle Street, Sligo
Tel: 071 63441

County Tyrone

Robert Elliott
Cookstown Clinic of Herbal Medicine, 4 Fairnhill Road, Cookstown BT80 8AG
Tel: 048 867 61661
E-mail: cherbalc@talk21.com

County Wicklow

John Kelly
72 Marlton Demesne, Marlton Road, Wicklow
Tel: 0404 67020
E-mail: aandjkelly@eircom.net

Homeopathy

County Clare

Christine Breen-Williams
Kiltumper, Kilmihil
Tel: 065 9050201

Nelleke Borgouts-McGrath
Riverstown Cottage, Corrofin
Tel: 065 6837555

Christine Jenkins
Cnocaibhinn, Liscannor
Tel: 065 7081129

Marie O'Sullivan
8 Parnell Street, Ennis
Tel: 065 684 0613

Liliane Tehery
Ballyknavin, Bridgetown
Tel: 061 377 443

Jane Tottenham
Mount Callan, Inagh
Tel: 065 683 6007

County Cork

Renita Ade
62 Asford Court, Grange, Douglas
Tel: 021 436 1944

Maura Ahern
LaVerna Medical Centre, Bishopstown Road, Cork
Tel: 021 434 8396

Mary Aspinwall
8 Wolfe Tone Street, Clonakilty
Tel: 023 34748

DUBLIN CITY

Ruth Appleby
168 Harold's Cross Road, Dublin 6W
Tel: 01 491 0387

Sandra Aungier
Hillcrest Veterinary Hospital, Dublin 15
Tel: 01 821 3189; E-mail: alexandra@iolfree.ie

Sheelagh Behan
32 Nassau Street, Dublin 2
Tel: 01 846 1276

Frances Bowe
66 Mount Anville Wood, Goatstown, Dublin 14
Tel: 01 278 3161

Joanne Breton
Harvest Moon Centre, 24 Lower Baggot Street, Dublin 2
Tel: 01 662 7556

Denise Clohessy
33 Niall Street, Dublin 7
Tel: 01 868 4429

James Dolan
Suite 4C, Olympia House, 62 Dame Street, Dublin 2
Tel: 01 677 3591

Brendan Fitzpatrick
115 Morehampton Road, Dublin 4
Tel: 01 269 7768

Madeline Gordon
119 Meadow Grove, Dundrum, Dublin 16
Tel: 01 298 6365

Declan Hammond
Kenmare Kill Lane, Foxrock, Dublin 18
Tel: 01 288 2422

Brian Kennedy
46 Lower Elmwood Avenue, Ranelagh, Dublin 6
Tel: 01 496 6481

Ursula Lynch
35 Cabra Park, Phibsboro, Dublin 7
Tel: 01 838 7796

Goodwin McDonnell
3 Ely Place Upper, Dublin 2
Tel: 01 661 6844

Maureen McLarnon
48 Castleknock Park, Castleknock, Dublin 15
Tel: 01 821 5121

Fergus Morrison
45 Marley Avenue, Rathfarnham, Dublin 16
Tel: 086 813 4022

Thomas Murphy
16 Castleknock Rise, Dublin 15
Tel: 01 821 6856

Pauline O'Reilly
52 Carnew Street, Dublin 7
Tel: 087 629 7708

Diane Sims
2 Killary Grove, The Danahies, Raheny, Dublin 13
Tel: 01 848 4868

Lloyd Smythe
29 Dame Street, Dublin 2
Tel: 01 679 4208

Karen Sweeney
53 Donnybrook Road, Donnybrook, Dublin 4
Tel: 087 272 8314

Ali Welfare
22 Ha'penny Bridge House, Lower Ormond Quay, Dublin 1
Tel: 01 872 4267

Gillian Wray
101 Collins Park, Donnycarney, Dublin 9
Tel: 01 831 6269 or 01 831 6269
E-mail: gwray@tinet.ie
Website: http://homepage.tinet.ie/~gwray

COUNTY DUBLIN

Nelleke Borgouts-McGrath
VICO Consultation Centre, 2 Dungar Terrace,
    Dun Laoghaire
Tel: 01 284 3336

Richard Fitzpatrick
196 Upper Glenageary Road
Tel: 01 285 4709

Peter McCulloch
Clonswords, Ballyboughal
Tel: 01 843 3166 or 01 843 3139

Peig McManus
Shorelark, The Burrow, Portrane
Tel: 01 843 6367

Marie Riordan
'Seafield', Ballmaorough, Donabate
Tel: 01 840 6707

Michael Smith
Old Quill House, Quill Road, Kilmacanogue
    Tel: 01 282 9461

Davis Emer Sweeney
Starboard Cottage, Nerano Road, Dalkey
Tel: 01 285 1144

Bernadette White
94 Lakelands Close, Stillorgan
Tel: 01 288 4959

COUNTY GALWAY

Karen Doherty
Irish Society of Homoeopaths, 35–37
    Dominick Street, Galway
Tel: 091 565 040 or 091 565 040
E-mail: ishom@eircom.net

COUNTY LAOIS

Paula Byrne
Kilvahan, Cullenagh, Portlaoise
Tel: 0502 27048

COUNTY LOUTH

Olli Kelly
32 Strand Street, Clogherhead
Tel: 041 982 2702

COUNTY MAYO

Stephen Blendell
6 Cherrington Place, Springfield, Castlebar
Tel: 094 21672

COUNTY OFFALY

Sheelagh Keenaghan
Cuba Avenue, Banagher
Tel: 0509 51383

COUNTY ROSCOMMON

Anne Walker
Carrigeen, Kilglass
Tel: 078 37221

COUNTY SLIGO

Stephen Blendell
6 Cherrington Place, Springfield, Castlebar
Tel: 094 21672

COUNTY TIPPERARY

Margaret Kenny
92 Connolly Street, Nenagh
Tel: 067 34677

COUNTY WATERFORD

Sally Ardis
1 Lower Yellow Road, Ballybricken
Tel: 051 643371

Kate Cross
3 Sexton Street, Abbeyside, Dungarvan
Tel: 058 45051

COUNTY WICKLOW

Lynda Ronayne
Bray Holistic Health Clinic, St George's,
    Herbert Road, Bray
Tel: 01 286 6611

MASSAGE – VARIOUS

COUNTY ANTRIM

Jean Sage
Therapy Matters, 'The Trees', 31 Fortwilliam
    Park, Belfast BT15 4AP
Tel: 02890 777830

COUNTY DOWN

Lesley Harvey
Accredited Bowen Therapists, Ireland, 230 Scrabo Road, Newtownards
Tel: 0801 247 826164
E-mail: intouchalternatives@nireland.com
Website: www.homestead.com/bowenireland

DUBLIN CITY

Margaret Brosnan
Irish Health Culture Association, Pecks Lane, Castleknock, Dublin 15
Tel: 01 820 1447

Hazel Byrne
The Holistic Sourcing Centre
67 Lower Camden Street, Dublin 2
Tel: 087 284 3079

Vickie Cahill
Harvest Moon Centre, 24 Lower Baggot Street, Dublin 2
Tel: 01 662 7556

Marie Carton
Beauty Days, Francis Street, Dublin 8
Tel: 01 454 9349

Michael Cantwell
Pat Henry's Figure & Fitness Centre, 14 Lower Pembroke Street, Dublin 2
Tel: 01 661 6195

Margaret Connolly
Harvest Moon Centre, 24 Lower Baggot Street, Dublin 2
Tel: 01 662 7556 or 087 239 2313

Anne Corcoran
Camden Court Hotel, Camden Street, Dublin 2
Tel: 01 475 9666

Margaret Crehan
Irish Health Culture Association, 1 Hainault Lawn, Foxrock, Dublin 18
Tel: 01 289 4779

Jenny Cuypers
2 Portersgate Way, Clonsilla, Dublin 15
Tel: 01 820 7369

Brenda Doherty
Odyssey Healing Centre, 15A Wicklow Street, Dublin
Tel: 01 677 1021

Helen Forde
Irish Health Culture Association, Meadowmount, Churchtown, Dublin 16
Tel: 01 298 7555

Claire Haugh
141 Roebuck Castle, Clonskeagh, Dublin 14
Tel: 01 283 3456

Declan Healy
Irish Health Culture Association, 126 Ranelagh, Dublin 6
Tel: 086 813 7880

Elizabeth Homan
Irish Health Culture Association, Orchardstown Avenue, Rathfarnham, Dublin 14
Tel: 01 494 3103

Sarah Howarth
Health & Beauty Clinic, 67A Vernon Avenue, Clontarf, Dublin 3
Tel: 01 853 1430

Grace Kelly
Irish Health Culture Association, Malahide Road, Dublin 13
Tel: 01 848 8125

Siobhán Kennedy
WestWood Club, Leopardstown Race Course, Foxrock, Dublin 18
Tel: 01 289 5665

Ann King-Hall
Melt: Temple Bar Natural Healing Centre, 2 Temple Lane South, Dublin 2
Tel: 01 679 8786 or 087 225 6053

Susanne Kunze
Harvest Moon Centre, 24 Lower Baggot Street, Dublin 2
Tel: 01 662 7556 or 086 304 7465
E-mail: healingway@hotmail.com

Tim Li
Harvest Moon Centre, 24 Lower Baggot Street, Dublin 2
Tel: 01 662 7556 or 086 847 0912

Sue Machesney
Bellaza Clinic, 27 Ranelagh Road, Dublin 6
Tel: 01 496 3484 or 086 810 5389

Shirley McClure
Odyssey Healing Centre, 15A Wicklow Street, Dublin 2
Tel: 01 286 5997 or 086 603 4481
E-mail: smcclure@ireland.com

Joseph McGuire
12 Grange Park View, Raheny, Dublin 5
Tel: 01 848 4270

Liam McGuirk
Harvest Moon Centre, 24 Lower Baggot Street, Dublin 2
Tel: 01 662 7556 or 087 292 4534

Nuala McNeeley
Irish Health Culture Association, 11 Westway Park, Blanchardstown, Dublin 15
Tel: 01 820 4125 or 087 284 7248

Patricia McWilliams
Donnybrook Medical Centre, 6 Main Street, Donnybrook, Dublin 4
Tel: 01 269 6588

Emily Miggin
5 Morehampton Road, Dublin 4
Tel: 01 668 3132 or 087 270 3119

Corona Morgan
Fairview Therapy Centre, 10 Fairview Strand, Dublin 3
Tel: 01 856 1289

Kay O'Connor
Irish Health Culture Association, Kingswood, Dublin 22
Tel: 01 451 8816

Anne O'Neill
Irish Health Culture Association, The Healing Oasis, Ranelagh, Dublin 6
Tel: 01 497 0774 or 086 222 5283

Nessa O'Shaughnessy
Stress Less Massage, 5 Tandy Court, Spitalfields, Dublin 8
Tel: 086 848 8442
E-mail: nessa@stressless.ie
Website: www.stressless.ie

Alan Pelly
Irish Health Culture Association, 7 Ardmore Park, Artane, Dublin 5
Tel: 01 847 6440 or 087 274 9011

Audrey Ross
Donnybrook Medical Centre, 6 Main Street, Donnybrook, Dublin 4
Tel: 01 269 6588

Sean Shortt
Irish Health Culture Association, Ashleen's Beauty Salon, Foxrock, Dublin 18
Tel: 01 289 3600 or 086 223 0066

Peter Walsh
Irish Health Culture Association, 10 Beaumont Drive, Churchtown, Dublin 14
Tel: 01 298 6015

Karen and Valerie Ward
Irish Health Culture Association, Rhiannon, St Paul's Grounds, Smithfield, Dublin 7
Tel: 01 670 4905 or 087 239 9571

Suzanne Wilson
22 Stapolin Lane, Baldoyle, Dublin 13
Tel: 01 839 2580

COUNTY DUBLIN
Anne Carter
Irish Health Culture Association, Adelaide Road, Dun Laoghaire
Tel: 01 284 1602

John Caviston
Sandycove Foot & Health Clinic, 57A Glasthule Road, Sandycove
Tel: 01 284 5287

Tony Coffey
Renaissance Hair & Beauty, 1 Newtown Park, Blackrock
Tel: 01 288 9520 or 086 243 5127

Maureen Coggins
Irish Health Culture Association, 110 Stillorgan Wood, Stillorgan
Tel: 01 288 1110

Martina Coyne
Inniú School of Healing, 11 Main Street, Lucan
Tel: 01 628 3467 or 086 821 3808

Barry Devlin
Irish Health Culture Association, 11 Grove Avenue, Blackrock
Tel: 086 814 6511

Anita Fessell
2 Castle Farm, Shankill
Tel: 01 272 1292

Sean George
Irish Health Culture Association, Portmarnock
Tel: 01 846 0952

Mairead McAnallen
Institute of Psychosocial Medicine, 2 Eden Park, Dun Laoghaire
Tel: 01 280 0084

COUNTY KERRY

Noeleen Tangey
Noeleen's Beauty Salon, 63 Main Street, Castleisland
Tel: 066 42609

COUNTY KILKENNY

Judith Ashton
The Blue Room Meditation & Healing Centre, Bennettsbridge, 147
Tel: 056 27004

COUNTY LOUTH

Mary Hutton
Main Street, Dunshaughlin
Tel: 01 825 0355

COUNTY MEATH

Martin Regan
'Millview', Station Road, Dunboyne
Tel: 01 825 5792

COUNTY WICKLOW

Kate Boyle
Newcourt Road, Bray
Tel: 01 286 0755

Kevin Clark
Willow Grove, Delgany
Tel: 01 287 6817 or 087 268 0572

Brenda Connolly
Irish Health Culture Association, Rathdown Park, Greystones
Tel: 01 287 6054 or 087 635 5172

Gretchen Thornton
Irish Health Culture Association, Kilmacanogue
Tel: 01 286 2504

NATUROPATHY

COUNTY CORK

Orla Broderick
Broderick's Pharmacy, 84 Barrack Street, Cork
Tel: 021 431 0191

Geraldine Gill
LaVerna Medical Centre, Bishopstown Road, Cork
Tel: 021 454 1806

Frank Hicks
8 Needham Place, Dunbar Street, Cork
Tel: 021 432 3296

Angela Kearney
Knockeens, Toormore, Goleen
Tel: 028 35182

Cathi Llewellyn-Davis
Flat 6, 14 Charlemont Terrace, Wellington Road, Cork
Tel: 087 235 8366

Anne Nidecker
Derrymihan, Castletownbere
Tel: 027 70801

Sandra Tyrrell
Reentrisk, Allihies, Beara
Tel: 027 73080

COUNTY DONEGAL

Mary Barr
Cooleen, St Oran's Road, Buncrana
Tel: 077 63769

Mary Bradley
Railway Road, Buncrana
Tel: 077 20691

Hans Weitbrecht
Tullynagreunu, Letterbarrow
Tel: 073 35319

DUBLIN CITY

Ruth Appleby
168 Harolds Cross Road, Dublin 6W
Tel: 01 491 0387

Frances Bowe
66 Mount Anville Road, Goatstown, Dublin 14
Tel: 01 278 3161

Joanne Breton
Harvest Moon Centre, 24 Lower Baggot Street, Dublin 2
Tel: 01 662 7556

Mary Bruen
44 Leinster Street, Phibsboro, Dublin 7
Tel: 01 830 4285

Hannah Chew
2 Belgrave Terrace, Rathmines, Dublin 6
Tel: 01 496 0792

Denyce Clohessy
15 Farranboley Park, Dundrum, Dublin 14
Tel: 01 296 8957

Martin Forde
66 Eccles Street, Dublin 7
Tel: 01 833 9902

Gwen Glasgow
85 Moyne Road, Ranelagh, Dublin 6
Tel: 01 497 6113

Declan Hammond
'Kenmare', Kill Lane, Foxrock, Dublin 18
Tel: 01 289 6293

Elizabeth Harrison
36 Oak Apple Green, Rathgar, Dublin 6
Tel: 01 486 5999

Ursula Lynch
35 Cabra Park, Phibsborough, Dublin 7
Tel: 01 838 7796

Anne McDevitt
11 Florence Street, Portobello, Dublin 2
Tel: 01 473 8121

Eileen Rock
29 Allenton Drive, Dublin 24
Tel: 01 462 3720

COUNTY DUBLIN

Evelyn Campbell-Tiech
Clonfadda Wood, 2 Waltham House, Mount Merrion Avenue, Blackrock
Tel: 01 278 6136

Helen DeVessey
Garden Apartment, 27 Corrig Avenue, Dun Laoghaire
Tel: 01 284 6968

Avril Ivory
Pine Hill, Vico Road, Dalkey
Tel: 01 285 9743

Claire Lysaght
51 Frascati Park, Blackrock
Tel: 01 278 2680

Roisin O'Kelly
86 Garrick Court, Portmarnock
Tel: 01 8740921

COUNTY GALWAY

Pauline Browne
Belville, Monivea
Tel: 091 849 098

Liz Burke
Tullykyne, Moycullen & Kirwin House, Flood
 Street, Galway
Tel: 091 555 687

Margo Diskin
51 Ocean View, Salthill
Tel: 091 529 941

Lucy Fahy
13 Mount Pleasant, Loughrea
Tel: 091 842 041

Lilian Higgins
Roveagh, Kilcolgan
Tel: 091 796 440

Anne Irwin
73 Rockfield Park, Rahoon, Galway
Tel: 091 523 993

Teresa Moloney
'Tara', Ennis Road, Gort
Tel: 091 632 258

Diane Rock
Norman Grove, Kinvara
Tel: 091 638 125

Clare Sheehan
11 Coole Park, Bohermore
Tel: 086 353 5910

Kate Soudant
Oldtown, Moycullen
Tel: 091 556 029

Jane Tottenham
Lower Cross Street, Galway
Tel: 065 683 6007

Lilian van Eyken
14 Pairc na gCaor, Moycullen
Tel: 091 555 810

COUNTY KERRY

David Cohen
10 Flemmings Lane, Killarney
Tel: 064 39535

Fran Malone
5 Knockmoyle, Tralee
Tel: 066 712 6437

Henk Meijnhardt
Greenane, Killarney
Tel: 064 82022

Ruth Appleby
The Healthy Way, Ralph Square, Leixlip
Tel: 01 624 4288

COUNTY KILDARE

Mary Manning
The Healthy Way, Ralph Square, Leixlip
Tel: 01 624 4288

Paul O'Connor
Riverview House, Chapel Lane, Newbridge
Tel: 045 431 518

Sheila Reidy
6 Ryston Close, Newbridge
Tel: 045 431 836

COUNTY KILKENNY

Sally Ardis
The Amcotts, Clonmore, Piltown
Tel: 051 643 371

COUNTY LAOIS

Paula Byrne
Kilvahan, Cullenagh, Portlaoise
Tel: 0502 27048

Paul Owens
38 Ardanglass, Mountrath Road, Portlaoise
Tel: 0502 60007

COUNTY LIMERICK

Peter Donnelan
Ballyleague, Lanesboro
Tel: 043 21284

Merle Madden
9 Ballykeelawn, Parteen
Tel: 061 343 490

Majella Scott
23 Caraballawn, Lower Park, Corbally
Tel: 061 349 741

County Longford
Betty White
Carbery, Clonrollagh
Tel: 043 45941

County Meath
John Byrne
26 Railway Street, Navan
Tel: 046 75781

County Monaghan
Kathleen Ward
Readuff, Loughmourne, Castleblaney
Tel: 042 974 5070

County Westmeath
Joy Judge
Gaulmoylestown, Crooked Wood, Mullingar
Tel: 086 815 4674

County Wexford
Gillian Dunlop
Youngstown, Taghmon
Tel: 053 39151

County Wicklow
Mairin Begley
Ballinaclash, Rathdrum
Tel: 0404 46761

Marita Byrne
6 Riverfield, Delgany
Tel: 01 287 7934 or 086 853 3601

Brenda Coller
Castlesallagh, Donard
Tel: 045 404 662

Lynda Gannon Ronayne
Holistic Health Clinic, St George's, Herbert Road, Bray
Tel: 01 286 6611

Michael Smith
Old Quill House, Quill Road, Kilmacanogue
Tel: 01 282 9461

Diane Stauder
Hazeldell, Avoca
Tel: 0402 35107 or 0401 33933

Nutrition Counselling
Siobhán Kennedy
WestWood Club, Leapardstown Racecourse, Foxrock, Dublin 18
Tel: 01 289 5665

Rebirthing
Brenda Doherty
Odyssey Healing Centre, 15 Wicklow Street, Dublin 2
Tel: 01 677 1021

Ann O'Brien
26 Lein Gardens, Raheny, Dublin 5
Tel: 0851 0943 (after 6 pm)
E-mail: rhaada@hotmail.com
Website: www.spiralconnections.com

Reflexology
County Antrim
Anne Arnold
'Fern Brook', Glenhugh Road, Ahoghill, Ballymena BT42 1JD
Tel: 01266 878 448

Eileen Baille
10 Cairnshill Crescent, Belfast BT8 6RL
Tel: 01232 703 012

Lorraine Clarke
17 Harwood Park, Carrickfergus BT38 7LZ
Tel: 02893 367 304

Aidan Corr
Cois Cluaine, 104 The Meadows, Randalstown BT41 2JB
Tel: 01849 478 127

Wendy Crawley
BIFHE School of Fashion & Beauty, Tower Street, Belfast BT5 4FH
Tel: 01232 265 269

Gavin Devlin
Complementary Care, 4 Glencroft Road, Newtownabbey BT36 5GD
Tel: 02890 832 966

Colin Doherty
29 Strandview Road, Ballycastle BT54 6AJ
Tel: 01265 762 843

Linda Eakin
21 Bendooragh Road, Ballymoney BT53 7NF
Tel: 01265 665 549

Barbara Farrell
19 Tudor Grange, Lisburn
Tel: 01846 601 613

Janice Flanigan
3 School Road, Crossnacreevy, Belfast BT5 7UA
Tel: 02890 448 829

Frances Gault
16 Dunfane Crescent, Ballymena BT43 7NF
Tel: 02825 644357

Christine Hoswell
14 Campbell Park Avenue, Belfast BT4 3FH
Tel: 02890 945 990

Diane Hume
5 Royal Lodge Gardens, Belfast BT8 7YS
Tel: 02890 799 942

Ivy Jamison
'Windyridge', 672 Saintfield Road, Carryduff, Belfast BT8 8BT
Tel: 02890 812 268

Rachel Lambert
Natural Health Care, 77 Belmont Road, Belfast BT4 2AA
Tel: 02890 471 905

Vanessa Lorimer
'Crossroads', 1 Largy Road, Crumlin BT29 4AH
Tel: 01849 452 491

Patricia McBrien
35 Belfast Road, Antrim BT41 1PB
Tel: 01849 467 929

Jennifer McCartney
221 The Woods, Larne BT40 1BD
Tel: 02828 279 413

Lorna McCooke
47 Blacksgrove, Grove Road, Ballymena BT43 6AS
Tel: 02825 632 106

Allison McCrea
4 Tynedale Crescent, Lisburn BT28 3JY
Tel: 01846 679 752

Donal McDaniel
Fortwilliam Reflexology, 537 Antrim Road, Belfast BT15
Tel: 08 01232 716 352

Martia McMullan
7 Royal Lodge Road, Belfast BT8 7UL
Tel: 02890 402 042

Noelle McNinch
'Tiptoe', 32 Meadowvale, Ballymena BT42 4EX
Tel: 02825 643 995

Mary Montgomery
6 Finlaystown Road, Portglenone, Ballymena BT44 8EA
Tel: 02825 821 438

Ivy O'Rawe
53 Castle Gardens, Belfast
Tel: 02890 771 944

Amanda Priestly
14 Hillcrest Crescent, Newtownabbey BT36 6EF
Tel: 02890 860 390

Jean Sage
Therapy Matters, 'The Trees', 31 Fortwilliam Park, Belfast BT15 4AP
Tel: 02890 777 830

Serena Sheppard
110 Carrickfergus Road, Larne BT40 3JX
Tel: 02828 260 710

Lindsey Shipley
Arena Health & Fitness Club, 100–150 York Gate Shopping Centre, Belfast BT15 1WA
Tel: 02890 741 235

Lorna Welsh
Dundonald Aromatherapy & Reflexology Clinic, 55A Comber Road, Dundonald, Belfast BT16 1AD
Tel: 01232 769 838

Carol Wray
Reflexology Clinic, 34 Lucerne Parade, Stranmillis, Belfast BT9 5FT
Tel: 01232 669 913

COUNTY ARMAGH

Lynn Hanna
Edenmore Lodge, 71 Drumnabreeze Road, Magheralin, Craigavon BT67 0RH
Tel: 02892 611 609

Patricia Kerr
41 Birches Road, Portadown, Craigavon BT62 1TL
Tel: 02838 851 226

Geraldine McCrory
10 Cathedral Villas, Cathedral Road, Armagh BT61 7QX
Tel: 01861 527 978

Deirdre Mitchell
7 Turmoyra Court, Lough Road, Lurgan, Craigavon BT66 6SD
Tel: 02838 346 076

Cathy Murray
11 Woodford Mews, Armagh BT60 2LW
Tel: 02837 526 493

Maria O'Neill
20 Main Street, Laurelvale, Tandragee, Craigavon BT62 2LN
Tel: 02838 841 524

Wendy Scott
90 Breezemount, Hamiltonsbawn, Armagh BT61 9SB
Tel: 02838 871 488

Anne Whittock
10 Waringfield Drive, Moira, Craigavon BT67 0FB
Tel: 01846 613 421

COUNTY CARLOW

Marianne Madden
'Nampara', Ballymurphy Road, Tullow
Tel: 0503 51681

Sharon Malloy
Ballytarsna, Nurney
Tel: 0503 27470

COUNTY CLARE

Eileen Addley
'Swallow Hill', Garraunboy, Killaloe
Tel: 061 375 997

Breeda Murphy
Creggaun, Ennis
Tel: 065 684 220

COUNTY CORK

Agnes Beary
Natural Healthcare Centre
17 Main Street, Kinsale
Tel: 021 774 907

Joanna Kavanagh
Weavers Square, Rathcooney, Glanmire
Tel: 021 482 1264

Rachel Lacey-Porter
'The Commons', Inchigeelagh, Near Macroom
Tel: 026 49254

Sandra Maher
'Oakdown', Moneygourney, Douglas
Tel: 021 436 4492

COUNTY DERRY

Rita Arbuthnot
1 Macknagh Road, Upperlands, Maghera BT46 5SG
Tel: 02879 644 087

Patricia Broderick
8 Mayogall Road, Knockloughrim, Magherafelt BT45 8PD
Tel: 01648 42136

Miriam Hunter
2 Glenesk Gardens, Coleraine BT52 1TG
Tel: 012 655 4601

Sandra Kilburn
75 Castle Park, Limavady BT49 0SW
Tel: 01504 762 967

Hazel McBrine
39 Seapark, Castlerock, Coleraine BT51 4TH
Tel: 02870 848 870

Olive McGarvey
76 Strand Road, Portstewart BT55 7LY
Tel: 01265 832 974

Margaret Watt
45 Coleraine Road, Garvagh, Coleraine BT51 5HP
Tel: 01266 558 739

Ann Wilson
15 Gortnahey Road, Dungiven, Derry BT47 4PY
Tel: 01504 741 458

County Donegal

Patricia Bailey
1 Millfield Heights, Buncrana
Tel: 077 20249

Joan O'Connell
'Airghialla', Lissadel Avenue, Magheracar, Bundoran
Tel: 072 41964

County Down

Beth Cully
Tudor Reflexology, 5 Tudor Abbey, Newtownards BT23 8YS
Tel: 02891 814 152

Paddy Hazel
Abbey Complementary & Sports Therapy Clinic, 70 Abbey Street, Bangor BT20 4JB
Tel: 02891 271984

Donna Kirk
11 Barclay Manor, Dromore BT25 2HX
Tel: 01238 533116

Mary Higgins
110 Newry Road, Kilkeel, Newry BT34 4ET
Tel: 01693 764 136

Mary Clare Killen
38 Lagan Court, Warrenpoint, Newry BT34 3SX
Tel: 02841 752 388

Dolores McCoy
3 Croft Park, Holywood BT18 0PF
Tel: 02890 424 604

Mary McGuiggan
16 Edenavaddy Road, Ballynahinch BT24 8JJ
Tel: 02897 561 345

Muriel McMurray
'Ashdene', 42 Banbridge Road, Rathfriland, Newry BT34 5PQ
Tel: 02840 630 842

Winifred Olive
'Morton', 22 Aughnacloy Road, Banbridge BT32 3RU
Tel: 01820 626 788

Karen Pickett
58 Upper Fathom Road, Cloughoge, Newry BT35 8NY
Tel: 02830 848 904

Maria Pundyke
15 Chatsworth, Bangor BT19 7WA
Tel: 02891 466 995

Heather Roylance
26 South Street, Newtownards BT23 4JT
Tel: 02891 469 731

Paul Smith
Spirals Natural Health Care, 61 Victoria Road, Bangor BT20 5ER
Tel: 01247 270 861

Patrick Thornton
Reflexology Clinic, 13 Lower Catherine Street, Newry BT35 6BE
Tel: 02830 252 950

Dublin City

Carol Allison
28 Manor Rise, Highfield Manor, Rathfarnham, Dublin 16
Tel: 01 494 5931

Carol Byrne
149 Kildare Road, Crumlin, Dublin 12
Tel: 01 453 8481

Margaret Connolly
Harvest Moon Centre, 24 Lower Baggot Street, Dublin 2
Tel: 01 662 7556 or 087 239 2313

Terry Kenny
1 Strand Road, Baldoyle, Dublin 13
Tel: 01 832 1398

Cora Lavin
Optimum Healthcare, Ranelagh, Dublin 6
Tel: 01 660 7903 or 087 687 8696

Valerie Lawrence
9 Balally Park, Dundrum, Dublin 16
Tel: 01 295 0390

Catherine MacBride
17 Cul na Greine, Old Bawn, Tallaght, Dublin 24
Tel: 01 451 9687

Patricia McWilliams
Donnybrook Medical Centre, 6 Main Street, Donnybrook, Dublin 4
Tel: 01 269 6588

Sean Nolan
31 Yellow Meadow Drive, Clondalkin, Dublin 22
Tel: 01 457 2565

Carol O'Byrne
66 Celtic Park Avenue, Whitehall, Dublin 6
Tel: 01 831 7621

Therésa O'Neill
Melt: Temple Bar Natural Healing Centre, 2 Temple Lane South, Dublin 2
Tel: 01 679 8786 or 01 456 7845

Yvonne O'Riordan
'St Jude's', Oldbridge Road, Templeogue, Dublin 16
Tel: 01 494 7821

Nessa O'Shaughnessy
Stress Less Massage, 5 Tandy Court, Spitalfields, Dublin 8
Tel: 086 848 8442
E-mail: nessa@stressless.ie
Website: www.stressless.ie

Margaret O'Shea
105 Darglewood, Knocklyon, Dublin 16
Tel: 01 495 0464

Audrey Ross
Donnybrook Medical Centre, 6 Main Street, Donnybrook, Dublin 4
Tel: 01 269 6588

Teresa Whelan
51 Beechlawn Green, Coolock, Dublin 5
Tel: 01 848 2499

COUNTY DUBLIN

Mary Canavan, International Institute of Reflexology (Ireland), Portmarnock
Tel: 01 846 1514

Martina Coyne
Inniú School of Healing, 11 Main Street, Lucan
Tel: 01 628 3467 or 086 821 3808

Carol Donnelly
Suaimhneas Reflexology, 74 The Dunes, Portmarnock
Tel: 01 846 2574
E-mail: easyfeet@hotmail.com
Website: www.suaimhneas.com

Carla Lonergan
The Ward, Ballymacarney
Tel: 01 835 1314

Lua McIlraith
'Phorus', 2 Sandycove Avenue North, Dun Laoghaire
Tel: 01 280 5014 or 086 813 8446

John Peter
Sandycove Foot & Health Clinic, Caviston, 57A Glasthule Road, Sandycove
Tel: 01 284 5287

COUNTY FERMANAGH

Sandra Quinn
Beech Lodge, 1 Killynure Wood, Enniskillen BT74 6FR
Tel: 01365 325 943

COUNTY GALWAY

Mary Irwin
Body & Sole Centre, Frenchville Lane, Off Eyre Square, Galway
Tel: 091 539 622

Jean Kelly
10 Lenaboy Gardens, Salthill
Tel: 091 526 693

Lucy Sullivan
Lavender Cottage, Kilteskle Road, Mason Brook, Loughrea
Tel: 086 877 9769

COUNTY KERRY

Teresa Kerins
Kilcummin, Killarney
Tel: 064 43113

COUNTY KILDARE

Bernadette Doyle
25 The Grange, Newbridge
Tel: 045 435 467

COUNTY LAOIS

Brenda Campion O'Toole
Stonehaven Cottage, Lea Road, Portarlington
Tel: 0105 024 3886

COUNTY LIMERICK

Mary Fitzgerald
Ballyneety
Tel: 061 351 369

Geraldine Kenny
Mikelle Health Studio, 153 Russell Court, Ballykeeffe
Tel: 061 227 981

Aileen O'Connor
2 County View Terrace, Ballincarra, Limerick
Tel: 061 228 860

Enid O'Leary
Ballymorrisheen, Ardagh
Tel: 069 77604

COUNTY MAYO

Margaret Graham
Logcurragh, Swinford
Tel: 094 65317

Martina Horan-Barrett
20 Pontoon Drive, Castlebar
Tel: 094 23161

COUNTY OFFALY

Michelle Healion
Ross Screggon, Tullamore
Tel: 0506 24558

COUNTY ROSCOMMON

Denise and Padraig King
Rossbeigh House, Wooden Bridge, Boyle
Tel: 079 64935

COUNTY TIPPERARY

Kathleen Droney
Ballyvandron, Nenagh
Tel: 067 31742

Helen Maher
Kennedy, Cloughjordan
Tel: 087 270 3959

COUNTY TYRONE

Jean Boyd
29 Benburb Road, Moy, Dungannon BT71 7SQ
Tel: 01868 784 597

Philomena Sweeney
'Mountfield', Mulnafye Road, Omagh BT79 0PG
Tel: 02880 771 381

COUNTY WESTMEATH

Britta Stewart
Unit 17, Enterprise Centre, Bishopsgate Street, Mullingar
Tel: 044 43444 or 044 48066 or 087 241 9156

County Wicklow

Kevin Clark
Delgany
Tel: 01 287 6917 or 087 268 0572

Helen Dring
3 Kilgarron Park, Enniskerry
Tel: 01 204 2864

Maria Lynch
'Brookside', Marlton Close, Wicklow
Tel: 0404 69045

Reiki

County Cork

Celine Spengeman
9 Castleowen, Blarney
Tel: 021 438 2235 or 087 965 2120

Dublin City

Siobhán Kennedy
WestWood Club, Leopardstown Racecourse, Foxrock, Dublin 18
Tel: 01 289 5665

Susanne Kunze
Harvest Moon Centre, 24 Lower Baggot Street, Dublin 2
Tel: 01 662 7556 or 086 304 7365
E-mail: healingway@hotmail.com

Tim Li
Harvest Moon Centre, 24 Lower Baggot Street, Dublin 2
Tel: 01 662 7556 or 086 847 0912

Patricia Woods
WestWood Club, Leopardstown Racecourse, Foxrock, Dublin 18
Tel: 087 236 8204

County Dublin

John Caviston
Sandycove Foot & Health Clinic, 57A Glasthule Road, Sandycove
Tel: 01 284 5287

Martina Coyne
Inniú School of Healing, 11 Main Street, Lucan
Tel: 01 628 3467 or 086 821 3808

Gwendolene MacGowan
Hamilton House, Turvey Avenue, Donabate
Tel: 01 840 7206

Peter McCulloch
Clonswords, Ballyboughal
Tel: 01 843 3166 or 01 843 3139

County Limerick

Aileen O'Connor
2 County View Terrace, Ballincarra
Tel: 061 228 860

Index of Centres

Aaron Acupuncture & Physiotherapy Clinic, Glengormley, 13
Abbey House Medical Centre, Navan, 164
Acorn Counselling & Holistic Therapy Centre, Drogheda, 152
Active Health, Dublin 6, 59
Acumedic, Dublin 1, 60
Acupuncture & Allergy Testing Clinic, Dublin 5, 61
Acupuncture & Sports Injury Clinic, Dublin 24, 62
Alara Beauty Salon, Dublin 6, 63
Amethyst, Killiney, 63
Annaghdown Seaweed Spas, Corrandulla, 131
Anam Cara, Bantry, 35
Anam Cara, Loughrea, 130
An Solas Healing Centre, Clogheen, 176
Anvil House & Therapeutic Centre, Foulksmills, 184
Aqua: The Art of Beauty, Stillorgan, 64
Ardagh Mobile Acupuncture Clinic, Blackrock, 65
Ashe Street Clinic, Tralee, 140
Atar Complementary Therapy Clinic, Wexford, 188

Ballycoursey Lodge & Health Spa, Enniscorthy, 185
Beauty Parlour, Dublin 6W, 66
Bellaza Clinic, Dublin 6, 67
Blarney Park Leisure Centre, Blarney, 26
Bliss – Beauty and Massage, Sandycove, 67
Blue Eriu, Dublin 2, 68
Blue Room Meditation & Healing Centre, Bennettsbridge, 147
Body & Beauty Spa, Dublin 15, 69
Body & Sole Centre, Galway, 132
Body Harmony Healing & Workshops, Dublin 3, 70
Bon Secours Health Lodge, Cork, 36
Bray Holistic Health Clinic, Bray, 196
Burren Holistic Centre, Tubber, 24
Burren Yoga & Meditation Centre, Kinvara, 122

Casement Centre of Complementary Therapies, Ballina, 157
Castlebar Health Care Clinic, Castlebar, 157
Castleknock Physiotherapy & Acupuncture Clinic, Dublin 15, 71
Celbridge Physiotherapy & Acupuncture Clinic, Celbridge, 144

Celtic Health Centre, Dublin 6, 72
Celtic Seaweed Baths, Strandhill, 173
Centre for Natural Therapies, Wexford, 189
Chinese Acupuncture Clinic, Dublin 2, 73
Chinese and Complementary Medicine Clinic, Belfast, 14
Chinese Medical Centre, Dun Laoghaire, 74
Chrysalis Holistic Centre, Donard, 190
Claureen Health Farm, Ennis, 19
Clinic of Alternative Medicine, Galway, 134
Clinic of Oriental & Traditional Chinese Medicine, Glanmire, 37
Cloona Health Centre, Westport, 153
Coiscéim Natural Therapy Centre, Tralee, 141
Complementary Healing Therapies, Dublin 7, 75
Complementary Health Clinic, Belfast, 15
Complementary House, Dublin 6W, 76
Complementary Medicine Clinic, Dublin 9, 77
Complementary Treatment Clinic, Athy, 145
Crystal Connection, Cork, 38

Dan-Tien, Dublin 8, 77
Delphi Mountain Resort & Spa, Leenane, 124
Diamus, Cork, 27
Dingle's Natural Therapy Centre, Dingle, 142
Douglas Day Spa, Douglas, County Cork, 39
Dungarvan Alternative Health Clinic, Dungarvan, 182

Endorphin Release Clinic, Dublin 12, 78
Eskine House of Silence, Sneem, 137

Fairgreen Holistic Clinic, Naas, 146
Fairview Therapy Centre, Dublin 3, 79
Flowing Unity, Cork, 40
Fortwilliam Reflexology, Belfast, 16
Freedom Holistic Centre, Midleton, 41
Freeing the Artist Within, Dalkey, 55

Galway Bay Health Farm, Oranmore, 126
Galway Rolfing Clinic, Moycullen, 135
Galway Yoga & Meditation Centre, Galway, 127
Greystones Physical Therapy Clinic, Greystones, 197
Grove House, Mallow, 29

Hagel Healing Farm, Bantry, 30
Hao Clinic for Traditional Chinese Medicine, Bangor, 17
Harmony Acupuncture & Angel Aromatherapy Clinic, Galway, 136

Harvest Moon, Dublin 2, 80
Healing House, Dublin 7, 82
Healing Place, Dublin 5, 83
Healing Room, Dublin 3, 84
Health and Harmony, Dublin 2, 84
Health Therapies Clinic, Waterford, 183
Herbal & Iridology Clinic, Dublin 2, 85
Holistic Healing Centre, Dublin 2, 86
Holistic Healing Centre, Graiguenamanagh, 149
Holistic Sourcing Centre, Dublin 2, 88

Ikebana Spirit Mind Body Centre, Dublin 6, 89
Impact Health, Beauty & Aromatherapy, Ballynahinch, 54
Inchydoney Lodge and Spa, Clonakilty, 31
Inner Adventure Company, Deansgrange, 90
Inner Circle Healing Centre, Dublin 13, 91
Innish Beg Cottages, Enniskillen, 118
Inniú School & Healing Centre, Lucan, 92
Inspirations, Dun Laoghaire, 93
Irish Institute for Integrated Psychotherapy, Monkstown, 94

Jan de Vries Healthcare Clinic, Dublin 1, 58
Jivan Clinic of Complementary Medicine, Cork, 42

Kelly's Resort Hotel, Rosslare, 187
Ki-Care Clinic, Cork, 33
Kilkee Thalassotherapy Centre & Guest House, Kilkee, 21

L.A. Beauty Salon, Clonakilty, 43
Lalloo's Medical Centre, Dublin 7, 95
Light Therapy Ireland, Swords, 96
Limerick Healing Centre of Colour & Light, Limerick, 151
Lios Dana Holistic Centre, Anascaul, 138
Lisdoonvarna Spa Wells Health Centre, Lisdoonvarna, 25
Little House of Avalon, Ballinasloe, 169

Macrobiotic Association, Dublin 12, 56
Malin Head Hostel, Inishowen, 50
Melt: Temple Bar Natural Healing Centre, Dublin 2, 97
Midas Touch Clinic, Tullamore, 168
Monaincha Health & Fitness, Roscrea, 178

Natural Healing Centre, Belmullet, 159
Natural Healing Centre and Natural Healing Institute of Ireland, Cork, 44
Natural Health Care Centre & Shop, Bantry, 45
Natural Therapy & Beauty Clinic, Dublin 15, 98
Natural Therapy Centre, Mallow, 46
Natural Therapy Clinic, Glanmire, 47
Nature Art Centre, Ballydehob, 34
Navan Holistic Therapy Centre, Navan, 165
Niamh's Beauty Salon, Athboy, 166
Nuala Woulfe, Sandycove, 99

Oasis Alternative Medical and Flotation Centre, Tralee, 143
Odyssey Healing Centre, Dublin 2, 100

Pat Henry Figure & Fitness Centre, Dublin 2, 102
Pine Lodge, Tullamore, 167
Poll na Lobhar Holistic Treatments, Kilnaboy, 22
Powerscourt Springs, Enniskerry, 192
Pu Shan Chinese Medicine Centre, Dublin 2, 103

Quayside Holistic Health Centre, Cork, 47
Quintessence Complementary Clinic, Belfast, 18

Rainbowhill Healing Centre, Boyle, 170
Raja Yoga Centre, Dublin 4, 104
Re:fresh, Dublin 18, 105
Rhiannon Clinic, Dublin 7, 106
Roseanna Crothers Beauty Salon, Dalkey, 107
Rosmoney Spa, Westport, 155

Sacred Journeys Ireland, Dublin 6, 193
Sanctuary Health & Holistic Centre, Kilross, 175
Sandycove Clinic, Sandycove, 108
Shamrock Health Clinic, Dublin 24, 109
Shoselish Holistic Healing Centre, Waterford, 179
Skerries Healing Centre, Skerries, 110
Slánú Cancer Help Centre, Moycullen, 129
Slí na Bande, Newtownmountkennedy, 194
Sligo Natural Health & Yoga Centre, Drumcliffe, 171
Suaimhneas Holistic Health Clinic, Buncrana, 52
Sureia Holistic Centre, Midleton, 48

T'ai Chi Ireland, Dublin 6, 111
Temple Country House & Health Spa, Moate, 180
Tethra Spa, Dublin 2, 112
Therapeutic Spa & Beauty Centre, Rosslare, 187
Three Rock Institute, Shankill, 113

Tinarana House, Killaloe, 23
Tír Na nÓg, Holistic Beauty Centre, Claremorris, 160
Transpersonal Centre, Navan, 163
Turning Point Positive Health Centre, Dun Laoghaire, 114

Walmer Clinic & College of Healing and Natural Therapies, Dublin 13, 115
Weekend Breaks at the Fisherman's Cottage, Aran Islands, 120

Yoga Therapy & Training Centre Ireland, Cabra, 53
Yoga Therapy Ireland, Killiney, 117

Index of Centres by County

County Antrim

Belfast: Chinese and Complementary Medicine Clinic, 14,
Belfast: Fortwilliam Reflexology, 16
Belfast: Quintessence Complementary Clinic, 18
Belfast: Complementary Health Clinic, 15
Glengormley: Aaron Acupuncture & Physiotherapy Clinic, 13

County Clare

Ennis: Claureen Health Farm, 19
Kilkee: Kilkee Thalassotherapy Centre & Guest House, 21
Killaloe: Tinarana House, 23
Kilnaboy: Poll na Lobhar Holistic Treatments, 22
Lisdoonvarna: Lisdoonvarna Spa Wells Health Centre, 25
Tubber: Burren Holistic Centre, 24

County Cork

Ballydehob: Nature Art Centre, 34
Bantry: Anam Cara, 35
Bantry: Hagel Healing Farm, Bantry, 30
Bantry: Natural Health Care Centre & Shop, 45
Blarney: Blarney Park Leisure Centre, 26
Clonakilty: Inchydoney Lodge and Spa, 31
Clonakilty: L.A. Beauty Salon, 43
Cork City: Bon Secours Health Lodge, 36
Cork City: Crystal Connection, 38
Cork City: Diamus, 27
Cork City: Flowing Unity, 40
Cork City: Jivan Clinic of Complementary Medicine, 42
Cork City: Ki-Care Clinic, 33
Cork City: Natural Healing Centre & Natural Healing Institute of Ireland, 44
Cork City: Quayside Holistic Health Centre, 47
Glanmire: Clinic of Oriental & Traditional Chinese Medicine, 37
Douglas: Douglas Day Spa, 39
Glanmire: Natural Therapy Clinic, 47
Mallow: Natural Therapy Centre, 46
Midleton: Freedom Holistic Centre, 41
Midleton: Sureia Holistic Centre, 48
Shanballymore: Grove House, 29

County Donegal

Buncrana: Suaimhneas Holistic Health Clinic, 52
Inishowen: Malin Head Hostel, 50

County Down

Ballynahinch: Impact Health, Beauty & Aromatherapy, 54
Bangor: Hao Clinic for Traditional Chinese Medicine, 17
Cabra: Yoga Therapy & Training Centre Ireland, 53

Dublin City

Dublin 1: Acumedic, 60
Dublin 1: Jan de Vries Healthcare Clinic, 51
Dublin 2: Blue Eriu, 68
Dublin 2: Chinese Acupuncture Clinic, 73
Dublin 2: Harvest Moon, 80
Dublin 2: Health and Harmony, 84
Dublin 2: The Herbal & Iridology Clinic, 85
Dublin 2: Holistic Healing Centre, 86
Dublin 2: Holistic Sourcing Centre, 88
Dublin 2: Melt: Temple Bar Natural Healing Centre, 97
Dublin 2: Odyssey Healing Centre, 100
Dublin 2: Pat Henry Figure & Fitness Centre, 102
Dublin 2: Pu Shan Chinese Medicine Centre, 103
Dublin 2: Tethra Spa, 112
Dublin 3: Body Harmony Healing & Workshops, 70
Dublin 3: Fairview Therapy Centre, 79
Dublin 3: Healing Room, 84
Dublin 4: The Raja Yoga Centre, 104
Dublin 5: Acupuncture & Allergy Testing Clinic, 61
Dublin 5: The Healing Place, 83
Dublin 6: Active Health, 59
Dublin 6: Alara Beauty Salon, 63
Dublin 6: Celtic Health Centre, 72
Dublin 6: Ikebana Spirit Mind Body Centre, 89
Dublin 6: Sacred Journeys Ireland, 193
Dublin 6: T'ai Chi Ireland, 111
Dublin 6W: The Beauty Parlour, 66
Dublin 6W: Complementary House, 76
Dublin 7: Complementary Healing Therapies, 75
Dublin 7: Lalloo's Medical Centre, 95
Dublin 7: The Healing House, 82
Dublin 7: Rhiannon Clinic, 106
Dublin 8: Dan-Tien, 77
Dublin 9: Complementary Medicine Clinic, 77
Dublin 12: Endorphin Release Clinic, 78
Dublin 12: Macrobiotic Association, 56
Dublin 13: Inner Circle Healing Centre, 91
Dublin 13: Walmer Clinic & College of Healing and Natural Therapies, 115
Dublin 15: Body & Beauty Spa, 69
Dublin 15: Castleknock Physiotherapy & Acupuncture Clinic, 71
Dublin 15: Natural Therapy & Beauty Clinic, 98
Dublin 18: Re:fresh, 105
Dublin 24: Acupuncture & Sports Injury Clinic, 62
Dublin 24: Shamrock Health Clinic, 109

County Dublin

Blackrock: Ardagh Mobile Acupuncture Clinic, 65
Celbridge: Celbridge Physiotherapy & Acupuncture Clinic, 144
Dalkey: Freeing the Artist Within, 55
Dalkey: Roseanna Crothers Beauty Salon, 107
Deansgrange: Inner Adventure Company, 90
Dun Laoghaire: Chinese Medical Centre, 74
Dun Laoghaire: Inspirations, 93
Dun Laoghaire: Turning Point Positive Health Centre, 114
Killiney: Amethyst, 63
Killiney: Yoga Therapy Ireland, 117
Lucan: Inniú School & Healing Centre, 92
Monkstown: The Irish Institute for Integrated Psychotherapy, 94
Sandycove: Bliss – Beauty and Massage, 67
Sandycove: Nuala Woulfe, 99
Sandycove: The Sandycove Clinic, 108
Shankill: Three Rock Institute, 113
Skerries: Skerries Healing Centre, 104
Stillorgan: Aqua: The Art of Beauty, 64
Swords: Light Therapy Ireland, 96

County Fermanagh

Enniskillen: Innish Beg Cottages, 118

County Galway

Aran Islands: Weekend Breaks at the Fisherman's Cottage, 120
Corrandulla: Annaghdown Seaweed Spas, 131
Galway city: Body & Sole Centre, 132
Galway city: Clinic of Alternative Medicine, 134
Galway city: Galway Yoga & Meditation Centre, 127
Galway city: Harmony Acupuncture & Angel Aromatherapy Clinic, 136
Kinvara: Burren Yoga & Meditation Centre, 122
Leenane: Delphi Mountain Resort & Spa, 124
Moycullen: Galway Rolfing Clinic, 135
Moycullen: Slánú Cancer Help Centre, 129

Oranmore: Galway Bay Health Farm, 126

COUNTY KERRY

Anascaul: Lios Dana Holistic Centre, 138
Dingle: Dingle's Natural Therapy Centre, 142
Sneem: Eskine House of Silence, 137
Tralee: Ashe Street Clinic, 140
Tralee: Coiscéim Natural Therapy Centre, 141
Tralee: Oasis Alternative Medical and Flotation Centre, 143

COUNTY KILDARE

Athy: The Complementary Treatment Clinic, 145
Naas: Fairgreen Holistic Clinic, 146

COUNTY KILKENNY

Bennettsbridge: The Blue Room Meditation & Healing Centre, 147
Graiguenamanagh: Holistic Healing Centre, 149

COUNTY LIMERICK

Limerick : Limerick Healing Centre of Colour & Light, 151

COUNTY LOUTH

Drogheda: Acorn Counselling & Holistic Therapy Centre, 152

COUNTY MAYO

Ballina: Casement Centre of Complementary Therapies, 157
Castlebar: Castlebar Health Care Clinic, 157
Claremorris: Tír na nÓg, Holistic Beauty Centre, 160
Belmullet: Natural Healing Centre, 159
Westport: Cloona Health Centre, 153
Westport: Rosmoney Spa, 155

COUNTY MEATH

Athboy: Niamh's Beauty Salon, 166
Navan: Abbey House Medical Centre, 164
Navan: Navan Holistic Therapy Centre, 165
Navan: The Transpersonal Centre, 163

COUNTY OFFALY

Tullamore: The Midas Touch Clinic, 168
Tullamore: Pine Lodge, 167

COUNTY ROSCOMMON

Ballinasloe: Little House of Avalon, 169

COUNTY SLIGO

Boyle: Rainbowhill Healing Centre, 170
Drumcliffe: Sligo Natural Health & Yoga Centre, 171
Strandhill: Celtic Seaweed Baths, 173

COUNTY TIPPERARY

Clogheen: An Solas Healing Centre, 176
Kilross: The Sanctuary Health & Holistic Centre, 175
Roscrea: Monaincha Health & Fitness, 178

COUNTY WATERFORD

Dungarvan: Dungarvan Alternative Health Clinic, 182
Waterford: Health Therapies Clinic, 183
Waterford: Shoselish Holistic Healing Centre, 179

COUNTY WESTMEATH

Moate: Temple Country House & Health Spa, 180

COUNTY WEXFORD

Enniscorthy: Ballycoursey Lodge & Health Spa, 185
Foulksmills: Anvil House & Therapeutic Centre, 184
Rosslare: Kelly's Resort Hotel, 187
Wexford town: Atar Complementary Therapy Clinic, 188
Wexford town: Centre for Natural Therapies, 189

COUNTY WICKLOW

Bray: Bray Holistic Health Clinic, 196
Donard: Chrysalis Holistic Centre, 190
Enniskerry: Powerscourt Springs, 192
Greystones: Greystones Physical Therapy Clinic, 197
Newtownmountkennedy: Slí na Bande, 194

Index by Therapy Type

Absent Healing
Suaimhneas Holistic Health Clinic, Buncrana, 52

Acupressure
Aaron Acupuncture & Physiotherapy Clinic, Antrim, 13
Chinese and Complementary Medicine Clinic, Belfast, 14
Sureia Holistic Centre, Midleton, 48
Chinese Medical Centre, Dun Laoghaire, 74
Complementary Medicine Clinic, Dublin 9, 77
Dan-Tien Complementay Health Studio, Dublin 8, 77

Acupuncture
Aaron Acupuncture & Physiotherapy Clinic, Antrim, 13
Chinese and Complementary Medicine Clinic, Belfast, 14
Hao Clinic for Traditional Chinese Medicine, Bangor, 17
Quintessence Complementary Clinic, Belfast, 18
Claureen Health Farm, Ennis, 19
Ki-Care Clinic, Cork, 33
Clinic of Oriental and Traditional Chinese Medicine, Cork, 37
Flowing Unity, Cork, 40
Natural Healing Centre & Natural Healing Institute of Ireland, Cork, 44
Jan de Vries Healthcare Clinic, Dublin 1, 58
Active Health, Dublin 6, 59
Acupuncture & Allergy Testing Clinic, Dublin 5, 61
Acupuncture & Sports Injury Clinic, Dublin 24, 62
Ardagh Mobile Acupuncture Clinic, Blackrock, 65
Castleknock Physiotherapy & Acupuncture Clinic, Dublin 15, 71
Celtic Health Centre, Dublin 6, 72
Chinese Acupuncture Clinic, Dublin 2, 73
Chinese Medical Centre, Dun Laoghaire, 74
Complementary House, Dublin 6W, 76
Dan-Tien Complementay Health Studio, Dublin 8, 77
Healing House, Dublin 7, 82
Health and Harmony, Dublin 2, 84
Holistic Sourcing Centre, Dublin 2, 88
Inner Adventure Company, Deansgrange, 90
Inner Circle Healing Centre, Dublin 13, 91
Lalloo's Medical Centre, Dublin 7, 95

Light Therapy Ireland, Swords, 96
Odyssey Healing Centre, Dublin 2, 100
Pu Shan Chinese Medicine Centre, Dublin 2, 103
Re:fresh, Dublin 18, 105
Sandycove Clinic, Sandycove, 108
Shamrock Health Clinic, Dublin 24, 109
Walmer Clinic & College of Healing and Natural Therapies, Dublin 13, 115
Clinic of Alternative Medicine, Galway, 134
Body & Sole Centre, Galway, 132
Harmony Acupuncture & Angel Aromatherapy Clinic, Galway, 136
Dingle's Natural Therapy Centre, Dingle, 142
Oasis Alternative Medical and Flotation Centre, Tralee, 143
Celbridge Physiotherapy & Acupuncture Clinic, Celbridge, 144
Complementary Treatment Clinic, Athy, 145
Fairgreen Holistic Clinic, Naas, 146
Acorn Counselling and Therapy Centre, Drogheda, 152
Abbey House Physiotherapy Clinic, Navan, 164
An Solas Healing Centre, Clogheen, 176
Dungarvan Alternative Health Clinic, Dungarvan, 182
Centre for Natural Therapies, Wexford, 189
Bray Holistic Health Clinic, Bray, 196
Greystones Physical Therapy Clinic, Greystones, 197

AEROBICS
Tinarana House, Killaloe, 23

AFRICAN MEDICINE
Anam Cara, Loughrea, 130

AIKIDO
Lios Dana Holistic Centre, Anascaul, 138

ALEXANDER TECHNIQUE
Body & Sole Centre, Galway, 132
Lios Dana Holistic Centre, Anascaul, 138
Chrysalis Holistic Centre, Donard, 190

ALGOTHERAPY See SEAWEED TREATMENTS

ALLERGY TESTING
Acupuncture & Allergy Testing Clinic, Dublin 5, 61

Acupuncture & Sports Injury Clinic, Dublin 24, 62
Ikebana Spirit Mind Body Centre, Dublin 6, 89
Lalloo's Medical Centre, Dublin 7, 95
Shamrock Health Clinic, Dublin 24, 109
Clinic of Alternative Medicine, Galway, 134
Galway Rolfing Clinic, Moycullen, 135
Oasis Alternative Medical and Flotation Centre, Tralee, 143
Ashe Street Clinic, Tralee, 140
Blue Room Meditation & Healing Centre, Bennettsbridge, 147
Natural Healing Centre, Belmullet, 159
Sanctuary Health & Holistic Centre, Kilross, 175

AMATSU BACK-PAIN THERAPY
Healing House, Dublin 7, 82

ANIMAL IMAGERY
Burren Holistic Centre, Tubber, 24

ANGEL THERAPY
Limerick Healing Centre of Colour & Light, Limerick, 151

AROMACEANE
Grove House, Mallow, 29

AROMATHERAPY/AROMATHERAPY MASSAGE
Complementary Health Clinic, Belfast, 15
Quintessence Complementary Clinic, Belfast, 18
Therapy Matters, Belfast, 19
Poll na Lobhar Holistic Treatments, Kilnaboy, 22
Tinarana House, Killaloe, 23
Anam Cara Natural Health Care Centre, Bantry, 35
Lisdoonvarna Spa Wells Health Centre, Lisdoonvarna, 25
Blarney Park Leisure Centre, Blarney, 26
Grove House, Mallow, 29
Hagel Healing Farm, Bantry, 30
Bon Secours Health Lodge, Cork, 36
Crystal Connection, Cork, 38
Douglas Day Spa, Cork, 39
Flowing Unity, Cork, 40
L.A. Beauty Salon, Clonakilty, 43
Natural Health Care Centre, Bantry, 45
Quayside Holistic Health Centre, Cork, 47
Sureia Holistic Centre, Midleton, 48
Derrynoid Centre, Draperstown, 49

Malin Head Hostel, Inishowen, 50
Impact Health, Beauty & Aromatherapy, Ballynahinch, 54
Jan de Vries Healthcare Clinic, Dublin 1, 58
Aqua, the Art of Beauty, Stillorgan, 64
Beauty Parlour, Dublin 6W, 66
Bellaza Clinic, Dublin 6, 67
Bliss – Beauty and Massage, Sandycove, 67
Blue Eriu, Dublin 2, 68
Celtic Health Centre, Dublin 6, 72
Complementary Medicine Clinic, Dublin 9, 77
Fairview Therapy Centre, Dublin 3, 79
Healing House, Dublin 7, 82
Healing Room, Dublin 3, 84
Holistic Healing Centre, Dublin 2, 86
Holistic Sourcing Centre, Dublin 2, 88
Inner Circle Healing Centre, Dublin 13, 91
Inspirations, Dun Laoghaire, 93
Light Therapy Ireland, Swords, 96
Melt: Temple Bar Healing Centre, Dublin 2, 97
Natural Therapy & Beauty Clinic, Dublin 15, 98
Nuala Woulfe, Sandycove, 99
Odyssey Healing Centre, Dublin 2, 100
Re:fresh, Dublin 18, 105
Roseanna Crothers Beauty Salon, Dublin 4, 107
Walmer Clinic & College of Healing and Natural Therapies, Dublin 13, 115
Innish Beg Cottages, Enniskillen, 118
Burren Yoga & Meditation Centre, Kinvara, 122
Delphi Mountain Resort & Spa, Leenane, 124
Galway Bay Health Farm, Oranmore, 126
Anam Cara, Loughrea, 130
Body & Sole Centre, Galway, 132
Harmony Acupuncture & Angel Aromatherapy Clinic, Galway, 136
Dingle's Natural Therapy Centre, Dingle, 142
Complementary Treatment Clinic, Athy, 145
Fairgreen Holistic Clinic, Naas, 146
Holistic Healing Centre, Graiguenamanagh, 149
Acorn Counselling and Therapy Centre, Drogheda, 152
Castlebar Health Care Clinic, Castlebar, 157
Tír na nÓg Holistic Beauty Centre, Claremorris, 160
Johnstown House Hotel & Spa, Enfield, 161
Midas Touch Clinic, Tullamore, 168
Little House of Avalon Holistic Health, Ballinasloe, 169
Celtic Seaweed Baths, Strandhill, 173
Sanctuary Health & Holistic Centre, Kilross, 175

An Solas Healing Centre, Clogheen, 176
Dungarvan Alternative Health Clinic, Dungarvan, 182
Shoselish Holistic Healing Centre, Waterford, 179
Ballycoursey Lodge Health Spa, Enniscorthy, 185
Therapeutic Spa & Beauty Centre, Rosslare, 187
Atar Complementary Therapy Clinic, Wexford, 188
Centre for Natural Therapies, Wexford, 189
Chrysalis Holistic Centre, Donard, 190
Powerscourt Springs, Enniskerry, 192
Greystones Physical Therapy Clinic, Greystones, 197

ART THERAPY

Hagel Healing Farm, Bantry, 30
Freeing the Artist Within, Dalkey, 55
Holistic Sourcing Centre, Dublin 2, 88
Irish Institute for Integrated Psychotherapy, Monkstown, 94
Melt: Temple Bar Healing Centre, Dublin 2, 97
Sandycove Clinic, Sandycove, 108
Turning Point Positive Health Centre, Dun Laoghaire, 114
Slánú Cancer Help Centre, Moycullen, 129

ASTROLOGY

Crystal Connection, Cork, 38
Healing Place, Dublin 5, 83
Melt: Temple Bar Healing Centre, Dublin 2, 97
An Solas Healing Centre, Clogheen, 176

AURA SOMA

Ikebana Spirit Mind Body Centre, Dublin 6, 89
Inner Adventure Company, Deansgrange, 90
Melt: Temple Bar Healing Centre, Dublin 2, 97
Body & Sole Centre, Galway, 132
Limerick Healing Centre of Colour & Light, Limerick, 151
An Solas Healing Centre, Clogheen, 176

AURA-WORK

Complementary House, Dublin 6W, 76
Limerick Healing Centre of Colour & Light, Limerick, 151
Midas Touch Clinic, Tullamore, 168
Rainbowhill Healing Centre, Boyle, 170

AURICULOTHERAPY

Dan-Tien Complementay Health Studio, Dublin 8, 77
Shamrock Health Clinic, Dublin 24, 109

AYURVEDA

Aqua, the Art of Beauty, Stillorgan, 64
Melt: Temple Bar Healing Centre, Dublin 2, 97

BACH FLOWER REMEDIES

Fortwilliam Reflexology, Belfast, 16
Quintessence Complementary Clinic, Belfast, 18
Inspirations, Dun Laoghaire, 93
Anam Cara, Loughrea, 130
Coiscéim Natural Therapy Centre, Tralee, 141
Oasis Alternative Medical and Flotation Centre, Tralee, 143

BALNEOTHERAPY

Kilkee Thalassotherapy Centre, Kilkee, 21
Tinarana House, Killaloe, 23
Inchydoney Lodge and Spa, Clonakilty, 31
Delphi Mountain Resort & Spa, Leenane, 124
Rosmoney Spa, Westport, 155

BEAUTY TREATMENTS

Complementary Health Clinic, Belfast, 15
Claureen Health Farm, Ennis, 19
Kilkee Thalassotherapy Centre, Kilkee, 21
Tinarana House, Killaloe, 23
Inchydoney Lodge and Spa, Clonakilty, 31
Douglas Day Spa, Cork, 39
L.A. Beauty Salon, Clonakilty, 43
Impact Health, Beauty & Aromatherapy, Ballynahinch, 54
Acupuncture & Sports Injury Clinic, Dublin 24, 62
Alara Beauty Salon, Dublin 6, 63
Aqua, the Art of Beauty, Stillorgan, 64
Beauty Parlour, Dublin 6W, 66
Bellaza Clinic, Dublin 6, 67
Bliss – Beauty and Massage, Sandycove, 67
Blue Eriu, Dublin 2, 68
Body & Beauty Spa, Dublin 15, 69
Light Therapy Ireland, Swords, 96
Natural Therapy & Beauty Clinic, Dublin 15, 98
Nuala Woulfe, Sandycove, 99
Roseanna Crothers Beauty Salon, Dublin 4, 107
Tethra Spa, Dublin 2, 112
Innish Beg Cottages, Enniskillen, 118

Delphi Mountain Resort & Spa, Leenane, 124
Galway Bay Health Farm, Oranmore, 126
Harmony Acupuncture & Angel Aromatherapy Clinic, Galway, 136
Dingle's Natural Therapy Centre, Dingle, 142
Rosmoney Spa, Westport, 155
His 'n' Hers Hair & Beauty Day Spa, Castlebar, 158
Tír na nÓg Holistic Beauty Centre, Claremorris, 160
Johnstown House Hotel & Spa, Enfield, 161
Niamh's Beauty Salon, Athboy, 166
Little House of Avalon Holistic Health, Ballinasloe, 169
Monaincha Health & Fitness, Roscrea, 178
Temple Country House and Health Spa, Moate, 180
Ballycoursey Lodge Health Spa, Enniscorthy, 185
Therapeutic Spa & Beauty Centre, Rosslare, 187
Atar Complementary Therapy Clinic, Wexford, 188
Powerscourt Springs, Enniskerry, 192

BELLY DANCING

Nature Art Centre for Drumming, Art and Healing, Ballydehob, 34
Irish Institute for Integrated Psychotherapy, Monkstown, 94

BIOCRANIAL THERAPY

Natural Healing Centre & Natural Healing Institute of Ireland, Cork, 44

BIODYNAMIC THERAPY

Anam Cara Natural Health Care Centre, Bantry, 35
Natural Health Care Centre, Bantry, 45
Sanctuary Health & Holistic Centre, Kilross, 175

BIOENERGY THERAPY

Complementary House, Dublin 6W, 76
Ikebana Spirit Mind Body Centre, Dublin 6, 89
Melt: Temple Bar Healing Centre, Dublin 2, 97
Odyssey Healing Centre, Dublin 2, 100
Oasis Alternative Medical and Flotation Centre, Tralee, 143
Fairgreen Holistic Clinic, Naas, 146
Acorn Counselling and Therapy Centre, Drogheda, 152
Castlebar Health Care Clinic, Castlebar, 157

Greystones Physical Therapy Clinic, Greystones, 197

BIORESONANCE TESTING
Quintessence Complementary Clinic, Belfast, 18
Coiscéim Natural Therapy Centre, Tralee, 141
Sanctuary Health & Holistic Centre, Kilross, 175

BIOTRIGGERNETICS
Atar Complementary Therapy Clinic, Wexford, 188

BLOOD ANALYSIS
Navan Holistic Therapy Centre, Navan, 165

BODY HARMONY
Body Harmony Healing, Dublin 3, 70
Odyssey Healing Centre, Dublin 2, 100

BODY PULSING
Poll na Lobhar Holistic Treatments, Kilnaboy, 22

BODY SCRUBS
Grove House, Mallow, 29
Impact Health, Beauty & Aromatherapy, Ballynahinch, 54
Aqua, the Art of Beauty, Stillorgan, 64
Bellaza Clinic, Dublin 6, 67
Blue Eriu, Dublin 2, 68
Body & Beauty Spa, Dublin 15, 69
Delphi Mountain Resort & Spa, Leenane, 124
Annaghdown Seaweed Spa, Corrandulla, 131
Harmony Acupuncture & Angel Aromatherapy Clinic, Galway, 136
Johnstown House Hotel & Spa, Enfield, 161
Ballycoursey Lodge Health Spa, Enniscorthy, 185
Therapeutic Spa & Beauty Centre, Rosslare, 187

BODY WRAPS
See also SEAWEED TREATMENTS
Tinarana House, Killaloe, 23
Grove House, Mallow, 29
Aqua, the Art of Beauty, Stillorgan, 64
Beauty Parlour, Dublin 6W, 66
Bliss – Beauty and Massage, Sandycove, 67
Blue Eriu, Dublin 2, 68
Body & Beauty Spa, Dublin 15, 69
Delphi Mountain Resort & Spa, Leenane, 124
Annaghdown Seaweed Spa, Corrandulla, 131

His 'n' Hers Hair & Beauty Day Spa, Castlebar, 158
Therapeutic Spa & Beauty Centre, Rosslare, 187

BOWEN TECHNIQUE
Dingle's Natural Therapy Centre, Dingle, 142

BREATH-WORK
Ikebana Spirit Mind Body Centre, Dublin 6, 89
T'ai Chi Ireland, Dublin 6, 11
Transpersonal Centre, Navan, 163
Temple Country House and Health Spa, Moate, 180
Slí na Bande, Newtownmountkennedy, 194

BRUMISATION
Inchydoney Lodge and Spa, Clonakilty, 31
Rosmoney Spa, Westport, 155

BUSH-FLOWER REMEDIES
Healing House, Dublin 7, 82
Anam Cara, Loughrea, 130

CELLULAR HEALING
Flowing Unity, Cork, 40
Inniú School & Healing Centre, Lucan, 92
Fairgreen Holistic Clinic, Naas, 146

CHAKRA-BALANCING
Flowing Unity, Cork, 40
Inner Circle Healing Centre, Dublin 13, 91
Body & Sole Centre, Galway, 132
Midas Touch Clinic, Tullamore, 168
Rainbowhill Healing Centre, Boyle, 170

CHELATION THERAPY
Tinarana House, Killaloe, 23

CHINESE MEDICINE
See also HERBAL MEDICINE
Hao Clinic for Traditional Chinese Medicine, Bangor, 17
Ki-Care Clinic, Cork, 33
Natural Therapy Centre, Mallow, 46
Chinese Medical Centre, Dun Laoghaire, 74
Dan-Tien Complementay Health Studio, Dublin 8, 77
Inner Adventure Company, Deansgrange, 90

Pu Shan Chinese Medicine Centre, Dublin 2, 103
Sandycove Clinic, Sandycove, 108
Clinic of Alternative Medicine, Galway, 134
Body & Sole Centre, Galway, 132
Oasis Alternative Medical and Flotation Centre, Tralee, 143
Dungarvan Alternative Health Clinic, Dungarvan, 182
Bray Holistic Health Clinic, Bray, 196

CHINESE TUI NA See TUI NA MASSAGE

CHIROPODY/PODIATRY
Complementary Health Clinic, Belfast, 15
Inner Circle Healing Centre, Dublin 13, 91

CHIROPRACTIC
Tinarana House, Killaloe, 23
Jan de Vries Healthcare Clinic, Dublin 1, 58
Harvest Moon Centre, Dublin 2, 80
Walmer Clinic & College of Healing and Natural Therapies, Dublin 13, 115
Dingle's Natural Therapy Centre, Dingle, 142
Dungarvan Alternative Health Clinic, Dungarvan, 182
Bray Holistic Health Clinic, Bray, 196

COGNITIVE THERAPY
An Solas Healing Centre, Clogheen, 176

COLONICS
Tinarana House, Killaloe, 23
Nuala Woulfe, Sandycove, 99
Re:fresh, Dublin 18, 105

COLOUR THERAPY
Complementary Health Clinic, Belfast, 15
Tinarana House, Killaloe, 23
Suaimhneas Holistic Health Clinic, Buncrana, 52
Impact Health, Beauty & Aromatherapy, Ballynahinch, 54
Anam Cara, Loughrea, 130
Coiscéim Natural Therapy Centre, Tralee, 141
Fairgreen Holistic Clinic, Naas, 146

COPING SKILLS
Bon Secours Health Lodge, Cork, 36

COUNSELLING
Anam Cara Natural Health Care Centre, Bantry, 35
Crystal Connection, Cork, 38
Natural Health Care Centre, Bantry, 45
Quayside Holistic Health Centre, Cork, 47
Sureia Holistic Centre, Midleton, 48
Suaimhneas Holistic Health Clinic, Buncrana, 52
Amethyst Resource for Human Development, Killiney, 63
Ardagh Mobile Acupuncture Clinic, Blackrock, 65
Complementary House, Dublin 6W, 76
Complementary Medicine Clinic, Dublin 9, 77
Fairview Therapy Centre, Dublin 3, 79
Harvest Moon Centre, Dublin 2, 80
Healing House, Dublin 7, 82
Healing Place, Dublin 5, 83
Holistic Sourcing Centre, Dublin 2, 88
Ikebana Spirit Mind Body Centre, Dublin 6, 89
Inner Adventure Company, Deansgrange, 90
Irish Institute for Integrated Psychotherapy, Monkstown, 94
Turning Point Positive Health Centre, Dun Laoghaire, 114
Slánú Cancer Help Centre, Moycullen, 129
Body & Sole Centre, Galway, 132
Eskine House of Silence, Sneem, 137
Coiscéim Natural Therapy Centre, Tralee, 141
Dingle's Natural Therapy Centre, Dingle, 142
Ashe Street Clinic, Tralee, 140
Fairgreen Holistic Clinic, Naas, 146
Blue Room Meditation & Healing Centre, Bennettsbridge, 147
Holistic Healing Centre, Graiguenamanagh, 149
Limerick Healing Centre of Colour & Light, Limerick, 151
Little House of Avalon Holistic Health, Ballinasloe, 169
Centre for Natural Therapies, Wexford, 189
Slí na Bande, Newtownmountkennedy, 194

CRANIO-SACRAL THERAPY
Anam Cara Natural Health Care Centre, Bantry, 35
Active Health, Dublin 6, 59
Healing House, Dublin 7, 82
Healing Place, Dublin 5, 83
Inspirations, Dun Laoghaire, 93
Melt: Temple Bar Healing Centre, Dublin 2, 97
Sandycove Clinic, Sandycove, 108

Shamrock Health Clinic, Dublin 24, 109
Walmer Clinic & College of Healing and Natural Therapies, Dublin 13, 115
Body & Sole Centre, Galway, 132
Dingle's Natural Therapy Centre, Dingle, 142
Oasis Alternative Medical and Flotation Centre, Tralee, 143
Temple Country House and Health Spa, Moate, 180

CREATIVE THERAPY
Ikebana Spirit Mind Body Centre, Dublin 6, 89

CRYOTHERAPY
Inchydoney Lodge and Spa, Clonakilty, 31
Rosmoney Spa, Westport, 155

CRYSTAL THERAPY
Body & Sole Centre, Galway, 132
Little House of Avalon Holistic Health, Ballinasloe, 169

CUPPING
Hao Clinic for Traditional Chinese Medicine, Bangor, 17
Ki-Care Clinic, Cork, 33
Dan-Tien Complementay Health Studio, Dublin 8, 77
Harmony Acupuncture & Angel Aromatherapy Clinic, Galway, 136

DANCE THERAPY
An Solas Healing Centre, Clogheen, 176

DEEP-TISSUE MASSAGE
Quintessence Complementary Clinic, Belfast, 18
Natural Healing Centre & Natural Healing Institute of Ireland, Cork, 44
Pat Henry Figure & Fitness Clinic, Dublin 2, 102
Harmony Acupuncture & Angel Aromatherapy Clinic, Galway, 136
Fairgreen Holistic Clinic, Naas, 146

DETOXIFICATION
Claureen Health Farm, Ennis, 19
Douglas Day Spa, Cork, 39
Re:fresh, Dublin 18, 105
Roseanna Crothers Beauty Salon, Dublin 4, 107
Burren Yoga & Meditation Centre, Kinvara, 122

Galway Yoga & Meditation Centre, Galway, 127
Cloona Health Centre, Westport, 153
Temple Country House and Health Spa, Moate, 180
Therapeutic Spa & Beauty Centre, Rosslare, 187
Powerscourt Springs, Enniskerry, 192

DIETARY COUNSELLING See NUTRITION COUNSELLING

DRAMA THERAPY
Turning Point Positive Health Centre, Dun Laoghaire, 114

DREAM-WORK
   See also JOURNALLING
Flowing Unity, Cork, 40
Complementary House, Dublin 6W, 76
Lios Dana Holistic Centre, Anascaul, 138
Blue Room Meditation & Healing Centre, Bennettsbridge, 147
Limerick Healing Centre of Colour & Light, Limerick, 151

DRUMMING
Nature Art Centre for Drumming, Art and Healing, Ballydehob, 34
Flowing Unity, Cork, 40
Healing House, Dublin 7, 82

EAR-CANDLING/EAR-CONING
Ki-Care Clinic, Cork, 33
Inner Circle Healing Centre, Dublin 13, 91
Casement Centre of Complementary Therapies, Ballina, 157
Navan Holistic Therapy Centre, Navan, 165

ELECTROLYSIS
Inchydoney Lodge and Spa, Clonakilty, 31

ELECTROMAGNETIC THERAPY/ELECTROTHERAPY
Chinese and Complementary Medicine Clinic, Belfast, 14
Jan de Vries Healthcare Clinic, Dublin 1, 58
The Complementary Medicine Clinic, Dublin 9, 77
Dan-Tien Complementay Health Studio, Dublin 8, 77

EMOTIONAL-RELEASE BODY-WORK
Natural Healing Centre, Belmullet, 159
Fairgreen Holistic Clinic, Naas, 146

ENDORPHIN-RELEASE THERAPY
Endorphin Release Clinic, Dublin 12, 78

ENERGY THERAPY
Freedom Holistic Centre, Midleton, 41
Jivan Clinic of Complementary Medicine, Cork, 42
Suaimhneas Holistic Health Clinic, Buncrana, 52
Inner Adventure Company, Deansgrange, 90
Inner Circle Healing Centre, Dublin 13, 91
Sandycove Clinic, Sandycove, 108
Body & Sole Centre, Galway, 132
Casement Centre of Complementary Therapies, Ballina, 157
Health Therapies Clinic, Waterford, 183

ENNEAGRAM
An Solas Healing Centre, Clogheen, 176

EUROWAVE
Complementary Treatment Clinic, Athy, 145

FACIALS
Claureen Health Farm, Ennis, 19
Kilkee Thalassotherapy Centre, Kilkee, 21
L.A. Beauty Salon, Clonakilty, 43
Aqua, the Art of Beauty, Stillorgan, 64
The Beauty Parlour, Dublin 6W, 66
Bliss – Beauty and Massage, Sandycove, 67
Blue Eriu, Dublin 2, 68
Body & Beauty Spa, Dublin 15, 69
Natural Therapy & Beauty Clinic, Dublin 15, 98
Nuala Woulfe, Sandycove, 99
Tethra Spa, Dublin 2, 112
Annaghdown Seaweed Spa, Corrandulla, 131
Harmony Acupuncture & Angel Aromatherapy Clinic, Galway, 136
Dingle's Natural Therapy Centre, Dingle, 142
His 'n' Hers Hair & Beauty Day Spa, Castlebar, 158
Tír na nÓg Holistic Beauty Centre, Claremorris, 160
Johnstown House Hotel & Spa, Enfield, 161
Monaincha Health & Fitness, Roscrea, 178
Temple Country House and Health Spa, Moate, 180
Ballycoursey Lodge Health Spa, Enniscorthy, 185
Therapeutic Spa & Beauty Centre, Rosslare, 187
Powerscourt Springs, Enniskerry, 192

FAMILY THERAPY
Body & Sole Centre, Galway, 132

FANGO
Tinarana House, Killaloe, 23

FASTING
Hagel Healing Farm, Bantry, 30

FELDENKRAIS
Melt: Temple Bar Healing Centre, Dublin 2, 97

FENG SHUI
Weekend Breaks at the Fisherman's Cottage, Aran Islands, 120
Burren Yoga & Meditation Centre, Kinvara, 122
Body & Sole Centre, Galway, 132
Namaste, Portlaoise, 150
An Solas Healing Centre, Clogheen, 176
Therapeutic Spa & Beauty Centre, Rosslare, 187

FLOTATION THERAPY
Harvest Moon Centre, Dublin 2, 80
Oasis Alternative Medical and Flotation Centre, Tralee, 143

FLOWER REMEDIES
See also BACH FLOWER REMEDIES AND BUSH-FLOWER REMEDIES
Body & Sole Centre, Galway, 132

FOCUSING
Poll na Lobhar Holistic Treatments, Kilnaboy, 22

FOOT-READING
Anam Cara, Loughrea, 130
Little House of Avalon Holistic Health, Ballinasloe, 169

GEMSTONE REMEDIES
Body & Sole Centre, Galway, 132

GESTALT THERAPY
Healing House, Dublin 7, 82

Guided Imagery
Bon Secours Health Lodge, Cork, 36

Hand Analysis
Complementary House, Dublin 6W, 76

Healing Prayer
Slánú Cancer Help Centre, Moycullen, 129

Heat Treatment
Chinese and Complementary Medicine Clinic, Belfast, 14

Herbal Medicine
Chinese and Complementary Medicine Clinic, Belfast, 14
Hao Clinic for Traditional Chinese Medicine, Bangor, 17
Tinarana House, Killaloe, 23
Ki-Care Clinic, Cork, 33
Acupuncture & Allergy Testing Clinic, Dublin 5, 61
Acupuncture & Sports Injury Clinic, Dublin 24, 62
Chinese Medical Centre, Dun Laoghaire, 74
Dan-Tien Complementay Health Studio, Dublin 8, 77
Health and Harmony, Dublin 2, 84
Herbal & Iridology Clinic, Dublin 2, 85
Melt: Temple Bar Healing Centre, Dublin 2, 97
Odyssey Healing Centre, Dublin 2, 100
Pu Shan Chinese Medicine Centre, Dublin 2, 103
Sandycove Clinic, Sandycove, 108
Shamrock Health Clinic, Dublin 24, 109
Weekend Breaks at the Fisherman's Cottage, Aran Islands, 120
Clinic of Alternative Medicine, Galway, 134
Body & Sole Centre, Galway, 132
Harmony Acupuncture & Angel Aromatherapy Clinic, Galway, 136
Oasis Alternative Medical and Flotation Centre, Tralee, 143
Complementary Treatment Clinic, Athy, 145
Navan Holistic Therapy Centre, Navan, 165
Temple Country House and Health Spa, Moate, 180
Chrysalis Holistic Centre, Donard, 190

Holistic Massage
Anam Cara Natural Health Care Centre, Bantry, 35
Sureia Holistic Centre, Midleton, 48
Complementary Healing Therapies, Dublin 7, 75
Healing Room, Dublin 3, 84
Walmer Clinic & College of Healing and Natural Therapies, Dublin 13, 115
Galway Bay Health Farm, Oranmore, 126
Body & Sole Centre, Galway, 132
Tír na nÓg Holistic Beauty Centre, Claremorris, 160
Sanctuary Health & Holistic Centre, Kilross, 175
Anvil House & Therapeutic Centre, Foulksmills, 184
Ballycoursey Lodge Health Spa, Enniscorthy, 185
Therapeutic Spa & Beauty Centre, Rosslare, 187

Holotropic Breath-work See Breath-work

Homeopathy
Tinarana House, Killaloe, 23
Clinic of Oriental and Traditional Chinese Medicine, Cork, 37
Natural Therapy Centre, Mallow, 46
Quayside Holistic Health Centre, Cork, 47
Jan de Vries Healthcare Clinic, Dublin 1, 58
Acupuncture & Allergy Testing Clinic, Dublin 5, 61
Fairview Therapy Centre, Dublin 3, 79
Ikebana Spirit Mind Body Centre, Dublin 6, 89
Irish Institute for Integrated Psychotherapy, Monkstown, 94
Lalloo's Medical Centre, Dublin 7, 95
Melt: Temple Bar Healing Centre, Dublin 2, 97
Re:fresh, Dublin 18, 105
Sandycove Clinic, Sandycove, 108
Shamrock Health Clinic, Dublin 24, 109
Anam Cara, Loughrea, 130
Clinic of Alternative Medicine, Galway, 134
Ashe Street Clinic, Tralee, 140
Fairgreen Holistic Clinic, Naas, 146
Blue Room Meditation & Healing Centre, Bennettsbridge, 147
Sanctuary Health & Holistic Centre, Kilross, 175
Centre for Natural Therapies, Wexford, 189
Chrysalis Holistic Centre, Donard, 190
Bray Holistic Health Clinic, Bray, 196

HOT-STONE THERAPY

Aqua, the Art of Beauty, Stillorgan, 64
Inniú School & Healing Centre, Lucan, 92
Johnstown House Hotel & Spa, Enfield, 161

HYDROTHERAPY

Tinarana House, Killaloe, 23
Inchydoney Lodge and Spa, Clonakilty, 31
Aqua, the Art of Beauty, Stillorgan, 64
Johnstown House Hotel & Spa, Enfield, 161
Temple Country House and Health Spa, Moate, 180
Powerscourt Springs, Enniskerry, 192

HYPNOTHERAPY

Complementary Health Clinic, Belfast, 15
Claureen Health Farm, Ennis, 19
Complementary House, Dublin 6W, 76
Complementary Medicine Clinic, Dublin 9, 77
Healing House, Dublin 7, 82
Holistic Sourcing Centre, Dublin 2, 88
Inner Circle Healing Centre, Dublin 13, 91
Walmer Clinic & College of Healing and Natural Therapies, Dublin 13, 115
Fairgreen Holistic Clinic, Naas, 146
Acorn Counselling and Therapy Centre, Drogheda, 152
Casement Centre of Complementary Therapies, Ballina, 157
Rainbowhill Healing Centre, Boyle, 170
Centre for Natural Therapies, Wexford, 189
Bray Holistic Health Clinic, Bray, 196

IMAGE CONSULTING

Galway Bay Health Farm, Oranmore, 126

INDIAN HEAD MASSAGE

Quintessence Complementary Clinic, Belfast, 18
Blarney Park Leisure Centre, Blarney, 26
Grove House, Mallow, 29
Ki-Care Clinic, Cork, 33
Crystal Connection, Cork, 38
Douglas Day Spa, Cork, 39
Flowing Unity, Cork, 40
Natural Therapy Centre, Mallow, 46
Natural Therapy Clinic, Glanmire, 47
Sureia Holistic Centre, Midleton, 48
Impact Health, Beauty & Aromatherapy, Ballynahinch, 54
Jan de Vries Healthcare Clinic, Dublin 1, 58

Celtic Health Centre, Dublin 6, 72
Complementary Healing Therapies, Dublin 7, 75
Complementary House, Dublin 6W, 76
Healing Room, Dublin 3, 84
Holistic Healing Centre, Dublin 2, 86
Ikebana Spirit Mind Body Centre, Dublin 6, 89
Inner Circle Healing Centre, Dublin 13, 91
Inspirations, Dun Laoghaire, 93
Light Therapy Ireland, Swords, 96
Melt: Temple Bar Healing Centre, Dublin 2, 97
Natural Therapy & Beauty Clinic, Dublin 15, 98
Odyssey Healing Centre, Dublin 2, 100
Re:fresh, Dublin 18, 105
Roseanna Crothers Beauty Salon, Dublin 4, 107
Shamrock Health Clinic, Dublin 24, 109
Innish Beg Cottages, Enniskillen, 118
Delphi Mountain Resort & Spa, Leenane, 124
Galway Bay Health Farm, Oranmore, 126
Anam Cara, Loughrea, 130
Body & Sole Centre, Galway, 132
Dingle's Natural Therapy Centre, Dingle, 142
Oasis Alternative Medical and Flotation Centre, Tralee, 143
Complementary Treatment Clinic, Athy, 145
Fairgreen Holistic Clinic, Naas, 146
Holistic Healing Centre, Graiguenamanagh, 149
Castlebar Health Care Clinic, Castlebar, 157
Natural Healing Centre, Belmullet, 159
Johnstown House Hotel & Spa, Enfield, 161
Little House of Avalon Holistic Health, Ballinasloe, 169
Rainbowhill Healing Centre, Boyle, 170
Dungarvan Alternative Health Clinic, Dungarvan, 182
Health Therapies Clinic, Waterford, 183
Temple Country House and Health Spa, Moate, 180
Powerscourt Springs, Enniskerry, 192

INFANT AND PREGNANCY MASSAGE

Bon Secours Health Lodge, Cork, 36
Re:fresh, Dublin 18, 105

INTEGRATED-ENERGY THERAPY

Burren Holistic Centre, Tubber, 24

INTUITIVE MASSAGE

Inniú School & Healing Centre, Lucan, 92
Chrysalis Holistic Centre, Donard, 190

IRIDOLOGY
Jan de Vries Healthcare Clinic, Dublin 1, 58
Herbal & Iridology Clinic, Dublin 2, 85
Navan Holistic Therapy Centre, Navan, 165
Centre for Natural Therapies, Wexford, 189

JAPANESE MEDICINE
Sandycove Clinic, Sandycove, 108

JOURNALLING
    See also WRITING THERAPY
Jivan Clinic of Complementary Medicine, Cork, 42
Slánú Cancer Help Centre, Moycullen, 129
Slí na Bande, Newtownmountkennedy, 194

KARATE
Natural Healing Centre & Natural Healing Institute of Ireland, Cork, 44

KI MASSAGE
Blarney Park Leisure Centre, Blarney, 26
Ki-Care Clinic, Cork, 33
Jivan Clinic of Complementary Medicine, Cork, 42
Complementary House, Dublin 6W, 76
Fairview Therapy Centre, Dublin 3, 79
Pat Henry Figure & Fitness Clinic, Dublin 2, 102
Rhiannon Clinic, Dublin 7, 106
Innish Beg Cottages, Enniskillen, 118
Anam Cara, Loughrea, 130
Complementary Treatment Clinic, Athy, 145
Holistic Healing Centre, Graiguenamanagh, 149
Acorn Counselling and Therapy Centre, Drogheda, 152
Midas Touch Clinic, Tullamore, 168
Powerscourt Springs, Enniskerry, 192

KINESIOLOGY
Complementary Health Clinic, Belfast, 15
Quintessence Complementary Clinic, Belfast, 18
Poll na Lobhar Holistic Treatments, Kilnaboy, 22
Freedom Holistic Centre, Midleton, 41
Celtic Health Centre, Dublin 6, 72
Ikebana Spirit Mind Body Centre, Dublin 6, 89
Melt: Temple Bar Healing Centre, Dublin 2, 97
Sandycove Clinic, Sandycove, 108
Walmer Clinic & College of Healing and Natural Therapies, Dublin 13, 115
Oasis Alternative Medical and Flotation Centre, Tralee, 143
Blue Room Meditation & Healing Centre, Bennettsbridge, 147
Natural Healing Centre, Belmullet, 159
Pine Lodge, Tullamore, 167
Little House of Avalon Holistic Health, Ballinasloe, 169
An Solas Healing Centre, Clogheen, 176
Shoselish Holistic Healing Centre, Waterford, 179
Temple Country House and Health Spa, Moate, 180

LA STONE THERAPY
Inniú School & Healing Centre, Lucan, 92

LIFE-COACHING
Complementary Health Clinic, Belfast, 15
Complementary House, Dublin 6W, 76

LIGHT THERAPY
Tinarana House, Killaloe, 23
Light Therapy Ireland, Swords, 96

LYMPHATIC TREATMENTS
Bon Secours Health Lodge, Cork, 36
Crystal Connection, Cork, 38
L.A. Beauty Salon, Clonakilty, 43
Complementary Medicine Clinic, Dublin 9, 77
Inner Circle Healing Centre, Dublin 13, 91
Melt: Temple Bar Healing Centre, Dublin 2, 97
Dingle's Natural Therapy Centre, Dingle, 142
Navan Holistic Therapy Centre, Navan, 165
Ballycoursey Lodge Health Spa, Enniscorthy, 185

MACROBIOTICS
Lios Dana Holistic Centre, Anascaul, 138

MAGNET THERAPY
Natural Healing Centre, Belmullet, 159
Anvil House & Therapeutic Centre, Foulksmills, 184

MAGNIFIED HEALING
Body & Sole Centre, Galway, 132
Fairgreen Holistic Clinic, Naas, 146
Casement Centre of Complementary Therapies, Ballina, 157

MANIPULATIVE THERAPY

Anam Cara Natural Health Care Centre, Bantry, 35
Celbridge Physiotherapy & Acupuncture Clinic, Celbridge, 144

MASSAGE (GENERAL)

>See also AROMATHERAPY MASSAGE, DEEP-TISSUE MASSAGE, HOLISTIC MASSAGE, INDIAN HEAD MASSAGE, INFANT AND PREGNANCY MASSAGE, INTUITIVE MASSAGE, KI MASSAGE, REMEDIAL MASSAGE, SPORTS AND SPORTS-INJURY MASSAGE, SWEDISH MASSAGE, THAI MASSAGE, THERAPEUTIC MASSAGE and TUI NA MASSAGE

Claureen Health Farm, Ennis, 19
Kilkee Thalassotherapy Centre, Kilkee, 21
Poll na Lobhar Holistic Treatments, Kilnaboy, 22
Anam Cara Natural Health Care Centre, Bantry, 35
Burren Holistic Centre, Tubber, 24
Lisdoonvarna Spa Wells Health Centre, Lisdoonvarna, 25
Blarney Park Leisure Centre, Blarney, 26
Grove House, Mallow, 29
Inchydoney Lodge and Spa, Clonakilty, 31
Douglas Day Spa, Cork, 39
Aqua, the Art of Beauty, Stillorgan, 64
Beauty Parlour, Dublin 6W, 66
Bliss – Beauty and Massage, Sandycove, 67
Body & Beauty Spa, Dublin 15, 69
Celtic Health Centre, Dublin 6, 72
Complementary Medicine Clinic, Dublin 9, 77
Fairview Therapy Centre, Dublin 3, 79
Harvest Moon Centre, Dublin 2, 80
Healing House, Dublin 7, 82
Holistic Healing Centre, Dublin 2, 86
Melt: Temple Bar Healing Centre, Dublin 2, 97
Pu Shan Chinese Medicine Centre, Dublin 2, 103
Re:fresh, Dublin 18, 105
Roseanna Crothers Beauty Salon, Dublin 4, 107
Shamrock Health Clinic, Dublin 24, 109
Innish Beg Cottages, Enniskillen, 118
Slánú Cancer Help Centre, Moycullen, 129
Coiscéim Natural Therapy Centre, Tralee, 141
Oasis Alternative Medical and Flotation Centre, Tralee, 143
Blue Room Meditation & Healing Centre, Bennettsbridge, 147
Cloona Health Centre, Westport, 153

Casement Centre of Complementary Therapies, Ballina, 157
His 'n' Hers Hair & Beauty Day Spa, Castlebar, 158
Natural Healing Centre, Belmullet, 159
Tír na nÓg Holistic Beauty Centre, Claremorris, 160
Johnstown House Hotel & Spa, Enfield, 161
Pine Lodge, Tullamore, 167
Sanctuary Health & Holistic Centre, Kilross, 175
Monaincha Health & Fitness, Roscrea, 178
Dungarvan Alternative Health Clinic, Dungarvan, 182
Health Therapies Clinic, Waterford, 183
Shoselish Holistic Healing Centre, Waterford, 179
Temple Country House and Health Spa, Moate, 180
Atar Complementary Therapy Clinic, Wexford, 188
Sacred Journeys Ireland, Dublin 6, 193
Bray Holistic Health Clinic, Bray, 196

MEDITATION

Burren Holistic Centre, Tubber, 24
Hagel Healing Farm, Bantry, 30
Bon Secours Health Lodge, Cork, 36
Crystal Connection, Cork, 38
Flowing Unity, Cork, 40
Jivan Clinic of Complementary Medicine, Cork, 42
Freeing the Artist Within, Dalkey, 55
Inner Circle Healing Centre, Dublin 13, 91
Raja Yoga Centre, Dublin 4, 104
T'ai Chi Ireland, Dublin 6, 111
Galway Yoga & Meditation Centre, Galway, 127
Slánú Cancer Help Centre, Moycullen, 129
Eskine House of Silence, Sneem, 137
Lios Dana Holistic Centre, Anascaul, 138
Dingle's Natural Therapy Centre, Dingle, 142
Blue Room Meditation & Healing Centre, Bennettsbridge, 147
Namaste, Portlaoise, 150
Limerick Healing Centre of Colour & Light, Limerick, 151
Natural Healing Centre, Belmullet, 159
An Solas Healing Centre, Clogheen, 176
Chrysalis Holistic Centre, Donard, 190
Slí na Bande, Newtownmountkennedy, 194

METAMORPHOSIS

Fortwilliam Reflexology, Belfast, 16

Tinarana House, Killaloe, 23
Natural Therapy & Beauty Clinic, Dublin 15, 98
Acorn Counselling and Therapy Centre, Drogheda, 152
Casement Centre of Complementary Therapies, Ballina, 157
Castlebar Health Care Clinic, Castlebar, 157

MOXABUSTION

Hao Clinic for Traditional Chinese Medicine, Bangor, 17
Chinese Medical Centre, Dun Laoghaire, 74
Health and Harmony, Dublin 2, 84
Harmony Acupuncture & Angel Aromatherapy Clinic, Galway, 136

MUSCLE STIMULATION

His 'n' Hers Hair & Beauty Day Spa, Castlebar, 158

NATURAL VISION IMPROVEMENT

Body & Sole Centre, Galway, 132
Natural Healing Centre, Belmullet, 159

NATUROPATHY

Navan Holistic Therapy Centre, Navan, 165

NEUROLINGUISTIC PROGRAMMING

Complementary Health Clinic, Belfast, 15
Burren Holistic Centre, Tubber, 24
Fairgreen Holistic Clinic, Naas, 146

NUMEROLOGY

Healing House, Dublin 7, 82

NUTRITION COUNSELLING

Complementary Health Clinic, Belfast, 15
Tinarana House, Killaloe, 23
Bon Secours Health Lodge, Cork, 36
Quayside Holistic Health Centre, Cork, 47
Jan de Vries Healthcare Clinic, Dublin 1, 58
Active Health, Dublin 6, 59
Acupuncture & Allergy Testing Clinic, Dublin 5, 61
Lalloo's Medical Centre, Dublin 7, 95
Light Therapy Ireland, Swords, 96
Nuala Woulfe, Sandycove, 99
Re:fresh, Dublin 18, 105
Rhiannon Clinic, Dublin 7, 106
Sandycove Clinic, Sandycove, 108

Galway Bay Health Farm, Oranmore, 126
Slánú Cancer Help Centre, Moycullen, 129
Oasis Alternative Medical and Flotation Centre, Tralee, 143
Acorn Counselling and Therapy Centre, Drogheda, 152
Little House of Avalon Holistic Health, Ballinasloe, 169
Sligo Natural Health & Yoga Centre, Drumcliffe, 171
Centre for Natural Therapies, Wexford, 189

OCCUPATIONAL THERAPY

Therapy Matters, Belfast, 19
Holistic Sourcing Centre, Dublin 2, 88

OSTEOPATHY

Jan de Vries Healthcare Clinic, Dublin 1, 58
Celtic Health Centre, Dublin 6, 72
Sandycove Clinic, Sandycove, 108
Clinic of Alternative Medicine, Galway, 134
Greystones Physical Therapy Clinic, Greystones, 197

OZONE BATHS

Tinarana House, Killaloe, 23

PAST-LIFE REGRESSION

Complementary House, Dublin 6W, 76
Holistic Sourcing Centre, Dublin 2, 88
Natural Healing Centre, Belmullet, 159

PERSONAL DEVELOPMENT

Diamus, Cork, 27
Nature Art Centre for Drumming, Art and Healing, Ballydehob, 34
Holistic Sourcing Centre, Dublin 2, 88
Odyssey Healing Centre, Dublin 2, 100
Turning Point Positive Health Centre, Dun Laoghaire, 114
Fairgreen Holistic Clinic, Naas, 146
Blue Room Meditation & Healing Centre, Bennettsbridge, 147
Acorn Counselling and Therapy Centre, Drogheda, 152
Rainbowhill Healing Centre, Boyle, 170
Ballycoursey Lodge Health Spa, Enniscorthy, 185
Chrysalis Holistic Centre, Donard, 190

PHYSICAL THERAPY/PHYSIOTHERAPY
Aaron Acupuncture & Physiotherapy Clinic, Antrim, 13
Acupuncture & Sports Injury Clinic, Dublin 24, 62
Castleknock Physiotherapy & Acupuncture Clinic, Dublin 15, 71
Complementary Medicine Clinic, Dublin 9, 77
Re:fresh, Dublin 18, 105
Shamrock Health Clinic, Dublin 24, 109
Ashe Street Clinic, Tralee, 140
Celbridge Physiotherapy & Acupuncture Clinic, Celbridge, 144
Abbey House Physiotherapy Clinic, Navan, 164
An Solas Healing Centre, Clogheen, 176
Greystones Physical Therapy Clinic, Greystones, 197

PILATES
Inner Circle Healing Centre, Dublin 13, 91
Melt: Temple Bar Healing Centre, Dublin 2, 97
Pat Henry Figure & Fitness Clinic, Dublin 2, 102
Burren Yoga & Meditation Centre, Kinvara, 122

PODIATRY See CHIROPODY

POLARITY THERAPY
Holistic Sourcing Centre, Dublin 2, 88
Melt: Temple Bar Healing Centre, Dublin 2, 97
Coiscéim Natural Therapy Centre, Tralee, 141
An Solas Healing Centre, Clogheen, 176
Health Therapies Clinic, Waterford, 183

PRANIC HEALING
Natural Healing Centre, Belmullet, 159

PRESENT-LIFE PROGRESSION
Complementary House, Dublin 6W, 76

PRESSOTHERAPY
Inchydoney Lodge and Spa, Clonakilty, 31
Rosmoney Spa, Westport, 155

PSYCHIC READINGS
Suaimhneas Holistic Health Clinic, Buncrana, 52
Complementary House, Dublin 6W, 76
Fairgreen Holistic Clinic, Naas, 146
Rainbowhill Healing Centre, Boyle, 170

PSYCHOLOGY
Bray Holistic Health Clinic, Bray, 196

PSYCHOTHERAPEUTIC MASSAGE
Irish Institute for Integrated Psychotherapy, Monkstown, 94

PSYCHOTHERAPY
Crystal Connection, Cork, 38
Quayside Holistic Health Centre, Cork, 47
Complementary House, Dublin 6W, 76
Fairview Therapy Centre, Dublin 3, 79
Healing House, Dublin 7, 82
Holistic Sourcing Centre, Dublin 2, 88
Ikebana Spirit Mind Body Centre, Dublin 6, 89
Inner Circle Healing Centre, Dublin 13, 91
Irish Institute for Integrated Psychotherapy, Monkstown, 94
Rhiannon Clinic, Dublin 7, 106
Sandycove Clinic, Sandycove, 108
Turning Point Positive Health Centre, Dun Laoghaire, 114
Walmer Clinic & College of Healing and Natural Therapies, Dublin 13, 115
Galway Bay Health Farm, Oranmore, 126
Dingle's Natural Therapy Centre, Dingle, 142
Fairgreen Holistic Clinic, Naas, 146
Blue Room Meditation & Healing Centre, Bennettsbridge, 147
Holistic Healing Centre, Graiguenamanagh, 149
Rainbowhill Healing Centre, Boyle, 170

QI GUNG
Crystal Connection, Cork, 38
Active Health, Dublin 6, 59
Chinese Medical Centre, Dun Laoghaire, 74
Sandycove Clinic, Sandycove, 108
T'ai Chi Ireland, Dublin 6, 111
Dungarvan Alternative Health Clinic, Dungarvan, 182
Slí na Bande, Newtownmountkennedy, 194

REBIRTHING
Flowing Unity, Cork, 40
Ikebana Spirit Mind Body Centre, Dublin 6, 89
Inner Circle Healing Centre, Dublin 13, 91
Odyssey Healing Centre, Dublin 2, 100
An Solas Healing Centre, Clogheen, 176
Slí na Bande, Newtownmountkennedy, 194

REFLEXOLOGY
Complementary Health Clinic, Belfast, 15
Fortwilliam Reflexology, Belfast, 16
Quintessence Complementary Clinic, Belfast, 18
Therapy Matters, Belfast, 19
Claureen Health Farm, Ennis, 19
Tinarana House, Killaloe, 23
Anam Cara Natural Health Care Centre, Bantry, 35
Lisdoonvarna Spa Wells Health Centre, Lisdoonvarna, 25
Blarney Park Leisure Centre, Blarney, 26
Grove House, Mallow, 29
Hagel Healing Farm, Bantry, 30
Inchydoney Lodge and Spa, Clonakilty, 31
Ki-Care Clinic, Cork, 33
Bon Secours Health Lodge, Cork, 36
Clinic of Oriental and Traditional Chinese Medicine, Cork, 37
Crystal Connection, Cork, 38
Douglas Day Spa, Cork, 39
Flowing Unity, Cork, 40 , 40
L.A. Beauty Salon, Clonakilty, 43
Natural Healing Centre & Natural Healing Institute of Ireland, Cork, 44
Natural Health Care Centre, Bantry, 45
Natural Therapy Centre, Mallow, 46
Natural Therapy Clinic, Glanmire, 47
Quayside Holistic Health Centre, Cork, 47
Sureia Holistic Centre, Midleton, 48
Derrynoid Centre, Draperstown, 49
Malin Head Hostel, Inishowen, 50
Impact Health, Beauty & Aromatherapy, Ballynahinch, 54
Jan de Vries Healthcare Clinic, Dublin 1, 58
Active Health, Dublin 6, 59
Acupuncture & Allergy Testing Clinic, Dublin 5, 61
Aqua, the Art of Beauty, Stillorgan, 64
Beauty Parlour, Dublin 6W, 66
Bliss – Beauty and Massage, Sandycove, 67
Body & Beauty Spa, Dublin 15, 69
Celtic Health Centre, Dublin 6, 72
Complementary Healing Therapies, Dublin 7, 75
Complementary House, Dublin 6W, 76
Complementary Medicine Clinic, Dublin 9, 77
Fairview Therapy Centre, Dublin 3, 79
Healing House, Dublin 7, 82
Healing Room, Dublin 3, 84
Herbal & Iridology Clinic, Dublin 2, 85
Holistic Healing Centre, Dublin 2, 86
Holistic Sourcing Centre, Dublin 2, 88
Ikebana Spirit Mind Body Centre, Dublin 6, 89
Inner Circle Healing Centre, Dublin 13, 91
Inniú School & Healing Centre, Lucan, 92
Inspirations, Dun Laoghaire, 93
Lalloo's Medical Centre, Dublin 7, 95
Melt: Temple Bar Healing Centre, Dublin 2, 97
Natural Therapy & Beauty Clinic, Dublin 15, 98
Nuala Woulfe, Sandycove, 99
Odyssey Healing Centre, Dublin 2, 100
Pat Henry Figure & Fitness Clinic, Dublin 2, 102
Pu Shan Chinese Medicine Centre, Dublin 2, 103
Re:fresh, Dublin 18, 105
Shamrock Health Clinic, Dublin 24, 109
Walmer Clinic & College of Healing and Natural Therapies, Dublin 13, 115
Delphi Mountain Resort & Spa, Leenane, 124
Galway Bay Health Farm, Oranmore, 126
Anam Cara, Loughrea, 130
Body & Sole Centre, Galway, 132
Harmony Acupuncture & Angel Aromatherapy Clinic, Galway, 136
Coiscéim Natural Therapy Centre, Tralee, 141
Dingle's Natural Therapy Centre, Dingle, 142
Oasis Alternative Medical and Flotation Centre, Tralee, 143
Complementary Treatment Clinic, Athy, 145
Fairgreen Holistic Clinic, Naas, 146
Holistic Healing Centre, Graiguenamanagh, 149
Acorn Counselling and Therapy Centre, Drogheda, 152
Cloona Health Centre, Westport, 153
Rosmoney Spa, Westport, 155
Casement Centre of Complementary Therapies, Ballina, 157
Castlebar Health Care Clinic, Castlebar, 157
Natural Healing Centre, Belmullet, 159
Tír na nÓg Holistic Beauty Centre, Claremorris, 160
Johnstown House Hotel & Spa, Enfield, 161
Navan Holistic Therapy Centre, Navan, 165
Pine Lodge, Tullamore, 167
Little House of Avalon Holistic Health, Ballinasloe, 169
Sanctuary Health & Holistic Centre, Kilross, 175
Monaincha Health & Fitness, Roscrea, 178
Dungarvan Alternative Health Clinic, Dungarvan, 182
Health Therapies Clinic, Waterford, 183
Shoselish Holistic Healing Centre, Waterford, 179

Temple Country House and Health Spa, Moate, 180
Anvil House & Therapeutic Centre, Foulksmills, 184
Therapeutic Spa & Beauty Centre, Rosslare, 187
Centre for Natural Therapies, Wexford, 189
Powerscourt Springs, Enniskerry, 192
Bray Holistic Health Clinic, Bray, 196
Greystones Physical Therapy Clinic, Greystones, 197

REGRESSION THERAPY

Limerick Healing Centre of Colour & Light, Limerick, 151

REIKI

Complementary Health Clinic, Belfast, 15
Quintessence Complementary Clinic, Belfast, 18
Poll na Lobhar Holistic Treatments, Kilnaboy, 22
Tinarana House, Killaloe, 23
Anam Cara Natural Health Care Centre, Bantry, 35
Burren Holistic Centre, Tubber, 24
Grove House, Mallow, 29
Hagel Healing Farm, Bantry, 30
Ki-Care Clinic, Cork, 33
Crystal Connection, Cork, 38
Douglas Day Spa, Cork, 39
Flowing Unity, Cork, 40
Jivan Clinic of Complementary Medicine, Cork, 42
Natural Health Care Centre, Bantry, 45
Natural Therapy Centre, Mallow, 46
Natural Therapy Clinic, Glanmire, 47
Quayside Holistic Health Centre, Cork, 47
Sureia Holistic Centre, Midleton, 48
Suaimhneas Holistic Health Clinic, Buncrana, 52
Impact Health, Beauty & Aromatherapy, Ballynahinch, 54
Jan de Vries Healthcare Clinic, Dublin 1, 58
Ardagh Mobile Acupuncture Clinic, Blackrock, 65
Complementary Healing Therapies, Dublin 7, 75
Fairview Therapy Centre, Dublin 3, 79
Healing Room, Dublin 3, 84
Holistic Sourcing Centre, Dublin 2, 88
Ikebana Spirit Mind Body Centre, Dublin 6, 89
Inner Circle Healing Centre, Dublin 13, 91
Inniú School & Healing Centre, Lucan, 92
Inspirations, Dun Laoghaire, 93
Lalloo's Medical Centre, Dublin 7, 95

Melt: Temple Bar Healing Centre, Dublin 2, 97
Natural Therapy & Beauty Clinic, Dublin 15, 98
Odyssey Healing Centre, Dublin 2, 100
Re:fresh, Dublin 18, 105
Innish Beg Cottages, Enniskillen, 118
Burren Yoga & Meditation Centre, Kinvara, 122
Galway Bay Health Farm, Oranmore, 126
Anam Cara, Loughrea, 130
Body & Sole Centre, Galway, 132
Harmony Acupuncture & Angel Aromatherapy Clinic, Galway, 136
Coiscéim Natural Therapy Centre, Tralee, 141
Dingle's Natural Therapy Centre, Dingle, 142
Oasis Alternative Medical and Flotation Centre, Tralee, 143
Fairgreen Holistic Clinic, Naas, 146
Blue Room Meditation & Healing Centre, Bennettsbridge, 147
Holistic Healing Centre, Graiguenamanagh, 149
Limerick Healing Centre of Colour & Light, Limerick, 151
Acorn Counselling and Therapy Centre, Drogheda, 152
Rosmoney Spa, Westport, 155
Casement Centre of Complementary Therapies, Ballina, 157
Castlebar Health Care Clinic, Castlebar, 157
Natural Healing Centre, Belmullet, 159
Tír na nÓg Holistic Beauty Centre, Claremorris, 160
Pine Lodge, Tullamore, 167
Midas Touch Clinic, Tullamore, 168
Little House of Avalon Holistic Health, Ballinasloe, 169
Rainbowhill Healing Centre, Boyle, 170
An Solas Healing Centre, Clogheen, 176
Health Therapies Clinic, Waterford, 183
Shoselish Holistic Healing Centre, Waterford, 179
Temple Country House and Health Spa, Moate, 180
Centre for Natural Therapies, Wexford, 189
Chrysalis Holistic Centre, Donard, 190

RELAXATION THERAPY

Aaron Acupuncture & Physiotherapy Clinic, Antrim, 13
Bon Secours Health Lodge, Cork, 36
Freedom Holistic Centre, Midleton, 41
Quayside Holistic Health Centre, Cork, 47
Derrynoid Centre, Draperstown, 49

Suaimhneas Holistic Health Clinic, Buncrana, 52
Freeing the Artist Within, Dalkey, 55
Active Health, Dublin 6, 59
Complementary Healing Therapies, Dublin 7, 75
Healing House, Dublin 7, 82
Healing Place, Dublin 5, 83
Holistic Sourcing Centre, Dublin 2, 88
Inner Circle Healing Centre, Dublin 13, 91
Irish Institute for Integrated Psychotherapy, Monkstown, 94
Re:fresh, Dublin 18, 105
Turning Point Positive Health Centre, Dun Laoghaire, 114
Slánú Cancer Help Centre, Moycullen, 129
Blue Room Meditation & Healing Centre, Bennettsbridge, 147
Limerick Healing Centre of Colour & Light, Limerick, 151
Acorn Counselling and Therapy Centre, Drogheda, 152
Casement Centre of Complementary Therapies, Ballina, 157
Transpersonal Centre, Navan, 163
An Solas Healing Centre, Clogheen, 176
Anvil House & Therapeutic Centre, Foulksmills, 184
Therapeutic Spa & Beauty Centre, Rosslare, 187
Centre for Natural Therapies, Wexford, 189
Chrysalis Holistic Centre, Donard, 190

REMEDIAL MASSAGE

Complementary Health Clinic, Belfast, 15
Active Health, Dublin 6, 59
Holistic Healing Centre, Dublin 2, 86
Sandycove Clinic, Sandycove, 108
Innish Beg Cottages, Enniskillen, 118
Casement Centre of Complementary Therapies, Ballina, 157
Navan Holistic Therapy Centre, Navan, 165
Greystones Physical Therapy Clinic, Greystones, 197

RESONANCE HEALING

Jivan Clinic of Complementary Medicine, Cork, 42

ROLFING

Galway Rolfing Clinic, Moycullen, 135

SACRED GEOMETRY

Namaste, Portlaoise, 150

SEAWEED TREATMENTS

Kilkee Thalassotherapy Centre, Kilkee, 21
Grove House, Mallow, 29
Hagel Healing Farm, Bantry, 30
Inchydoney Lodge and Spa, Clonakilty, 31
Douglas Day Spa, Cork, 39
L.A. Beauty Salon, Clonakilty, 43
Impact Health, Beauty & Aromatherapy, Ballynahinch, 54
Macrobiotic Association, Dublin 12, 56
Blue Eriu, Dublin 2, 68
Body & Beauty Spa, Dublin 15, 69
Nuala Woulfe, Sandycove, 99
Annaghdown Seaweed Spa, Corrandulla, 131
Rosmoney Spa, Westport, 155
Celtic Seaweed Baths, Strandhill, 173
Kilcullen's Seaweed Baths & Tea Rooms, Enniscrone, 174
Temple Country House and Health Spa, Moate, 180
Ballycoursey Lodge Health Spa, Enniscorthy, 185
Therapeutic Spa & Beauty Centre, Rosslare, 187

SEICHIM

Crystal Connection, Cork, 38
Flowing Unity, Cork, 40
Ikebana Spirit Mind Body Centre, Dublin 6, 89
Limerick Healing Centre of Colour & Light, Limerick, 151
Casement Centre of Complementary Therapies, Ballina, 157
Castlebar Health Care Clinic, Castlebar, 157
Rainbowhill Healing Centre, Boyle, 170
Centre for Natural Therapies, Wexford, 189

SHAMANISM

Nature Art Centre for Drumming, Art and Healing, Ballydehob, 34
Flowing Unity, Cork, 40
Transpersonal Centre, Navan, 163
Rainbowhill Healing Centre, Boyle, 170
An Solas Healing Centre, Clogheen, 176

SHEN THERAPY

Healing Place, Dublin 5, 83
Holistic Sourcing Centre, Dublin 2, 88

SHIATSU

Anam Cara Natural Health Care Centre, Bantry, 35
Hagel Healing Farm, Bantry, 30
Natural Health Care Centre, Bantry, 45
Macrobiotic Association, Dublin12, 56
Celtic Health Centre, Dublin 6, 72
Fairview Therapy Centre, Dublin 3, 79
Healing Place, Dublin 5, 83
Irish Institute for Integrated Psychotherapy, Monkstown, 94
Melt: Temple Bar Healing Centre, Dublin 2, 97
Odyssey Healing Centre, Dublin 2, 100
Re:fresh, Dublin 18, 105
Sandycove Clinic, Sandycove, 108
Weekend Breaks at the Fisherman's Cottage, Aran Islands, 120
Burren Yoga & Meditation Centre, Kinvara, 122
Body & Sole Centre, Galway, 132
Lios Dana Holistic Centre, Anascaul, 138
Dingle's Natural Therapy Centre, Dingle, 142
Oasis Alternative Medical and Flotation Centre, Tralee, 143
Fairgreen Holistic Clinic, Naas, 146
Cloona Health Centre, Westport, 153
Little House of Avalon Holistic Health, Ballinasloe, 169
Sligo Natural Health & Yoga Centre, Drumcliffe, 171
Temple Country House and Health Spa, Moate, 180

SKENAR THERAPY

Galway Rolfing Clinic, Moycullen, 135

SOUND THERAPY

An Solas Healing Centre, Clogheen, 176

SPINE-WORK

Midas Touch Clinic, Tullamore, 168
Centre for Natural Therapies, Wexford, 189

SPIRITUAL HEALING

Suaimhneas Holistic Health Clinic, Buncrana, 52
Complementary House, Dublin 6W, 76
Healing House, Dublin 7, 82
Holistic Sourcing Centre, Dublin 2, 88
Inner Adventure Company, Deansgrange, 90
Raja Yoga Centre, Dublin 4, 104
Fairgreen Holistic Clinic, Naas, 146

Limerick Healing Centre of Colour & Light, Limerick, 151

SPORTS AND SPORTS-INJURY MASSAGE

Anam Cara Natural Health Care Centre, Bantry, 35
Douglas Day Spa, Cork, 39
Flowing Unity, Cork, 40
Natural Healing Centre & Natural Healing Institute of Ireland, Cork, 44
Natural Therapy Clinic, Glanmire, 47
Active Health, Dublin 6, 59
Complementary House, Dublin 6W, 76
Fairview Therapy Centre, Dublin 3, 79
Inner Circle Healing Centre, Dublin 13, 91
Melt: Temple Bar Healing Centre, Dublin 2, 97
Re:fresh, Dublin 18, 105
Shamrock Health Clinic, Dublin 24, 109
Body & Sole Centre, Galway, 132
Complementary Treatment Clinic, Athy, 145
Fairgreen Holistic Clinic, Naas, 146
Acorn Counselling and Therapy Centre, Drogheda, 152
Casement Centre of Complementary Therapies, Ballina, 157
Tír na nÓg Holistic Beauty Centre, Claremorris, 160
Therapeutic Spa & Beauty Centre, Rosslare, 187
Atar Complementary Therapy Clinic, Wexford, 188

SPORTS MEDICINE

Ashe Street Clinic, Tralee, 140
Celbridge Physiotherapy & Acupuncture Clinic, Celbridge, 144

STEAM BATH/SHOWER

Aqua, the Art of Beauty, Stillorgan, 64
Celtic Seaweed Baths, Strandhill, 173
Kilcullen's Seaweed Baths & Tea Rooms, Enniscrone, 174

STRESS-MANAGEMENT THERAPY See RELAXATION THERAPY

SULPHUR BATHS

Lisdoonvarna Spa Wells Health Centre, Lisdoonvarna, 25

Sweat-lodge Ceremonies

An Solas Healing Centre, Clogheen, 176
Sacred Journeys Ireland, Dublin 6, 193
Slí na Bande, Newtownmountkennedy, 194

Swedish Massage

Quayside Holistic Health Centre, Cork, 47
Impact Health, Beauty & Aromatherapy, Ballynahinch, 54
Active Health, Dublin 6, 59
Bellaza Clinic, Dublin 6, 67
Celtic Health Centre, Dublin 6, 72
Complementary House, Dublin 6W, 76
Healing Room, Dublin 3, 84
Melt: Temple Bar Healing Centre, Dublin 2, 97
Odyssey Healing Centre, Dublin 2, 100
Re:fresh, Dublin 18, 105
Roseanna Crothers Beauty Salon, Dublin 4, 107
Burren Yoga & Meditation Centre, Kinvara, 122
Galway Bay Health Farm, Oranmore, 126
Harmony Acupuncture & Angel Aromatherapy Clinic, Galway, 136
Navan Holistic Therapy Centre, Navan, 165
Atar Complementary Therapy Clinic, Wexford, 188

T'ai Chi

Anam Cara Natural Health Care Centre, Bantry, 35
Natural Healing Centre & Natural Healing Institute of Ireland, Cork, 44
Active Health, Dublin 6, 59
Celtic Health Centre, Dublin 6, 72
Chinese Medical Centre, Dun Laoghaire, 74
Holistic Sourcing Centre, Dublin 2, 88
Melt: Temple Bar Healing Centre, Dublin 2, 97
T'ai Chi Ireland, Dublin 6, 111
Lios Dana Holistic Centre, Anascaul, 138
Sligo Natural Health & Yoga Centre, Drumcliffe, 171
An Solas Healing Centre, Clogheen, 176
Dungarvan Alternative Health Clinic, Dungarvan, 182

Tantra

Burren Holistic Centre, Tubber, 24
Inner Adventure Company, Deansgrange, 90

Tarot

Complementary House, Dublin 6W, 76
Healing House, Dublin 7, 82
Crystal Connection, Cork, 38
Flowing Unity, Cork, 40
Fairgreen Holistic Clinic, Naas, 146
Casement Centre of Complementary Therapies, Ballina, 157
Midas Touch Clinic, Tullamore, 168

Team-building

Irish Institute for Integrated Psychotherapy, Monkstown, 94
Delphi Mountain Resort & Spa, Leenane, 124

Thai Massage

Celtic Health Centre, Dublin 6, 72
Ikebana Spirit Mind Body Centre, Dublin 6, 89
Melt: Temple Bar Healing Centre, Dublin 2, 97
Odyssey Healing Centre, Dublin 2, 100
Little House of Avalon Holistic Health, Ballinasloe, 169

Thalassotherapy

Rosmoney Spa, Westport, 155

Therapeutic Massage

Therapy Matters, Belfast, 19
Tinarana House, Killaloe, 23
Blarney Park Leisure Centre, Blarney, 26
Hagel Healing Farm, Bantry, 30
Ki-Care Clinic, Cork, 33
Bon Secours Health Lodge, Cork, 36
Flowing Unity, Cork, 40
Jivan Clinic of Complementary Medicine, Cork, 42
Natural Healing Centre & Natural Healing Institute of Ireland, Cork, 44
Natural Health Care Centre, Bantry, 45
Natural Therapy Centre, Mallow, 46
Natural Therapy Clinic, Glanmire, 47
Blue Eriu, Dublin 2, 68
Holistic Sourcing Centre, Dublin 2, 88
Ikebana Spirit Mind Body Centre, Dublin 6, 89
Inner Circle Healing Centre, Dublin 13, 91
Inniú School & Healing Centre, Lucan, 92
Inspirations, Dun Laoghaire, 93
Melt: Temple Bar Healing Centre, Dublin 2, 97
Sandycove Clinic, Sandycove, 108
Delphi Mountain Resort & Spa, Leenane, 124

Galway Bay Health Farm, Oranmore, 126
Castlebar Health Care Clinic, Castlebar, 157
Anvil House & Therapeutic Centre, Foulksmills, 184
Centre for Natural Therapies, Wexford, 189

THERAPY-LAMP TREATMENT
Jan de Vries Healthcare Clinic, Dublin 1, 58

TRAGER
Ikebana Spirit Mind Body Centre, Dublin 6, 89
Melt: Temple Bar Healing Centre, Dublin 2, 97
Fairgreen Holistic Clinic, Naas, 146

TRANSFORMATIONAL THERAPY
Ikebana Spirit Mind Body Centre, Dublin 6, 89

TRANSPERSONAL THERAPY
Fairgreen Holistic Clinic, Naas, 146

TUI NA MASSAGE
Active Health, Dublin 6, 59
Acupuncture & Allergy Testing Clinic, Dublin 5, 61
Melt: Temple Bar Healing Centre, Dublin 2, 97
Odyssey Healing Centre, Dublin 2, 100
Oasis Alternative Medical and Flotation Centre, Tralee, 143

VEGA TESTING See ALLERGY TESTING

VICHY SHOWER
Rosmoney Spa, Westport, 155

VISUALISATION THERAPY
Sandycove Clinic, Sandycove, 108
Slánú Cancer Help Centre, Moycullen, 129

VITAMIN INFUSION
Tinarana House, Killaloe, 23

VOICE-WORK
Transpersonal Centre, Navan, 163

VORTEX HEALING
Natural Therapy Centre, Mallow, 46
Ikebana Spirit Mind Body Centre, Dublin 6, 89
Body & Sole Centre, Galway, 132

WAX-BATH TREATMENT
Lisdoonvarna Spa Wells Health Centre, Lisdoonvarna, 25

WOMEN'S HEALTH
Ashe Street Clinic, Tralee, 140

WRITING THERAPY
    See also JOURNALLING
Lios Dana Holistic Centre, Anascaul, 138
Sligo Natural Health & Yoga Centre, Drumcliffe, 171
An Solas, Cougheen, 176
Chrysalis Holistic Centre, Donard, 190

YOGA
Claureen Health Farm, Ennis, 19
Tinarana House, Killaloe, 23
Anam Cara Natural Health Care Centre, Bantry, 35
Crystal Connection, Cork, 38
Natural Healing Centre & Natural Healing Institute of Ireland, Cork, 44
Natural Health Care Centre, Bantry, 45
Yoga Therapy and Training Centre Ireland, Cabra, 53
Celtic Health Centre, Dublin 6, 72
Harvest Moon Centre, Dublin 2, 80
Healing House, Dublin 7, 82
Holistic Healing Centre, Dublin 2, 86
Holistic Sourcing Centre, Dublin 2, 88
Ikebana Spirit Mind Body Centre, Dublin 6, 89
Irish Institute for Integrated Psychotherapy, Monkstown, 94
Melt: Temple Bar Healing Centre, Dublin 2, 97
Pat Henry Figure & Fitness Clinic, Dublin 2, 102
Raja Yoga Centre, Dublin 4, 104
Rhiannon Clinic, Dublin 7, 106
Yoga Therapy Ireland, Killiney, 117
Innish Beg Cottages, Enniskillen, 118
Burren Yoga & Meditation Centre, Kinvara, 122
Galway Yoga & Meditation Centre, Galway, 127
Eskine House of Silence, Sneem, 137
Lios Dana Holistic Centre, Anascaul, 138
Dingle's Natural Therapy Centre, Dingle, 142
Blue Room Meditation & Healing Centre, Bennettsbridge, 147
Limerick Healing Centre of Colour & Light, Limerick, 151

Acorn Counselling and Therapy Centre, Drogheda, 152
Cloona Health Centre, Westport, 153
Casement Centre of Complementary Therapies, Ballina, 157
Sligo Natural Health & Yoga Centre, Drumcliffe, 171
An Solas Healing Centre, Clogheen, 176
Monaincha Health & Fitness, Roscrea, 178
Temple Country House and Health Spa, Moate, 180
Anvil House & Therapeutic Centre, Foulksmills, 184
Ballycoursey Lodge Health Spa, Enniscorthy, 185
Slí na Bande, Newtownmountkennedy, 194

The Little House Of Avalon

Holistic Health Farm

Enjoy the simple Luxury of our mountain style Health Village surrounded by Nature's tranquillity and fresh country air. You have the privacy of your own little Chalet (en-suite) with all the pleasures of 18 relaxing, de-stressing health treatments to choose from, ranging from Oriental Style to Alternative and French Luxury Beauty treatments - detox in the Sauna and recline in our open-air Jacuzzi overlooking the country-side.

A small number of guests guarantees You to be the centre of our discreet, but always available attention, for the pampering of not only your body, but also your soul.

Please call for a brochure **0905 83 002**
We are looking forward to welcoming you!
Bernadette and Anthony
Smith-McGowan and Team

Holistic Breaks at Innish Beg, Fermanagh

A Peaceful Retreat by the Lakes

Innish Beg is located on a 170 acre farm overlooking the Fermanagh lakelands. Here on the shores of Lough Erne you can eliminate stress and regenerate your mind, body and soul.

Holistic Breaks available
Weekend breaks
Week breaks
Pamper days
Painting Break

Services and treatments available:
Yoga classes, aromatherapy, reflexology, Ki massage, Indian head massage, Reiki, body massage, painting, beauty treatments, aerobic classes.

Contact: Gabriele Tottenham, Innish Beg, Blaney,
Tel/Fax: 028 6864 152 www.innishbegcottages.com
As featured on Country Times programme, BBC 1

Yoga Therapy Ireland

20 Auburn Drive, Killiney,
County Dublin
Tel/Fax: 01 235 2120

Yoga Therapy Ireland is a recognised charity dedicated to practising, teaching and researching yoga, particularly for specific health-related problems.

Yoga Therapy Ireland offers
* On-going weekly yoga classes, suitable for all level practitioners.
* Yoga therapy for groups(e.g. Arthritis, M.S.)
* Individual sessions designed to meet the needs of clients with specific medical conditions.
* Interactive Yoga 'Open Days' and complementary healthcare weekends.
* A fully accredited Yoga Teacher Training course (university recognition in progress).

www.YogaTherapyIreland.com
Member of International Association of Yoga Therapists

Celtic Health Centre,

117-119 Ranelagh, Dublin 6
www.celtichealth.com
Tel: 01 4910689

Specialists in Bodywork Massage:
Swedish massage
Traditional Thai massage
Indian head massage
Myofascial release
Reflexology

The Celtic School of Bodyworks (Registered ITEC College)
Offers diplomas and courses in all of the above therapies.
Yoga classes nightly.

Irish Association of Medical Herbalists

Western herbal medicine, which has its roots in Greek and Roman medical traditions, uses herbs to support the body in its healing processes. Use of the herbs is based on traditional understanding and modern research.

Members of the Irish Association of Medical Herbalists follow a prescribed course of training to degree level.
This training covers both herbal medicine, medical science, and possible interactions between herbal medicine and medically prescribed medication.
Members are regulated and fully insured and they will have the letters MNIMH and MIAMH after their names.

Contact: Rosari Kingston (Chair) 028 22803 or Anna-Maria Keaveney (Secretary) 01 6281362 / 087 2378183 for a Medical Herbalist in your area.

ABBEYVALE HOUSE
Cashel Road
Holycross Co Tipperary
Tel: 0504 43032
www.tipperarytours.com
Abbeyval@gofree.indigo.ie

Here at **Abbeyvale House** we work with individuals to discard daily pressure and stress of every day life. In the **peaceful tranquil setting** of this beautiful energising village we help you to **unwind, relax and rejuvenate**, going away in a calmer cheerful mood. All our treatments and facilities are available to individuals or groups: body massage, reflexology, yoga, facials, hair treatments, Indian head massage, stress management and aromatherapy.

2 nights (full Board)	3 nights (full Board)
plus 2 therapies	plus 3 therapies
€215	€320

No single supplement. Extra therapies by arrangement.

CLOONA HEALTH CENTRE

Retreat from the habitual.

*Three-day and five-day cleansing/de-tox programs.
*Structured energising daily sequence of activities.
*Simplicity of content, simplicity of form.

Contact: Cloona **Health Centre**
Westport
County Mayo
Tel: (098) 25251
e-mail: info@cloona.ie
www.cloona.ie
See our entry p.153 for further details

Shoselish Holistic Healing Centre
Crystal School of Complementary Medicine
Blenheim Cross
Dunmore Road Waterford

The Crystal school of Complementary Medicine is situated three and a half miles from Waterford city centre on one and a quarter acres. Our centre is a self-contained dormer bungalow with four out of the five rooms completed with natural wood of teak, beech or pine. Within the beautiful landscaped grounds you can enjoy our dolmen, stream, orchard, organic garden, rockeries and fountain.

Therapies offered:	Professional courses conducted:
Reflexology	Reflexology
Aromatherapy	Aromatherapy
Therapeutic massage	Massage/Indian head massage
Indian head massage	Basic Kinesiology
Basic kinesiology/	
Muscle testing	
Reiki healing	

Contact: Joe McCormack, BA (Health Economics), DIP-REF, M.A.R, RN, MNRRI **Tel/Fax: 051 875444**

Bon Secours Health Lodge

Beside Cork Clinic, Western Road, Cork

Our **Complementary Medicine Health Service** has been active for the past five years. It was officially opened and recognised by the Minister for Health and Children, Micheal Martin T.D. We have a recognised integrated service in our general hospital. We offer an extensive range of services, and **each therapist is a state-registered nurse** with other nursing specialities.

List of therapies:
* Aromatherapy
* Holistic Massage
* Reflexology
* Manual Lymph Drainage
* Meditation/Spirituality
* Nutrition & Diet Theory
* Coping Skills
* Visualization
* Mother & Baby Massage.
* Remedial Sport massage

Therapies available: Monday – Saturday
Tel: 021 4347351
Email: bonsecourshealthlodge@eircom.net

CONSULT MEDICAL HERBALIST

Rosari Kingston BA MNIMH, MIAMH

for treatment of
Acne, eczema, psoriasis, arthritis, varicose ulcers, PMT, menopausal problems, IBS stress, anorexia etc
at

The Herb Clinic
Skibbereen
County Cork
Tel. 028 22803

Consultations by appointment only.

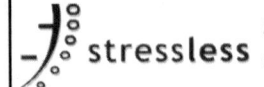

---

stressless

StressLess Massage is a Dublin based company, which offers seated acupressure massage for the workplace, as a cost effective method of reducing stress in the workplace.

Seated acupressure massage is a 15-minute massage based on the Japanese form of Shiatsu. It uses a unique series of acupressure points and stretches covering the back, neck and shoulder area, specifically designed to reduce muscle tension and stress. This leaves you feeling **physically relaxed, invigorated and energised** and ready to return to work with renewed concentration. As this is a fully clothed, non-invasive massage, it is ideal to be performed in any workplace on a custom-designed mobile chair, during a coffee break, perfect for those who are sitting at a computer thoughout the day.

Benefits for You:

* Stress reduction
* Reduces muscular tension and associated pain
* Lowers blood pressure
* Helps relieve headaches and backache
* Increases energy levels
* Improves mental alertness and concentration
* Boosts memory
* Increases Circulation
* Calms the nervous system
* Relaxes mind and body

Benefits for Your Company:

* Relieves stress
* Improves employee morale
* Enhances quality of work
* Reduces absenteeism
* Reduces healthcare costs
* Leads to fewer accidents
* Bonus for those working overtime or on special projects
* Reward or incentive
* Gift to corporate clients
* Enhances corporate image both internally and externally
* Shows staff you care

Nessa O'Shaughnessy B.Sc., I.T.E.C. Dip., AOR, mGCP nessa@stressless.ie, www.stressless.ie
To arrange a complimentary demonstration or for more information call: **(086) 8488442.**